AI and the Transformation of Visual Culture, Art, and Design

And Algül
https://orcid.org/0000-0001-5516-5249
Üsküdar University, Turkey

IGI Global
Scientific Publishing
Publishing Tomorrow's Research Today

Published in the United States of America by
IGI Global Scientific Publishing
701 East Chocolate Avenue
Hershey, PA, 17033, USA
Tel: 717-533-8845 | Fax: 717-533-7115
Website: https://www.igi-global.com E-mail: cust@igi-global.com

Library of Congress Cataloging-in-Publication Data

Names: Algül, And, 1973- editor
Title: AI and the transformation of visual culture, art, and design / edited by And Algül.
Description: Hershey, PA : IGI Global Scientific Publishing, [2027] | Includes bibliographical references and index. | Summary: "This book explores how AI is transforming art, design, and visual culture by reshaping creativity, authorship, and communication. It examines interdisciplinary practices, ethical challenges, and human-AI collaboration, highlighting how intelligent systems influence artistic production, cultural representation, and the future of creative expression"-- Provided by publisher.
Identifiers: LCCN 2026031967 (print) | LCCN 2026031968 (ebook) | ISBN 9798260027110 hardcover | ISBN 9798260027127 paperback | ISBN 9798260027134 ebook
Subjects: LCSH: Art and technology | Artificial intelligence | LCGFT: Essays
Classification: LCC N72.T4 A37 2027 (print) | LCC N72.T4 (ebook)
LC record available at https://lccn.loc.gov/2026031967
LC ebook record available at https://lccn.loc.gov/2026031968

British Cataloguing in Publication Data
A Cataloguing in Publication record for this book is available from the British Library.

Editorial Advisory Board

Uğur Efe Uçar, *Department of Interior Architecture, İstanbul Technical University, Turkey*
Dicle Yıldırım, *Faculty of Communication, Üsküdar University, Turkey*

Table of Contents

Detailed Table of Contents

This chapter examines the characteristics of artificial intelligence (AI)-generated art through the semiotic and linguistic concept of redundancy. Its purpose is to define AI art, evaluate its advantages and limitations in comparison to human-created works, and analyze its communicative and aesthetic properties. Drawing on concepts such as redundancy, Baroque, eclecticism, and laconicism, the chapter argues that the semiotic redundancy frequently present in AI art (marked by dense sign systems and elaborate compositions) derives from the vast computational capabilities. By contrast, historical art movements such as the Baroque and Eclecticism used redundancy as an intentional strategy to express ideology, often supported by the material wealth of their cultural context. The analysis concludes that while AI art may share aesthetic parallels with these movements, its redundancy is technologically driven rather than ideologically motivated.

The integration of AI applications into art has transformed the creative process and expression. This transformation has caused ethical debates about authorship in the art field and encouraged a re-evaluation of artistic and business practices in the digital age. In this context, we aim to examine the impact of AI-generated art on online artists. In 2024, through a quantitative approach we surveyed 220 traditional and AI practicing artists to assess their attitudes regarding aesthetic value and originality, authorship and co-creation, and the ethical and economic issues surrounding data use, attribution, and compensation. Through our findings it was clear that many artists welcomed AI as a helpful collaborator but still held human creativity at the core of their practice. At the same time, most called for clear data policies, proper credit, and fair pay when their work is used in AI datasets. Together, these responses reveal a tension between embracing new technological possibilities and protecting the uniquely human aspects of art.

The preservation and transmission of intangible cultural heritage, particularly traditional tales, legends, and myths, are increasingly challenged by the dominance of digital media and the changing habits of younger generations. In this context, the adoption of contemporary digital strategies becomes essential to ensure the continuity and relevance of oral traditions. This approach proposes a web storytelling application, structured through a seven-stage methodological framework. The case study focuses on a digital adaptation of Little Red Riding Hood, reimagined through a dark aesthetic approach combining illustration, sound, and interactive transitions to enhance narrative immersion. The resulting application demonstrates how web storytelling can function both as a tool for safeguarding intangible cultural heritage and as a pedagogical strategy that bridges creativity, technology, and education. By aligning cultural transmission with digital literacy, the project highlights the potential of interdisciplinary design practices in sustaining heritage within the digital age.

This study analyzes the contradictions inherent in digital environmentalism from opposing perspectives within the context of new ecological realities shaped by digital art and AI-driven creations, examining both the contribution of the digitalization of art to sustainability and its impact on the overall carbon footprint. While digital art offers significant contributions to sustainability goals through functions such as raising awareness of the environmental crisis and conveying scientific knowledge in a more accessible and visually impactful manner, the technical infrastructure of digitalization, particularly large data centers, AI modeling processes, and digital art applications, creates a significant environmental cost due to high-energy consumption and carbon emissions, which often conflicts with sustainability values. The primary objective of the study is to argue that, a more holistic understanding of digital environmentalism can be developed that also questions the field's internal carbon footprint and ethical responsibilities.

This study examines the social and emotional dimensions of streamer–viewer interaction on Twitch through thematic analysis of viewer comments. As users shift from passive consumers to active participants, interaction practices in live streaming have transformed. Twitch's real-time communication enables collective and interactive experiences while fostering dynamic parasocial relationships. The study applies qualitative thematic content analysis to 3,000 randomly selected comments from gaming, reaction, and chatting streams of a highly viewed Turkish streamer. Using NLP-assisted pre-coding and manual validation, themes were identified as direct address, humor, positive and negative emotion, toxic language, and content reaction. Findings show that behavior varies by stream type: positive emotions dominate gaming (13%), humor reaction streams (10%), and direct address chatting streams (35%), while toxic language remains low (0.3%). Results position Twitch as a digital public space where users engage emotionally, co-produce meaning, and compete for visibility.

This study critically examines Google Gemini 3 Pro as an AI-based visual production system, analyzing how it constructs cultural representations of urban space through the lenses of Nicholas Mirzoeff's Visual Culture Theory and Stuart Hall's Representation Theory. Rather than treating AI-generated images as neutral outputs, the research positions them as culturally mediated representations shaped by dominant ideological structures. Using visual content and frequency analysis across all 81 provinces of Turkey, findings reveal that AI-generated visuals rely on Western-centric aesthetic codes and generalized cultural markers, simplifying local identities. These results demonstrate that AI-based visual production actively participates in reproducing cultural meaning, positioning artificial intelligence as a cultural agent that reshapes the relationships between space, identity, and visual representation in digital environments.

Speculative design is a critical design approach that aims to question existing social and technological orders through images of alternative futures. The integration of generative AI tools into design practices is opening up a new arena of discussion regarding the visual strategies of this critical practice. This study aims to make this transformation visible by examining speculative design projects produced before and after the era of generative AI through a comparative visual rhetorical analysis. The analysis is based on a framework that combines Barthes' concepts of denotation, connotation, and myth with Aristotle's concept of pathos and Auger's perceptual bridge approach. The findings indicate that generative AI tools can, in some cases, reproduce dominant visual aesthetics, thereby creating tendencies toward aesthetic convergence. It has been observed, however, that projects that position AI as a critical design object can preserve the critical potential of speculative design.

Artificial intelligence stands out as a central technological paradigm transforming the current design ecosystem. The discussion revolves around computer systems moving beyond passive tools to become creative agents that organically partner with designers and incorporate their aesthetic preferences into the process. This study analyzes how artificial intelligence transforms design practices within the framework of Lev Manovich's new media approach, encompassing epistemology, phenomenology, and ontology. Adopting a mixed-methods approach, the research combines quantitative data with expert opinions. The findings demonstrate that artificial intelligence is positioned as an agent in the design process, while users are transformed from technical implementers into curators/selectors managing the process. Consequently, a hybrid subjectivity model is proposed, where agency in design is distributed between humans and algorithms; and the necessity of a human-centered transformation in design education is argued.

This chapter examines the intersection of generative artificial intelligence and immersive virtual reality as a transformative shift in the communicative structure of architectural representation. It aims to reconceptualize representation not as a linear process of visual production but as a multilayered system of mediation through which spatial meaning is progressively constructed. The chapter outlines how linguistic input, algorithmic interpretation, visual synthesis, volumetric modeling, and immersive experience operate as interconnected stages within a unified framework. Through this perspective, representation is positioned as a dynamic and iterative process shaped by feedback loops between human intention and computational systems. The proposed AI–IVR mediated framework highlights how design knowledge is generated, evaluated, and reformulated across semantic, visual, geometric, and experiential domains, offering a conceptual model for understanding contemporary interior architectural practice.

Artificial intelligence (AI) introduces a new cognitive condition in design communication, where human interpretative reasoning operates alongside computational processes. This chapter examines this relationship through distinct cognitive mechanisms and discusses how design thinking is transformed through the interaction between textual narrative and AI-mediated visualization. To investigate this framework, a speculative design workshop conducted in interior architecture education is presented, analyzing how narrative-based human reasoning and AI-generated imagery interact within a shared design process. The findings indicate that while human cognition enables interpretative depth and conceptual expansion, artificial intelligence supports rapid ideation and variation through computational visualization, yet may also limit spatial diversity by reinforcing recurring tendencies. This interaction reveals a cognitive divergence between human reasoning and

Preface

Artificial Intelligence (AI) is rapidly transforming the ways in which visual culture is produced, interpreted, distributed, and experienced. Across the fields of art, design, and visual communication, AI-driven technologies are redefining creative processes, challenging traditional notions of authorship, and opening new possibilities for innovation and interdisciplinary collaboration. As the boundaries between human creativity and computational intelligence continue to evolve, there is a growing need for scholarly inquiry that critically examines the opportunities, challenges, and implications of these developments. *AI and the Transformation of Visual Culture, Art, and Design* has been developed to address this need by bringing together diverse perspectives from across disciplines that are shaping the future of creative practice and visual communication.

This volume provides a comprehensive exploration of current theoretical and applied research at the intersections of artificial intelligence, design, art, and communication. Through interdisciplinary approaches and innovative methodologies, the chapters examine how emerging AI technologies influence artistic production, visual storytelling, design processes, cultural representation, audience engagement, and communication practices. The contributions also investigate how social, cultural, ethical, and technological contexts shape the adoption and impact of AI within creative industries and visual environments.

The increasing integration of AI into creative disciplines raises important questions regarding originality, aesthetics, authorship, ethics, accessibility, and the evolving relationship between humans and intelligent systems. Rather than viewing AI solely as a technological tool, this book positions it as a transformative force that is reshaping visual culture itself. The contributors explore both the practical applications and conceptual implications of AI-driven creativity, offering critical insights into how designers, artists, communicators, and scholars can engage with these emerging technologies in meaningful and responsible ways.

One of the defining strengths of this volume is its interdisciplinary perspective. The chapters draw upon knowledge from design studies, visual communication, media studies, computer science, cultural studies, art theory, and related fields to provide a holistic understanding of AI's influence on contemporary creative practices. By bringing together theoretical developments alongside practical examples and case studies, the book encourages dialogue across disciplinary boundaries and highlights the value of collaborative approaches to understanding complex technological transformations.

The contributors represent a diverse community of internationally recognized academics, creative professionals, and interdisciplinary researchers. Their expertise spans a wide range of topics and perspectives, ensuring that the discussions presented in this volume remain relevant, balanced, and forward-looking. Through their collective efforts, the book offers readers an opportunity to engage with emerging trends, innovative methodologies, and critical debates that are shaping the future of visual culture, art, and design.

As editor, I hope that this volume serves as an important resource for researchers, educators, students, artists, designers, visual communication specialists, and industry professionals seeking to better understand the evolving relationship between artificial intelligence and creative practice. Beyond its role as a reference work, I hope it inspires new research, encourages interdisciplinary collaboration, and stimulates thoughtful discussion about the opportunities and responsibilities associated with AI-driven innovation.

The future of visual culture will be shaped not only by technological advancement but also by the ways in which individuals and communities choose to engage with these technologies. By fostering critical reflection and interdisciplinary exploration, this book contributes to a broader conversation about creativity, communication, and human expression in an increasingly intelligent and interconnected world. It is my sincere hope that the insights presented throughout this volume will support ongoing scholarship and inspire new directions for research and practice in the years ahead.

ORGANIZATION OF THE BOOK

Chapter 1 examines the emergence of AI-generated art through a semiotic perspective, focusing on the concept of redundancy as a defining characteristic of machine-produced visual works. By comparing contemporary AI-generated imagery with historical artistic movements such as Baroque and Eclecticism, the chapter explores how dense visual sign systems and elaborate compositions are created through computational processes rather than ideological intent. This contribution offers a valuable framework for understanding the communicative and aesthetic dimensions of AI-generated art while highlighting important distinctions between human artistic expression and algorithmically generated creativity.

Chapter 2 explores the growing influence of AI-generated art on online artistic communities and creative practices. Through survey-based research involving both traditional and AI-assisted artists, the chapter investigates evolving attitudes toward originality, authorship, collaboration, and ethical concerns surrounding data use. The findings reveal a complex relationship between technological innovation and artistic identity, as many creators embrace AI as a collaborative tool while continuing to emphasize the importance of human creativity. The chapter provides important insights into the ethical, economic, and professional challenges accompanying the integration of artificial intelligence into contemporary artistic production.

Chapter 3 addresses the preservation of cultural heritage in the digital age through an innovative web storytelling framework that combines design, illustration, sound, and interactive media. Using a contemporary adaptation of a traditional narrative, the chapter demonstrates how digital platforms can serve as powerful tools for transmitting cultural knowledge to younger generations while fostering creativity and digital literacy. This contribution highlights the role of interdisciplinary design approaches in sustaining intangible cultural heritage and illustrates how technology can be leveraged to bridge tradition and innovation.

Chapter 4 critically examines the environmental paradoxes associated with digital art and AI-driven creative production. While digital media and AI technologies offer new opportunities to raise awareness of environmental issues and support sustainability goals, the chapter also draws attention to the significant carbon footprint associated with data centers, computational infrastructures, and large-scale AI systems. By exploring the tensions between ecological advocacy and technological consumption, the chapter encourages a more holistic understanding of sustainability within contemporary digital culture and creative practice.

Chapter 5 investigates the social, emotional, and participatory dimensions of live-streaming culture through an analysis of viewer interactions on Twitch. Focusing on the relationships between streamers and audiences, the chapter explores how digital platforms facilitate collective experiences, emotional engagement, and the co-creation of meaning. The findings reveal how different forms of interaction emerge across various content formats and position Twitch as an influential digital public sphere shaped by visibility, participation, and affective communication. This contribution enhances understanding of audience behavior within contemporary digital media environments.

Chapter 6 examines artificial intelligence as a cultural agent through an analysis of AI-generated representations of urban space across Turkey. Drawing on theories of visual culture and representation, the chapter demonstrates how AI image-generation systems often reproduce dominant cultural narratives and aesthetic conventions. The findings reveal tendencies toward generalized and Western-centric representations that simplify local identities and cultural diversity. Through this critical perspective, the chapter highlights the role of AI technologies in shaping visual culture, identity formation, and the production of cultural meaning in digital environments.

Chapter 7 explores the evolving relationship between speculative design and generative artificial intelligence through a comparative visual rhetorical analysis. The chapter investigates how AI-generated imagery influences the critical and imaginative capacities of speculative design practices. While identifying tendencies toward aesthetic standardization and convergence, the study also demonstrates how AI can be strategically employed as an object of critique within design processes. This contribution offers valuable insights into the opportunities and challenges presented by AI technologies for designers seeking to envision alternative futures and question dominant technological narratives.

Chapter 8 examines the shifting role of artificial intelligence within contemporary design ecosystems, focusing on its emergence as an active creative agent rather than a passive technological tool. Through a combination of empirical research and theoretical analysis, the chapter explores how AI reshapes traditional understandings of creativity, authorship, and design practice. The findings suggest that designers increasingly operate as curators and decision-makers within collaborative human-machine systems. By proposing a model of distributed agency, the chapter contributes to ongoing discussions regarding the future of design education and the evolving nature of creative work in AI-enhanced environments.

Chapter 9 investigates the convergence of generative artificial intelligence and immersive virtual reality within interior architectural representation. Moving beyond conventional approaches to visualization, the chapter presents a conceptual framework that understands representation as a dynamic and iterative process involving linguistic, visual, geometric, and experiential layers. By emphasizing the interaction between human intention and computational systems, the chapter offers a forward-looking perspective on how design knowledge is generated, communicated, and refined through emerging immersive technologies. This contribution highlights the transformative potential of AI-driven workflows within contemporary architectural practice.

Chapter 10 explores the relationship between human cognition and artificial intelligence in design communication, focusing on their distinct yet complementary modes of reasoning. Drawing upon a speculative design workshop in interior architecture education, the chapter examines how narrative-based human thinking interacts with AI-generated visualizations during the creative process. The findings reveal that while AI supports rapid ideation and visualization, human reasoning remains essential for conceptual depth, interpretation, and critical reflection. The chapter contributes to a deeper understanding of hybrid cognitive environments and offers important insights into the future of design thinking, communication, and education in an era increasingly influenced by artificial intelligence.

CONCLUDING REMARKS

The chapters gathered in *AI and the Transformation of Visual Culture, Art, and Design* collectively illuminate the profound and multifaceted ways in which artificial intelligence is reshaping creative practice, visual communication, and cultural production. Rather than presenting AI as a singular technological phenomenon, this volume demonstrates that its influence extends across aesthetics, ethics, cognition, sustainability, media participation, heritage preservation, and the very structures through which visual meaning is produced and interpreted.

Throughout the book, contributors critically examine the opportunities and tensions that emerge when computational systems enter traditionally human-centered creative domains. The discussions reveal a recurring theme: AI is not simply replacing existing artistic or design practices, but transforming the conditions under which creativity, communication, and representation take place. Whether through generative art, immersive environments, participatory digital cultures, or hybrid human-machine design processes, the chapters show how AI is becoming embedded within the infrastructures of contemporary visual culture.

At the same time, this volume underscores the importance of maintaining a critical and human-centered perspective. Questions of authorship, originality, cultural representation, environmental responsibility, cognitive diversity, and ethical governance appear throughout the contributions, reminding us that technological innovation must be accompanied by thoughtful reflection and interdisciplinary dialogue. The book's contributors demonstrate that meaningful engagement with AI requires not only technical understanding but also cultural sensitivity, philosophical inquiry, and social responsibility.

One of the most significant insights emerging from this collection is the growing need for collaboration across disciplines. The intersection of artificial intelligence with art, design, architecture, communication, media studies, and cultural theory creates new spaces for research and practice that cannot be fully understood within isolated academic boundaries. By bringing together diverse methodologies and perspectives, this volume contributes to a richer and more nuanced understanding of how AI is transforming visual culture on a global scale.

As editor, I hope this book serves as both a scholarly resource and a catalyst for future inquiry. It is intended to support researchers, educators, students, designers, artists, and communication professionals who seek to navigate the rapidly evolving relationship between human creativity and intelligent technologies. More importantly,

I hope it encourages readers to approach AI not with uncritical enthusiasm or apprehension, but with curiosity, reflection, and a commitment to shaping technologies that enhance human expression and cultural diversity.

The transformation of visual culture through AI is still unfolding. The ideas and debates presented in this volume represent an important step in understanding that transformation and in imagining the creative, ethical, and interdisciplinary futures that lie ahead.

Chapter 1
Accelerated and Redundant Development of Art Generated by Artificial Intelligence: Semiotic Aspects

Christo Kaftandjiev
http://orcid.org/0000-0002-4655-7408
Sofia University, Bulgaria

ABSTRACT

This chapter examines the characteristics of artificial intelligence (AI)-generated art through the semiotic and linguistic concept of redundancy. Its purpose is to define AI art, evaluate its advantages and limitations in comparison to human-created works, and analyze its communicative and aesthetic properties. Drawing on concepts such as redundancy, Baroque, eclecticism, and laconicism, the chapter argues that the semiotic redundancy frequently present in AI art (marked by dense sign systems and elaborate compositions) derives from the vast computational capabilities. By contrast, historical art movements such as the Baroque and Eclecticism used redundancy as an intentional strategy to express ideology, often supported by the material wealth of their cultural context. The analysis concludes that while AI art may share aesthetic parallels with these movements, its redundancy is technologically driven rather than ideologically motivated.

DOI: 10.4018/979-8-2600-2711-0.ch001

INTRODUCTION

The purpose of this chapter is to analyze some of the most important caracteristics of art created by artificial intelligence (AI) from the perspective of basic semiotic concepts.

This chapter will address the following key topics -defining AI-generated art and its basic characteristics; examining the advantages and disadvantages of AI-generated art in comparison to human-made art; analyzing AI art through the lens of semiotics; exploring AI art from the perspective of the semantic concept of redundancy; studying AI art through the concepts of Baroque and eclecticism and examining AI art in relation to the concepts of laconicism (zero morpheme) and Bauhaus.

The primary method used in this chapter is this of semiotics, enhanced by theories of communication, narratives, and artificial intelligence.

This chapter does not claim to be an exhaustive or comprehensive semiotic analysis of art created by artificial intelligence. The main reason for this limitation is that semiotics is a very broad discipline with no fewer than two hundred key concepts, while the chapter must be approximately 10,000 words.

Literature Review

The book "The Art and the Artificial Intelligence: How the Value of Real Art is Increased" examines the great potential of artificial intelligence in the arts, while simultaneously emphasizing the irreplaceable role of creative human potential. A central conclusion is that AI does not diminish human creativity; rather, it amplifies it, enabling new heights of artistic expression (Herpers, 2023). Building on this perspective, "Artificial Intelligence and the Arts: Computational Creativity, Artistic Behavior, and Tools for Creatives" examines psychological phenomena such as emotions, imagination, and creative processes, analyzing their influence on the development of AI. The volume gives particular attention to the interplay between computational creativity and human intelligence, highlighting how the two can complement one another in artistic practice (Greenfield et al., 2021). While these works focus on creativity, other authors emphasize ethical and aesthetic considerations. In "The Art of Artificial Intelligence: New Frontiers of Creativity", issues of authenticity and responsibility are central, alongside analyses of AI's applications across diverse fields such as cinema, literature, and painting. This positions AI both as a creative tool and as a cultural agent (Amoris, 2025) Philosophical reflections deepen this discussion. "The Art of Artificial Intelligence: Philosophical Keywords" investigates how humans might interact with AI without succumbing to subordination, analyzing creativity from both human and artificial perspectives and offering insights into their respective possibilities and limitations (Barale, 2024). Complementing these perspectives, "Art and Artificial Intelligence" revisits the long-standing debate on whether computers merely reproduce artistic patterns or are capable of genuine artistic creation. Several hypotheses are examined, highlighting how rapid technological progress continues to reshape the boundaries of artistic production (Hermerén, 2024). The discussion also extends to AI's evaluative capacities. "Artificial Intelligence for Art Creation and Understanding" underscores AI's ability not only to generate but also to interpret artworks, presenting case studies such as robotic theatre projects that integrate elements of Chinese folk traditions. This highlights AI's potential role in both creative innovation and cultural preservation (Mou, 2024). In addition to individual case studies, collective scholarly efforts provide a broader perspective. A collection of 26 articles from a major European conference in 2022 demonstrates AI's application across artistic forms such as architecture, video, and visual imagery. Through a multidisciplinary approach, the volume combines aesthetics, ethics, communication studies, and computer science to underscore AI's transformative impact on the arts (Rodríguez et al., 2022). The potential of collaboration between humans and AI is further emphasized in "Artificial Intelligence, Co-Creation and Creativity: The New Frontier for Innovation". This research illustrates how such partnerships can lead to increasingly sophisticated and high-quality artistic works, pushing the boundaries of co-creation (Moura, 2024). Beyond the arts, AI also shapes communication practices. The customization of media content has become a dominant trend in contemporary society, with AI enabling rapid and efficient production of personalized messages across political, cultural, and economic contexts (Jana et al., 2025). Another emerging field of inquiry concerns interactive art forms. Research in this area highlights AI's capacity to foster participation, engagement, and novel creative practices, thereby broadening the scope of artistic experience (Shen et al., 2021). Despite these advancements, questions of authenticity remain at the forefront of scholarly debate. While AI has achieved significant progress in architecture, music, and the visual arts, uncertainty persists over whether its outputs can truly be considered authentic artistic creations (Cheng, 2022). In parallel, studies on audience perception shed light on the reception of AI-generated artworks. Findings indicate that audiences often respond positively, though reactions vary across artistic mediums such as music and visual art. Ethical considerations remain central to this discussion, as highlighted in analyses of the advantages and dilemmas inherent in AI-human artistic collaborations (Moura et al., 2023; Yusa et al., 2022). Nevertheless, skepticism continues to shape the discourse. Although AI artworks are sometimes indistinguishable from human-made pieces, doubts remain widespread. This skepticism may be explained by anthropocentric thinking, which tends to undervalue AI-generated art and influences copyright debates. Further studies also point to the growing sophistication of AI systems, which adds to the complexity of the issue (Kalpokienė et al., 2023; Samo et al., 2023).

The question of artistic value therefore remains unresolved. Assessing whether AI creations possess artistic merit requires consideration of whether AI can approximate qualities associated with natural intelligence, such as emotional capacity, which remain integral to the human creative process (Liu, 2023). Finally, research has also addressed the role of AI in education. One study reviews the current state of AI integration in art teaching, identifies related challenges, and proposes strategies such as adaptability enhancement, intelligent instructional modes, and enriched artistic experiences. Using analytic hierarchy process (AHP) and grey clustering methods, the research demonstrates practical ways to evaluate and advance AI's role in art education (Kong, 2020).

Semiotics offers considerable opportunities in the analysis of communications generated by artificial intelligence. Semiotics, a discipline at the intersection of communication science and anthropology, explores the cultural codes that shape communication, value, spatial experience, and social change. One important contribution to this field is "Doing Semiotics", which introduces the principles and methods of applied semiotics while demonstrating their use in branding, strategic decision-making, cross-cultural marketing, and consumer experience through practical exercises and projects (Oswald, 2020). Building on foundational semiotic approaches, new research addresses the challenges posed by artificial intelligence. A revised framework for Multimodal Social Semiotics (MSS) has been proposed to account for autonomous AI systems capable of producing multimodal ensembles without direct human intentionality. By restructuring the hierarchy between sign designers and sign makers, this framework allows MSS to classify AI-generated signs as motivated while still preserving its theoretical integrity (Tomalin, 2025). In parallel, other scholarship examines the historical and semiotic dimensions of art and technology. This work analyzes how AI influences the intermedial landscape, reshaping co-creative practices and expanding the notion of distributed agency. Drawing on the theoretical insights of Walter Benjamin, Roland Barthes, Gilles Deleuze, and N. Katherine Hayles, the study explores how AI might embody forms of cognitive nonconsciousness and imaginative capacity (López-Varela Azcárate, 2023). Semiotic traditions are also revisited through the study of physiognomy and face reading, interpreted as enduring forms of semiotic practice. Contemporary research bridges ancient methods of analyzing the visage as a text with modern AI applications, offering new insights into human behavior and identity perception. At the same time, these interpretations raise critical questions about their cultural and technological implications (Gramigna, 2023). The cinematic domain provides another important site for applying semiotic principles to AI. Given the problems of neural networks in generating illogical or unintended visual content, one study proposes a production method grounded in iconography, symbols, and film semiotics. By leveraging rule-based semiotic AI, this approach seeks to mitigate issues of falsity and disconnectedness, ensuring closer alignment between creative intention and final output (Jeon, 2024). Beyond semiotics, artificial intelligence has also emerged as a transformative force in linguistics research. Using methods from Natural Language Processing (NLP), Machine Learning (ML), and Deep Learning (DL), AI enables the automated analysis of large linguistic datasets. These approaches assist researchers in modeling language development, predicting learning trajectories, and gaining deeper insights into linguistic phenomena (Singla, 2024). Finally, the broader implications of AI in applied linguistics have been examined through systematic content analysis. A study of 73 scholarly articles highlights both the promise and the limitations of AI tools such as GPT models for language teaching and research. While AI provides new opportunities for pedagogy and inquiry, its use also raises ethical concerns, challenges of content quality, and the demand for new digital competencies among educators and researchers (Alaqlobi et al., 2024).

One of the most important concepts in both semiotics and artificial intelligence is redundancy. Expanding beyond Russian academic contexts, one study investigates syntagmatic redundancy, particularly concord, to evaluate its status as a linguistic universal. Based on data from 50 languages, the research demonstrates that argumentative and temporal concord are nearly universal, while negative and multiple concord are not. These findings reveal two distinct functional principles: accuracy-driven redundancy and emphasis-driven redundancy, which differ in both communicative purpose and historical development (Leufkens, 2020). Further insights are offered by studies that distinguish between deliberate and accidental redundancy. Deliberate redundancy—manifested in devices such as anaphora and cataphora—enhances information structure, discourse cohesion, and readability. Accidental redundancy, in contrast, often results from syntactic transformations and lexical overlaps, potentially diminishing communicative efficiency (Pericliev, 2015). The paradoxical relationship between redundancy and language complexity has also been examined. Redundancy can simplify language processing and acquisition by providing cues for understanding, yet it may simultaneously complicate communication by violating principles of linguistic economy. A cross-linguistic study measuring four types of concord empirically demonstrates significant variation across languages, further underscoring this paradox (Leufkens, 2022). At a broader level, redundancy has been analyzed across multiple layers of language and communication. One paper investigates redundancy at the phonemic, syntactic, and semantic levels, as well as in complementary communication channels such as kinesics and situational context. The findings highlight redundancy's key role in language learning, concluding with pedagogical exercises designed to help students exploit redundancy in foreign language acquisition (Darian, 1979). Stylistic overload has also been studied in academic writing contexts. Research on Russian-language education articles shows that redundancy and wordiness cluster within specific rhetorical steps, particularly in sections where authors seek to establish the importance of their topic or articulate research objectives. These patterns suggest that redundancy in academic writing is systematic rather than accidental (Tikhonova et al., 2025). Finally, the pedagogical dimensions of redundancy have been explored in classroom discourse. A study of 20 primary education mathematics teachers across five schools found that redundancy was most prevalent in third-grade instruction. By defining the concept of redundancy and analyzing its occurrence in teaching practice, the research underscores its potential value as a pedagogical tool (Horváthová, 2017).

Redundancy is an integral part of the baroque and eclectic architectural styles and is completely foreign to Japanese culture. The book „Rethinking Architecture" compiles key writings on architecture by influential 20th-century philosophers and cultural theorists. Aimed at students in the social sciences and humanities, the collection challenges conventional architectural theory by reframing the built environment through a wider cultural lens, thereby integrating architectural discourse with broader debates in cultural theory (Leach, 1997). Extending this dialogue between philosophy and cultural theory, one article draws on Gilles Deleuze's "The Fold: Leibniz and the Baroque" to establish a connection between Baroque aesthetics and Juri Lotman's concept of the semiosphere. By examining these systems side by side, the author identifies conceptual parallels such as the monad and the fold, ultimately concluding that Lotman's work introduces a "folded" or Baroque boundary between structuralist and post-structuralist thought (Vidugirytė, 2022). A similar engagement with the Baroque can be found in Angela Ndalianis's book, which investigates the intersections between 17th-century Baroque aesthetics and contemporary entertainment media. Ndalianis argues that modern cultural forms such as films, video games, and theme parks are infused with a neo-Baroque aesthetic. This phenomenon, however, is not simply a repetition of historical art but emerges from technological innovation and shifting economic conditions (Ndalianis, 2003). The authors of one article focus on the divisive concept of Eclecticism, constructing "Eclectic Attribute Models" using the Cartography of Controversies and Actor-Network-Theory (ANT) to visually clarify it. The research concludes that contemporary eclecticism encompasses six key attributes: Pluralism, Historicity, Elitism, Decoration, Innovation, and Symbolism. (Cheng et al., 2022) In "Empire of Signs", Roland Barthes offers a fragmented, semiotic look at Japanese culture, which he views as a "rich, mobile, and subtle" system of signs.

Rather than providing a traditional analysis of the country, he uses his observations—from the arrangement of a dinner tray to the use of chopsticks—to explore the absence of a "deep meaning" or "precious heart." This leads him to a meditation on Tokyo as a city with an "empty" center, a concept that challenges Western notions of a symbolic core. (Barthes, 1982)

The artificial intelligence is analysed in different technological, artistic, educational, and cultural contexts, with particular attention to its social, ethical, and narrative implications. The book "AI Con: How to Fight Big Tech's Hype and Create the Future We Want" of Bender and Hanna critically examines the prevalent narratives surrounding artificial intelligence, showing how corporate AI "hype" can mask social, economic, and ethical concerns. The authors examine how the language of "intelligence" is often used to justify automation and control, rather than reflecting real intellectual capabilities. (Bender & Hanna, 2025) Barrat in his book "The Intelligence Explosion: When AI Beats Humans at Everything" examines the possible development of AI to levels where systems surpass human capabilities. He analyses both the potential benefits and serious risks of opaque and highly automated systems, including the economic and social consequences of an "intelligence explosion." (Barrat, 2025) This review article "Narratology meets text-to-image: A survey of consistency in AI generated storybook illustrations" presents a combination of narrative theory and text-to-image model analysis, highlighting the challenges of semiotic and plot consistency in AI-generated illustrations. The authors propose a six-dimensional framework model for assessing consistency in sequential visual narratives. (Lin et al. 2026) The article "When Stories Get a Visual Voice: AI-Generated Images, a Visual Pedagogy for Enhancing Student Engagement and Critical Analysis in World Literature" explores the impact of AI-generated images on visual perception and literary criticism. Using Reader Response theory, the authors show how algorithmic visual elements can enhance students' emotional and analytical engagement, but also narrow interpretive diversity. (Dakamsih et al. 2025) An article "Imagining AI futures in mainstream cinema: socio-technical narratives and social imaginaries. AI & Society" analyses how mainstream cinema shapes social and technical narratives about the future of AI, identifying dominant plot patterns (dystopian, hybrid, etc.) and their influence on public imagination and perceptions of AI technologies. (Valdivia, 2026).

MAIN ANALYSIS

Artificial intelligence (AI) is computational creator that generates various artifacts, including poetry, paintings, films, and music by the use of specific prompts and algorithms, along with the analysis of relevant databases with varying degrees of human involvement.

The initial stage of any new art form is the imitation or mimicry of an existing paradigm. It is widely anticipated that AI will soon move beyond merely replicating existing artistic poetics and paradigms. The technology is expected to largely emancipate itself from human prompts and begin to independently seek new and original creative solutions.

Similarly, human-led art creation has followed a parallel trajectory. Early cinema, for instance, uncritically adopted the poetics of theater, which led to its initial classification as "filmed theater." However, cinema gradually emancipated itself from the theatrical stage, progressively discovering and developing its own unique poetics.

AI-generated art will follow a similar developmental path. For example, in the near future, AI may begin to generate its own high-quality prompts without significant human intervention. This process is known as self-supervised prompt optimization.

From a semiotic standpoint, AI-generated art can be defined as the creation of artistic texts built upon multiple integrated sign systems, including symbolic, iconic, and indexical signs.

From the perspective of narrative theory, AI-generated art is a communicative phenomenon in which prompts are used to generate various narrative characters, their dramatized narrative actions, and their chronotopes.

The human role remains critical for defining goals and ensuring ethical integrity, factual accuracy, and contextual relevance. AI struggles to handle nuances, ambiguities, and phenomena related to ethics and social responsibility. This highlights the crucial role of humans in these specific interactions.

Artificial intelligence offers several key advantages in the artistic process, distinguishing its capabilities from those of human creators:

- Efficiency and Automation: AI develops self-supervised learning to optimize prompts, allowing it to achieve effective results with minimal human intervention. This automation is a significant advantage.
- Scale and Cost-Effectiveness: AI's ability to generate an immense number of creative variations easily and inexpensively is a key feature that distinguishes its creative process from that of humans.
- Speed: AI generates artistic works with exceptional speed, often in a matter of seconds.
- Personalization and Data Interpretation: AI can easily individualize creative works for specific users (e.g., based on social profiles), process vast amounts of scientific and other data, and interpret multiple perspectives.
- Reduced Labor: While some artistic creations may require months of costly, labor-intensive work from a human artist, AI can generate similar works almost for free through algorithmic modeling.
- Consistency and Precision: AI is also distinguished by its ability to effortlessly and consistently reproduce complex patterns—a level of precision that is often unattainable for most human creators.

Redundancy as a Key Semiotic Concept in this Article

The American semiotician Charles Morris introduced pragmatics as a central component of semiotics in his seminal work, "Foundations of the Theory of Signs" (1938). The author of this article, whose expertise is primarily in marketing communications and marketing semiotics, recognizes that two of the most fundamental characteristics of marketing communications are the demands for their efficiency and the active utilization of numerous sign systems. This duality is precisely what emphasizes the importance of semiotics for marketing.

From the perspective of communication efficiency, pragmatics plays a key role. The concept of pragmatics itself is a product of American cultural models, which are deeply defined by the practical results and effectiveness. It is these same applied characteristics of artificial intelligence (AI) that make redundancy a crucial semiotic concept for this analysis.

Redundancy is most commonly defined in linguistics and semiotics as the repetition or predictability of signs within a communication process. This predictability helps to reduce uncertainty during the interpretation of some text.

The concept originates from Claude Shannon's information theory, which posits that redundancy is the portion of a message that can be removed without the loss of essential information. This is because the meaning is already understood from its context.

In semiotic terms, this means that additional signs, repetitions, or patterns facilitate the decoding of meaning, even when certain elements of the message are missing or distorted.

In linguistics, redundancy is expressed by the use of more words than are strictly necessary. In semiotics, it manifests as a surplus of iconic, symbolic, and indexical signs. Within narratives, redundancy can involve an excess of characters or their actions, while in communication, it can be seen in the use of multiple interactions, communicative genres, and media.

The Transmedia is the ultimate demonstration of communicatve redunadancy because the Transmedia communicators could actualize all media and their genres, channels, etc.

The primary function of redundancy is to ensure the accurate and complete understanding of information in critical situations. For example, it is crucial for conversations between aircraft pilots and air traffic controllers to prevent potentially fatal misinterpretations.

Redundancy also plays a significant role in interpersonal communication, such as in a heated argument in the family, where repeated phrases or gestures might be used to emphasize a point and ensure the message is received despite the emotional noise.

The meaning of redundancy can vary slightly depending on its context, ranging from everyday use to more technical applications in linguistics and communication theory.

In the context of semiotics, redundancy in art is actualized when multiple distinct and abundant sign systems work together to express the same meaning. This creates what is known as multichannel reinforcement, where several visual elements—such as color, composition, gesture, and iconography—collaborate to provide repetitive clues for the viewer, thereby facilitating the decoding of the intended meaning.

Redundancy also serves to narrow the polysemy of signs. A single sign can often be interpreted in multiple ways; however, several signs constrain the viewer's interpretation toward a desired understanding.

An excellent example of this is Pierre-Auguste Renoir's painting *Le Déjeuner des canotiers*. In this work, the primary theme is "civilized pleasure." The artist masterfully conveys this abstract concept of paradise, civilization and happiness by the redundancy of various visual (iconic) signs, including the depiction of beautiful, well-dressed people, their harmonious and peaceful interactions, and the beautiful, fresh nature and time (chronotope).

All of these visual cues reinforce the central meaning, making it easy for the viewer to grasp the intended message.

We can define redundancy in art as "excessive signification" when multiple sign systems—including iconic, symbolic, and indexical signs—are used simultaneously to express a single, unambiguous meaning. The most important characteristic of this process is that these diverse sign systems are all governed by one primary code.

For instance, if we use the code of hellish evil, a painting might depict devils and dragons (iconic signs), use dark colors (coloremes), and show a subterranean space with erupting lava (indexical signs). The meaning in such a painting is duplicated not through homogeneous signs but through entirely different sign systems. Each of these systems expresses the same meaning, yet with distinct signs.

Redundancy is only effective if the sender and receiver of the message share the same cultural and semiotic codes. A person from China, for example, would likely have great difficulty interpreting the "hellish" painting discussed previously. The reason lies in the differences in cultural symbolism.

In China, the color white, not black, is the sign for death. It symbolizes death, endings, and transition, which is why people wear white clothes or white armbands at funerals and mourning ceremonies. In contrast, while black is a color of mourning in many Western cultures, in China it typically represents solemnity and formality, not grief.

Furthermore, the dragon, which is a malicious creature of hell in European mythology, is a kind and powerful being in Chinese culture. The Chinese dragon embodies:

- Goodness and Power: It controls water, rain, rivers, and seas.;
- Fertility and Life-Giving Force: It brings rain and good harvests.;
- Harmony: It acts as a mediator between the heavens and the earth.;
- Longevity and Prosperity: The dragon brings luck, protection, and success.

These examples illustrate that the effectiveness of redundancy and "excessive signification" depends entirely on the shared understanding of the underlying cultural and semiotic codes. Without this shared context, the intended meaning of a message can be completely lost or misinterpreted.

Redundancy can also be understood as a form of semiotic and communicative excess that arises from ideological, financial, or technological motivations. This particular definition is the core concept analyzed in this article.

A typical example of this is Baroque and Eclectic art and architecture, which are definitively redundant in their nature. The Baroque style, which flourished during the 17th and 18th centuries, is renowned for its dramatic, intricate, and lavishly decorated character. It often emerged as a reaction to the more balanced and restrained art of the Renaissance.

The key characteristics of the Baroque style, which contribute to its redundancy, include:

- Grandeur and Drama: A sense of awe is created through monumental scale, dramatic lighting, and a feeling of movement.;
- Abundance of Detail: Every surface is typically filled with intricate ornamentation, such as ornate carvings, twisting columns, and elaborate frescoes.;
- *Horror vacui*: A Latin phrase meaning "the fear of empty space," which drives the tendency to fill every part of a surface or design with details.;
- Sensory Appeal: The goal was to evoke strong emotions in the viewer through a rich, multisensory experience that redundantly combines painting, sculpture, music, architecture, cloths, etc.

The Baroque style, a flamboyant and extravagant artistic movement, required substantial funding due to its opulence. The primary financial sources were:

- The Catholic Church and the Counter-Reformation: The Church in Rome used the Baroque style to reassert its power after the Protestant Reformation. Popes and religious orders commissioned magnificent churches, elaborate frescoes, and sculptures, financed by the wealthy Catholic system.
- European Monarchies and Aristocracy: Absolute monarchs and the super-rich aristocracy employed Baroque art to glorify their reigns and display their power. The Palace of Versailles, built for King Louis XIV, is a prime exam-

ple. Spanish and Portuguese monarchies also commissioned opulent Baroque palaces and churches to emphasize their dominance and Catholic faith.

- Trade and Colonialism: Colonial conquests and global trade brought immense wealth from gold, silver, and other valuable goods. These funds enriched monarchies, aristocrats, and the new merchant class, who in turn commissioned palaces, chapels, and portraits to showcase their status and sophistication.

Combined, these sources provided the financial power for the grandeur and magnificence—the semiotic, narrative, and communicative redundancy—of Baroque art, making it a symbol of both religious and secular authority.

Redundancy and Architectural Eclecticism (19th Century)

Architectural eclecticism, a prominent style in the second half of the 19th century, is characterized by its intentional mixing of elements from various historical styles such as Gothic, Romanesque, Baroque, and Neoclassical.

This approach was a reaction against the strict, singular canons of earlier periods. Rather than adhering to a "pure" style, eclectic architecture utilizes a redundant catalog of forms, resulting in complex and often overly ornate compositions. The famous Opéra Garnier in Paris is a prime example of this eclectic architectural style.

Interestingly, this type of redundancy is also characteristic of AI-generated art, but it stems from fundamentally different reasons. While the redundancy in Baroque and Eclectic art reflected the ideology and immense wealth of the ruling classes of those eras, the redundancy in AI art is a direct result of the incredible computational capabilities available today.

A pragmatic analysis demonstrates that redundancy can serve as a communication strategy born out of an abundance of resources.

In the case of the Baroque period, this "rich reality" was the vast financial wealth acquired from colonial possessions. This wealth enabled the creation of a stylistically redundant art form characterized by its opulence and overabundance of signs.

Similarly, in the case of artificial intelligence (AI), its continuous use of redundancy as a communicative strategy is a direct result of its near-limitless computational capabilities. These capabilities allow it to tirelessly generate a massive quantity of sign-rich texts—including images, music, and video—at virtually no cost.

Where possible, we can structure semantic concepts and the corresponding stylistic figures as pairs of oppositions.

The opposition to the concept of redundancy (excess) is the concept of zero morpheme (laconicism).

Redundancy means that we communicate with the maximum amount of signs, that is, we are maximally explicit. The zero morpheme is exactly the opposite – the explicitness is minimal. In this case, we can communicate without any signs, as long as we actualized the relevant text in a favorable context.

The stylistic figure hyperbole corresponds to the concept of redundancy, and the stylistic figure litotes corresponds to the concept of laconism (zero morpheme).

In grammar, a zero morpheme is a morpheme without a phonetic constituent. In English, for example, the noun sheep is unchanged in the plural: Here, the zero morpheme (∅) expresses the plural form solely with the help of the context.

AI frequently generates redundant images that re-envision Baroque art (Figure 1).

Figure 1. Redundant AI painting, intertextualizing Baroque art

This is a quite natural, considering the profound relationship between the two phenomena. The images are characterized by an abundance of depicted elements.

The space is cluttered with architectural and decorative elements such as sculptures, columns, arches, gilded furniture, and a massive chandelier. There is no "empty" or negative space; the majority of the composition is filled with ornaments, figures, and intricate details. Only a small portion of the floor is relatively naked.

The same principle of abundance applies to the figures within the artwork; the aristocrats are dressed in lavish clothing, adopting theatrical poses and gestures. This image is a typical example of a communication strategy based on the semiotic concept of redundancy.

All the semiotic systems—architecture, decor, figures, gestures—express the notions of wealth, grandeur, and power through a multitude of signs. This repetition embodies Baroque rhetoric, where hyperbole and allegory are employed to amplify the impact.

Thus, a clear connection between the Baroque and AI-generated art can be established. In classical Baroque art, the excess was a product of the material and financial prosperity of the ruling classes, derived from colonial wealth, political power, and monarchical prestige.

In AI-generated art, however, this excess arises as a result of technological power. The machine can produce an infinite number of images, often cluttered with details to the point of hyperrealism.

The AI-generated image (Figure 2) is inspired by the Baroque and Rococo styles, particularly in how it depicts excess and decorativeness.

Figure 2. AI-generatedpainting inspired by Baroque and Rococo styles

The artificial intelligence achieved this through two primary methods:

- Accumulation of Objects: The AI filled the space with numerous artifacts, including gilded picture frames, heavy curtains, crystal chandeliers, and decorative items such as vases with flowers and bowls on a table. Every surface is saturated with texture and ornaments, creating a sense of opulence and clutter characteristic of the era.
- Interpretation of the Subject: The AI interprets the central female figure through the visual codes of power and dominance. She is portrayed as sophisticated, beautiful, young, and aristocratic. Her dress—an extremely lavish (redundant) gown made of satin and richly embroidered—along with her ornate hairstyle and abundant jewelry, further reinforces this theme.

An essential characteristic of the Baroque is theatricality. The figure is in a clearly theatrical pose—she is static, with a dramatic expression and a gaze directed to the side, creating a sense of contemplation or detachment.

Here, the central code is again that of dominance and power. The woman is beautiful and sophisticated, placed in an expensive setting—a beautiful room with costly furniture, gold, etc. The image recreates the atmosphere of the 17th-18th-century French court, where luxury was a sign of the grandeur of the king, the monarchy, and the aristocracy. This painting is a visual apology for elitism.

In this way, the Baroque and technological redundancies align perfectly.

The semiotic mechanism is similar in an AI-generated painting created based on surrealistic excess (Figure 3).

The painting uses the poetics of Hieronymus Bosch's work, and he certainly painted redundantly.

In this case, we can define several types of redundancy:

The painting harmoniously combines elements from medieval and Renaissance art (tall towers, architecture, primitive figures) with futuristic and science fiction elements (a rocket, flying ships, spherical buildings). This creates a visual abundance of unrelated eras.

Figure 3. AI-generated painting based on poetics of Hieronymus Bosch

The space is not realistic but fantastic. It resembles a floating island or a strange world where the land is broken, and below it, there is another, no less strange world. This is an abundance of absurd and unexpected combinations.

A multitude of different creatures are accumulated—humans, angels, monsters, strange animals, and mechanisms. Each of them is detailed, but the meaning of their existence is not clear.

The painting does not tell a single story but many small, unclear narratives. Each group of figures is engaged in some action—sitting, standing, flying—but it is not clear exactly what is happening or how all these many stories are connected in the overall pictorial text.

The unifying code here is likely that of the Apocalypse, which AI interprets based on the redundant artistic code of Hieronymus Bosch, specifically his painting, “The Garden of Earthly Delights.” The apocalyptic redundancy of Bosch is a natural result of the terrifying time and place of deadly and widespread inquisition in which this great Flemish artist worked.

The painting is also an excellent example of AI's ability to synthesize and combine elements from completely different sources—medieval and Renaissance art, science fiction, and surrealism—into a new and coherent whole.

This excess is generated by the rapid processing of unlimited data in the fields of art history and theory, combined with exceptional computer programs and excellent, competent prompts.

The Viennese decadence of the late 19th and early 20th centuries is a classic example of civilizational redundancy. The main reason for this was the highly wealthy and civilized Vienna of that era—a capital and a focal point of impressive wealth and civilizational achievements in science, arts, architecture, urban planning, administration, the military, and so on.

All these elements are naturally reflected in the paintings of the great Gustav Klimt, which are overflowing with gold, Byzantine poetics, beautiful women, fabulous dresses, sophisticated jewelry, and more. A painting created by AI, inspired by Gustav Klimt's aesthetic, is a present-day interpretation of the artistic poetics of Viennese fin de siècle (Figure 4):

Figure 4. AI generated painting, inspired by Gustav Klimt art style

It captures and transfers the characteristic features of Art Nouveau—decorative abundance, golden ornamentation, symbolism, and the aesthetics of decadence—into a digital context. At the same time, the work builds upon and "overloads" its archetypes, transforming Klimt's refined poetics into a digital redundancy.

The gold in this painting is a redundant sign for Byzantine civilization. It's the dominant semiotic system in the composition. Much like Klimt, who drew inspiration from the Byzantine mosaics in Ravenna, the golden background here creates an aura of eternity and transcendence.

Gold acts as both a decorative and a spiritual element—a sign of wealth, cultural elevation, and a striving for the absolute.

What's important in this specific case is the overwhelming abundance of gold. More than 90% of the painting is composed of signs that express gold: golden ornaments, golden jewelry, golden dresses, golden architecture, and golden backgrounds.

The painting is also a typical example of abundant architectural and ornamental eclecticism. The background presents an architectural fantasy in which domes, arches, and facades representing Baroque, Orientalist, and Modernist styles are mixed.

This amalgamation is characteristic of the age of eclecticism, but in the digital image, it reaches an extreme—every surface is covered with endless ornaments and oversaturated decorations. This accumulation functions as a visual expression of the cultural sophistication and civilized luxury of late 19th-century Vienna, where architecture, art, and social life were maximally aestheticized.

The female figure embodies decadent poetics. The central character is a stylish and civilized beauty, whom the AI has interpreted entirely within the poetics of Klimt.

From the perspective of this article, her most important feature is the redundancy of her dress. It is entirely gold and overflowing with beautiful floral and other ornaments. In this way, the dress fits completely into the ideology of Austrian civilization, the poetics of Klimt, and its redundant digital interpretations.

The conclusion is that AI has fully interpreted the philosophy and ideology of sophisticated and redundant Viennese eclecticism and has interpreted it very subtly in its numerous paintings influenced by the poetics of Gustav Klimt.

This Paris born style, also bears the characteristics of redundancy, thanks to the wealth and highly developed culture of the city in the late 19th and early 20th centuries. The analyzed image (Figure 5) successfully interprets the core elements of Alphonse Mucha's style—the rich semantic field of female beauty, interpreted through numerous signs of grace, an abundance of decorations, exquisite clothing, floral motifs, and so on.

Figure 5. AI generated painting, inspired by Alphonse Mucha art style

A crucial part of Alphonse Mucha's poetics is his treatment of idealized female beauty. He interprets women through their ideal forms, ensuring there are no physical imperfections in his figures. This approach to perfection is a hallmark of his style.

The AI creates the female figures in an identical manner. In this case, the central figure is a beautiful woman, a distinctive feature of Mucha's work. She is idealized and romanticized, serving as the focal point of the composition.

The AI's rendering intensifies this idealization, making her features perfect (like a deity's) and elevating the "poetics" to a hyper-stylized level. Her pose and expression are serene, embodying the aesthetic of graceful femininity characteristic of the era.

The floral motifs in the AI-generated painting are just as abundant as in Mucha's posters. Therefore, in both bodies of work, we can certainly speak of floral hyperbole.

We can also definitively observe decorative excess. The decorative details in this image are numerous and repetitive. The circular medallion behind the woman, a classic Mucha motif, is cluttered with intricate ornamentation. Nearly the entire space of the painting is ornamented to align with the overarching principle of redundancy.

The same applies to the chromatic signs—a rich color palette is used—and the decorative signs—for example, the woman's hairstyle is also complex and composed of many details.

Due to all these elements, we can certainly describe the composition as hyperbolized or exaggerated (redundant).

AI's interpretations of African art are also very interesting (Figure 6):

Figure 6. AI interpretation of African art

The artificial intelligence has excellently captured the poetics of African art and, due to its redundant nature, has created an abundance of African abstract images and symbols (likely around one hundred). Each individual image is simple and clear, but their accumulation creates a sense of visual and spatial density. This phenomenon can be described as a visual rhetoric of accumulation. Instead of using words, the painting accumulates visual signs to create a specific rhetoric of abundance, which immerses the viewer in a world of signs. This highlights how AI can apply the principle of redundancy to different cultural aesthetics.

There is a semantic excess in the interpretations; the images are numerous and abstract, and their meanings are unknown to the viewer. Therefore, each person can interpret the multiple images and their corresponding meanings as they wish.

This also leads to syntactic excess—these images arrange a connected text, which is a syntactic phenomenon. However, since the interpreters do not know the meanings, each one perceives the connections in the image differently.

Finally, there is narrative abundance. Each image is a potential idea or story. Together, they create a "narrative mix" where the images can tell us multiple stories.

The Baroque is not the only redundant European architectural style. Architectural eclecticism in Western Europe, especially in France during the mid-to-late 19th century, is also a typical example of architectural excess.

The reasons for its emergence and flourishing are, to a large extent, similar to those of the Baroque. Both styles appeared during wealthy and prosperous times when large fortunes were accumulated, which could finance the lavish Baroque and Eclectic projects.

The main characteristic of this style is the combination of elements from different periods, such as Gothic, Renaissance, Baroque, Rococo, Neoclassicism, and even Oriental motifs. For instance, a single building might feature Gothic windows, a Renaissance facade, and Baroque ornaments.

Eclectic buildings are often heavily ornamented, utilizing richly decorated facades, cornices, columns, and sculptures that are characteristic of various historical periods. The elements used are chosen to express specific meanings. For example, elements from Greek and Roman architecture might symbolize power and grandeur, while Gothic elements convey mysticism and spirituality.

Eclecticism can be defined as a lavish style, a direct result of Europe's financial prosperity in the second half of the 19th century. It originated in an era of rapid industrialization and the accumulation of bourgeois wealth.

It perfectly allowed the rich and often less-educated bourgeoisie to flaunt their wealth and taste through magnificent and richly decorated, albeit somewhat kitschy, buildings. This makes architecture a quintessential semiotic and communicative phenomenon.

The use of elements from other historical styles, such as Baroque and Rococo, which are known for their extravagant decoration, further emphasizes this trend. The financial boom in Europe during this period provided the necessary funds for the construction of large-scale and lavishly redundant projects.

Similarly, artificial intelligence communicates its creative capabilities by generating elaborate images. It is not by chance that some of these images interpret eclectic architecture (Figure 8) as a scene depicting a cityscape from the late 19th or early 20th century:

This image illustrates architectural eclectic redundancy. The main building on the left combines various architectural elements. Its facade is complex, with numerous windows and decorative cornices reminiscent of the French Second Empire, particularly the mansard roof. The adjacent buildings have more classical lines but are also richly decorated in a mixture of historical styles.

Figure 7. AI painting intepreting architectural eclectic style

The facades of the buildings, streetlights, and even the cars are ornately decorated. These features are not purely functional but rather decorative. Details such as figures, cornices, and intricate window shapes serve as a form of visual pleonasm, conveying the wealth, opulence, success, and prosperity of the era.

The excess is not just in the architecture, however in the overall busy city life—the multitude of people, carriages, tramlines, and wet streets reflecting the city lights. This abundance of objects contrasts with the empty, clean spaces often found in many Renaissance paintings.

The AI once again demonstrates its ability to generate a wealth of artifacts, natural scenes, and intricate details.

Similar to architectural eclecticism, the AI "mixes" different visual "styles" and elements from its database. The result is a hybrid painting that appears to be a classical work but with a level of detail only possible through modern algorithms. This is a form of "technological eclecticism," where styles and eras merge into a new, unique image.

The visual style of the analyzed image can be classified as a variant of hyperrealism, yet with a distinct regional and cultural specificity that may provisionally be referred to as *"Brazilian Hyperrealism."*

Hyperrealism, which emerged in the 1970s, is characterized by a meticulous and detailed imitation of photographic imagery that often exceeds the reality, thereby emphasizing particular phenomena through aesthetic exaggeration. In this case, what is observed is not merely an obedience to this aesthetic paradigm but also its integration with a cultural code associated with Brazilian, and more broadly, Latin American traditions.

In art theory, the term *"Brazilian Hyperrealism"* does not formally exist. It is introduced here to express the cultural mixture between the global style of hyperrealism and the vividly emphasized aesthetics of the South American context.

This aesthetic is marked by the abundance of warm, saturated, and contrasting colors, dynamic composition, and heightened expressivity. Such features correspond to well-known characteristics of Brazilian culture: joyfulness, sensuality, bodily expressiveness, and a pronounced affinity for ornamentation (Figure 9):

Figure 8. AI painting in a Brazilian Hyperrealism style

From a semiotic perspective, the image is full with *redundancies*—repetitive signifying elements that amplify the central message. Several principal levels of redundancy may be identified:

Chromatic redundancy - Bright and warm hues—orange, red, yellow, green, and pink—dominate the composition and form its primary aesthetic layer. The saturation of color exceeds mere functional necessity and shifts into pure decorativeness.

Redundancy in the female figure - The depicted woman functions as the central visual sign, embodying the erotic and hedonistic dimensions of Latin American culture. Her minimal clothing may be conceptualized as a "zero morpheme"—minimal in quantity, yet compensated through maximal ornamentation.

The attire is adorned with colors, patterns, jewelry, tattoos, and accessories, thereby generating additional redundancy.

Redundancy in decorèmes (accessories and details) - sunglasses, hairstyle, jewelry, necklaces, and tattoos form a secondary field of signs that reinforce the sense of excess, opulence, and cultural hyperbole. Each element may function independently as a signifier, yet in their cumulative presence they create a form of "visual noise" that is simultaneously superfluous and indispensable for producing the intended effect of oversaturation.

Redundancy in the surrounding ornamentation (the vehicle) - The bus-like vehicle is covered with vivid graffiti, verbal inscriptions, and images, functioning as an active semiotic field rather than a neutral background. It creates contextual reinforcement for the central female figure, effectively acting as a parallel redundant narrative layer.

Taken together, these redundancies produce a cultural message that may be defined as an apotheosis of bodily and aesthetic expressivity, typical of Latin American traditions.

This semiotic oversaturation can be interpreted as a symbol of "liberated erotic culture," which, in its bright and exuberant form, may appear highly attractive to societies where corporeality, expressivity and redundancy are socially valorized (e.g., in Latin America and Southern Europe).

Laconism (zero morpheme)

The semantic concept that forms the opposition to redundancy is laconism or the zero morpheme. While redundancy actualizes an extralinguistic phenomenon with an abundance of different signs, laconism uses a minimal number of signs, or they are even completely absent.

Entire cultures are built and function on the basis of these two concepts. In this article, the Baroque era was analyzed as an example of redundancy.

However, Japanese culture functions on the basis of laconism. Roland Barthes insightfully analyzed this in his book, "Empire of Signs".

One of the main ideas of his book is the concept of emptiness and the absence of a center in Japanese culture—for example, the empty space in architecture, silence in communication, and the mildness (delicatness) of forms.

European Baroque is superabundant—full of ornaments, cluttered compositions, rhetorical figures, and theatricality. The Baroque aims to overwhelm the senses, leaving no "empty" space and no room for silence or absence.

Japanese laconism, however, is anti-Baroque. Where the Baroque clutters, Japan simplifies; where the Baroque fills, Japan leaves empty space; where the Baroque insists on meaning, Japan defers or disperses it.

This difference is clearly seen when we analyze a Japanese garden and a Baroque cathedral. In a Japanese garden, the space is minimalist, with large empty zones (sand, stones, a few trees). The important element is the interval—the emptiness between the elements—and meaning comes from contemplation and silence. The Japanese garden does not "impose" a meaning but offers an open field for meditation.

In a Baroque cathedral, the space is maximally filled with frescoes, sculptures, gilding, dynamic lines, and an abundance of details.

Of course, we should not make general conclusions. One of the most famous Japanese painting, "The Great Wave off Kanagawa," is definitely redundant, while the functional architectural styles of Bauhaus and of the world-renowned architect Le Corbusier are laconic.

Traditional Japanese painting is characterized by minimalism and restraint, where a few visual signs are sufficient to convey complex philosophical or aesthetic meanings.

In contrast, the AI-generated image (Figure 10) demonstrates a radically different sensibility:

Figure 9. AI painting inspired by the traditional Japanese art style

Instead of economy, the composition is redundant and saturated, resembling more to the abundance of European Baroque than to the austerity of Japanese scroll painting.

The women are dressed in richly decorated kimonos and elaborate headdresses, recalling both classical Japanese courtly culture and idealized portraiture.

Their porcelain-like, flawless faces exemplify the AI's tendency to generate an *aesthetic of perfection* that transcends traditional painterly limitations. The pairing of the figures echoes Baroque double portraits, where multiplicity and ornamentation connote grandeur.

The abundance of lotuses and blossoms creates decorative excess. While in traditional Japanese aesthetics a single flower could express an entire philosophy, here flowers multiply, representing an almost Western sense of abundance.

The background merges calligraphy, birds, abstract circular forms, and splashes of red. Rather than serving as an empty space (*ma*)—a central principle in Japanese art—the background becomes a site of visual noise, demanding as much attention as the central figures themselves.

SOLUTIONS AND RECOMMENDATIONS

A solution typically refers to the process of addressing or resolving a problem. In this context, the issue does not lie in the quantity or quality of works of art produced by artificial intelligence (AI), as these are not currently problematic.

Instead, the challenge concerns human artists who create original works of art. Competing with AI-generated creativity may prove difficult for these individuals, potentially leading to severe economic and psychological consequences, including financial problems and, in extreme cases, suicide.

One potential solution is for artists to develop the skills necessary to collaborate effectively with AI. Through such teamwork, it is possible to create artistic masterpieces that integrate human creativity with technological innovation.

FUTURE TRENDS

The article emphasizes the benefits of artificial intelligence (AI) in artistic production, including efficiency and automation, scalability and cost-effectiveness, speed, personalization, and consistency. Collectively, these features represent a positive trend, as AI enables the creation of vast amounts of artistic production.

Various forms of art—including literature, painting, comics, and both live-action and animated films—are rapidly evolving through integration with AI and other advanced technologies.

One notable example of this trend is the rise of immersive exhibitions featuring artists such as Vincent van Gogh, Gustav Klimt, and Salvador Dalí. These exhibitions have transformed museums by making them more accessible, democratic, and appealing to broader audiences.

Of course, there are also quite a few negative trends. It is entirely possible that artificial intelligence will bring us some social dystopia as the book 1984 or will destoy the human civilization – as in the film The Matrix.

THE MAIN SCIENTIFIC CONTRIBUTIONS OF THIS ARTICLE

The main scientific contributions of this study can be summarized as follows:

First, the analysis identifies a connection between redundancy in the Baroque aesthetic and redundancy in artificial intelligence (AI). Although redundancy emerges from different causes in each case, it constitutes a defining characteristic of both phenomena. This observation is one of the most significant trends in the development of AI-generated art.

Second, three additional trends are highlighted: (a) the capacity of AI to generate multiple variants of the same work, (b) the frequent use of the semantic concept of intertextuality, and (c) the application of the semantic dichotomy of synchrony and diachrony as communicative strategies. These trends have been examined in detail in my previous scientific articles.

Third, the research establishes a link between the semantic concept of redundancy and the stylistic figure of hyperbole, as well as between the semantic concept of laconicism (zero morpheme) and the stylistic figure of litotes.

Finally, the findings demonstrate that AI redundancy can be systematically contextualized in relation to architectural styles such as Baroque and Eclecticism, which historically employed ornamental excess as a semiotic strategy of grandeur, abundance, and ideological authority.

CONCLUSION

This chapter has conceptualized artificial intelligence (AI) art as a distinct form of computational creativity that employs prompts, algorithms, and machine learning techniques to generate a wide variety of artistic artifacts—including painting, music, and cinema—across a continuum of human involvement. AI art is not merely a technological novelty but a phenomenon that challenges and redefines traditional boundaries of artistic authorship, creativity, and meaning-making.

From a semiotic perspective, AI art may be interpreted as a multimodal text constructed through the interplay of different sign systems—iconic, symbolic, and indexical. The semiotic lens provides a framework for understanding AI-generated works as complex structures in which meaning is produced not only through the algorithmic processes themselves but also through their integration with human prompts, interpretive practices, and cultural contexts.

A central issue addressed in this chapter concerns the notion of redundancy as a semiotic concept. Drawing upon Claude Shannon's (1948) information theory, redundancy is traditionally defined as the repetition or predictability of signs within a communicative system. However, in the artistic domain, redundancy assumes a different function.

Rather than operating as predictability, it often manifests as what might be described as "excessive signification," wherein multiple semiotic systems—such as color, composition, and iconography—interact to produce texts that are saturated with meaning. This form of redundancy transcends informational efficiency and instead highlights artistic abundance, complexity, and richness.

The analysis has further demonstrated that AI technologies accelerate the development of artistic production along two principal dimensions: the speed of generating creative artifacts and the degree of their semiotic redundancy. This dual acceleration introduces new dynamics into the cultural field, enabling rapid experimentation and iterative creation while simultaneously producing works that are densely layered with signs.

Moreover, the chapter has situated AI art within broader art-historical frameworks by drawing comparisons between the redundancy of AI-generated works and that observed in earlier artistic styles and movements, particularly the Baroque and Eclecticism. Both historical and contemporary examples reveal that redundancy functions as a critical semantic and stylistic principle that shapes the evolution of artistic expression.

By placing AI art within this lineage, the study underscores continuity between traditional aesthetic practices and technologically mediated forms of creation.

The general conclusion emerging from this inquiry is that the artistic landscape has already been profoundly reshaped by AI. This transformation extends beyond the fine arts to encompass creative industries, entertainment, marketing and mass communications, music, architecture, and other cultural domains.

The impact of AI on speed, quality, affordability, and accessibility, as well as its ability to generate entirely new aesthetic possibilities, signals an irreversible shift in how art is conceptualized, produced, and consumed. Nevertheless, this is only the beginning of a broader transformation whose long-term consequences remain to be fully understood.

Consequently, the systematic study of AI art should be integrated into educational curricula at both the primary, secondary and higher education levels. Only through such sustained engagement can society adequately prepare for the profound reconfigurations of creativity and meaning-making that AI technologies will continue to bring.

REFERENCES

Alaqlobi, O., Alduais, A., Qasem, F., & Alasmari, M. (2024). Artificial intelligence in applied (linguistics): A content analysis and future prospects. *Cogent Arts & Humanities, 11*(1), 1–19. DOI: 10.1080/23311983.2024.2382422

Amoris, A. (2025). *The art of artificial intelligence: New frontiers of creativity.* CBF Publishing.

Barale, A. (2024). *The art of artificial intelligence: Philosophical keywords.* Cambridge Scholars Publishing.

Barrat, J. (2025). *The Intelligence Explosion: When AI Beats Humans at Everything.* St. Martin's Press.

Barthes, R. (1982). *Empire of Signs* (Howard, R., Trans.). Hill and Wang. (Original work published 1970)

Bender, E. M., & Hanna, A. (2025). *The AI Con: How to Fight Big Tech's Hype and Create the Future We Want.* Harper/The Bodley Head.

Cheng, K., & Neisch, P. (2022). A new perspective on eclectic attributes in architecture: Taking eclectic architecture in Beijing and Hong Kong as an example. *Journal of Asian Architecture and Building Engineering, 22*(3), 1126–1145. DOI: 10.1080/13467581.2022.2074017

Cheng, M. (2022). The creativity of artificial intelligence in art. In *Proceedings of the 2021 Summit of the International Society for the Study of Information. Proceedings, 81*(1), 110. Retrieved January 22, 2025, from. DOI: 10.3390/proceedings2022081110

Dakamsih, N., Alshunnag, M., & Alkayid, A. (2025). When Stories Get a Visual Voice: AI-Generated Images, a Visual Pedagogy for Enhancing Student Engagement and Critical Analysis in World Literature. *Educational Process: International Journal, 18*(1), e2025416. DOI: 10.22521/edupij.2025.18.416

Darian, S. (1979). The role of redundancy in language and language teaching. *System, 7*(1), 47–59. DOI: 10.1016/0346-251X(79)90022-8

Gramigna, R. (2023). *The visage as text: physiognomy, semiotics, and face reading from antiquity to artificial intelligence.* Chinese Semiotic Studies.

Greenfield, G., Romero, J., & Machado, P. (Eds.). (2021). *Artificial intelligence and the arts: Computational creativity, artistic behavior, and tools for creatives.* Springer International Publishing.

Hermerén, G. (2024). *Art and artificial intelligence*. Cambridge University Press. DOI: 10.1017/9781009431798

Herpers, Y. P. (2023). *The art and the artificial intelligence: How the value of real art is increased*. Herpers Publishing International.

Horváthová, K. (2017). Redundancy in the verbal communication of teachers in primary education. *Journal of Language and Cultural Education*, *5*(3), 93–107. DOI: 10.1515/jolace-2017-0030

Jana, M., & Banerjee, S. (2025). *Artificial intelligence and contemporary media*. Notion Press.

Jeon, B. (2024). Studies of Artificial Intelligence (AI) Cinema: The necessity for studying AI film making methodologies that apply iconography, semiotics, and film semiotics theories. *The Korean Journal of Arts Studies*.

Kalpokienė, J., & Kalpokas, I. (2023). Creative encounters of a posthuman kind – anthropocentric law, artificial intelligence, and art. *Technology in Society*, *72*, 102197. DOI: 10.1016/j.techsoc.2023.102197

Kong, F. (2020). Application of artificial intelligence in modern art teaching. [iJET]. *International Journal of Emerging Technologies in Learning*, *15*(13), 1863–1870. DOI: 10.3991/ijet.v15i13.15351

Leach, N. (Ed.). (1997). *Rethinking architecture: A reader in cultural theory*. Routledge.

Leufkens, S. (2022). Measuring redundancy: The relation between concord and complexity. *Linguistics Vanguard : Multimodal Online Journal*, *9*(s1), 95–106. Advance online publication. Retrieved January 22, 2025, from. DOI: 10.1515/lingvan-2020-0143

Leufkens, S. C. (2020). A functionalist typology of redundancy. *Revista da Abralin*, *19*(3), 79–103.

Lin, Z., Wang, Z., Liu, Q., Zhang, X., & Liu, J. (2026). Narratology meets text-to-image: A survey of consistency in AI generated storybook illustrations. *Artificial Intelligence Review*, *59*(2), 83. DOI: 10.1007/s10462-025-11482-6

Liu, B. (2023). Arguments for the rise of artificial intelligence art: Does AI art have creativity, motivation, self-awareness and emotion? *Arte. Individuo y Sociedad*, *35*(3), 811–822. DOI: 10.5209/aris.83808

López-Varela Azcárate, A. (2023). Intermedial semiotics in the age of artificial intelligence. Challenges and opportunities for the arts. *Techno Humanities*, *3*(2), 108–116. DOI: 10.1016/j.techum.2024.04.001

Morris, C. W. (1938). Foundations of the theory of signs. In O. Neurath (Ed.), International Encyclopedia of Unified Science (pp. 1–59). Chicago University Press., https://www.mpi.nl/publications/item2364493/foundations-theory-signs, Retrieved February 15, 2026, from.

Mou, L. (Ed.). (2024). *Artificial intelligence for art creation and understanding*. CRC Press. DOI: 10.1201/9781003406273

Moura, F. T. (Ed.). (2024). *Artificial intelligence, co-creation and creativity: The new frontier for innovation*. Taylor & Francis. DOI: 10.4324/9781003453901

Moura, F. T., Castrucci, C., & Hindley, C. (2023). Artificial intelligence creates art? An experimental investigation of value and creativity perceptions. *The Journal of Creative Behavior*, *57*(4), 534–549. DOI: 10.1002/jocb.600

Ndalianis, A. (2003). Architectures of the senses: Neo-Baroque entertainment spectacles. In D. Thorburn & H. Jenkins (Eds.), *Rethinking media change: The aesthetics of transition* (pp. 355–374).[1] The MIT Press.

Oswald, L. R. (2020). *Doing semiotics: A research guide for marketers at the edge of culture* (E-book ed.). OUP Oxford.

Pericliev, V. (2015). On Redundancy in Describing Linguistic Systems. In Bolić, P. A., & Tselinska, D. A. (Eds.), *Proceedings of the 13th International Conference on the Lexical-Functional Grammar* (pp. 125–136). CSLI Publications.

Rodríguez-Fernández, N., Rebelo, S. M., & Martins, T. (Eds.). (2022). *Artificial intelligence in music, sound, art and design: 11th International Conference, EvoMUSART 2022, held as part of EvoStar 2022, Madrid, Spain, April 20–22, 2022, proceedings*. Springer International Publishing.

Samo, A., & Highhouse, S. (2023). Artificial intelligence and art: Identifying the aesthetic judgment factors that distinguish human- and machine-generated artwork. *Psychology of Aesthetics, Creativity, and the Arts*, *19*(5), 1084–1098. Advance online publication. Retrieved January 22, 2025, from. DOI: 10.1037/aca0000570

Shen, Y., & Yu, F. (2021). The influence of artificial intelligence on art design in the digital age. *Scientific Programming*, *2021*(1), 4838957. Retrieved January 22, 2025, from. DOI: 10.1155/2021/4838957

Singla, P. (2024). *Artificial Intelligence in Linguistics Research: Applications in Language Acquisition and Analysis*. NATURALISTA CAMPANO.

Tikhonova, E., Zavolskaya, O., & Mekeko, N. (2025). Stylistic Redundancy and Wordiness in Introductions of Original Empirical Studies: Rhetorical Risks of Academic Writing. *Journal of Language and Education*, *11*(2), 125–136. DOI: 10.17323/jle.2025.27389

Tomalin, M. (2025). Multimodal social semiotics and the challenge of artificial intelligence. *Multimodality & Society*, *5*(2), 223–244. Advance online publication. Retrieved January 22, 2025, from. DOI: 10.1177/26349795251327939

Valdivia Alonso, D. (2026). Imagining AI futures in mainstream cinema: Socio-technical narratives and social imaginaries. *AI & Society*. Advance online publication. DOI: 10.1007/s00146-026-02880-7

Vidugirytė, I. (2022). Lotman and the Baroque. *Semiotika*, *17*(32), 164–177.

Yusa, I. M. M., Yu, Y., & Sovhyra, T. (2022). Reflections on the use of artificial intelligence in works of art. *Journal of Aesthetics, Design, and Art Management*, *2*(2), 152–167. Advance online publication. Retrieved January 22, 2025, from. DOI: 10.58982/jadam.v2i2.334

Chapter 2
Code and Canvas: Exploring How AI-Generated Art Impacts Online Artists

And Algül
http://orcid.org/0000-0001-5516-5249
Üsküdar University, Turkey

Hiba Narmouq
http://orcid.org/0009-0009-4110-5312
Üsküdar University, Turkey

ABSTRACT

The integration of AI applications into art has transformed the creative process and expression. This transformation has caused ethical debates about authorship in the art field and encouraged a re-evaluation of artistic and business practices in the digital age. In this context, we aim to examine the impact of AI-generated art on online artists. In 2024, through a quantitative approach we surveyed 220 traditional and AI practicing artists to assess their attitudes regarding aesthetic value and originality, authorship and co-creation, and the ethical and economic issues surrounding data use, attribution, and compensation. Through our findings it was clear that many artists welcomed AI as a helpful collaborator but still held human creativity at the core of their practice. At the same time, most called for clear data policies, proper credit, and fair pay when their work is used in AI datasets. Together, these responses reveal a tension between embracing new technological possibilities and protecting the uniquely human aspects of art.

DOI: 10.4018/979-8-2600-2711-0.ch002

INTRODUCTION

Technology does not seem to be slowing down in terms of advancements any time soon, and that is especially evident in the AI field, through the milestones they have achieved in a relatively short period of time. The field of AI has developed in multiple ways in just the last century. Starting from the age-old fascination with the 'other', themes such as creation, ethics and the consequences of achieving the impossible have emerged (Cave & Dihal, 2019; Fakhar, 2024), it developed into machine learning (Alpaydın, 2020: 1-4), neural networks, deep learning (Aggarwal, 2018: 1-2), and Big Data (Mayer-Schönberger & Cukier, 2013). Artificial Intelligence has undoubtedly served innovation by making what was once thought to be impossible possible. Although such rapid growth comes with growing concerns and even questioning our perception of reality. It is even argued that the rapid advancements in the field of AI would eventually threaten human societies (Shermer, 2017: 29; Schellmann, 2024). The technical achievements of AI are certainly impressive, from mastering complex games like Go (Silver et al., 2016) to generating human-like language (Brown et al., 2020), but when it comes to art and creativity, the impact of generative AI in particular has captured the attention of the public and the artists alike, causing serious debate in the art scene (Peters & Peters, 2013; Boden, 2016). Raising questions about originality, authorship, aesthetics, and the value of creative labor. These generative AI models are trained on large datasets which are collections of existing artworks, illustrations, and media collected from the internet (Snijders et al., 2012; Islam, 2023). All that data basically forms the foundation of the model's ability to produce images, sounds or even videos that resemble art in seconds (Zylinska, 2020). AI is considered not just as a tool, but even a medium to some (Mazzone & Elgammal, 2019), capable of both enhancing and challenging artistic practices. Through Fuch's ideas on digital capitalism (Fuchs & Mosco, 2015), as well as postmodernist and metamodernist theory, we discuss the similarities between how postmodernism questions traditional ideas on aesthetics and authorship, and how AI-generated art challenges traditional creative practices by blending diverse styles and creating new forms of expression (Duchamp, 1973; Barthes, 1977; Lyotard, 1984; Jameson, 1991; Jameson, 1998; Boden, 2016). While on the other hand metamodernism embraces a balance between optimism and skepticism, perhaps offering a different perspective regarding the role of AI in art (Vermeulen & van den Akker, 2010). Such theories will help us better understand these different perspectives regarding AI-generated art and its effects on artists and different creative practices.

The aim of this study is to examine ideas of aesthetics, authenticity, and authorship and how it all translates into recent developments in creative practices involving AI generated art and its reception. By conducting quantitative analysis through a survey-based approach in 2024, we were able to capture perspectives and gather data from 220 artists online that provided valuable insight and answered key questions. To better understand the issues AI generated art affects, a deeper dive into AI generated art models and applications is needed, starting by examining how the introduction and popularization of AI has impacted both art creation and the artists themselves. Also how such technologies are shaping artistic expression.

Computational Creativity And Artificial Intelligence In Art

The use of computations in art creation dates back to the 1960s. Early digital pioneers like Vera Molnar, Frieder Nake, and Desmond Paul Henry treated code as an art tool, using simple rule-based programs to generate abstract, plotter-drawn patterns (Reichardt, 1968; Taylor, 2014; Franco, 2022). In those experiments, artists wrote every instruction and maintained direct control over form and composition Manovich, 2001: 32-33; McCormack & d'Inverno, 2012). With the integration of technological advancements into artistic practices came the term "digital art", which was first introduced by G. Cohen in the 1980s, referring to the use of digital tools in creative processes (Cohen, 1994). Harold Cohen's "Aaron" program produced black-and-white drawings semi-autonomously, yet still required artistic supervision (McCorduck, 1991: 210; Arantes et al., 2019: 1–8; Kovalova et al., 2022). These early experiments showed both the possibilities and the limitations of code-based art, as they were fresh, abstract designs that still felt obviously computer-made. Advancements in Deep Learning opened up new possibilities, especially neural networks (LeCun et al., 2015) which allows the transfer of one artistic style to another image (Venkatesan & Li, 2017). GANs Generative Adversarial Networks (Goodfellow et al., 2014) on the other hand can produce completely new images and later evaluate outcomes. One can not mention GANs and AI generated art without the mention of the "Portrait de Edmond de Belamy" by Obvious. Belamy, the name is a tribute to Ian Goodfellow. It reached the news when it was announced to be sold in a Christie's art auction and was sold for a large amount of 432,500$ (Alleyne, 2018). Making it the first AI artwork featured in Christie's art auction. The piece was produced by an algorithm code trained on a set of 15,000 portraits from WikiArt, from the 14th to the 19th century (Nugent, 2018). From this, we see how AI art transformed from a niche experiment into a global phenomenon.

Advancements like CLIP (Radford et al., 2021) and diffusion models made AI art accessible to a much wider audience. The innovation of CLIP (Contrastive Language-Image Pretraining) lies in its ability to understand the relationships between words and images, which paved the way for text-based prompt artificial intelligence generators. That type of AI art generator has gained the most popularity with the general public in recent years. Diffusion models solve the limitation

GANs models had, when it comes to computational cost and performance, also the possibility to generate diverse outputs. That made diffusion models alternatives to GANs. Other than generating detailed images from descriptive text, it can also be applied to tasks such as image-to-image translations guided by text prompt, and image modifications (Diffuse The Rest, 2022). With that 2022 would be the year AI art became a mainstream form of art. Text-to-image platforms such as DALL-E 2, and Midjourney, removed technical barriers, democratizing image-making for the public and artists alike (Bak Herrie et al., 2024; Guinness, 2023). The September 2023 launch of DALL-E 3 within ChatGPT further cemented AI art's place in everyday creativity, sparking both widespread excitement and concern over its impact on artistic practices (Pearl, 2023). The abundance of such accessible tools has not only made art creation more inclusive but also driven a rise of commercial platforms and subscription services (Bak Herrie et al., 2024). The general public's creations on such tools feed back into the same large datasets they were trained on, powering further advances. Although the initial excitement around generative models has subsided somewhat, trends emerge whenever new features or technologies are introduced, reflecting continued public interest and commercial opportunities in AI-driven creativity. It is crucial to recognize how and why AI-generated art has gained widespread popularity, engaging the public and encouraging more people to experiment with these tools. This increased interest has not only democratized access to creative technologies but has also paved the way for the commercialization and further development of AI applications beyond image generation.

THEORETICAL FRAMEWORK

Digital Capitalism Through Postmodern Thought

When it comes to changes in the art field, we can see parallels to postmodernism's aesthetic principles. During the research period, we expanded on our ideas, beyond postmodern aesthetics and authorship to include Fuchs's analysis of digital labor and capitalism, along with Marxist critiques. Exploring such theories and seeing the parallels between them and what artists experience in the digital age, particularly when it comes to AI-generated art, enhanced the depth and relevance of the study by providing information into the interaction between technology, art, and society structures of today.

Postmodernism, with its emphasis on the blurring of boundaries between various styles, the rejection of grand narratives, and the celebration of diverse influences (Jameson, 1991: 54), finds similarities in how AI-generated artworks are created. When it comes to aesthetics, postmodernism introduced elements of "commercialism, kitsch and a general camp aesthetic"; by taking styles from past periods, and mixing them, sometimes ignoring their original use in their artistic movement (Duchamp, 1973). The diversity of styles, the embrace of technology, and the challenge to traditional unities in AI-generated art mirrors postmodern aesthetic features. At the same time, Fuchs' insights on digital labor can help us understand the current economic dynamics (Fuchs & Mosco, 2015). The creation of AI-generated art involves not only the artistic input but also the labor of algorithms and use of vast datasets (Wissner-Gross, 2016; Zylinska, 2020; Filimowicz, 2023; Vergil et al., 2025) which many artists view as nonconsensual use. In this context, issues of ownership, control, and compensation relate to Marxist concerns about how issues of labor in a capitalist society become central. Wittel's examination of digital media dives into labor, value, property, and struggle. He notes that while information production becomes more accessible in the digital age, information distribution remains controlled by the capitalist class (Wittel, 2012). This observation is clear when exploring AI generators and the datasets they operate on, revealing an imbalance in ownership and distribution rights, as expressed by artists online during discussions about the research (Radsch, 2024). At the same time AI generator users, instead of writing every line of code, they can now curate datasets operating these models, becoming "prosumers", which to Fuchs are those who both produce and consume digital media, and this unpaid input generates surplus value for platforms (Fuchs, 2012; Fuchs & Mosco, 2015). This creates uncertainty over who counts as the artist and who counts as the consumer. Through all this we can see how with machines setting aesthetic norms and corporations owning distribution channels, questions of data ownership, fair compensation, and creative control have never been more urgent.

The digital economy's impact on traditional artists, if explored through Marxist ideas, raises questions about fair opportunities, power dynamics, and potential exploitation, which we can see within the evolving field of AI-generated art. Marx talked about two forms of alienation that did not exist prior to capitalism (Marx, 2012: 77-78; Fuchs, 2014). The first is where the worker is unable to use his own product for his living. The second refers to the workers' inability to organize the process of work as it is controlled by the capitalist owning the means of production (Beinin, 1994: 187-188; Wittel, 2012). We can apply the same to artworks in the current digital age, especially after the popularization of AI art generators. Some concerns that creators in the digital age of today have revolve around the possibility of these technologies being monopolized (Stokes et al., 2023; Radsch, 2024). Further discussing ideas of postmodernism and digital labour, we will be citing Shusterman and his work on postmodernity and aesthetics. The concepts of postmodernity and digital labor reveal the transformation of aesthetics in postmodernity. Shusterman states that Lyotard introduces postmodernity by its history relating to postindustrial age, and the transformation and commercialization of knowledge in computer-aided societies (Shusterman, 2009). Regarding that Lyotard states that with the "commodification of knowledge" in what he described as late capitalist society, unity is no longer what is aspired for, but endless rapid growth through competition (Lyotard 1994). Which we can see in recent developments concerning AI art generators and models. Each model comes challenging its competitors like the case of DALL-E3 (Buhl, 2023).

Commodifying knowledge and information mean turning them into commodities, removing their inherent value. They can't possess surplus value themselves. Instead, any profits from knowledge come indirectly, as "knowledge rents," which comes from economic activities that generate value elsewhere, such as marketing and selling them (Vidal et al., 2019). Such ideas are evident in the advancements of AI, datasets and rapid emergence of various subscription-based applications (Zee, 2025; Srnicek, 2017: 72) with little to no regard to artists' copyrights, fair use and consent. Large tech companies monopolize AI through control of training datasets. This relates to concerns about fair access to AI tools and the ethical use of artists' works. It strengthens the argument for regulations that ensure transparency, attribution, and compensation for artists whose work is included in training datasets (Radsch, 2024). If we compare this to Marx's perspective on capitalism, we see how he emphasizes the commodity as a fundamental element of capitalism, and an exchange of quantifiable goods in return for money. Commodification, in Marxian terms, is the transformation of social relations into buyer-seller exchanges. We can see that in various internet studies, discussing the commodification of the Internet, online privacy, and community in the digital age, along with the online commodification of personal information (Fuchs, 2012). Pasquinelli further emphasizes the exploitation of free labor, particularly within non-profit digital sites, discussing dynamics of commodification and labor exploitation in the digital age (Pasquinelli, 2015). We also see how this relates to the current situation with AI generated art with the exploitation of free labor in digital spaces, such as the unpaid contributions of artists whose works are used to build AI models (Radsch, 2024). Considering how fast and easy it is to generate images these days, art can begin to be viewed as a mere mass-produced commodity rather than a personal creative expression of value (Robhestand1, 2024).

From Postmodernism to Metamodernism: A Changing Aesthetic

Postmodern artists often borrowed and blended different styles, often removing them from their original context, creating art pieces that are overtly commercial, with a kitsch and camp aesthetic (Duchamp, 1973). AI generators operate similarly in a way, trained on vast, diverse datasets, they blend everything from classical portraits to pop-culture imagery in an instant. Like postmodernism's key features of, irony, playful appropriation, mixing of styles, and a deliberate superficiality that mocks traditional unity (Jameson, 1991), AI-generated art seems to celebrate and highlight the same features, making both challenge established aesthetics by turning past forms into possibilities for repurposing.

The challenge of accepting generative AI as art is quite similar to the historical development of photography. Hertzman (2018) and Aguera y Arcas (2016) have explored the struggles faced by photography in gaining recognition as a legitimate form of art. The debates surrounding the artistic value of photography is similar to the ones we see today when it comes to Artificial Intelligence. Postmodernism was against how modernity disregarded aesthetic and artistic importance of industrial and popular arts, by showing how art is inseparable to other aspects of life and culture. Social and political issues, popular arts, and everyday aesthetic issues all become important for aesthetic theory. That tells us that creativity and originality can still be explored and celebrated when borrowed tools and materials are used. Postmodernism can be considered not just as a "cynical rejection of aesthetics, but as a celebration" (Shusterman, 2009). When it comes to AI generated art, this is evident in the use of algorithms based on datasets, going beyond fixed artistic styles and mixing diverse elements, to create different outcomes, as well as the democratization of creation, making it available for anyone willing to try AI tools.

While Postmodernism embraced irony, borrowing, and blending of styles, it often approached ideas like originality and authorship with detachment and skepticism. In contrast, metamodernism, which is a philosophical and artistic movement that emerged in response to the advancements in digital technology and its integration into daily life (Kovalova et al., 2022), balances between opposing ideas, such as unity and plurality, totality and fragmentation or tradition and innovation. It embraces "oscillatio" meaning a constant shifting between these contrasting views, and "pragmatic idealism" which refers to balancing hope and ambition with realism and practicality (Vermeulen & van den Akker, 2010). Metamodernism works towards meaningful change and progress while acknowledging limitations and constraints. From that we can see it as described by Moyo Okediji as an artistic movement that both builds upon and critiques modernist and postmodernist ideas (Storm, 2021: 5). The relevance of metamodernism to this study lies in its flexibility to incorporate the contradictory elements of modern optimism and postmodern skepticism, making it a useful perspective to help examine the evolving role of AI in art. Storm even argued that rather than viewing metamodernism as just a "response" to postmodernism or an oscillation between modernist and postmodernist ideas, metamodernism is an "overcoming" of both (Storm, 2021: 18). Metamodernism builds on this celebration of pluralism, which refers to the recognition and embrace of diverse perspectives, ideas, cultures, and approaches but shifts the focus from deconstruction to reconstruction, emphasizing the coexistence of sincerity and irony (Vermeulen & van den Akker, 2010; Mul, 1999: 18-26). Metamodernism's re-signification of familiar cultural forms, attempts to give them new meaning and context is similar to the way AI tools take existing datasets and transform them into different expressions that oscillate between the familiar and the unfamiliar. This dynamic emphasizes the metamodern idea of "making the impossible possible" that involves joining contradictory ideas in pursuit of new artistic expression. Which relates to what we discussed earlier on, with how AI made the impossible possible. For example, the commercialization and kitsch elements of AI generators, that we discussed earlier in our postmodern analysis, become opportunities for metamodern re-signification (Vermeulen & van den Akker, 2010). Artists can transform these tools into instruments of both critique and creation, joining outputs with perceived creative value. This aligns with the metamodern idea of "pragmatic idealism," which can be a way to approach AI art, both as a critique of traditional practices and an exploration of new possibilities. As Kovalova et al. discussed in their paper how creatives should embrace interdisciplinary trends in both culture and art as a whole (Kovalova et al., 2022).

This metamodern approach can be a constructive way in which we move forward regarding AI generated art, and even other technological advancements. Hutcheon acknowledges that while the postmodern era has ended, its critical approaches and ideological challenges continue (Hutcheon, 1989). Similarly, Vermeulen and van den Akker argue that postmodern ideas have not entirely disappeared but are evolving into new forms with new meaning and direction (Vermeulen & van den Akker, 2010). This perspective aligns with our research approach, as we examine how artistic expression and reception change in response to emerging technologies like AI-generated art. Just as postmodernism questioned authorship and originality, these ideas are now changing within the metamodern framework, shaping contemporary discussions on creativity, digital labor, and authorship.

Based on theories mentioned, we can reach our first hypothesis, Hypothesis 1: Influence of AI on Creative Expression. Artists adopting a metamodern approach towards digital labor are more likely to incorporate artificial intelligence tools in their creative process.

Death and Rebirth of the author, Authorship and Ethics.

The Death of the Author revolves around the changing nature of authorship. In his theory, Roland Barthes challenges the notion of the authors as having all the power over creation, where they also give meaning to their work. Barthes calls for the "liberation of interpretation from the author's authority", calling for the art and consumer to break free from the artist, allowing them to create their own meanings

(Barthes, 1977: 142-148; Burke, 2008). We discuss this here in relation to the collaborative nature of AI generated art, challenging traditional authorship. A comparison to language is how Rorty explains that "language is a tool for creation" (Rorty, 1989: 5), in a liberal postmodern society, that puts more value on individual freedom, each person is encouraged to take from past vocabulary and ideas, apply them into current context, and producing new ideas through them, "to make of oneself a work of art" (Rorty, 1989: 27-29, 98). Which is what most visions for AI generated models hope to achieve. By giving the ability of creation to almost anyone willing to try and explore their tools. One can state that questioning the presence of a single author is no recent matter, since artists have been producing "anti-art" from the beginning of the twentieth century, with the intent to defy notions of authorship and to even attempt to redefine what is considered art in the first place (Storm, 2021: 33).

Taking our previous point into consideration, who can we regard as the artist when it comes to AI art generators? Elgammal, speaking about his own experiments, says that if you look at AI art creation, focusing on only the basis of it, ignoring what the artwork is trying to convey, then you would of course see the algorithm as only generating "forms" and following artistic styles and principles from already existing art. But if you look at the bigger picture, then you might see it as "conceptual art" rather than traditional artwork. He views it as follows: A loop, containing a human, one that is asking a machine questions, and getting answers in return. He sees that whole process as "the art", not only the images/artworks generated. He describes it as a collaboration between what he considers two artists; the human and the machine. He later says that his vision for the future of AI art generators is them being considered a medium for art, not only a tool (Elgammal 2019). In this context, we are recognising the role of algorithms as active contributors of the creative process. We question whether people would agree with Elgammal and consider them as co-authors.

Based on Elgammal ideas we can discuss how metamodernism shifts from the postmodern deconstruction of the author towards a reconstruction. It proposes a "rebirth" of the author, where the creator is not entirely erased but is redefined. This perspective aligns with the nature of AI art creation. While AI tools may generate the artwork, human creators curate, guide, and interpret the process, forming a shared authorship, as Elgammal described it previously. In this way, the artisan, whether human or machine, is reintroduced, not as the sole creator but perhaps as part of a collaborative, dynamic process (Miller, 2022). The idea that "art constitutes itself by excluding the artisan" relates to the concepts of the death and rebirth of the author, particularly in the context of metamodernism and AI-generated art (Power, 2020; Storm, 2021, 70). While postmodernism deconstructs the notion of a single author, metamodernism suggests a different perspective, one that embraces collaboration and co-authorship, oscillating between individual and collective agency. In the context of AI-generated art, this oscillation allows for a refined engagement that both acknowledges the mechanical, data-driven nature of AI and treats it as a genuine collaborator in the creative process. This all reflects how metamodernism shifts the focus from postmodern detachment to an "informed naivety" or "pragmatic idealism". This duality reflects the metamodern attitude of "believing as if" (Vermeulen & van den Akker, 2010), where artists and audiences engage with AI art in creative expression, while still recognizing that it is a result of algorithms and datasets. The collaborative nature described earlier by Elgammal is what presents challenges in determining authorship, attribution, and copyright issues. Especially considering the involvement of algorithms and datasets. Even if we view AI art generators as a shared effort and a collaboration, we cannot forget to highlight the importance of preserving authorship rights and avoiding exploitation of human creativity. In 2023, a federal judge in the United States ruled that AI artwork does not meet "federal copyright standards" because "Copyright law is limited to the original intellectual conceptions of the author". Focusing on considering human beings as an important part of a valid copyright claim. Recently after the popularization of AI generated art, and due to the nonconsensual use of artists' work and styles in both datasets and image prompts, several artists have filed lawsuits in the US against companies commercially using image generators (Vincent, 2023). From what we can see, Fair use and copyright policies need critical reconsiderations. We can also see how important development of both fair use and copyright policies should be for policy makers. Accountability is also incredibly vital in cases of infringements (Jiang et al., 2023). This all further highlights the ever arising need to take action (European Parliament, 2025).

This leads us to our 2nd and 3 hypotheses.

Hypothesis 2: Changing perception of authorship. Artists show an overall bias against considering AI generative art creators as artists.

Hypothesis 3: Authorship and Attribution Ethics. Artists showing a negative bias against AI generated art consider the non-consensual use of art as data in the field of AI unethical and an infringement.

RESEARCH METHODOLOGY

Recent developments in computer technologies, especially in the field of artificial intelligence have led to the arising questions and concerns in creative and artistic industries. In 2024, a structured survey was utilised to address the research hypotheses, with the objective of gathering numerical data that could be statistically analysed. The survey was designed to identify any emerging patterns, address questions, and reach clear conclusions, with the aim of enhancing understanding of the influence of such technology. Questions were directed at both AI artists and traditional artists. The primary method involves a structured online survey that was distributed in 2024 to a diverse sample of artists within online art communities, from various social media platforms after it was approved by the ethics committee on the 31st, January of 2024.

Participants

The sample of this study is a collection of over 220 diverse artists from various backgrounds. Over 1700 artists were contacted regarding the survey, and we received over 220 entries as a result. It is considered that the participants are actively engaged and familiar with the internet and new technologies, also they are exposed to various forms of art, including AI-generated creations. Ensuring a broad representation or perceptions, we targeted artists across multiple social media in the recruitment process. Participants were drawn from platforms such as Reddit, Discord, Instagram, and Survey Swap, in hopes to include different online communities and demographics, representing various backgrounds. We hoped to gather a comprehensive view of the artists' attitudes towards AI-generated art. Inclusion Criteria:

- Target both traditional artists and AI-focused artists.
- Artists that are active on social media in order to be able to reach out to them.
- Consider participants from diverse geographical locations, age groups, and artistic backgrounds to enhance the generalizability of findings.

Procedures

A set of statements or questions is formulated to capture the diverse dimensions of artists' attitudes towards AI-generated art. These statements are carefully crafted to cover a spectrum of opinions and experiences within the research domain. First, to gather some information about the participants general demographic questions were asked as well as inquiring about their primary field of art, as we wanted to cover a diverse sample. The Likert scale is utilized to measure participants' perceptions and feelings regarding various aspects related to the impact of AI-generated art on artists. Participants were given 31 statements where they got to express their attitude towards them on a scale from (1-5) ranging from (Strongly Disagree) to (Strongly Agree).

The survey is designed to address a series of hypotheses through a set of questions. The questions are structured to measure artists' opinions on various aspects related to AI-generated art, covering topics such as its impact on creative work, perceptions of authorship, ethical considerations, and the influence on the broader digital art scene.

Hypotheses and Supporting Questions:

Hypothesis 1: Influence of AI on Creative Expression. Artists adopting a meta-modern approach towards digital labor are more likely to incorporate artificial intelligence tools in their creative process. Supporting Questions: Q1 - Q9

Hypothesis 2: Changing perception of authorship. Artists show an overall bias against considering AI generative art creators as artists. Supporting Questions: Q11 - Q19

Hypothesis 3: Authorship and Attribution Ethics. Artists showing a negative bias against AI generated art consider the non consensual use of art as data in the field of AI unethical. Supporting Questions: Q10 and Q20 - Q31

The survey questions are strategically aligned with each hypothesis to capture the perspectives of artists. Data collected through the survey responses was later subjected to statistical analysis, allowing for quantitative interpretation, we identified trends and correlations, later drawing conclusive insights into the impact of AI-generated art on artists in today's digital age.

FINDINGS

Quantitative Data Analysis & Discussion.

Through quantitative methods, we analyzed over 220 responses. In this phase, we aim to identify attitudes, patterns and key trends to answer our questions and measure the impact such technological advancements in art production have, when it comes to how artists perceive AI-generated art. We can start the data analysis by providing some information regarding the demographic composition of our participants. Including age, geographic location, and field of art. Limitations to our study are evident, as due to time constraints and self-selection bias, the predominant represented age groups in our gathered responses were (19-24) 44.7% and (25-34) 38.7%. This affected generalizability. Perhaps future research would include a better representation of diverse age groups. Similar observations were made in geographic locations, around 24% of the sample were from Asia, 36% from Europe, and 27.4% from North America.

Other limitations to the study are evident in the primary field of art for participants (Figure 1), although we tried reaching out to both sides of the online art discourse, AI artists' input only represented around 5% of the sample gathered. Multiple factors play a role in this, one of them is the existing discourse happening online between AI artists and traditional artists, especially after major companies announced endorsing AI art and even using it in their productions and marketing, such as Disney creating a task force aimed at AI exploration (Chmielewski & Hu, 2023). As well as Wacom and Wizards of the Coast receiving backlash for reportedly using AI generated images in their presence campaigns (Weatherbed, 2024). Such news created tension between both sides on social media, and as a result AI artists grew increasingly pensive about being as cooperative or even reachable online. Other factors include time constraints faced during the research period. We are hoping further research will be able to cover a wider sample size presenting AI artists and their views on the matters of authorship and ethics surrounding AI art generators.

To measure how widely spread AI generated art is online, the following question was asked: How often do you see AI generated art shared on online platforms? Only 3.1% of participants said they "rarely" see it, while 46% said they see it "very often", 17.8% said they "occasionally" see it and 32% answered with "often". Considering how accessible AI image generators have become, the percentage makes sense in regard to the traffic the technology is attracting. And the number of products and images generated being shared on various social media. That tells us that certain regulations need to take place, as you are overwhelmed with the amount of AI generated images you encounter even when you are looking up a famous artist's work.

Figure 1. Primary field of art of participants

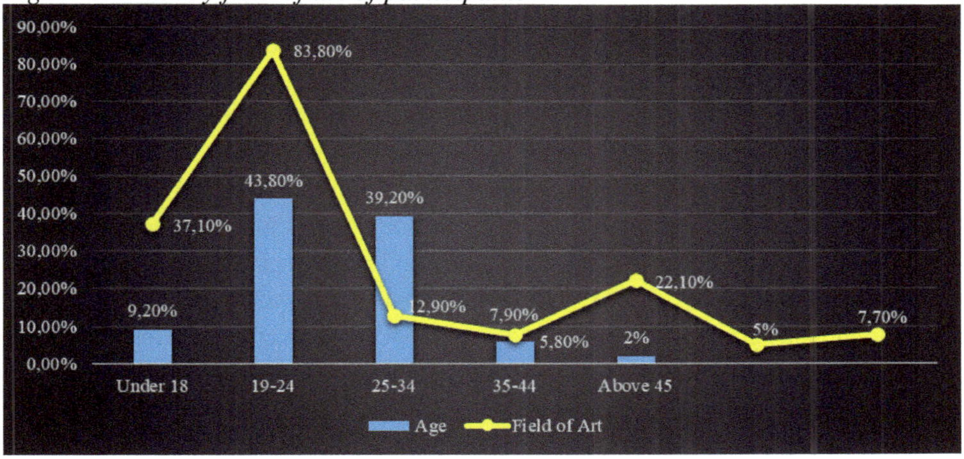

To understand how we quantified data and on what basis, we will provide an explanation on how we structured the likert statements to gather data that could provide information that either supports or contradicts each of our hypotheses in this research.

(H1) Hypothesis 1: Influence of AI on Creative Expression. Artists adopting a metamodern approach towards digital labor are more likely to incorporate artificial intelligence tools in their creative process.

Our first hypothesis suggested that artists with post and meta modernist views on creative practices are more likely to be open to incorporating AI in their creations. In return, the survey included inquiring participants about their openness to embracing technological advancements, the perceived importance of challenging traditional practices, and their views on the inclusivity of AI generated art. Rather than directly asking participants whether they "like" AI art, we first assessed their openness to new technologies and metamodern attitudes with Q1-Q4, and from the answers we got a subgroup. We then examined how their answers correlated with their responses to the remaining questions, to check if having a metamodern outlook on digital labor aligns with more positive views of AI's role in art.

The analysis of the responses reveals certain attitudes. From Q1-Q4 10% (21) of all participants had a positive attitude towards being open to embracing new technologies, challenging norms, and finding AI more inclusive. We then compared the 10% subgroup, the overall sample and AI artists, presenting it in a figure to be able to better notice the attitude of each group towards AI art and its creation:

In Figure 2 we notice that artists in the 10% subgroup (those who scored 4 or 5 on Q1-Q4), consistently had a more positive attitude towards AI's creative role than the overall sample. Looking first at aesthetics (Q7), the metamodern group averaged 3.4 (somewhat agree) versus just 1.9 (somewhat disagree) overall. They also reported greater hands-on use of AI tools (Q8: 3.2 vs. 1.6) and saw AI's overall impact favorably (Q10: 3.1 vs. 1.5). Even on Q9 (valuing traditional art more) they still agreed (4.1) that more human made art holds special worth, even if it is slightly less than the overall sample (4.7). Through figure 2 we also notice that the 10% subgroup line sits well above the green overall sample line and is closer to and sometimes only slightly below the yellow AI-artist line. This pattern confirms Hypothesis 1. From our findings we accept H1, stating that artists who embrace metamodern attitudes do indeed show greater willingness to adopt AI in their work. However, even within this group, traditional art remains highly valued (average attitude of 4.1 on Q9), suggesting that despite the use of AI, artists still value human-made art more.

Figure 2. Attitudes towards AI creations

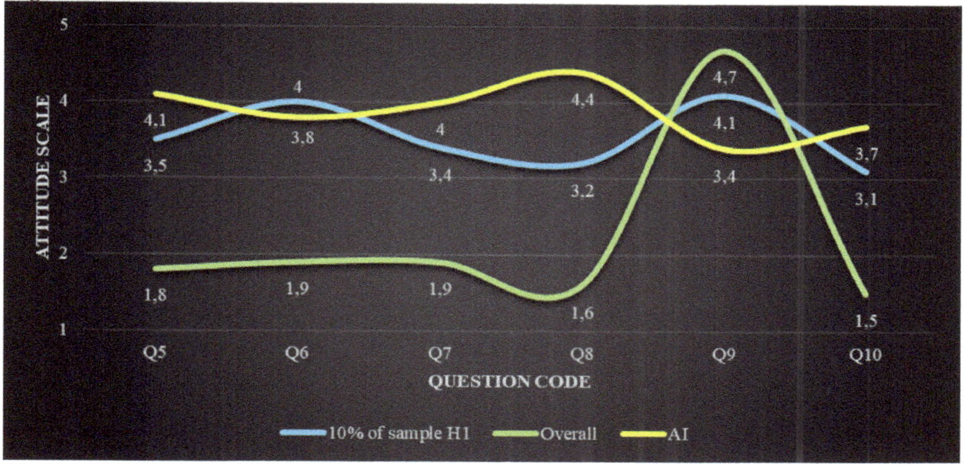

Moving on to our second Hypothesis:

(H2): Changing perception of Authorship. Artists show an overall bias against considering AI generative art creators as artists.

To test our second hypothesis stating that artists hold a bias against recognizing AI art creators, and generators as artists, we needed questions that assess both basic acceptance and other aspects of authorship. Q11 and Q12 directly ask whether participants see AI art creators as equal to artists. Q13 and Q14 further assess how authorship is perceived by asking whether AI algorithms can be considered as co-creators and whether they can think creatively. Finally, Q15 and Q16 measure openness to working alongside AI (synergy and collaboration), while Q17 to Q19 explore effects of AI art on perception, whether AI limits artistic freedom, and calls for more control over AI tools usage.

Combining the attitudes towards all the statements (Q11-Q14) addressing the authorship of AI generated art, we collected a sample where they had a negative attitude towards all 4 statements, that was around 1 (strongly disagree) to Q11 to Q13, in Q14 stating that AI algorithms lack creative thinking, they had an average attitude of 4.9 (strongly agree) which also translates to having a negative bias against AI art. According to that we found that 67% (148) of artists had a negative bias against considering AI creators as artists. We took that as a subgroup to compare it to the overall and AI artists's attitudes as you see in Figure 3.

From the figure we see that all artists do not see AI systems as true "artists." Both the overall sample and the 67% negative bias subgroup rated statements on AI as equal creators at just around 1-1.5 on a 5 point scale, even AI artists' attitudes were neutral 3.1-3.3 (Q11, Q12, Q13). AI artists displayed a slightly positive attitude (average 3.3) when it comes to Q13 (I see AI algorithms as co-creators of the artistic process), indicating they are more open to acknowledging AI as a legitimate participant in the creative process. This aligns with their frequent use of AI tools and willingness to integrate these technologies into their work. Other artists, on the other hand, rated this much lower (average of 1.1 and 1.6), showing skepticism or discomfort towards attributing artistic agency to machines and algorithms (Figure 3).

Nearly everyone agreed (4.4 - 4.9) that AI lacks the ability to think creatively Q14, AI artists' attitude was neutral (3.3). We notice a difference in attitudes at Q15, Q16 where both the overall sample (2.4, 2.3) and artists with a bias against AI (1.9, 1.8) had a negative attitude towards seeing a potential for collaboration and synergy, while AI artists had a very positive attitude (4.7, 4.8). At Q18 we notice a difference in attitudes between groups. Both the overall sample and the subgroup with a bias against AI agree to the statement of Q17 all artists seem to be more skeptical about the authenticity of art shared online with attitudes of (4.3, 4.2 and 3.7).

Figure 3. Figure of attitude towards considering AI art creators as artists

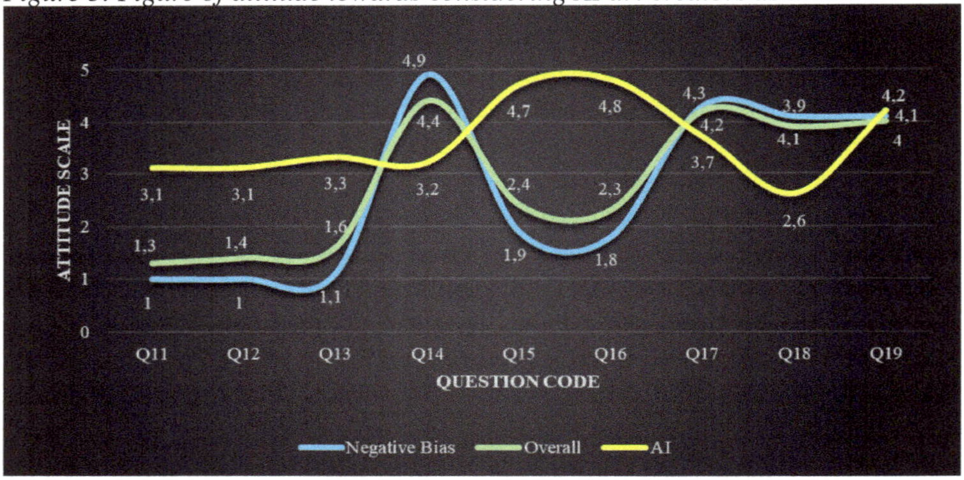

We can see that perspectives differ at Q18 regarding limiting the freedom of the artist, but not that greatly, that aligns with our hypothesis stating that traditional artists would have a bias against AI art creations, while AI artists have a negative attitude meaning they don't consider AI art generators as limiting freedom (Figure 3). Those results may also be affected by the fact that AI artists are more familiar with art generators. And that they view it as a democratization of art creation, where it can be more inclusive, which is why they do not view it as limiting as traditional artists do. When it comes to Q19 (Artists should have more control over algorithms) shows a shared awareness of the ethical implications of the use of AI algorithms. Both groups agree that greater transparency and control are necessary. This highlights a balanced perspective (Figure 3). These patterns confirm Hypothesis 2: artists exhibit a clear bias against recognizing AI generators as equal creators. This shows us that currently, traditional artists are more likely to view AI-generated art as a disruption rather than a useful tool or medium. We therefore accept H2.

(H3): Authorship and Attribution Ethics. Artists showing a negative bias against AI generated art consider the non-consensual use of art as data in the field of AI unethical.

To test our third hypothesis, stating that artists who view AI-generated art negatively against the non-consensual use of their work, we focused on questions regarding ethical and economic concerns (Q26-Q31). Q26 (finding it unethical to collect artists' works in artificial intelligence databases) and Q27 (finding it unethical to collect artist styles in artificial intelligence databases) directly relating to our hypothesis. As well as Q28 (considering art used in AI databases without the consent of the artists as theft). Questions Q29 (thinking artists should be paid for the use of their works in digital databases) and Q30 (thinking there should be more legal regulations protecting art and artists when it comes to AI art) assess demands for fair compensation and stronger legal safeguards. Finally, Q31 (thinking that legal regulations regarding art produced with artificial intelligence will restrict creativity in AI-generated art) captures another perspective regarding regulations. From responses to Q10, 85% of artists viewed the overall impact of AI generated art as negative, compared to 55% out of AI artists. We took that as a subgroup and based our analysis on their average attitude on Q26 till Q31. Comparing the 85% to AI artists in Figure 4 below.

Figure 4. Attitudes towards attribution and ethics

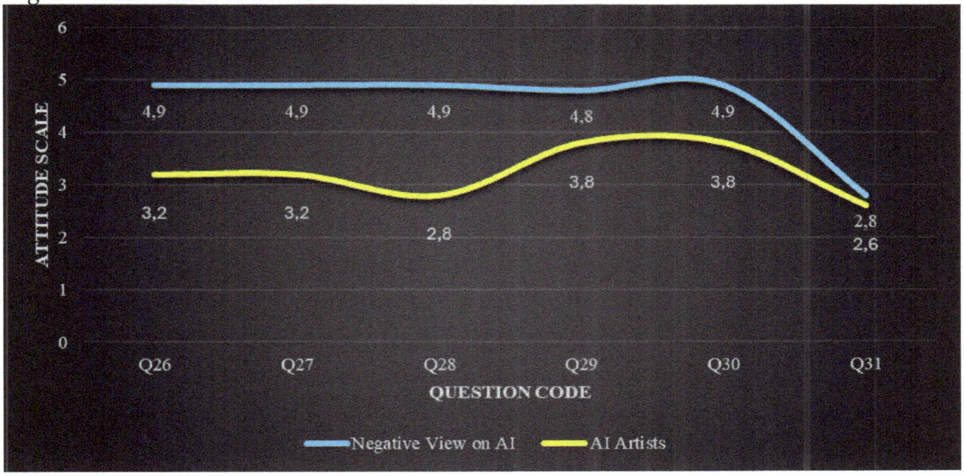

It becomes evident that artists who view AI–generated art negatively also express strong ethical concerns about how their work is used in AI training (Figure 4). In our negative view on AI subgroup, average agreement was overwhelmingly high on questions of non-consensual data use: Q26-Q29 all scored around 4.8-4.9 (find it unethical to collect works/styles, regard unconsented use as theft, insist on payment and legal protections). Even among AI-focused creators, these scores remain elevated (3.2, 3.2, 2.8, 3.8, 3.8, 2.6), indicating broad support for attribution rights and better regulation. For Q31, while in the figure the average attitude is 2.8 and 2.6, when you actually look at the responses, opinions were somewhat different: about 24% agreed that regulations would restrict AI art, 25% were neutral, and 41% disagreed. And that was shared with us during the research period by some participants. They stated that big companies pushing stricter copyright laws might just limit creative expression overall, and only monopolize creativity. As some artists said that companies might end up with copyright to entire art styles and techniques and viewed that as extreme restriction. This concern ties back to Fuchs's critique of digital capitalism, where platform owners employ unpaid creative labor and turn it into profit, and to Marx's notion of alienation, as artists lose both control over their work and any personal benefit when corporations claim exclusive rights to styles and techniques. It is also important to note that even AI artists' average attitude towards Q24 is 4.3, which is only 0.5 different from the overall attitude 4.8 (Figure 5). According to such responses we accept hypothesis H3 stating that artists showing negative bias against AI generated art, view the nonconsensual use of their data as unethical.

The figures of overall attitudes versus AI artists' attitudes was added to help us observe the bigger picture, where we can spot broader patterns like peaks, valleys, and crossover points, that were not obvious when we focused only on Hypotheses 1-3. From Figure 5 above we can observe some fluctuations, we see the contrast in attitude at certain points in the figure, with the following question: Q4, Q5, Q6, Q7 Q8, Q15, Q16, Q18. Traditional artists show higher skepticism, while AI artists demonstrate consistently positive attitudes toward questions on creativity, collaboration, and inclusivity. On the other hand, in Figure 6 the lines appear closer together for questions addressing ethical concerns (Q20-Q31), showing relative agreement between all artists on the importance of consent, attribution, and proper legal regulations. We observe significant opposition in questions like Q15-Q16 (collaboration and synergy) AI artists rated it higher (average 4.7, positive), reflecting their optimism toward collaborative practices that blend AI and traditional methods. On the other hand, traditional artists were less enthusiastic (average 2.4, negative), suggesting that they view AI-generated art as incompatible with traditional artistic values. Which may reflect concerns that AI is disrupting traditional artistic methods or affecting the value of human creative expression.

Figure 5. Crosstab of attitudes of AI artists vs. overall sample (Q1-Q18)

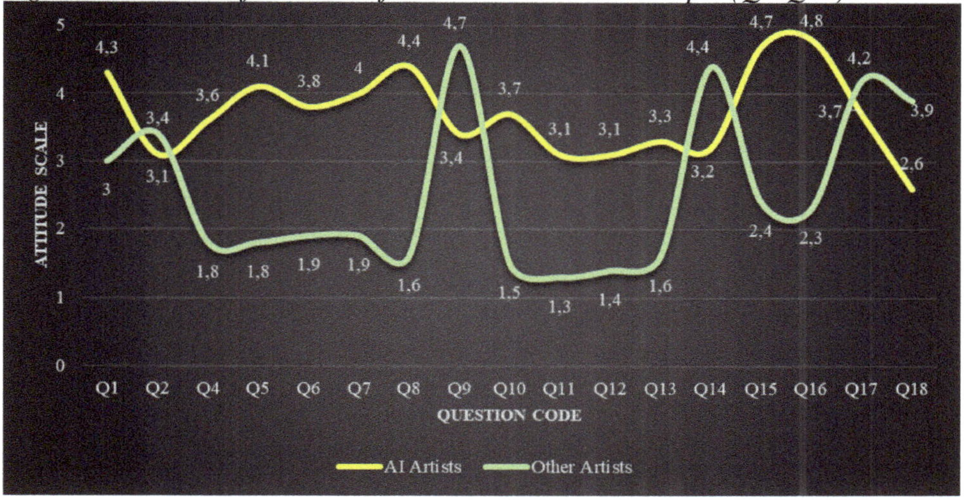

Figure 6. Crosstab of attitudes of AI artists vs. overall sample (Q19-Q31)

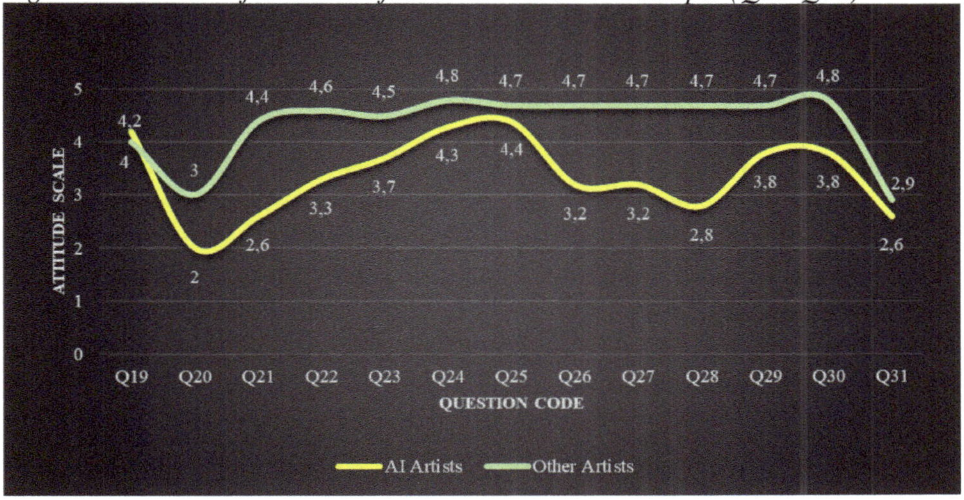

The strong positive responses to Q24-Q29 (artists' consent for database inclusion, proper attribution, ethical data collection) highlights the overall agreement on the need to protect artists' rights in the age of AI-generated art. Both AI and traditional artists view unauthorized use of art in databases as unethical (Q26-Q28). This reflects a shared concern about exploitation and the commodification of creative labor, which relates to postmodern critiques of digital capitalism and authenticity. Also, attitudes toward Q30 (There should be more legal regulations protecting art and artists) are positive, demonstrating a unified desire for formal protections to safeguard creative industries and most importantly creative individuals from exploitation (Waters, 2025) (Figure 5).

Overall, it seems like AI artists appear more optimistic and collaborative in their attitudes toward AI as a creative partner, reflecting their closer relationship with AI technologies. While traditional artists show more skepticism, possibly driven by concerns about authorship, authenticity, or the loss of traditional artistic values. This contrast in attitude highlights the ongoing tension between tradition and AI generated art in today's art scene. However, traditional artists, while less enthusiastic, still show moderate agreement, suggesting the possibility to accept AI in creative practices. But with major consideration towards their art and the protection of their creative rights. Which all aligns with metamodern ideas, where the blending of ideas and constructive collaboration are welcomed.

DISCUSSION AND CONCLUSION

Creative technologies such as generative AI are certainly affecting how artists and art creation work, raising urgent questions about authorship, fairness, and value while maybe offering new opportunities for collaboration. Our survey of 220 artists in 2024, viewed through the frameworks of digital capitalism, postmodernism, and metamodernism, revealed the possibility of AI tools to expand creative possibilities and where they threaten traditional artistic practices. By examining issues of commodification, authorship, and ethical accountability, we've identified both the promise of AI generated art and the pressing need for policies that protect artists' rights and livelihoods.

The first hypothesis suggests that artists who adopt postmodernist practices are more likely to incorporate AI into their creative process. This was supported by findings that indicate artists with a progressive attitude toward challenging traditional norms and embracing technological advancements are open to experimenting with AI tools. This way of thinking where questioning old ideas while staying open to new creative possibilities reflects a metamodern approach. Artists who see AI not just as a tool but as a potential creative partner show the possibility for technology and human expression to work together. Our findings suggest that artists aligned with these ideals are more willing to explore the capabilities and limits of AI-generated art and see the possibility of a real collaboration and synergy between AI and art, human and machine. The second hypothesis explored the perception of authorship and revealed a significant bias among artists against recognizing AI as an autonomous creator, as well as viewing AI generated art creators as artistic equals. Survey responses indicated that artists strongly believe creativity and authorship are fundamentally human. While postmodernism deconstructed authorship, metamodernism seeks to reconstruct it in ways that integrate human agency with technological innovation. This shift points to the potential of AI moving from being a mere tool to a co-author, working alongside human artists. Under a metamodern framework, technology and tradition combine, where AI can contribute fresh ideas and techniques, while protecting artists. The third hypothesis revealed a shared worry regarding the exploitation of artists' labor, when their work ends up in training AI datasets without consent or compensation. Participants called for clear data transparency, proper credit, and fair pay, which are demands that echo Fuchs's critique of digital capitalism, where unpaid "prosumers" fuel corporate profits, and Marx's insight into how workers become alienated from their products. Meeting these concerns means supporting regulations that respect artists' rights, guarantee fair compensation, and ensure AI tools enhance rather than harm creative practice.

The potential for exploitation of artists' labor only grows with time, whether by tech giants and their datasets storing basically free labor, or by other big corporations enforcing strict copyright laws that only restrict the creative freedom for everyone but them. An example would be if a big production company would buy access to such AI technologies, with their large, close-sourced datasets and models from already existing intellectual property, and as a result, AI would replace people, as it is considered much faster, and cheaper. On the other hand, small and independent creators and any regular user would not be allowed to access those same datasets, so they don't potentially present a threat or become competition to the companies in question. This is why people suggest the availability of open-source datasets as a possible solution to such concerns. In conclusion, it was evident that the issues presented are complex and involve various stakeholders. It is also important to acknowledge the concerns of both traditional and AI focussed artists, prioritizing their rights and creative freedom, because unless all concerns are addressed, the outcomes will mostly affect all stakeholders negatively, especially small artists. Presented solutions need to prioritize artists' rights while maintaining their creative freedom. Proposing regulations or revising any laws require an in-depth understanding of the potential impacts on creators everywhere. Ensuring their protection against any exploitation of labor and ensuring fair attribution, compensations and copyright practices should be a focal point to any proposed framework. Our study highlights the urgent need for policy changes, where we need clear disclosure of the data and methods behind AI models, guard against companies monopolizing datasets and tools, and expand open, affordable access to these technologies. Only by building transparency, competition, and inclusivity into the AI advancements can we protect artists' rights, preserve creative freedom, and ensure that everyone, not just big corporations, can shape the future of art.

We hope that future research continues to explore and uncover the complexities of this subject, aiming for a solution benefiting all stakeholders without being only in favor of the monopolizing powers of the economy, as Marx theorized. The goal is to reach the perfect balance, embracing the potential to enrich human creativity rather than replacing or exploiting it, to hopefully create a space where innovation is welcomed without compromising the rights and livelihood of those at the heart of creative expression; the artists.

REFERENCES

Aggarwal, C. C. (2018). *Neural Networks and Deep Learning: A Textbook*. Springer International Publishing. DOI: 10.1007/978-3-319-94463-0

Aguera y Arcas, B. (2016, February 23). *Art in the Age of Machine Intelligence*. Medium. Retrieved September 21, 2024, from https://medium.com/artists-and-machine-intelligence/what-is-ami-ccd936394a83

Alleyne, A. (2018, October 25). *A sign of things to come? AI-produced artwork sells for $433K, smashing expectations*. CNN. Retrieved November 18, 2024, from https://edition.cnn.com/style/article/obvious-ai-art-christies-auction-smart-creativity/index.html

Alpaydın, E. (2020). *Introduction to Machine Learning*. MIT Press.

Arantes, P., Sa, V. J., Veiga, P. D. D., & Fernandes-Marcos, A. (Eds.). (2019). *Proceedings of the 9th International Conference on Digital and Interactive Arts*. Portugal. 2019. New York: Association for Computing Machinery. ACM ISBN: 978-1-4503-5273-4 978-1-4503-7250-3.

Bak Herrie, M., Maleve, N. R., Philipsen, L., & Bryld Staunæs, A. (2024). Democratization and generative AI image creation: Aesthetics, citizenship, and practices. *AI & Society*, *40*(5), 3495–3507. DOI: 10.1007/s00146-024-02102-y

Barthes, R. (1977). The death of the author. In *Image, music, text* (Heath, S., Trans.; pp. 142–148). Hill and Wang.

Barthes, R. (1977). The death of the author. In *Image–music–text* (pp. 142–148). Hill and Wang.

Beinin, J. (1994, March/April). Marxism and Postmodernism. *Middle East Report*, 187–188.

Boden, M. A. (2016). *AI: Its nature and future*. Oxford University Press.

Brown, T., Mann, B., Ryder, N., Subbiah, M., Kaplan, J. D., Dhariwal, P., Neelakantan, A., Shyam, P., Sastry, G., Askell, A., Agarwal, S., Herbert-Voss, A., Krueger, G., Henighan, T., Child, R., Ramesh, A., Ziegler, D., Wu, J., Winter, C., Hesse, C., Chen, M., Sigler, E., Litwin, M., Gray, S., Chess, B., Clark, J., Berner, C., McCandlish, S., Radford, A., Sutskever, I., & Amodei, D. (2020). Language Models are Few-Shot Learners. *Advances in Neural Information Processing Systems 33 (NeurIPS 2020)*. Retrieved November 18, 2024, from https://arxiv.org/abs/2005.14165

Buhl, N. (2023, September 21). *OpenAI's DALL-E 3 Explained: Generate Images with ChatGPT*. Encord. Retrieved November 18, 2024, from https://encord.com/blog/openai-dall-e-3-what-we-know-so-far/

Burke, S. (2008). *The Death and Return of the Author* (3rd Edition ed.). Edinburgh University Press. DOI: 10.1515/9781474482172

Cave, S., & Dihal, K. (2019). Hopes and fears for intelligent machines in fiction and reality. *Nature Machine Intelligence, 1*(2), 74–78. Retrieved November 18, 2024, from. DOI: 10.1038/s42256-019-0020-9

Chmielewski, D., & Hu, K. (2023, August 10). Disney creates task force to explore AI and cut costs - sources. *Reuters*. Retrieved November 18, 2024, from https://www.reuters.com/technology/disney-creates-task-force-explore-ai-cut-costs-sources-2023-08-08/

Cohen, H. (1994). The further exploits of Aaron, painter. *Stanford Humanities Review, 2*(4), 141–158.

Diffuse The Rest. (2022, September 5). Hugging Face. Retrieved November 18, 2024, from https://huggingface.co/spaces/huggingface-projects/diffuse-the-rest

Duchamp, M. (1973). *The writings of Marcel Duchamp* (Sanouillet, M., & Peterson, E., Eds.). Da Capo Press.

Elgammal, A. (2019). *AI Is Blurring the Definition of Artist*. American Scientist. Retrieved November 18, 2024, from https://www.americanscientist.org/article/ai-is-blurring-the-definition-of-artist

European Parliament. (2025, February 19). *EU AI Act: first regulation on artificial intelligence Topics*. European Parliament. Retrieved May 5, 2025, from https://www.europarl.europa.eu/topics/en/article/20230601STO93804/eu-ai-act-first-regulation-on-artificial-intelligence

Fakhar, A. (2024, January 11). *Religious Ethics in the Age of Artificial Intelligence and Robotics: Exploring Moral Considerations and Ethical Perspectives*. AI and Faith. Retrieved May 5, 2025, from https://aiandfaith.org/insights/religious-ethics-in-the-age-of-artificial-intelligence-and-robotics-exploring-moral-considerations-and-ethical-perspectives/

Filimowicz, M. (2023). *AI and the Future of Creative Work Algorithms and Society*. Routhledge. DOI: 10.4324/9781003299875

Franco, F. (2022). *The Algorithmic Dimension: Five Artists in Conversation*. Springer International Publishing. DOI: 10.1007/978-3-319-61167-9

Fuchs, C. (2012). Towards Marxian Internet Studies. *Marx is Back-The Importance of Marxist Theory and Research for Critical Comm, 10*(2). 392-412.

Fuchs, C. (2014). *Digital Labour and Karl Marx.* Routhledge. DOI: 10.4324/9781315880075

Fuchs, C., & Mosco, V. (Eds.). (2015). *Marx in the Age of Digital Capitalism.* Brill.

Goodfellow, I. J., Pouget-Abadie, J., Mirza, M., Xu, B., Warde-Farley, D., Ozair, S., Courville, A., & Bengio, Y. (2014) Generative Adversarial Nets. *Proceedings of the 27th International Conference on Neural Information Processing Systems,* 2, 2672-2680.

Guinness, H. (2023). *The 30+ top AI art generators in 2025.* Zapier. Retrieved May 5, 2025, from https://zapier.com/blog/ai-art-generator/#jasper-art

Hutcheon, L. (1989). *The Politics of Postmodernism.* Routhledge.

Islam, A. (2023, March). *A History of Generative AI: From GAN to GPT-4.* Marktechpost. Retrieved May 5, 2025, from https://www.marktechpost.com/2023/03/21/a-history-of-generative-ai-from-gan-to-gpt-4/

Jameson, F. (1991). *Postmodernism, or, The cultural logic of late capitalism.* Duke University Press. Retrieved May 5, 2025, from https://web.education.wisc.edu/halverson/wp-content/uploads/sites/33/2012/12/jameson.pdf

Jameson, F. (1998). *The cultural turn: Selected writings on the postmodern, 1983–1998.* Verso.

Jiang, H., Brown, L., Cheng, J., Artist, A., Khan, M., Gupta, A., Workman, D., Hanna, A., Flowers, J., & Gebru, T. (2023, 08 08-10). AI Art and its Impact on Artists. *AAAI/ACM Conference on AI, Ethics, and Society*, 12. DOI: 10.1145/3600211.3604681

Kovalova, M., Alforova, Z., Sokolyuk, L., Chursin, O., & Obukh, L. (2022). The digital evolution of art: Current trends in the context of the formation and development of metamodernism. *Amazonia Investiga, 11*(56), 114–123. DOI: 10.34069/AI/2022.56.08.12

LeCun, Y., Bengio, Y., & Hinton, G. (2015, May 27). Deep Learning. *Nature, 521*(7553), 436–444. DOI: 10.1038/nature14539 PMID: 26017442

Lyotard, J.-F. (1984). *The postmodern condition: A report on knowledge* (Bennington, G., & Massumi, B., Trans.). University of Minnesota Press.

Lyotard, J.-F. (1994). *Das postmoderne Wissen: ein Bericht* (Engelmann, P., Ed.). Passagen-Verlag.

Manovich, L. (2001). *The Language of New Media*. MIT Press.

Marx, K. (2012). *Economic and Philosophic Manuscripts of 1844*. Dover Publications.

Mayer-Schönberger, V., & Cukier, K. (2013). *Big Data: A Revolution That Will Transform How We Live, Work, and Think*. Houghton Mifflin Harcourt.

Mazzone, M., & Elgammal, A. (2019, February 21). Art, Creativity, and the Potential of Artificial Intelligence. Retrieved May 5, 2025, from https://www.mdpi.com/2076-0752/8/1/26

McCorduck, P. (1991). *Aaron's Code: meta-art, artificial intelligence, and the work of Harold Cohen*. W.H. Freeman.

McCormack, J., & d'Inverno, M. (Eds.). (2012). *Computers and Creativity*. Springer Berlin Heidelberg. DOI: 10.1007/978-3-642-31727-9

Miller, J. (2022, December). *The Rebirth of the Author*. Medium. Retrieved May 5, 2025, from https://jjosephmiller.medium.com/the-rebirth-of-the-author-ca6bcc085c89

Mul, J. d. (1999). *Romantic Desire in (Post)modern Art and Philosophy*. State University of New York Press.

Nugent, C. (2018, August 20). *Can Artificial Intelligence Create Art? Buyers Think So*. Time. Retrieved November 18, 2023, from https://time.com/5357221/obvious-artificial-intelligence-art/

Pasquinelli, M. (Ed.). (2015). *Alleys of Your Mind: Augmented Intelligence and Its Traumas*. Meson Press.

Pearl, M. (2023, September 21). *OpenAI just demoed its most sophisticated image generator yet, DALL-E 3*. Mashable. Retrieved September 21, 2024, from https://in.mashable.com/tech/60582/openai-just-revealed-dall-e-3-its-newest-image-generator

Peters, B., & Peters, T. (2013). *Inside smartgeometry: Expanding the architectural possibilities of computational design*. Wiley. DOI: 10.1002/9781118653074

Power, A. J. (Ed.). (2020). *The Birth and Death of the Author: A Multi-Authored History of Authorship in Print*. Taylor & Francis. DOI: 10.4324/9780429459023

Radford, A., Kim, J. W., Hallacy, C., Ramesh, A., Goh, G., Agarwal, S., Sastry, G., Askell, A., Mishkin, P., Clark, J., Krueger, G., & Sutskever, I. (2021, February 26). *Learning Transferable Visual Models From Natural Language Supervision*. arXiv. Retrieved November 18, 2024, from https://arxiv.org/abs/2103.00020

Radsch, C. (2024, October 9). *Dismantling AI Data Monopolies Before it's Too Late | TechPolicy.Press*. Tech Policy Press. Retrieved October 9, 2024, from https://www.techpolicy.press/dismantling-ai-data-monopolies-before-its-too-late

Reichardt, J. (1968). *Cybernetic serendipity: The computer and the arts*. Studio International.

Robhestand1. (2024, October). *AI and the Commodification of Art: Protecting Creative Integrity*. A.I. in Screen Trade. Retrieved October 8, 2024, from https://aiinscreentrade.com/2024/10/08/ai-and-the-commodification-of-art-protecting-creative-integrity/

Rorty, R. (1989). *Contingency, Irony, and Solidarity*. Retrieved October 8, 2024, from DOI: 10.1017/CBO9780511804397

Schellmann, H. (2024). *The Algorithm: How AI Can Hijack Your Career and Steal Your Future*. Hachette Books.

Shermer, M. (2017). Why Artificial Intelligence Is Not An Existential Threat. *Skeptic*, •••, 2.

Shusterman, R. (2009, January). Aesthetics and Postmodernism. *The Oxford Handbook of Aesthetics, Chapter 47*, 771-782.

Silver, D., Huang, A., Maddison, C. J., Guez, A., Sifre, L., van den Driessche, G., Schrittwieser, J., Antonoglou, I., Panneershelvam, V., Lanctot, M., Dieleman, S., Grewe, D., Nham, J., Kalchbrenner, N., Sutskever, I., Lillicrap, T., Leach, M., Kavukcuoglu, K., Graepel, T., & Hassabis, D. (2016). Mastering the game of Go with deep neural networks and tree search. *Nature*, *529*(7587), 484–489. DOI: 10.1038/nature16961 PMID: 26819042

Snijders, C., Matzat, U., & Reips, U.-D. (2012). Big Data': Big gaps of knowledge in the field of Internet. *International Journal of Internet Science*, *7*(1), 1–5.

Srnicek, N. (2017). *Platform Capitalism*. Polity Press.

Stokes, J., Greene, R., Paul, R., de Rugy, V., Camp, E., & Petti, M. (2023, January 19). Don't Let Disney Monopolize A.I.-Generated Art. *Reason Magazine*. Retrieved January 22, 2025, from https://reason.com/2023/01/19/dont-let-disney-monopolize-a-i-generated-art/

Storm, J. A. J. (2021). *Metamodernism: The Future of Theory*. University of Chicago Press. Retrieved January 22, 2025, from DOI: 10.7208/chicago/9780226786797.001.0001

Taylor, G. D. (2014). *When the machine made art: The troubled history of computer art*. Bloomsbury Academic.

Venkatesan, R., & Li, B. (2017). *Convolutional Neural Networks in Visual Computing: A Concise Guide*. CRC Press. DOI: 10.4324/9781315154282

Vergil, H., Kaplan, M., İbrahim, M. M., Hasan, A. D., & Khan, A. U. I. (2025). *Beyond Algorithms: Artificial Intelligence's Impact and Applications in Economics and Finance*. Ibn Haldun University.

Vermeulen, T., & van den Akker, R. (2010). Notes on Metamodernism. *Journal of Aesthetics & Culture*, *2*(1), 1–14. Retrieved January 22, 2025, from https://www.tandfonline.com/doi/epdf/10.3402/jac.v2i0.5677?needAccess=true. DOI: 10.3402/jac.v2i0.5677

Vidal, M., Smith, T., Rotta, T., & Prew, P. (Eds.). (2019). *The Oxford Handbook of Karl Marx*. Oxford University Press. DOI: 10.1093/oxfordhb/9780190695545.001.0001

Vincent, J. (2023). AI art tools Stable Diffusion and Midjourney targeted with copyright lawsuit. *The Verge*. Retrieved January 22, 2025, from https://www.theverge.com/2023/1/16/23557098/generative-ai-art-copyright-legal-lawsuit-stable-diffusion-midjourney-deviantart

Waters, J. K. (2025). *Meta AI Releases Open Source Machine Learning Library to Tackle Dataset Management Challenges*. Campus Technology. Retrieved January 22, 2025, from https://campustechnology.com/Articles/2025/01/22/Meta-AI-Releases-Open-Source-Machine-Learning-Library.aspx

Weatherbed, J. (2024, January 9). Artists keep rallying against creative companies for using AI. *The Verge*. Retrieved January 22, 2025, from https://www.theverge.com/2024/1/9/24031468/wacom-wizards-of-the-coast-mtg-artists-against-generative-ai

Wissner-Gross, A. (2016). *Datasets Over Algorithms*. Edge. Retrieved October 8, 2024, from https://www.edge.org/response-detail/26587

Wittel, A. (2012). Digital Marx: Toward a Political Economy of Distributed Media. Triple C. Communication Capitalism & Critique. *Open Access Journal for Global Sustainable Information Society*, *10*(2), 313–333.

Zee. (2025). *Artificial Intelligence Apps Gain Global Popularity, Report Finds*. TechRound. Retrieved January 22, 2025, from https://techround.co.uk/news/ai-apps-global-popularity/

Zylinska, J. (2020). *AI Art. Machine Visions and Warped Dreams*. Open Humanities Press.

Chapter 3
Traditional Narratives in the Digital Era:
Web Storytelling Through Design, Illustration, and Sound

Madalena Gonçalves Ribeiro
http://orcid.org/0000-0003-1228-2845
Techn&Art, Polytechnic University of Castelo Branco, Portugal

Lara Cardoso Marques
http://orcid.org/0009-0002-4742-2537
Polytechnic University of Castelo Branco, Portugal

Toni Jorge Gameiro
http://orcid.org/0009-0001-0146-8663
Polytechnic University of Castelo Branco, Portugal

ABSTRACT

The preservation and transmission of intangible cultural heritage, particularly traditional tales, legends, and myths, are increasingly challenged by the dominance of digital media and the changing habits of younger generations. In this context, the adoption of contemporary digital strategies becomes essential to ensure the continuity and relevance of oral traditions. This approach proposes a web storytelling application, structured through a seven-stage methodological framework. The case study focuses on a digital adaptation of Little Red Riding Hood, reimagined through a dark aesthetic approach combining illustration, sound, and interactive transitions to enhance narrative immersion. The resulting application demonstrates how web storytelling can function both as a tool for safeguarding intangible cultural heritage

DOI: 10.4018/979-8-2600-2711-0.ch003

and as a pedagogical strategy that bridges creativity, technology, and education. By aligning cultural transmission with digital literacy, the project highlights the potential of interdisciplinary design practices in sustaining heritage within the digital age.

INTRODUCTION

The preservation and transmission of cultural heritage have long relied on oral traditions, which serve as powerful carriers of memory, identity, and community values. Oral heritage - including myths, legends, songs, proverbs, and personal testimonies - embodies a dynamic and collective form of knowledge. Traditionally passed from generation to generation through face-to-face interaction, these narratives not only safeguard historical continuity but also provide frameworks for interpreting the present.

In an increasingly digital society, however, the ways in which these stories are communicated, shared and experienced are undergoing profound transformation. The widespread use of electronic devices has reshaped media habits, especially among younger audiences often described as "digital natives" (Dingli, 2015). Images, video, sound, and animation now play a central role in capturing attention and shaping engagement, while the introduction of the hyperlink (Berners-Lee, 1989) enabled non-linear, interconnected forms of navigation that profoundly influence contemporary modes of storytelling.

Within this context, web-based storytelling has emerged as a powerful tool for mediating and revitalizing intangible cultural heritage. By combining text, visuals, sound, and interactive elements, digital storytelling environments offer immersive and participatory experiences that differ fundamentally from traditional oral transmission. This hybrid mode of communication opens new possibilities for preserving the authenticity of cultural traditions while fostering innovative approaches to interpretation and engagement.

Drawing on these opportunities, the present project uses Portuguese tales, myths, and legends as its foundation. These narratives, deeply rooted in national cultural memory, face growing challenges in reaching younger audiences shaped by pervasive digital media. Adapting them to a web-based environment seeks to counter this trend, enhancing their relevance and ensuring their continued accessibility.

To pursue this objective, undergraduate students in Communication Design and Audiovisual Arts developed a series of web storytelling applications. The methodological approach emphasized the integration of illustration, animation, and interactivity as core elements of narrative design. These components were strategically employed to intensify immersion, stimulate engagement, and support meaningful interaction with content.

Among the several works produced, this article presents a single selected project as a case study - specifically, the digital adaptation of a traditional story to the principles of web storytelling - used to illustrate the creative process and the methodological decisions involved.

Ultimately, the project demonstrates how interdisciplinary collaboration - bringing together cultural heritage studies, design practices, and digital technologies - can generate innovative storytelling experiences that preserve tradition while meaningfully engaging contemporary, digitally oriented audiences.

THEORETICAL FRAMEWORK

Intangible Cultural heritage

In 2003, the concept of intangible cultural heritage (ICH) was formally consolidated in the UNESCO Convention for the Safeguarding of the Intangible Cultural Heritage (UNESCO, 2003a), following a decade of preliminary references and discussions within UNESCO documents. In the text document of the convention, the article 2 stands the ICH definition as "Cultural heritage does not end at monuments and collections of objects. It also includes traditions or living expressions inherited from our ancestors and passed on to our descendants, such as oral traditions, performing arts, social practices, rituals, festive events, knowledge and practices concerning nature and the universe or the knowledge and skills to produce traditional crafts." (UNESCO, 2003a).

The safeguarding of intangible cultural heritage (ICH) is of vital importance, as it embodies the living culture of communities and sustains their sense of identity and continuity across time. Beyond its symbolic value, ICH contributes directly to the well-being of people and the vitality of territories, reinforcing cultural distinctiveness, fostering social cohesion, and enriching human diversity. However, globalization and cultural homogenization have weakened the natural mechanisms of intergenerational transmission, threatening languages, practices, and know-how once passed down spontaneously (Lenzerini, 2011). This author underscores his concern by asserting that "the cultural diversity of humanity is steadily and dangerously moving toward uniformity".

Indeed, understanding and valuing heritage across all generations - particularly among younger people - is crucial for fostering identity and a sense of belonging to the territory in which they live. It is therefore essential to design initiatives that actively encourage communities to connect with their region's cultural heritage. In this regard, it becomes imperative to devise innovative and engaging strategies for the transmission of ICH, ensuring both its preservation and its capacity to remain meaningful in contemporary societies.

Oral traditions – tales, myths and legends

The ICH branch of Oral Traditions embraces a wide range of spoken forms - such as tales, legends, and myths - that serve not only as entertainment but also as powerful vehicles for transmitting cultural knowledge and reinforcing social and moral values. In fact, these narratives play a central role in keeping cultures alive, connecting generations, preserving the collective memory and culture of communities and shaping and strengthening their identities and supporting social cohesion (UNESCO, 2003c). Its roles span historical, political, aesthetic, and social dimensions.

The individual and collective human experience is shaped by a narrative repertoire, both oral and written, often blending factual elements with the imaginary and the surreal. Tales, myths and legends, embody concepts, values, anxieties, and forms of popular wisdom, serving as cultural frameworks through which communities seek to explain events and interpret reality. According to (Junior, 2021) "legends are literary narratives that have elements that characterize the society in which they are narrated", being sources of memories preservation and local and social historical particularities, which allow us to go back in time.

Stories, Narratives and Storytelling

Stories have always been part of human cultural development, functioning as a means of transmitting knowledge, experiences, and values across generations. Rooted in the identity of communities, traditional stories embody moral teachings, practical wisdom, proverbs, and social norms that help interpret the world and guide behaviour (Benjamin, 1994). Initially conveyed through visual representations, these narratives later evolved into oral language, written texts, and eventually a synthesis of writing and imagery.

Frequently, stories are communicated through narratives - structured sequences of events that together form a coherent plot with a beginning, middle, and end. A narrative unfolds within a specific spatial and temporal setting, which may correspond to a real historical moment or a completely fictional world. Characters - human, animal, inanimate, or imaginary - are defined by physical and psychological traits that support the development of the plot. As Simon-Shoshan notes, establishing a narrative structure involves organizing events into an interconnected system that conveys meaning in a clear and accessible way (Simon-Shoshan, 2013).

Narratives can take diverse expressive forms, including oral or written language, static or moving images, gestures, or combinations of these media (Barthes, et al.,

2011). A well-constructed narrative supports comprehension, while the plot provides emotional and intellectual engagement, sustaining attention and enhancing the communicative impact.

Storytelling refers to the process of crafting and delivering stories in an engaging and meaningful manner. Defined as the use of narratives to share, value, and transmit knowledge (Serrat, 2017), storytelling involves establishing a connection with the audience through language, performance, or visual and auditory elements. When effectively executed, storytelling transforms information into memorable experiences, making it a powerful tool for communication, education, and cultural transmission.

Figure 1. Representation of the relation between story and storytelling

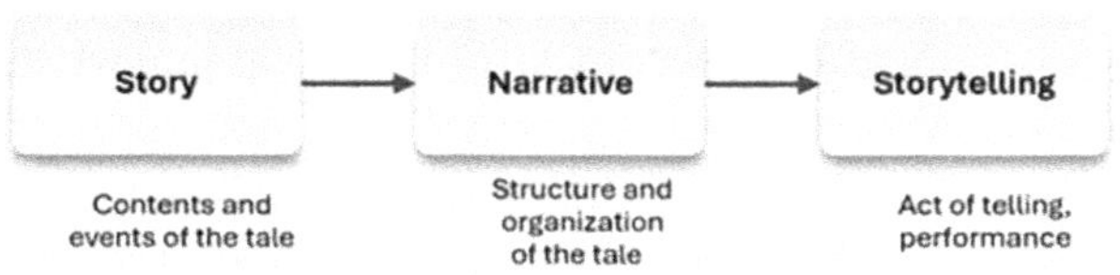

In sum, *stories*, *narratives*, and *storytelling* represent complementary layers of the same communicative phenomenon. While the *story* provides the foundational events and meanings, the *narrative* structures these elements into a coherent and intelligible sequence, and *storytelling* transforms this structure into an expressive act capable of engaging audiences and conveying knowledge (see Figure 1). Understanding the correlation among these three dimensions not only clarifies the nature of traditional accounts but also highlights their potential as cultural and educational resources, particularly when reinterpreted through contemporary media.

DIGITAL STORYTELLING

Analog or digital, storytelling can be conveyed through a wide range of media. Nevertheless, electronic devices - such as laptops, tablets, and mobile phones - have become central to everyday communication for most users. Combined with the prevalence of social media and online platforms, where multimedia content is continually disseminated, this widespread use has fostered a growing public interest in digital formats across all age groups.

At the same time, the expanding domain of digital technologies offers new opportunities for the sphere of cultural heritage, enabling innovative approaches to the creation, management, presentation and dissemination of content. Because digital storytelling can incorporate diverse technologies and media - audio, video, text,

3D graphics, and animation - it supports the development of dynamic, engaging, and sometimes disruptive interpretative strategies. This versatility underscores its potential as a compelling and effective alternative to traditional forms of narrative communication (Robin, 2008).

Interactivity plays a central role in this context. According to Miller, interactive elements are fundamental for effective comprehension and are integral to digital storytelling, as they offer more distinctive and engaging narrative experiences (Miller, 2019). Through mechanisms such as user choices, integrated multimedia content, and immediate feedback, digital narratives enable audiences to explore different pathways within the story. This active involvement enhances immersion, strengthens emotional and cognitive engagement, and transforms users from passive viewers into participants.

The importance of interactivity becomes even more evident when considering the habits of younger generations, who often struggle to maintain sustained attention. Gen Z, for instance, exhibits an average attention span of about 8 seconds - considerably shorter than that of Millennials, who average around 12 seconds (Shatto & Erwin, 2016). As a result, digital content has a narrow window in which to capture and retain interest within a culture driven by immediacy and instant gratification.

Interactivity helps address this challenge in two key ways. First, elements such as branching choices and real-time feedback extend users' engagement by encouraging them to remain involved in the narrative for longer periods. Second, the ability to influence the progression of the story or discover alternative paths enhances the sense of agency and uniqueness of the experience. More broadly, interactivity enriches user experience by providing feedback, encouraging exploration, and supporting intuitive navigation - qualities that are beneficial in storytelling as well as in any digital environment.

The Role of Digital Storytelling in Sustaining Intangible Cultural Heritage

Employing digital storytelling's potential as an effective communication tool and the popularity of digital resources and multimedia information, this mechanism has been applied for a few decades in a variety of contexts, including marketing, education, leisure, and cultural heritage. In truth, there are numerous examples of how digital storytelling has been used successfully to teach and disseminate heritage, particularly the culture of a region, its communities, and its history, with the goal of enhancing citizens' sense of identification.

Europeana (Europeana, 2019), a, a foundation funded by the European Union, plays a central role in driving the digital transformation of the cultural heritage sector across Europe. By aggregating digital collections and developing storytelling initiatives, it contributes to the preservation, accessibility, and reinterpretation of Europe's shared cultural memory. Inspired by Europeana, the Digital Public Library of of America[1] (DPLA) also promotes digital storytelling projects that explore historical and social themes, while serving as a national repository.

Complementing these efforts, the StoryCenter (founded in 1994 as the Center for Digital Storytelling) in California has been a pioneer in using digital storytelling as a means of personal and community expression. The methodology developed by its founder, Joe Lambert (Lambert & Hessler, 2018), has inspired numerous initiatives worldwide - including the BBC's *Capture Wales* project in the United Kingdom, *Patient Voices* in the field of healthcare storytelling, StoryCenter Australia's focus on community and Indigenous narratives, and various programs across Latin America and Africa.

Together, these initiatives demonstrate the transformative potential of narrative, media, and digital storytelling to foster social inclusion and safeguard intangible heritage. As a result, digital storytelling emerges as an effective means of sustaining intangible cultural heritage. It also serves as an effective means of expressing another dimension of intangible cultural heritage - the oral traditions of places, particularly the telling of stories, legends, and myths. The integration of multiple media formats, the potential for diverse forms of interaction, and the possibility of permanent accessibility all contribute to its capacity for wide dissemination and engagement.

Web Storytelling

At approximately the same time as digital storytelling, the expansion of networked communication made it possible to publish digital narratives online, greatly increasing their accessibility. With the advent of Web 2.0 (Aronsson & Solsjo, 2022; Alexander., 2017), the concept of Web 2.0 Storytelling emerged, defined as the creation and sharing of stories through web-based tools, technologies, and participatory platforms (Alexander & Levine, 2008). More recently, new technological dimensions - such as virtual reality, augmented reality, artificial intelligence, and Web 3D - have given rise to Web Storytelling 3.0, expanding the possibilities for immersive and adaptive narrative experiences (Weston, 2023).

Within the broader field of web storytelling, two main approaches can be identified. The first involves digital stories originally created for non-web platforms but later published online through HTML, such as embedded audio clips, streaming video, or animations. The second approach consists of narratives conceived directly for the web, developed using hypermedia elements distributed across interconnected web pages via hyperlinks (Alexander & Levine, 2008). This latter modality has become increasingly relevant, as the web evolves from a simple channel of dissemination into a dynamic environment for cultural expression, creative experimentation, and narrative reinvention.

This second perspective on web storytelling is particularly promising, as the web environment provides a flexible and inclusive framework capable of integrating multiple forms of media and interaction. The combined use of HTML, CSS, and JavaScript supports the coherent incorporation of diverse digital content - text, sound, image, animation, and interactivity - within a unified narrative space. Together, these technologies offer structural, aesthetic, and functional foundations that allow stories to unfold dynamically across digital interfaces.

HTML establishes the narrative structure and enables the inclusion of multimodal content. CSS (Cascading Style Sheets) enhances visual expressiveness and aesthetic coherence; with the advancements introduced by CSS3, transitions and animations contribute not only to stylistic refinement but also to rhythm, atmosphere, and emotional tone. JavaScript introduces interactivity and responsiveness, transforming otherwise static stories into participatory experiences in which the audience can explore, navigate, or influence the narrative in non-linear and immersive ways.

In sum, web storytelling refers to the creative use of digital platforms and interactive media to craft, disseminate, and experience narratives within online environments, enabling reinterpretations of traditional stories while exploring the expressive potential of contemporary web technologies.

Multimedia Contents for Web Storytelling

The convergence of diverse media - visual, aural, and interactive - has the potential to transform traditional narratives into multisensory and immersive experiences. Storytelling becomes more compelling when it integrates multiple forms of media, such as images, text, music, audio, video, animation, or other forms of 2D and 3D virtual elements. Together, these components contribute collectively to establishing context, constructing meaning, and convey emotional depth, enabling users to engage with and experience the narrative in a more profound and immersive way (Psomadaki et al., 2019).

Visual Contents –Image. It has been used for about thirty thousand years and, now more than ever, serves as a powerful means to tell stories (Graf, 2017). Sequences of images can depict events, symbolize abstract ideas, or convey emotions that text alone cannot express. Myths and legends, in particular, have long relied on visual imagery to complement verbal narration and stimulate imagination. In digital contexts, static visuals function both as narrative structures and aesthetic vehicles, contributing to cohesion and emotional resonance. In web-based narratives, illustrations, photographs, and 2D or 3D models are essential, as they anchor meaning, evoke atmosphere, and guide interpretation - enhancing audience engagement.

Visual Contents – Animation. Bridging the static and dynamic dimensions of visual communication, animation infuses narratives with rhythm, transformation, and vitality. By simulating temporal progression or guiding attention, animation reinforces narrative coherence and drives emotional engagement (Rizvic et al., 2017). Subtle movements - such as flickering light, flowing water, or the gradual appearance of a character - can enrich atmosphere and sensory immersion. Conversely, more pronounced animated actions can emphasize narrative turning points or symbolic moments, lending vitality and depth to the story. In web environments, technologies such as CSS3 transitions, keyframe animations, and JavaScript effects enable the seamless integration of animation and interactivity. When used as an intrinsic narrative layer rather than mere decoration, animation transforms web storytelling into a living, evolving experience that heightens both cognitive and emotional involvement.

Aural Contents – Sound. Yet often underestimated in digital storytelling, sound constitutes a powerful dimension. Within multimedia narratives, aural elements introduce emotional nuance, spatial depth, and rhythm, intensifying immersion and engagement (Salselas & Penha, 2019; Privitera et al., 2024). The narrator's voice conveys information, emotion, and tone, shaping audience perception. Ambient sounds - such as natural environments, urban noise, or human activity - help establish atmosphere and situate the story within a specific context. Likewise, music and sound effects can heighten tension, signal transitions, or evoke wonder and enchantment. When thoughtfully designed, sound becomes a guiding thread that orchestrates attention, amplifies emotion, and transforms digital narratives into deeply affective multisensory experiences.

Interactivity. It is core element that distinguishes digital storytelling from traditional narrative forms, enabling the audience from passive spectators into active participants who influence, navigate, or co-create the unfolding story. Through mechanisms such as hyperlinks, branching paths, clickable objects, or responsive interfaces, interactivity introduces activity and personalization, allowing each user to construct a unique narrative experience (Ryan, 2015). Beyond its functional role, interactivity deepens emotional and cognitive engagement, fostering immersion through choice, exploration, and feedback (Murray, 2017). In web-based storytelling, it thus operates not merely as a technological feature but as an expressive language - one that empowers users to inhabit, shape, and reinterpret the story world.

APROACH

Recognizing the significant value of traditional stories as fundamental elements of oral tradition and intangible cultural heritage, a project was conceived with the aim of revitalizing, for new generations, the legacy contained in these narratives - their wisdom, knowledge, customs, experiences, and regional traditions.

PROPOSAL

During the 2024/2025 academic year, a creative challenge was launched for 65 third-year students of the Communication Design and Audiovisual degree program. They were invited to employ digital and web-based environments to reinterpret and present a traditional story in an engaging and compelling way, directed at a specific target audience (to be defined). The task consisted of developing a web-based storytelling application that reimagines and communicates a traditional tale.

Web Storytelling was chosen as the development approach, as the web offers an ideal medium for reinterpreting traditional tales through contemporary digital practices. Its global accessibility, interactive potential, and capacity to merge different sensory modalities enable a renewed narrative experience - one that preserves the essence of oral and visual traditions while embracing the expressive possibilities of the digital age.

The initiative was intended not only to stimulate valuable creative exploration but also to encourage students to reconceptualize the web - traditionally used for conventional websites - as a dynamic environment for experimental narratives and innovative structures. Moreover, it aimed to foster the intersection of design, storytelling, illustration and technology, promoting a multidisciplinary approach, where photography, video, illustration, animation, and interactivity served as complementary narrative instruments. The integration of these media facilitates intuitive and engaging experiences, provided there is a harmonious relationship between the various elements - an aspect that demands a well-defined methodological framework.

METHODOLOGY

The present case study was developed by applying the methodology proposed in *"Methodology for Storytelling"* (Ribeiro & Almeida, 2024), which was specifically designed to guide the creation of web storytelling applications. This methodological framework was conceived to address a clear gap: while existing approaches to *digital storytelling* and traditional *website development* provide useful insights, neither of them proves adequate when the objective is to design interactive narratives for the web that combine multiple media resources in a coherent and engaging way.

The methodology encompasses seven main stages:

1. Choosing the tale and collecting information;
2. Planning and conceptualization of the digital narrative;
3. Design;
4. Structure creation, content insertion, and interaction implementation;
5. Creation and integration of multimedia content;
6. Evaluation and refinement;
7. Sharing and publishing.

These stages form a sequential process, ensuring narrative coherence, visual consistency, and usability throughout the development of a web-based storytelling application. The method not only structures the workflow but also provides the flexibility to adapt to the specificities of each story and the digital medium chosen for its adaptation.

First stage - *Choosing the Tale and Collecting Information.* The selected story is thoroughly researched to gather relevant details such as its origin, historical context, themes, and underlying metaphors. Additional information, including references to settings, clothing, and cultural elements, is collected to ensure authenticity and depth. At this stage, the target audience is also defined, and inspirational materials such as images, colors, fonts, symbols, sounds, and videos are compiled to create a Moodboard, which serves as a visual and conceptual guide for the subsequent stages of the project.

Figure 2. Web storytelling application's methodology diagram

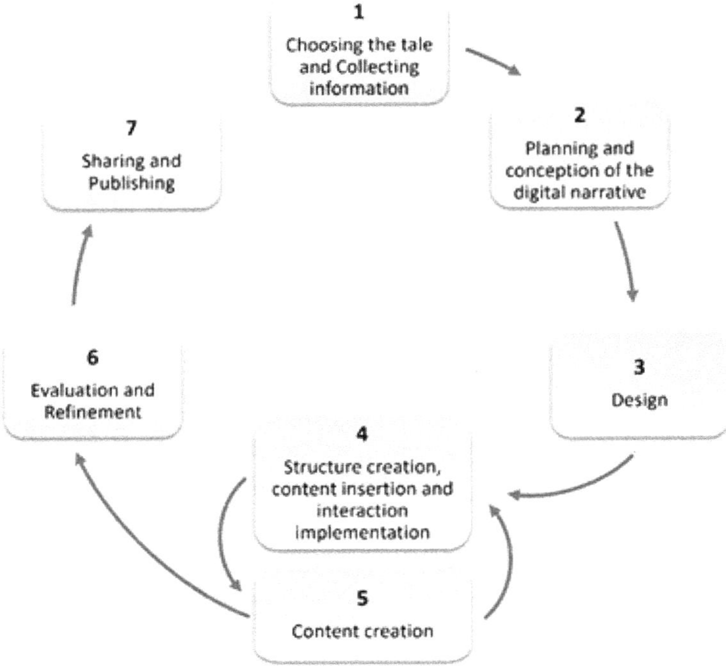

Second stage - *Planning and Conception*. Focuses on identifying and structuring the key moments of the story, defining transitions between them, and outlining possible interactions. Two essential tools are used in this process: the script and the storyboard. The script, developed first, presents the entire narrative scene by scene, describing actions, dialogues, settings, characters, gestures, and expressions. Its main goal is to distill the story into a coherent sequence of meaningful moments that guide the viewer through the narrative flow.

From the script, the storyboard is created as a visual representation that translates written content into a structured sequence of scenes. It specifies how each scene will be depicted, including visual composition, media types (such as audio, video, or animation), and interactive elements that enhance engagement. This stage is decisive, as it determines the coherence and effectiveness of the final application. However, both tools should remain flexible and open to refinement during later stages, with the aid of digital software that facilitates the visualization and adjustment of scenes, characters, and interactions.

Third stage - *Design*. All visual and auditory elements of the digital narrative are defined, guided by the outcomes of the planning phase and the previously developed

Moodboard. This includes establishing typographic choices, color schemes, and image styles, as well as determining the characteristics of each media component - such as sound effects, background audio, narration, or interactive responses. Like film production, this stage shapes the narrative's atmosphere and identity, ensuring coherence between aesthetic and emotional dimensions.

Fourth stage - Structure Creation. The narrative framework is defined before adding content. Different formats can be used, from a simple page-by-page layout resembling a digital book to more dynamic structures where the story unfolds on a single page. User interactions such as scrolling, opacity changes, or overlapping effects can make transitions smoother and the experience more engaging.

This stage requires proficiency in HTML, CSS, and JavaScript, as these languages enable structure, styling, and interactivity. In practice, it often overlaps with content insertion, since adjustments to layout and interactions are made along the way to ensure consistency and narrative flow.

Fifth stage - *Content Creation and Insertion.* Multimedia elements such as images, audio, and video are produced or gathered following the storyboard as a guide. These components bring the story to life and must be prepared in formats compatible with web standards (HTML, CSS, and modern browsers). This phase often overlaps with structural adjustments, as integrating content may require refining layouts, transitions, and interactive effects to ensure seamless functionality and narrative coherence.

Sixth stage - *Evaluation and Refinement.* The application undergoes usability testing to identify and correct errors, inconsistencies, or design flaws before its release. Evaluation may involve expert reviews or user testing to gather feedback on functionality and user experience. Based on these insights, necessary adjustments are made to enhance efficiency, usability, and engagement, resulting in a more polished and effective web storytelling application.

Seventh stage - *Sharing and publishing*. When the web storytelling application is finalized, it should be published, easily accessed and experienced on any computer or tablet through a standard web browser, without the need for additional software or installation.

In summary, the methodology applied in this case demonstrates how a structured, step-by-step approach to web storytelling can be enriched by interdisciplinary contributions. The integration of illustration and design into the methodological framework not only strengthened the aesthetic dimension of the application but also enhanced its capacity to engage users. By combining technical rigor with creative artistry, the project illustrates the potential of web storytelling to reinvent traditional tales for contemporary audiences, providing applications that are not only functional and accessible but also visually compelling and emotionally engaging.

Web Storytelling Case Study

The case under discussion pertains to a project undertaken by two students within a multidisciplinary framework that integrated the subjects "Illustration" and "Web Design and Development" from the Communication Design and Audiovisual degree program. The primary objective of the project was to convey a traditional story in an engaging and captivating manner through a web-based storytelling application.

The methodological procedure described in section 3.3 is applied in this case-study, step-by-step. Before the implementation, there are preliminary moment involving the preparation of the narrative, data collecting, planning and concepting, and design, determinant stages for the result – a web storytelling story. This section will outline the development process of a web-based storytelling tool designed to convey a traditional narrative.

Stage 1 - Choosing the tale and collecting information

The traditional tale chosen for the web storytelling application is the well-known "Little Red Riding Hood", a legend that originates from central Europe, which was transmitted orally until its first publication in the book "*Histoires ou Contes du Temps Passé*" (Perrault, 1697). This story, entitled "Le Petit Chaperon Rouge", was intended to transmit some morality, as is the case with many traditional stories. Since then, this story has already given rise to several different versions.

To this case, the underlying idea is to preserve the emotional resonance and originality, while introducing elements of suspense and a darker atmosphere. As a result, a version that adheres to that spirit was suggested, as the summary of the story that follows illustrates.

> *"Once upon a time, in a village forgotten by time - where nights were long and the moon shone brighter than the sun - there lived a girl known to all as Little Red Riding Hood, for she always wore the red hood made by her grandmother. Legend had it that, at birth, she was cursed by a forest spirit, and whenever she cried, her dark aura became visible to ordinary human eyes.*
>
> *The villagers believed that Little Red left the village each night to visit her grandmother, who lived deep in the woods. In truth, however, she had learned the art of witchcraft from her grandmother, a powerful sorceress. After her grandmother's death, Little Red transformed the old house into a sanctuary and profane altar, where she would summon and return creatures to the earth - her fated purpose since birth.*
>
> *On one particular night, she felt the forest grow restless; the animals had fled, and danger lingered nearby. Preparing herself, she stood her ground as the creature aproached, thirsting for blood. Without hesitation, she faced it head-on,*

and with two swift blows, she severed its head. Carrying it to her grandmother's house, she completed the ritual - returning the creature to the earth. Bound by her destiny, Little Red could only wait for the next being that would come for her soul, ready once again to fulfill her dark prophecy."

Given the nature of the narrative, the project sought to identify visual elements capable of conveying its atmosphere and underlying symbolism, supported by research focused on visual mood. In alignment with the intended visual expression, which served as a source of inspiration, a Moodboard was developed, as illustrated in Figure 3.

It expresses a sense of mystery, tension, and moral ambiguity. The mood is dark, eerie, and almost psychological due to the heavy usage of dark tones, blacks, grays, and deep reds. The images imply a more reflective and mature world where danger, wonder, and dread coexist rather than a naive children's story. As if nothing is entirely obvious, there is also a sense of suspense and suspicion: the woods are more maze-like than setting, the wolf and the girl appear to be sharing secrets, and crimson is no longer just a symbol of innocence but also of danger and blood.

Though the tale of *Little Red Riding Hood* is widely known from children's storybooks, the version intended to be presented here is not designed for a very young target people. Therefore, both the narrative and the subsequent creative process must be adapted accordingly to reflect a more mature and complex interpretation.

Figure 3. Moodboard for the dark "Little Red Riding Hood" story

Stage 2 - Planning and Conception

At this stage, there are several key tasks that must be undertaken to enable consistent planning of the application. These include defining the organizational structure, developing the story script, and creating a storyboard based on the script.

A. Structure of the Web Storytelling application

The initial task involved establishing the overall structural framework of the web application. In this case, it is composed of four main nodes: a home page, a story cover page, the story page itself, and a final epilogue page. Navigation between these nodes follows a linear structure (see Figure 4).

Figure 4. Storytelling application site map

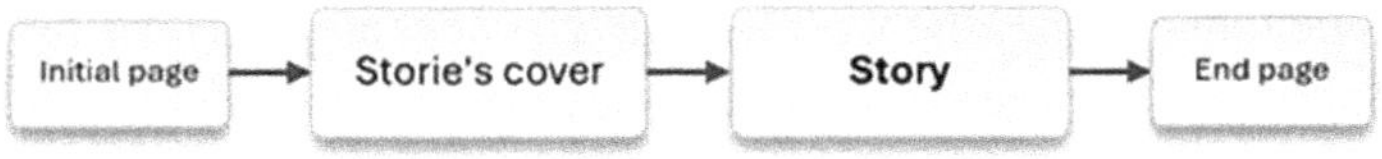

In the initial page, the user chooses the preferred language (English and Portuguese) and in the last one, the sentence "And so, the story ends" serves as a traditional closing formula, marks the narrative's conclusion and reinforces the storytelling frame typical of oral or folk narratives. The focus, however, is on second and the third node - the story's cover and particularly, the story page.

The cover page is intended to be impactful, integrating multiple media elements to enhance user immersion. The combination of a strong image, interactivity or animation, and a suggestive sonority can stimulate the user's curiosity and encourage engagement with the story being conveyed. Regarding the story, it should be presented on a single node (web page), where a sequence of narrative scenes unfolds laterally from right to left.

It is intended to provide harmonious and disguised passages between the different each pair of successive narrative scenes, thereby ensuring cohesion and continuity.

The "Story" page structure

The scenes of the narrative will be created in overlapping layers, from the first to the last scene. The passage from a scene to the successor is performed by clicking in an arrow (located in the right side of the scene). At that moment, the layer containing the scene shifts to the left, disappearing completely, and the next scene becomes visible.

Figure 5. Representation of the scenes of the narrative on the web page

To ensure seamless and visually harmonious transitions between scenes, a specific mechanism was conceived to create discreet and aesthetically pleasant shifts. During each passage, as the background and all visual elements of the preceding scene slide to the left, an image positioned on the right side of the screen begins to move simultaneously. Initially, only half of this image is visible; as the motion unfolds, it gradually reveals itself in full. When the shift is complete, only the right half remains visible, perfectly aligned with the left edge of the screen, where it becomes integrated into the subsequent scene.

In transitions between scenes with white backgrounds, continuity is achieved through connecting elements such as a tree or a house (see Figure 12). In scenes with black backgrounds, the linkage is accomplished using vertical gradient bars along the lateral edges, ensuring an equally smooth and elegant passage.

B. Story's Script

Based on the story, the script identifies the key scenes of the narrative, allowing the establishment of a coherent storyline that enables the reader to comprehend the story through a logical flow of events. At this point, factors that contribute to the story's interest and engagement can already be identified, namely, elements that provide interaction, animation, immersion, content of a diverse nature (multimodal) and emotional involvement (suspense, fear, etc.), among others.

In this case, there was identified a set of eight key scenes of the "Little Red Riding Hood" story, hereinafter referred to as scenes in the Table 1. Each one is characterized through the description of the environment and what happens there and the type of audiovisual plan (long shot, aerial plan, etc). Additionally, considering that was planned to include a narrator and ambient sound throughout the entire narrative, both these two media elements are specified in the script.

Table 1. Narrative's script of the "Little Red Riding Hood" tale (alternative version).

<table>
<tr><td>Scene 1</td><td>Extreme long shot: An ancient village, surrounded by dense forest. It appears to be being watched evasively from some distance.
Action: None.
Sound: Typical sounds of the countryside and animals (dogs, birds, owls, etc.) + distant howls.</td></tr>
<tr><td colspan="2">Narrator (voice-over): "Once upon a time there was a village forgotten by time, where the nights were long and the moon shone brighter than the sun itself, sheltered by the forest and its animals."</td></tr>
<tr><td>Scene 2</td><td>Long shot: In a scene with streets of the village, Little Red Riding Hood moves along a street, crossing the plane.
Action: Little Red Riding Hood moving through the streets.
Sound: Typical sounds of the countryside and animals (dogs, birds, owls, etc.) + the sound of footsteps walking on the sidewalk.</td></tr>
<tr><td colspan="2">Narrator (voice-over): "There lived a girl known to everyone as Little Red Riding Hood, because she always wore the red hood made by her grandmother."</td></tr>
<tr><td>Scene 3</td><td>Group shot: Silhouette of a group of villagers whispering, watching a crib with a baby.
Action: Waves swirling beneath the cradle, enveloping it.
Sound: Group of voices whispering (somewhat muffled) + a baby crying.</td></tr>
<tr><td colspan="2">Narrator (voice-over): "They say that when she was born, Little Red Riding Hood was cursed by a forest spirit, and that when she cried, her dark aura could be seen by the naked eye of mere humans."</td></tr>
<tr><td>Scene 4</td><td>Extreme long shot: It's night. A lonely house in the middle of the woods looks abandoned. Candles are lit. In the distance, the top of the church tower can be seen.
Action: None.
Sound: Typical night sounds in the forest (birds and other animals).</td></tr>
<tr><td colspan="2">Narrator (voice-over): "The villagers believed that Little Red Riding Hood left the village every night to visit her grandmother, who lived deep in the forest, but the reality went far beyond their imagination. In fact, Little Red Riding Hood learned all kinds of spells from her grandmother, who was an incredibly powerful witch. After her grandmother's death, Little Red Riding Hood began using her grandmother's house as a sanctuary and unholy altar, where she would attract creatures and return them to the earth; this had been her purpose since birth."</td></tr>
<tr><td>Scene 5</td><td>Aeria plan: It's night. A path lined with trees can be seen on both sides (above). The atmosphere is suspenseful.
Action: Little Red Riding Hood moves along the path. Birds' eyes appear above the trees, giving the impression that the birds are watching.
Sound: Typical night sounds in the forest (birds and other animals) + sound of footsteps walking in the forest.</td></tr>
<tr><td colspan="2">Narrator (voice-over): "On that night, Little Red Riding Hood could feel the trees becoming more agitated as she walked through the forest. All the small animals had fled. She prepared herself for what was to come, but she didn't expect the danger to be so close."</td></tr>
<tr><td>Scene 6</td><td>Full shot: It's night. Little Red Riding Hood stands with her arms open in a defiant stance, ready for attack/defense, wearing warrior garb beneath her red hooded cape.
Action: Little Red Riding Hood crouches, preparing to attack. The silhouettes of the trees disappear, and the enormous eyes of a creature appear.
Sound: Typical nighttime sounds in the forest (birds and other animals). When Little Red Riding Hood crouches, a (muffled) sigh of anxiety is heard; when the creature's eyes appear, a (muffled) growl is heard.</td></tr>
<tr><td colspan="2">Narrator(voice-over): "It was there and now, she opened her arms, and without retreating or looking back, she crouched down and took a deep breath, preparing to face the creature that was approaching, thirsty for blood."</td></tr>
</table>

continued on following page

Table 1. Continued

Scene 7	Close-up: Head of a wolf. Action: Two cross sword strikes are created on the wolf's head. Sound: Typical nighttime sounds in the forest (birds and other animals). When the strike occurs, the cutting sound of the sword blade is heard simultaneously.
Narrator (voice-over): "With his head held high, he looked into the creature's eyes and with two deep blows ripped off its head."	
Scene 8	Full shot: Surrounded by fan-shaped trees, Little Red Riding Hood stands in front of the wolf lying dead on the ground, perched on a five-pointed star. At each point, a candle burns. Action: Candle fire animation. Sound: Typical night sounds in the forest (birds and other animals) + strong wind in the leaves of the trees.
Narrator(voice-over): "She took the head near her grandmother's house and fulfilled her purpose, the earth took what was rightfully hers, and Little Red Riding Hood had no option but to wait for the next creature to come after her soul and fulfill her prophecy."	

C. Storybooard

Based on the information provided in the script, a storyboard was developed to plan the visual interpretation of each scene, illustrated in Figure 6. In this case, only one frame was drawn per scene of the script, as the numerous animations and other visual effects would otherwise require the production of multiple frames for each. Instead, each frame is accompanied by detailed descriptive annotations that convey the intended visual and narrative dynamics (see Table 2).

Figure 6. Storyboard. The height scenes of the script are represented by the images, from (a) scene 1 to (h) scene 8, respectively

The actions that occur in each scene are described in detail (see Table 2). These specifications should be sufficiently descriptive and comprehensive to support stage 4 (particularly, the interaction implementation) and stage 5 (content creation). They should enable inferences regarding which CSS properties will be modified, what geometric transformations will be applied (such as rotation, translation or scale), and whether multiple images will be generated to produce an animation, among other aspects.

Table 2. Identification and specification of the animations to perform in each scene of the narrative

#Scene	Actions in the scene
Scene 1	None.
Scene 2	Summary: Little Red Riding Hood is moving through the streets. 1. The girl's image translates and, additionally, rotates to the left and right, as it moves (simulating the steps).
Scene 3	Summary: Waves swirling beneath the cradle, enveloping it. 1. An image with irregular, circular, and concentric lines repeatedly expand and contracts as it rotates (this image is partially overlapped by the still image of the cradle).
Scene 4	None.
Scene 5	Summary: Little Red Riding Hood moves along the path. Birds' eyes appear above the trees, giving the impression that the birds are watching. It is an aerial view. 1. The background image, with the path (center) lined with trees, translates horizontally from right to left; 2. The image of the girl translates horizontally, from the left side of the screen, and stops in the center; 3. But, simultaneously, the girl's image rotates to the left and right as it moves (simulating the steps). 4. Pairs of eyes appear, remain and disappear slowly, in different places, as time goes by. In the animation of the eyes appearing, their shape changes, giving the sensation that they are opening (and the inverse when they are disappearing.
Scene 6	Summary: Little Red Riding Hood crouches, preparing to attack. The silhouettes of the trees disappear, and the enormous eyes of a creature appear. 1. First, the image of the girl appears in the scene, standing. 2. However, the eyes (of a creature) gradually appear; 3. The image of the standing girl gradually disappears, and soon after, the image of the girl in an alert/attack position gradually appears; 4. The creature's eyes change shape, closing slightly, expressing its aggression.
Scene 7	Summary: Two cross sword strikes are created on the wolf's head. 1. In the bottom of the screen, an arm appears, with a sword in the hand, making a rotational movement to the left, until it disappears; then the arm appears again, making a rotational movement to the right (until it disappears), over the image of a wolf; 2. Simultaneously, a blow is drawn over the wolf's snout when it is cut by the sword. First, it is created gradually the cut made from right to left; then, it is created gradually the cut made from left to right, making a crosscut.
Scene 8	Summary: Candle fire animation. 1. The fire shape changes gradual and repeatedly, to simulate the fire candle.

Stage 3 - Design

The design phase is primarily concerned with defining the visual and interactive elements of the application prior to development. During this stage, key aspects such as colors, typography, icons, and overall graphic style are established, along with the visual styling of any images to be incorporated. In addition, the sketches of scene transitions may be produced, sustained by the outputs of the (preceding) planning and conception stage, particularly by the script and the storyboard.

Specifications developed during this phase should be sufficiently detailed to ensure a smooth and coherent progression to the implementation stage.

A. Colors

In alignment with the inspiration derived from the Moodboard (see Figure 3), black, white, and dark red were the primary colors employed. When necessary, shades of gray may also be incorporated. The inherent qualities of these colors help to emphasize the intended atmosphere of suspense, melancholy and mystery, suggesting a dark narrative tone.

B. Images

The illustration style to be applied should be minimalist and linear. The absence of color, complex shadows, or elaborate textures reinforces a sketched and almost monochromatic aesthetic, conveying a sense of simplicity and intentional incompleteness. At the beginning of the narrative, a light background with black lines should be used, which will later be inverted. Certain details should appear in dark red to create a striking visual contrast.

The illustrations should evoke the atmosphere of a fairy tale or fable.

C. Sound

The integration of both ambient and action sounds enhances the user's immersion in the narrative experience. Ambient sounds should reflect the atmosphere of each scene, while action sounds should represent specific interactions - such as the movement of objects, human activities, and other contextual elements.

Furthermore, audio narration will be incorporated to support individuals with dyslexia and those who prefer to engage more deeply with the narrative details. The narrator's voice should adopt a grave tone, reinforcing the sense of suspense that the story aims to convey.

D. Typography

"Cinzel Decorative" is a typeface inspired by first-century Roman inscriptions and grounded in classical proportions. However, it is not merely a revivalist design; while it evokes the ancient heritage of the Latin alphabet, it simultaneously integrates a contemporary sensibility (Gama, 2012). This old-style typeface also conveys a medieval artistic character, enhancing its historical and aesthetic resonance.

Figure 7. EB Cinzel Decorative (Gama, 2012)

LITTLE RED RIDING HOOD

Due to its characteristics, this typeface aligns with the atmosphere intended to be conveyed. Nevertheless, it is not applied within the narrative itself but rather used at the beginning of the application for small visual highlights.

Stage 4 - Creating Structure, Inserting Content, and Implementing Interactivity Stage

Structure. Regarding the structure of the narrative scenes, it consists of eight overlapping layers (HTML sections), where scene one is the first and scene eight is the last. The transition between two successive scenes is accomplished by moving the cursor to the left of the previous scene, revealing the subsequent scene, which was hidden by the overlap, which becomes visible.

After the implementation of this primary structure, it is warned to start the content creation, namely with the creation of the background images. In fact, this stage is interlaced with the "content creation" stage.

Inserting images. After creating illustrations (in stage 5), they should be integrated into the HTML sections, starting by the background images and then the other images, in the positions.

Adding interactions. Since the focus was placed on animation, interactivity was limited to two elements: one on the cover, where a wolf's eye moves in response to the cursor's position, and navigation arrows that allow the user to move between different scenes in the story.

The interaction on the cover takes place within a striking and aggressive image of a wolf (depicted in Figure 8) and is further complemented by a rhythmic sound that suggests imminent danger. Its purpose is to create anticipation and stimulate interest in exploring the story. In contrast, the interaction via the arrows is minimal, serving solely to advance to the next scene in the narrative.

Figure 8. Interaction with the wolf's eyes: (a) when the cursor is in the bottom left side of the screen and (b) when the cursor is in the right side of the screen

Integrating animations. In accordance with the conceived animations, CSS3 is used for the implementation, resort to JavaScript to resolve more complex situations, when necessary.

Incorporating Sound. Immediately following the transition to a new scene, the background sound begins to establish the atmosphere and continues throughout. Immediately afterwards, the narrator's voice emerges, guiding the viewer into the unfolding story.

Stage 5 – Creating Contents

Considering the visual line defined in mind, it is appropriate to start the images achievement, illustrations in this case.

Illustrations

Created through freehand drawing, using a digital tablet, the illustrations were inspired by Moodboard (Figure 3) and the style in the Design stage. As for the role of the constructed illustrations, one can point three categories: backgrounds, scene components and other complementary elements as illustrated in Figure 9.

Figure 9. Illustrations for the web-based storytelling application. (a) Wolf featured on the cover page; (b) navigation arrow leading to the next scene; (c) typographic sample used to number the narrative scenes

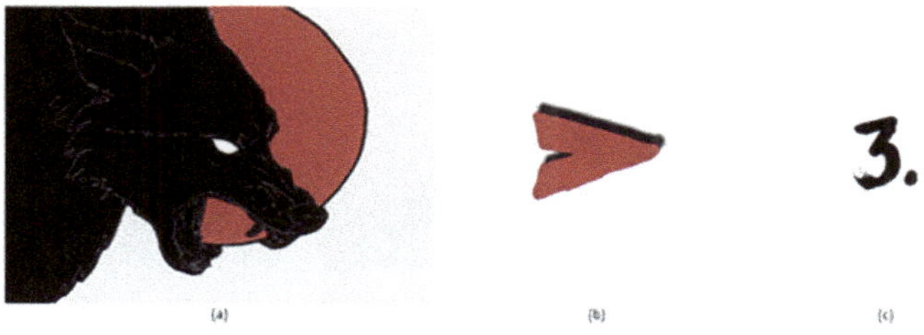

Figure 10 presents two background illustrations. In Figure 10(b), the background image features a patterned design, created to support continuous horizontal scrolling without revealing any visible seams or connection points. At the beginning of the narrative, the white background serves to introduce the characters and the story. As the narrative progresses, a darker mood is conveyed when the background shifts to black and the illustrations appear in white.

Figure 10. Background of scenes 2 (in white) and 5 (in black), respectively

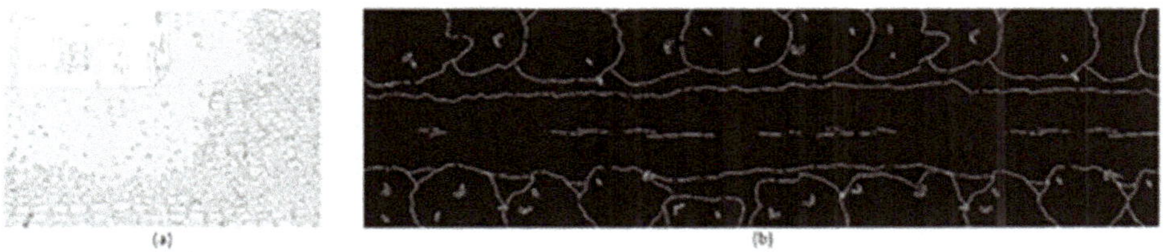

The story's scenes also include additional illustrations, which were drawn separately - both to allow animation (mainly implemented through CSS3) or to enable the overlapping of visual elements, as shown in Figure 11.

Figure 11. (a) Illustration of Little Red Riding Hood (for scene 2); (b) Illustration of Little Red Riding Hood (for scene 6); and (c) circular lines surrounding the cradle (for scene 3)

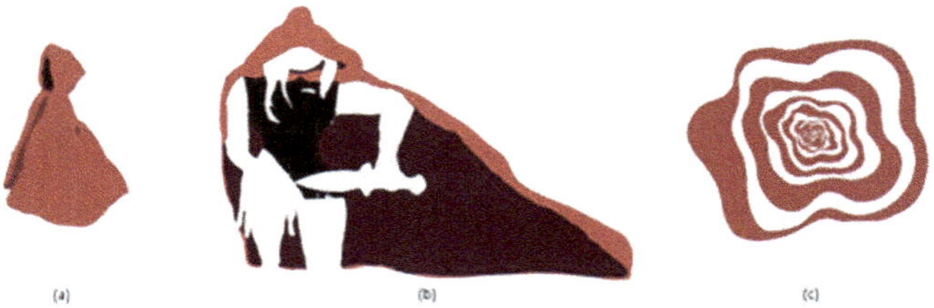

To ensure a harmonious transition between the scenes (previously described in Stage 2), those with white backgrounds include specific "connecting elements," such as a tree or a house (see Figure 12). The tree visible on the right side of Scene 1 remains on screen throughout the transition, gradually moving to the left as the background of Scene 1 slides away. Once the shift is complete, the tree is positioned on the left side, now integrated into Scene 2.

Figure 12. Backgrounds of scenes (a) one and (b) two, and their connecting element - a tree

Animations

The various scenes of the narrative are represented on pages with alternating black and white backgrounds, with the illustration lines rendered in inverse colors.

In general, the illustrations are divided into three distinct layers: fixed planes, transition planes, and objects (namely characters or specific parts such as eyes). For the transitions between the scenes represented by white backgrounds, connecting elements such as trees or houses are created. In the scenes represented on black backgrounds, planes are designed with a vertical gradient line that, when turning the page, seamlessly merges the illustrations in a way that remains imperceptible.

Sound

For each scene, two distinct audio components were produced: the environmental sound and the narrator's voice, both exported in MP3 format. The background sound operates as a continuous ambient layer, remaining active for the entire duration of the user's presence in the scene and contributing to the establishment of tone and atmosphere. In contrast, the narrator's voice is triggered shortly after the scene is entered and plays a single time, ensuring a controlled, non-repetitive delivery of the verbal narrative and preventing overlap or auditory fatigue.

RESULT

The resultant application can be achieved in https://mribeiro.ipcb.pt/samples/Story/LaraMarq_TonyGam/index.html.

CONCLUSION

The dissemination and revitalization of intangible cultural heritage - particularly traditional tales, myths, and legends transmitted through oral tradition - were the central motivations of this project. In an age dominated by digital media, such narratives risk fading from collective memory, especially among younger generations whose cultural experience no longer includes communal storytelling. By translating these traditional stories into digital, web-based narratives, this project sought not only to safeguard their symbolic and pedagogical value but also to render them relevant and appealing to today's audiences.

The initiative demonstrated that web storytelling can serve as an effective vehicle for cultural preservation and education, combining artistic expression, narrative design, and technological development. Through illustration, animation, sound, and interactivity, students reinterpreted ancestral stories, giving them new life in the digital sphere. The guiding concept of edutainment - learning through creative and playful experiences - proved essential to fostering engagement and deepening understanding among younger users, who are naturally attuned to multimodal and interactive forms of communication.

Equally significant was the project's multidisciplinary character, which united fields such as design, illustration, storytelling, sound design, and web development. This convergence enabled students to approach the same narrative from different disciplinary perspectives, promoting collaboration, critical thinking, and integrative problem-solving. The results confirmed that interdisciplinarity not only enhances the aesthetic and communicative quality of the applications but also strengthens their educational and cultural impact. In this sense, the project also functioned as a pedagogical laboratory in which students learned to integrate technology, creativity, and cultural interpretation - skills that are increasingly essential in contemporary design and digital media practice.

From a research standpoint, the project contributed valuable insights into the conceptual, methodological, and technological strategies most effective in web storytelling for cultural heritage. The knowledge generated here lays a foundation for future initiatives that may explore advanced technologies - such as virtual or augmented reality, artificial intelligence, or web 3D - to further expand the immersive potential of digital narratives. Moreover, the methodological process developed throughout the project demonstrates strong potential for replication and adaptation in other educational contexts, cultural institutions, or community-based initiatives seeking to revitalize traditional narratives through digital means.

Ultimately, the project illustrates how creativity, technology, and cultural memory can intersect to sustain intangible heritage in the digital era. By reimagining traditional storytelling through a multidisciplinary and human-centered design approach, it reaffirms the enduring power of narrative as both a cultural artifact and a tool for education, innovation, and connection across generations. Its outcomes show that when students actively engage with cultural heritage through digital creation, they not only contribute to its preservation but also develop meaningful competencies that extend beyond the scope of the classroom.

ACKNOWLEDGEMENT

Work funded by national funds through the Portuguese National Funding Agency for Science, Research and Technology (FCT) under the project UID/05488/2025 (https://doi.org/10.54499/UID/05488/2025).

REFERENCES

Alexander, B. (2017). *The New Digital Stotytelling*. Bloomsbury Publishing. DOI: 10.5040/9798400690839

Alexander, B., & Levine, A. (2008). Web 2.0 Storytelling: Emergence of a New Genre. *EDUCAUSE, 43*(6), 41–56.

Aronsson, S., & Solsjo, C. (2022). *Transmedia Storytelling & Web 4.0 - an upcoming love story*. Jonkoping.

Barthes, R., Greimas, A. J., Bremond, C., Eco, U., Gritti, J., Morin, V., Metz, C., Todorov, T., & Genette, G. (2011). *Análise Estrutural da Narrativa* (7th ed.). Editora Vozes.BBC (Ed.). *Digital Stories*. Retrieved 2025, from BBC Capture Wales: Retrieved from March 02, 2026, https://www.bbc.co.uk/wales/audiovideo/sites/galleries/pages/digitalstorytelling.shtml

BBC (Ed.). (n.d.). *Digital Stories*. Retrieved 2025, from BBC Capture Wales: Retrieved from March 02, 2026, https://www.bbc.co.uk/wales/audiovideo/sites/galleries/pages/digitalstorytelling.shtml

Benjamin, W. (1994). O narrador: considerações sobre a obra de Nikolai Leskov. In *Magia e técnica, arte e política: ensaios sobre literatura e história da cultura* (Vol. 1. Série Obras Escolhidas, pp. 197-221). São Paulo: Brasiliens.

Berners-Lee, T. (1989). Information Management: A Proposal. CERN. Geneva: CERN.

Dingli, A. S. (2015). Who Are the Digital Natives? In *The New Digital Natives*. Springer-Verlag., DOI: 10.1007/978-3-662-46590-5_2

Europeana. (2019). Retrieved 2025, from Europeana: https://www.europeana.eu/

Gama, N. (2012). *Cinzel Decorative*. Google Fonts. Retrieved from https://fonts.google.com/specimen/Cinzel+Decorative/about?preview.text=Little%20Red%20Riding%20Hood&query=Natanael+Gama

Graf, C. (2017). Narrating through Images. In Johnston, S. I. (Ed.), *Religion: Narrating Religion* (pp. 157–175). Macmillan Reference USA.

Junior, F. (2021). *Entre Lendas e História - Narrativas que Representam a Identidade de São Luís*. Appris Editora.

Lambert, J., & Hessler, B. (2018). *Digital Storytelling: Capturing lives, creating community* (5th ed.). Routledge. DOI: 10.4324/9781351266369

Lenzerini, F. (2011). Intangible Cultural Heritage: The living culture of peoples. *European Journal of International Law*, *22*(1), 101–120. DOI: 10.1093/ejil/chr006

Miller, C. H. (2019). *Digital Storytelling - A creator's guide to interactive entertainment*. Routledge. DOI: 10.1201/9780429440045

Murray, J. (2017). *Hamlet on the Holodeck: The Future of Narrative in Cyberspace*. MIT Press.

Perrault, C. (1697). *Histoires ou Contes du Temps Passé.*

Privitera, A. G., Fontana, F., & Geronazzo, M. (2024). The Role of Audio in Immersive Storytelling: A Systematic Review in Cultural Heritage. *Multimedia Tools and Applications*, *84*(16), 16105–16143. DOI: 10.1007/s11042-024-19288-4

Programme, P. V. (n.d.). *Insight through first-person stories...* Retrieved 2025, from Patient Voices: https://www.patientvoices.org.uk/

Psomadaki, O. I., Dimoulas, C. A., Kalliris, G. M., & Paschalidis, G. (2019). Digital storytelling and audience engagement in cultural heritage management: A collaborative model based on the Digital City of Thessaloniki. *Journal of Cultural Heritage*, *36*, 12–22. DOI: 10.1016/j.culher.2018.07.016

Ribeiro, M., & Almeida, M. (2024). Methodology to develop Web Storytelling Applications. In D. Raposo, J. Neves, R. Silva, L. C. Castilho, & R. Dias, *Advances in Design, Music and Arts III* (pp. 426-436). SPRINGER. DOI: 10.1007/978-3-031-73705-3_32

Rizvic, S., Djapo, N., Alispahic, F., Hadzihalilovic, B., Cengic, F., Imamovic, A., & Boskovic, D. (2017). Guidelines for interactive digital storytelling presentations of cultural heritage. *9th International Conference on Virtual Worlds and Games for Serious Applications (VS-Games)* (pp. 253-259). Athens: IEEE. DOI: 10.1109/VS-GAMES.2017.8056610

Robin, B. R. (2008). Digital Storytelling: A powerful technology tool for the 21st century classroom. *Theory into Practice*, *47*(3), 220–228. DOI: 10.1080/00405840802153916

Ryan, M.-L. (2015). *Narrative as Virtual Reality 2: Revisiting Immersion and Interactivity in Literature and Electronic Media*. Johns Hopkins University Press. DOI: 10.1353/book.72246

Salselas, I., & Penha, R. (2019). The role of sound in inducing storytelling in immersive environments. *14th International Audio Mostly Conference: A Journey in Sound.* Nottingham: ACM. DOI: 10.1145/3356590.3356619

Serrat, O. (2017). Storytelling. In O. Serrat, *Knowledge Solutions*. DOI: 10.1007/978-981-10-0983-9_91

Shatto, B., & Erwin, K. (2016). Moving on From Millennials: Preparing for Generation Z. *Journal of Continuing Education in Nursing*, *47*(6), 253–254. DOI: 10.3928/00220124-20160518-05 PMID: 27232222

Simon-Shoshan, M. (2013). Narrativity and textuality in the study of stories. *Workshop on Computational Models of Narrative (CMN 2013).* Hamburg. DOI: 10.4230/OASIcs.CMN.2013.228

UNESCO. (2003a). *Text of the Convention for the Safeguarding of the Intangible Cultural Heritage.* Paris: UNESCO. Retrieved from https://ich.unesco.org/en/convention

UNESCO. (2003b). *Manual on Oral Traditions and Expressions.* UNESCO, Paris. Retrieved from https://ich.unesco.org/doc/src/00114-EN.pdf

Weston, G. (2023, March 22). *The rise of Web3 Storytelling*. (101 Blockchains) Retrieved February 22, 2024, from 101 Blockchains: https://101blockchains.com/web3-storytelling/

ENDNOTES

1 nationwide network that brings together collections from libraries, universities, and museums across the country.

Chapter 4
Eco-Realities and Ecological Tensions in Digital Art:
Contradictions Between Sustainability and Carbon Footprint

Ezgi Tokdil
http://orcid.org/0000-0003-2701-0842
Burdur Mehmet Akif Ersoy University, Turkey

ABSTRACT

This study analyzes the contradictions inherent in digital environmentalism from opposing perspectives within the context of new ecological realities shaped by digital art and AI-driven creations, examining both the contribution of the digitalization of art to sustainability and its impact on the overall carbon footprint. While digital art offers significant contributions to sustainability goals through functions such as raising awareness of the environmental crisis and conveying scientific knowledge in a more accessible and visually impactful manner, the technical infrastructure of digitalization, particularly large data centers, AI modeling processes, and digital art applications, creates a significant environmental cost due to high-energy consumption and carbon emissions, which often conflicts with sustainability values. The primary objective of the study is to argue that, a more holistic understanding of digital environmentalism can be developed that also questions the field's internal carbon footprint and ethical responsibilities.

DOI: 10.4018/979-8-2600-2711-0.ch004

INTRODUCTION

In recent years, digital technologies have played an increasingly active role in monitoring environmental processes, data analysis, and the dissemination of ecological information. Remote sensing systems, environmental sensor networks, and big data infrastructures have made it possible to monitor and visualize environmental processes, such as climate change, air pollution, and ecosystem transformations, on a broader scale (Kitchin, 2014; Gabrys, 2016). While these developments create new opportunities for the production and circulation of environmental data in the public sphere, issues such as the energy consumption of digital infrastructures, the carbon footprint of data centers, and the material resource usage of computing processes are also increasingly becoming subjects of debate. The literature on digital sustainability and/or digitalization for sustainability acknowledges that information and communication technologies offer important tools for monitoring and managing environmental processes, yet it also demonstrates that these technologies rely on physical infrastructures that are significantly dependent on energy and resource consumption (Hilty & Aebischer, 2015; Jones, 2018). While research on the environmental impacts of digital infrastructure is widespread in the current literature, studies examining how these technologies relate to environmental representation and ecological awareness in cultural production fields, particularly in digital art practices, remain limited.

In this context, environmentally focused digital art practices are recognized as an important field of production that brings to light the tension between digital technologies and ecological representation. Today, many artists are engaged in work that visualizes environmental data, models ecological processes using algorithmic systems, and creates digital environments that invite viewers to reflect on environmental issues (Paul, 2015; Grau, Hoth, & Wandl-Vogt, 2019). However, since these productions, which rely on digital technology in both production and dissemination processes, are linked to data processing infrastructures, algorithmic systems, and energy-intensive computational processes, it is necessary to consider the environmental impacts of both the represented content and the technological infrastructure that enables these representations together. In this context, the research aims to examine the ecological tensions emerging in environmentally focused digital art practices and to develop an analytical framework that evaluates digital art creations within the context of different ecological positions through the relationship between representation and the technological infrastructure that enables it.

THEORETICAL FRAMEWORK

The Environmental Paradoxes of Digitalization: Sustainability or Consumption?

Digital technologies have long been regarded as a key component of sustainability discussions, and this positioning places these technologies within a dual paradoxical framework. In particular, the capacity of information and communication technologies to optimize production processes, monitor energy usage, and analyze environmental data more effectively has led to their being viewed as important tools for achieving sustainable development goals. The existing literature, which argues that energy consumption can be reduced and environmental resources can be used more efficiently through smart infrastructure systems, data-driven management mechanisms, and digital monitoring technologies, emphasizes the importance of digitalization and digital tools for sustainability (GeSI, 2015; Hilty & Aebischer, 2015). From the perspective advanced by these studies, digitalization is recognized as a transformative field that facilitates the implementation of sustainability policies by providing new management and analytical capabilities for addressing environmental challenges.

However, recent studies on the environmental impacts of digital technologies reveal significant limitations in this optimistic approach. While digitalization is important for sustainability, the ecological footprint of digital technologies is also one of the greatest contradictions facing environmental sustainability. Data centers, global network systems, and computational processes requiring high processing power, which enable digital infrastructure to function, consume significant amounts of energy and result in an ever-growing ecological footprint. Furthermore, the rare metals used in the production of digital devices, the generation of electronic waste, and short product life cycles link the environmental impacts of the digital economy to broader resource use that extends beyond energy consumption (Hilty & Aebischer, 2015; Malmodin & Lundén, 2018). Therefore, the environmental impacts of digitalization require a holistic perspective that encompasses the production, use, and waste processes of technological infrastructure alongside efficiency gains. This dual structure clearly highlights the environmental paradoxes of digital technologies.

This paradox is related to the "multi-layered environmental impacts of ICT" framework, that is, the first-, second-, and third-order effects framework, used in the literature to explain the environmental impacts of digital technologies (Berkhout & Hertin, 2001; Hilty & Aebischer, 2015: 21). Conceptualized by Berkhout and Hertin, these effects are classified as the direct environmental impacts of technology production and use (negative impact), primary effects resulting from changes in production and distribution systems (negative and positive impacts), and secondary indirect environmental impacts stemming from effects on lifestyles and value systems (long-term systemic impact) (2001: 2). From this perspective, the environmental impacts of digital technologies should not be limited to direct effects such as energy consumption, resource use, and/or carbon footprint, but must also be evaluated through transformations in other areas and long-term changes in social behavior. Consequently, the structural characteristics of digitalization and ICT reveal the existence of two opposing fronts, as "part of the problem" and "a tool for the solution," which further deepens the paradoxical structure defined above (Hilty, 2008). While current technology, in terms of energy efficiency, data-driven management, and resource optimization, can play a facilitating role in addressing environmental issues, it may also introduce new environmental burdens. Through the mechanism known as the "rebound effect," technological efficiency reduces costs, thereby increasing consumption and potentially leading to a resurgence in overall environmental impact (Hilty & Aebischer, 2015: 22). In particular, the rapid proliferation of digital services, the expansion of data storage capacity, and the growth of online content production are continuously increasing the energy demand of digital infrastructures. This situation demonstrates that the environmental impacts of digitalization cannot be assessed as a linear improvement process but instead produce a paradox shaped by the tension between efficiency and consumption.

Consequently, digitalization is recognized as a complex field of transformation that holds both potential solutions and new risks from a sustainability perspective, and this contradictory structure becomes even more visible, particularly in the realm of cultural production. While digital media and art practices have the potential to make environmental issues visible and foster ecological awareness, most of these productions rely on data processing that requires high computational power and large-scale digital infrastructure. Therefore, evaluating the environmental impacts of environmentally focused digital art practices requires a more holistic analysis that also considers the material and energy-based conditions of the technological systems in which these narratives are produced. In this context, environmentally focused digital art productions, due to their inherent conditions of existence, can be approached as "contradictory practices," and it can be argued that these practices contribute to the formation of new "eco-realities" through the tension between the ecological impacts of digital technologies and their forms of cultural representation.

Contradictory Practices and the Production of New Eco-Realities

Discussions regarding the environmental impacts of digital technologies are closely linked not only to energy consumption and the use of infrastructural resources but also to how these technologies are utilized in cultural production spheres.

In particular, digital art and data-driven visualization practices are producing new aesthetic and experiential spaces that transform the way environmental issues are perceived. In this context, digital art plays a significant role in making environmental crises visible and raising public awareness. Numerous studies examining the relationship between art and environmental awareness have shown that art's modes of representation can influence how environmental problems are perceived through emotional connection and "play a significant role in shaping pro-environmental attitudes" (Curtis, 2009; Froehlich et al., 2010; Berney et al., 2024). However, environmentally focused digital art productions, much like the environmental impacts of digitalization itself, often deepen the existing paradox. While they make changes in attitudes and behaviors regarding the environment visible, they also result in significant energy consumption through data processing, algorithmic computing systems, and high-performance digital infrastructure. Maxwell and Miller (2012: 4), while defining the invisible environmental costs of digital culture through the material infrastructure of media technologies, noted that "the magic created by media technology" overshadows much of accepted historical knowledge and "makes it difficult to perceive the material connection to ecological collapse." Therefore, when evaluating the environmental role of digital technologies, it is important to critically examine and properly contextualize the cultural production forms created by technology from opposing perspectives.

As in Berkhout and Hertin's (2001) conceptualization of the environmental impacts of ICT, it is possible to evaluate environmentally focused digital art practices through three distinct ecological positions: applications that reproduce exploitative infrastructures (negative impact), applications that seek to balance relatively low impact infrastructures with environmental awareness (balancing practices), and applications that propose alternative eco-social models (positive contribution). Consequently, it is observed that the sociological dimensions of digital art practices have a significantly negative impact in terms of energy consumption and carbon footprint; they occupy a partially neutral position in terms of relying on relatively low-resource infrastructures and balancing ecological data with infrastructural sustainability; and they offer a positive contribution in terms of proposing alternative eco-social models. This tension highlights the paradoxical relationship between environmental impact and positive contribution, thereby contributing to the formation of a broader eco-political and eco-social framework within which digital art practices can be evaluated. Therefore, to understand environmentally focused digital art productions, an analytical framework is needed that evaluates the relationship between the ecological narratives represented and the technological infrastructures in which these narratives are produced. In this study, the proposed framework suggests a model that examines digital art practices through three distinct ecological positions based on their environmental impacts and the social contributions they offer. The table below summarizes how environmentally focused digital art practices can be classified according to this three-part structure.

*Table 1. Ecological positions of environmental digital art practices**

Ecological Position	Environmental Characteristics	Artistic Strategy	Representative Examples
Negative Impact	High-energy computational infrastructures, large-scale data processing, and a significant carbon footprint	Data-driven aesthetic representations that rely on intensive digital infrastructures	Refik Anadol
Balancing Practices	Relatively low-impact infrastructures, environmental data visualization, and efforts to balance environmental awareness with resource use	Making environmental data visible through sensors, visualization systems, and public installations	Tega Brain, Joana Moll, Andrea Polli
Positive Contribution	Proposing alternative eco-social models, linking art with environmental justice and sustainable living	Artistic projects that integrate ecological practices with social and political engagement	Forensic Architecture

*The classification proposed in this table was developed by the author as an analytical framework for evaluating the ecological implications of environmentally focused digital art practices.

The first category includes art practices that are directly related to the high-energy-consuming infrastructure of digital technologies and therefore create a negative impact in terms of environmental costs. Since they are often produced through systems requiring large datasets, intensive computational processes, and high processing power, and since their physical existence depends on the presence of these technologies, the environmental impact is predominant, regardless of whether the art is environmentally focused. The second category consists of practices that aim to make ecological issues visible through environmental data production and visualization processes and thus strive to strike a balance between environmental awareness and technological infrastructure. While such initiatives aim to increase the visibility of environmental problems by utilizing environmental data streams, sensor technologies, or low-resource digital systems, they also strive to minimize the environmental costs they themselves generate. The third category encompasses practices focused on making a positive contribution by using digital technologies to develop alternative environmental models. In such projects, digital technologies are approached as part of broader scale transformations, such as the design of eco-social systems, making environmental justice visible, or supporting sustainable living practices. This three-pronged approach, conceptualized through outputs and ecological costs, also makes it possible to evaluate environmentally focused digital art practices as cultural technologies embedded within a complex production field that generates ecological impacts. Therefore, the analysis of environmentally focused digital art practices requires a critical approach that considers not only the images of nature represented by artworks but also the ecological impacts of the technological systems that make these representations possible.

CONTRADICTORY PRACTICES IN ENVIRONMENTAL DIGITAL ART

Negative Impact: The Environmental Cost of Data-Driven Art

From the perspective of the critical approach outlined above, the primary ecological position regarding environmental digital art practices consists of modes of production that are directly linked to the material infrastructure of digital technologies and occupy a contradictory position in terms of environmental costs. Although digital culture is often perceived as immaterial or "cloud" based systems (Hu, 2015; Crawford, 2021), the current media and technology-focused literature demonstrates that these systems are connected to large-scale energy infrastructures, massive data centers, and global resource networks (Maxwell & Miller, 2012; Parikka, 2015). Therefore, it is possible to describe digital art productions as part of complex technological production processes supported by data processing, algorithmic modeling systems, and high-performance computing infrastructure, and in this sense, they entail an "invisible" ecological cost.

Studies on the environmental impacts of information and communication technologies (ICT) demonstrate that digital infrastructures generate significant energy consumption and carbon emissions on a global scale. For example, research examining the carbon footprint of ICT reveals that data centers, network infrastructures, and computing systems account for an increasingly large share of global greenhouse gas emissions (Belkhir & Elmeligi, 2018; Malmodin & Lundén, 2018). Consequently, the use of digital technologies for aesthetic productions that represent environmental crises also brings with it the ecological impacts of the technological infrastructures that make these productions possible. The fundamental contradiction of environmentally focused digital art emerges at this point. The representation of nature is often produced through technological processes that can harm nature itself. As discussed in the previous section, although ICT infrastructure is significantly associated with energy consumption and carbon emissions, this infrastructural condition becomes particularly evident in data-driven art and design practices within the context of digital art.

This contradiction appears to be linked to a strong belief in the capacity of digital technologies to provide solutions to environmental problems. This approach, termed "technological digital solutionism," is based on the assumption that complex social and environmental problems can be solved through technological systems (Morozov, 2013; Tonkinwise, 2014; Heikkurinen & Ruuska, 2021). From the perspective of design practices, this assumption is most often represented through speculative digital ecosystems and/or technological simulations. For example, Stephanie Rothenberg's *Aquadisia* (2022) project, which simulates a biological organism to establish a tactile connection with the life cycle by utilizing oysters, a marine creature capable of filtering polluted water, has produced a speculative digital ecosystem environment (Singh & Tholia, 2022). However, as in the aforementioned project, which envisions creating a "magical kind of bioengineering product" addressing industrial degradation and the recovery of natural resources, such digital ecosystem simulations carry the risk of reproducing the solutionist assumption that environmental crises can always be resolved through technological modeling.

Discussions regarding the use of artificial intelligence systems in environmental decision-making processes also reveal similar epistemological limitations. *Asunder* (2019), an AI-based art project designed by Tega Brain, Julian Oliver, and Bengt Sjölén, consists of an algorithmic system that analyzes global-scale environmental datasets to generate potential solution scenarios for the planet's ecological problems (Brain, 2019). However, the solutions generated by the system often yield ethically problematic or overly reductive results, and in this regard, the project challenges the optimistic assumptions that AI systems can solve complex environmental problems. On the other hand, this critical perspective is supported by research findings that question the relationship between artificial intelligence and sustainability, demonstrating that algorithmic decision systems may harbor significant risks in environmental decision-making mechanisms due to data dependency and modeling limitations (Vinuesa et al., 2020). Consequently, three major tensions can be identified in speculative ecological simulations: the persistence of technological determinism, the epistemic limitations of algorithmic decision-making systems, and the aestheticization of ecological data alongside the invisibility of infrastructural resource usage in large-scale installations.

This debate is even more pronounced in data-driven digital art production. For instance, the works of artists such as Refik Anadol, who use large datasets and machine learning models to transform themes such as nature, architecture, and collective memory into large-scale visual experiences, are among the most environmentally contentious art practices due to their reliance on high-energy and resource consumption. Anadol's work titled *Machine Hallucinations: Nature Dreams* (2021) consists of large-scale data visualizations created by processing visual data related to nature through artificial intelligence and deep learning models (Anadol, 2021). In this and similar projects, experiences related to nature are transformed into datasets and reinterpreted through algorithmic processes, and the resulting aesthetic experience relies on data processing infrastructures requiring high computational power. On the other hand, while data related to nature is transformed into immersive visual compositions, the energy consumption and infrastructural resource usage of the data centers enabling these representations are often invisible, referred to as infrastructural invisibility, revealing the existence of a contradiction, a cost/benefit balance, that must be properly managed between the visual experience and the material conditions of the technological systems enabling it. Consequently, the "negative impact" category describes a situation in which, despite digital art's aim to make environmental crises visible, it reproduces technological systems reliant on intensive energy consumption during production processes. Works in this category generate high environmental costs due to data centers, algorithmic computing systems, and high-performance computing infrastructures, necessitating a proper positioning of the contradiction between the potential of environmentally themed and data-driven digital art to foster environmental awareness and the ecological cost of the technological infrastructure.

Seeking Balance: Strategies for Visibility

Environmentally oriented digital art practices engage with the complex relationship between the environmental costs generated by data-intensive infrastructures and the potential to foster ecological awareness. In this context, some artists intentionally employ digital technologies to render environmental issues visible and to open critical discussion on the material consequences of digital infrastructures. Although these artists' digital cultural productions do not eliminate the environmental costs associated with data-driven art, they have facilitated the emergence of practices that seek to establish a balance between technological production and ecological consciousness.

These practices of environmentally focused digital art can be analyzed through three interrelated strategies: (1) making data on digital pollution visible, (2) reducing the use of infrastructural resources, and (3) critically redefining the relationship between natural ecosystems and data systems. These strategies make a significant contribution to the ongoing discourse on ecological costs, as they directly address the environmental impacts of digital technologies, invite audiences to reflect on the often-invisible ecological dimensions embedded within technological systems, and offer alternative narratives for advancing sustainability in the design field.

Making Data on Digital Pollution Visible

One of the most common strategies in the quest for balance is making the invisible data flows produced by digital systems visible. Rather than directly representing the invisible infrastructure and environmental impacts of digital technologies, this strategy positions itself at the center of the current debate by aestheticizing data production processes, thereby prompting viewers to rethink the relationship between technology and the environment. In terms of data visibility, Tega Brain and Sam Lavigne's *Synthetic Messenger* (2022), Joana Moll's *The Hidden Life of an Amazon User* (2019), and *Inanimate Species* (2022) are among the key works that exemplify this quest for balance.

Developed by Brain and Lavigne, *Synthetic Messenger* (2022) intervenes in online information flows by using a bot system that automatically responds to climate change denial narratives circulating on social media platforms; in doing so, it opens up a discussion not only on the visibility of misinformation but also on the political and ecological consequences of digital communication systems (Brain, 2021; Brain & Lavigne, 2021). Unlike Brain and Lavigne, who demonstrate the critical potential of data-driven art by showing how online data circulation shapes public perception of the climate crisis, Joana Moll's study titled *The Hidden Life of an Amazon User* (2019), on the other hand, calculates the energy consumption generated by an Amazon user's online activity through data centers, thereby directly revealing the hidden environmental costs of digital consumption and digital infrastructure (Figure 1). This project concretizes the hidden ecological cost of the capitalist economic system, which, under the guise of being "customer focused," forces the average user to navigate through vast amounts of code and various interfaces, equivalent to 8,724 A4 pages of printed code and 87.33 MB of data, simply to purchase a single book on Amazon's official website. In doing so, it transforms this process into a tangible product and converts the ecological blindness underlying Heikkurinen and Ruuska's (2021) concept of "digital solutionism," defined as the contribution of digitalization and ICT to sustainability, into a cultural narrative.

Figure 1. Joana Moll, The Hidden Life of an Amazon User, 2019, Utrecht, The Netherlands

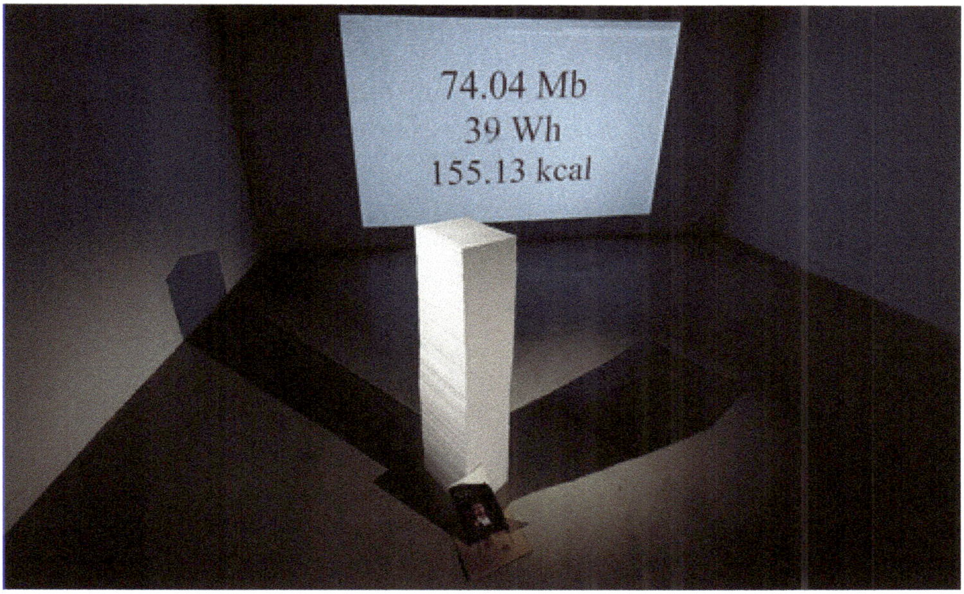

Building on Chakrabarty's (2009: 208) statement that "most of our freedoms are energy-intensive," and as Parikka (2019) also argues, noting that this is particularly true of much libertarian digital discourse, there exists a reality far more significant than the non-discursive code language hidden behind the enthusiasm of technology advocates, interface effects, and screenshots of contemporary logistics. The energy consumed to load the code and the human energy required to navigate it constitute a process directly linked to the larger-scale economy-cum-ecology of contemporary digital culture. Consequently, in Moll's project, the idea, as defined by Cubitt (2017), that the use of digital media occurs at the cost of "an immense ecological footprint and environmental degradation", despite providing the ability to communicate with and understand the world, becomes tangible. Furthermore, the notion, as emphasized by Parikka (2019), that energy costs are externalized both to the user and to the environment, brings to light the concept of "integral waste" (Cubitt, 2015) underlying this process.

Another concrete example of the quest for balance in making data visible is "an interface that registers its own existence as part of a larger ecology of energy" (Parikka, 2019), exemplified by the CO2GLE (2014) project, a symbolic tool that "aims to reveal the material impacts of human actions on the physical world" by visualizing the constant energy consumption underlying "digital comfort" throughout the user experience (Moll, 2018). In this project, which reveals the carbon footprint and data mining behind consumer actions, search engine user interactions continuously increase the carbon emission rate on the screen, thereby generating a form of balance that supports the predictions of existing scientific research suggesting that cost awareness can lead to behavioral change (Inie et al., 2025; Anthony et al., 2020). A similar approach is also evident in Moll's project *Inanimate Species* (2022), which highlights the contradiction between technology and nature, where the environmental impacts of internet infrastructure, such as energy consumption and carbon footprint, are conveyed through data visualization. By establishing a correlational relationship between the rise in the number of microprocessors and computational power and mass extinctions in wildlife, the project reveals that technological progress transforms ecosystems "by deceiving" them and that "techno capitalism" accelerates climate change and undermines fundamental life systems (Moll, 2022). Therefore, it is clear that these examples must be evaluated outside design forms, such as those by artists like Anadol, which rely on high-energy consumption and result in high environmental costs, where data is used solely to create visual aesthetics. While the existence of these works entails a certain digital burden, it can be argued that this burden serves as a tool to make the burden of the ongoing capitalist system, economic digital capitalism, visible and highlights the power of awareness to minimize environmental costs. As Cucuzzella also emphasizes, these works "do not simply attempt to persuade the viewer of ecological priorities"; they are also shaped by the need to shed light on a specific aspect of the current ecological crisis and assert that "action, even cognitive action, is a moral imperative" (2021: 3).

Reducing the Use of Infrastructure Resources

The second key strategy in the quest for balance, as seen in the works of artists such as Moll and Brain, involves approaches that rely on more concrete action rather than merely aiming to make the materiality of infrastructure and the contradictions of digital capitalism visible. These approaches seek to carry out data visualization and environmental information production through technological systems that consume as few resources as possible. These works, as seen in the case of Anadol and others, prefer methods with relatively low infrastructure requirements, such as sensor technologies, real-time data streams, and public space installations, rather than producing design strategies based on deep learning models and algorithmic systems or utilizing large-scale data infrastructures that rely on high-energy consumption.

Figure 2. Andrea Polli, Particle Falls, 2015, in the ARTsySTEM Project at Utah State University, USA

One notable example of this approach is Andrea Polli's work titled *Particle Falls*, which visualizes data from sensors that measure air pollution levels in the urban atmosphere in real-time via projection systems installed in public spaces (Figure 2). The project, which measures fine particulate matter concentration, down to PM2.5, using a nephelometer, consists of a beam of light projected into the air that changes color from blue to yellow and red, depending on the pollution level, based on real-time air quality data (Meier, 2015). Consequently, the project demonstrates how air quality data is transformed from abstract scientific measurements into a directly experiential visual form. While highlighting the potential of digital data visualizations to raise awareness, it also demonstrates that environmental data can be made visible in public spaces with relatively low infrastructure requirements. In this sense, while Polli's work could also be categorized as a positive contribution, it can be described as continuing the "making visible" strategy pursued in Moll's projects, which aims to change individual preferences rather than trigger systemic change. However, as with the other studies examined, the act of making pollution visible creates a new pollution zone through light. Moreover, even though it is a public art project operating with minimal infrastructure requirements, the fact that digital technology itself brings this complex and systemic issue to the forefront creates a new paradox. This paradox, as Cucuzzella also emphasizes, raises the question of whether the individual change assumed to be possible is truly necessary or sufficient to reverse the depicted harms (2021). Therefore, while these works cannot be directly categorized as having a negative impact due to their dependence on the very digital technologies they critique, they can be described as relatively beneficial, though balanced in terms of cost/benefit, because of their pragmatic structures shaped around awareness beyond their physical reality.

Critically Redefining the Relationship between Natural Ecosystems and Data Systems

The third strategy regarding cultural forms of representation in the context of the environmental pressure exerted by digitalization and ICT involves artistic approaches that aim to critically rethink the relationship between digital data systems and natural life. These works, in connection with the concepts of data activism and eco aesthetics, which have been increasingly discussed in the literature on digital art and activism in recent years (Demos, 2016; Miles, 2014), open up a discussion on the relationship between nature and data through the question of how algorithmic systems define and reproduce nature.

For example, the Cesar and Lois collective's installation titled *Degenerative Cultures* (2018) was designed as a mechanism that makes visible the interaction between living organisms, digital networks, and artificial intelligence (Figure 3). In this installation, which depicts humanity's dominance over nature, or the impulse to reshape nature, on a physical book, "the growth of the smart microorganism *Physarum polycephalum* is mimicked by artificial intelligence". The microorganism's microbiological development, which reduces the readability of the pages and, over time, physically erases the text, that is, the growth of the biological culture, is analyzed and parameterized by artificial intelligence. Subsequently, similar documents related to humanity's intervention in nature are searched for online, and digital fungi, an NLP-based artificial intelligence algorithm, reorganize these documents (Solomon et al., 2022; Singh & Tholia, 2022). In this way, living and non-living ecosystems are brought into interaction, making the connection between artificial technological networks and living non-human intelligences, such as slime molds and fruiting mushrooms visible (Solomon et al., 2022). As the artists have also described, this entire cycle leads to the intermingling of different information systems. Human knowledge about nature in written texts, "human technological systems for communicating similar concepts", and the knowledge of nature inherent in the organic growth patterns of living organisms in our environment all reveal the epistemological limits of algorithmic production processes through the ways data-driven systems represent nature (Cesar & Lois, 2018).

Figure 3. Cesar & Lois (Lucy HG Solomon and Cesar Baio), Degenerative Cultures, 2018, in Uncommon Natures at the Brighton Digital Festival, UK

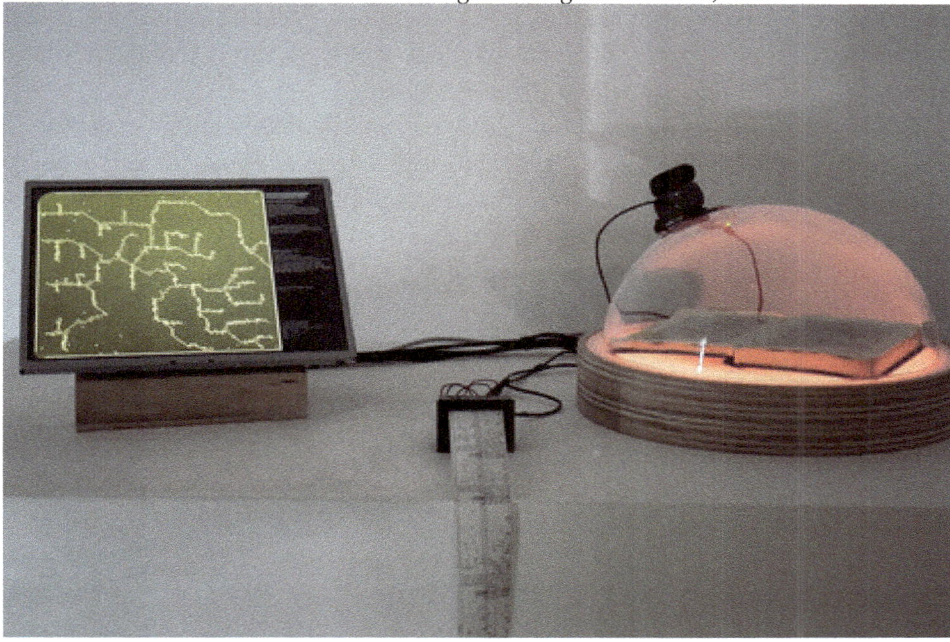

As Cubitt (2017) emphasizes in his analysis of the ecological footprint of digital media and its impact on environmental degradation, arguing that the solution lies in an eco-political media aesthetics in which "people use media to shift their relationships to the environment", the Cesar and Lois installation removes media from being an end in itself and transforms it into a cultural research space that enables reflection on a hybrid alternative way of life, as envisioned by Latour (2004) in his prediction of "new inclusive communities of human and non-human entities". Consequently, as demonstrated by this project, which can be understood as a product of the quest for balance between technological infrastructure and the natural environment, it is not possible to categorically assess information and communication technologies, digital tools, and artificial intelligence algorithms as having a negative impact based solely on environmental costs under all circumstances. Some of these studies, as in the case of *Degenerative Cultures*, question the possibility of a symbiotic relationship between natural and artificial ecosystems by opening up data production, algorithmic infrastructures, and environmental knowledge to public debate, in contrast to Polli's awareness-based approach. In this potential relationship, the environmental cost of the technological infrastructure certainly does not disappear entirely. However, data visualization and knowledge production transform into forms of cultural intervention that critically interrogate the environmental impacts of digital technologies. This strategy, serving as an alternative to design processes that reduce the environment to data, as seen in artists such as Anadol, facilitates the emergence of a speculative and post-humanist approach that integrates data into nature, ensuring that the negative impact remains secondary to the positive contribution.

Unlike other categories, the boundaries between the exploration of symbiotic living possibilities, the final category in the quest for balance, and environmentally focused art practices that make a positive contribution are permeable; indeed, it is often impossible to distinguish these approaches from one another without considering the cost/benefit balance. Nevertheless, in works that can be evaluated within the context of positive contribution, efforts to encourage alternative eco-social modes of thinking and to improve the current situation through new possibilities, as seen in geoengineering's utopian solutions and related approaches, are noteworthy. These works have also emerged from the idea that digital art can be used as an intervention tool in parallel with the increasing problems created by human environment and machine interactions in the current century; the search for balance has increasingly given way to active participation in the solution process.

Positive Contribution: Alternative Eco-Political and Eco-Social Approaches

There is no doubt that the skies are closing in.
But we all share the universal right to breathe
(Mbembe, 2020; Albano, 2022).

In the context of positive contribution, the third ecological position of environmentally focused digital art practices, it is observed that the digital technologies employed in such works, as noted above, serve as tools for intervention in areas such as environmental justice, the production of public knowledge, and political awareness. Much like the relationship established by the Cesar and Lois collective between "artificial intelligence and other non-human living intelligences", many works that generate positive value also establish a similar relationship between environmental data and public knowledge, positioning technology, while acknowledging it as a system that generates environmental costs, as a tool that can be utilized for environmental responsibility and collective action. In this context, it is also possible to define these works as research areas that enable reflection on alternative social and ecological models.

One significant example of this approach is the *Cloud Studies* project developed by Forensic Architecture, an organization composed of researchers specializing in human rights violations, state violence, and environmental crimes (Figure 4). The project focuses on the interconnectedness of global atmospheres, including gases used to suppress protests, emissions from petrochemical plants, herbicides sprayed to destroy farmland, and the burning of forests for industrial plantations, and consists of eight studies under the theme of toxic clouds, which combine open source data, witness testimonies, and digital modeling techniques to analyze the spatial and temporal distribution of chemical gas attacks (Forensic Architecture, 2020). The project creates a digital research environment that reconstructs the dispersion of chemical gases by combining atmospheric data analysis with architectural modeling and visual simulation techniques; thus, environmental data, the subject of scientific measurements, becomes part of discussions on legal and political accountability. In this regard, the *Cloud Studies* project demonstrates that digital visualization techniques, beyond producing immersive visual experiences as seen in the works of artists such as Anadol, can also play a pragmatically significant role in documenting crimes and shaping public discourse.

Figure 4. Forensic Architecture, Cloud Studies, 2021, in In the Air (2022), Wellcome Collection, London, UK

In relation to this work, Albano (2021) defines such practices as "an embodied and performative response" within "the politics of breathing", while Lee Morrison (2021) conceptualizes them as mechanical landscapes by critiquing the creation of cloudscapes using "machinic vision" technologies. In this context, Forensic Architecture's work is a clear example of the use of digital modeling and data analysis techniques to highlight environmental accountability. Visual reconstructions created through atmospheric data modeling, video analysis, and spatial simulations make environmental disasters visible by reconstructing the movement of gas clouds and the areas they affect, while also demonstrating, as Cubitt (2017) emphasizes, that digital technologies can become part of discussions on environmental justice. Therefore, evaluating the narrative forms of projects such as *Cloud Studies*, as with others, solely based on the environmental costs created by technological infrastructure would be an incomplete and flawed approach. Of course, while the high-energy consumption of digital technologies and the environmental costs associated with data infrastructure apply to the Forensic Architecture example as well, given the stages of data analysis, interpretation, and presentation, the same technology can at times also serve as a crucial tool in processes such as documenting environmental disasters, raising public awareness, and establishing environmental accountability (Weizman, 2019).

DISCUSSION: ENVIRONMENTAL DIGITAL ART AND THE MANAGEMENT OF CONTRADICTORY PRACTICES BETWEEN REPRESENTATION AND INFRASTRUCTURE

As examined, the analysis of environmentally focused digital art demonstrates that evaluating the environmental impacts of digital technologies solely through measurable indicators such as energy consumption or carbon emissions is insufficient. These works should be approached as fields of cultural research that make visible the relationship between digital infrastructures, data production processes, and forms of cultural representation. The co-construction of environmental data and visual data should be recognized as a significant cultural mechanism capable of transforming the public circulation and modes of perception of environmental information.

As studies focusing on media ecology and the infrastructural analysis of digital technology also argue (Maxwell & Miller, 2012; Parikka, 2015), the perception of digital culture as immaterial systems causes the ecological burden of energy infrastructures and data centers to remain overshadowed by the visual appeal of representation. Consequently, the fundamental tension in environmentally focused digital art emerges not from the question of how nature is represented, but from the environmental impacts of the digital systems that make these representations possible. This tension becomes particularly pronounced in data-driven art productions. While art practices generated through algorithmic modeling processes and computational systems requiring high processing power may directly or indirectly highlight environmental crises, they also reproduce the material conditions of digital infrastructures based on energy consumption. However, environmentally focused digital art practices are not limited to works that reproduce the environmental costs created by digital infrastructures. Many artists use digital technologies to make environmental data visible, open up discussions on environmental risks in the public sphere, and reestablish the relationship between environmental information and public awareness. Through sensor technologies, data visualization systems, and public installations, environmental data can transcend scientific measurements to become an integral part of the public experience. Studies on the role of art in the production of environmental knowledge and social awareness also demonstrate that such practices can transform the way environmental issues are perceived (Miles, 2014).

In this context, an approach to ecological responsibility is proposed for environmentally focused digital art practices, one that requires evaluating the environmental impact of digital art on three levels: the energy and resource consumption of the digital infrastructures used; the environmental costs of data production and processing; and the role of art in generating environmental knowledge and public awareness. It is possible to define such an approach as one that facilitates the emergence of more responsible cultural practices that address digital art production in conjunction with the ecological impacts of the technological infrastructure.

CONCLUSION: TOWARD CRITICAL DIGITAL ENVIRONMENTALISM

This study demonstrates the need for a more systematic evaluation of the environmental impacts of technological infrastructures in the development of environmentally focused digital art. In particular, the emergence of energy consumption and carbon footprint calculations as significant areas of discussion in AI-based art production, which relies on data-intensive computational processes, necessitates a reevaluation of the technological infrastructure used in digital art production from a sustainability perspective. In this context, this study proposes an analytical framework that examines the relationship between the ecological themes represented in environmentally focused digital art practices and the technological infrastructures that enable these representations. This framework facilitates the assessment of the environmental impacts of digital art productions through infrastructural conditions such as data generation, computational processes, and energy consumption, and enables the evaluation of environmentally focused digital art practices across different ecological contexts. This approach not only increases the visibility of the environmental costs generated by data-driven projects but also highlights the critical potential offered by research-based art practices that bring environmental data into the public sphere.

In this context, three fundamental approaches stand out for environmentally focused digital art practices. First, it is of critical importance for artists and actors in the creative industries to shift toward alternative production strategies, such as relatively low-resource digital infrastructures, sensor-based data collection systems, and local data production models, rather than data processing processes that rely on high-energy consumption. Second, making the environmental impacts of the data and technological infrastructures used in digital art projects visible can contribute to raising awareness regarding the material ecology of digital culture. Third, the development of environment-themed digital art practices as critical research practices capable of contributing to eco-social and eco-political transformation discussions facilitates the dissemination of sustainable design.

REFERENCES

Albano, C. (2021). To 'Hold In-Common' in the Midst of Clouds' Drift. *Performance Research, 26*(7), 38–43. DOI: 10.1080/13528165.2021.2059286

Albano, C. (2022). Out of Breath: Vulnerability of Air in Contemporary Art. University of Minnesota Press, 2022. DOI: 10.5749/9781452968193

Anadol, R. (2021). *Machine Hallucinations- Nature Dreams* [AI installation]. Retrieved January 22, 2026, from https://refikanadol.com/works/machine-hallucinations-nature-dreams/

Anthony, L. F. W., Kanding, B., & Selvan, R. (2020). CarbonTracker: Predicting the Carbon Footprint of Training Deep Learning Models. *arXiv.* DOI: 10.48550

Belkhir, L., & Elmeligi, A. (2018). Assessing ICT global emissions footprint: Trends to 2040 & recommendations. *Journal of Cleaner Production, 177*, 448–463. DOI: 10.1016/j.jclepro.2017.12.239

Berkhout, F., & Hertin, J. (2001). Impacts of Information and Communication Technologies on Environmental Sustainability: Speculations and Evidence. *Report to the OECD.* Retrieved January 22, 2026, from https://www.oecd.org/dataoecd/4/6/1897156.pdf

Berney, M., Ouaazki, A., Macko, V., Kocher, B., & Holzer, A. (2024). Care-based eco-feedback augmented with generative AI: Fostering pro-environmental behavior through emotional attachment. In *Proceedings of the CHI Conference on Human Factors in Computing Systems (CHI '24),* May 11-16, 2024, USA. DOI: 10.1145/3613904.3642296

Brain, T. (2019). *Asunder* [AI installation]. Tega Brain Studio. Retrieved January 22, 2026, from https://tegabrain.com/Asunder

Brain, T. (2021). *Synthetic Messenger* [Art project]. Retrieved January 25, 2026, from https://tegabrain.com/Synthetic-Messenger

Brain, T., & Lavigne, S. (2021). The Battle to Control the Carbon Media Cycle, *Ding Magazine.* Retrieved January 25, 2026, from https://dingdingding.org/issue-4/the-battle-to-control-the-carbon-media-cycle/

Cesar & Lois. (2018). *Degenerative Cultures* [Artwork]. Retrieved January 22, 2026, from https://cesarandlois.org/digitalfungus/

Chakrabarty, D. (2009). The climate of history: Four theses. *Critical Inquiry, 35*(2), 197–222. DOI: 10.1086/596640

Crawford, K. (2021). *Atlas of AI: Power, Politics, and the Planetary Costs of Artificial Intelligence*. Yale University Press.

Cubitt, S. (2015). Integral waste. *Theory, Culture & Society*, *32*(4), 133–145. DOI: 10.1177/0263276414537316

Cubitt, S. (2017). *Finite Media- Environmental Implications of Digital Technologies*. Duke University Press.

Cucuzzella, C. (2021). Making the invisible visible: Eco-art and design against the anthropocene. *Sustainability (Basel)*, *13*(7), 3747. DOI: 10.3390/su13073747

Curtis, D. J. (2009). Creating inspiration: The role of the arts in creating empathy for ecological restoration. *Ecological Management & Restoration*, *10*(3), 174–184. DOI: 10.1111/j.1442-8903.2009.00487.x

Demos, T. J. (2016). *Decolonizing Nature, Contemporary Art and the Politics of Ecology*. Sternberg Press.

Forensic Architecture. (2020). *Cloud Studies* [Artwork]. Retrieved January 22, 2026, from https://forensic-architecture.org/investigation/cloudstudies

Froehlich, J., Findlater, L., & Landay, J. (2010). The design of eco-feedback technology. In *Proceedings of the SIGCHI Conference on Human Factors in Computing Systems*. New York: ACM Press. DOI: 10.1145/1753326.1753629

Gabrys, J. (2016). *Program Earth: Environmental Sensing Technology and the Making of a Computational Planet*. University of Minnesota Press. DOI: 10.5749/j.ctt1b7x5gq

GeSI. (2015). *SMARTer2030: ICT solutions for 21st century challenges.* https://gesi.org/research/smarter2030

Grau, O., Hoth, J., & Wandl-Vogt, E. (2019). *Digital Art through the Looking Glass: New Strategies for Archiving, Collecting and Preserving in Digital Humanities*. Edition Donau-Universität Krems.

Heikkurinen, P., & Ruuska, T. (Eds.). (2021). *Sustainability Beyond Technology: Philosophy, Critique, and Implications for Human Organization*. Oxford University Press. DOI: 10.1093/oso/9780198864929.001.0001

Hilty, L. M. (2008). *Information Technology and Sustainability. Essays on the Relationship between ICT and Sustainable Development*. Books on Demand, Norderstedt.

Hilty, L. M., & Aebischer, B. (2015). ICT for Sustainability: An Emerging Research Field. In Hilty, L., & Aebischer, B. (Eds.), *ICT Innovations for Sustainability. Advances in Intelligent Systems and Computing* (Vol. 310, pp. 3–36). Springer. DOI: 10.1007/978-3-319-09228-7_1

Hu, T.-E. (2015). *A Prehistory of the Cloud*. The MIT Press. DOI: 10.7551/mitpress/9780262029513.001.0001

Inie, N., Falk, J., & Selvan, R. (2025). How CO2STLY Is CHI? The carbon footprint of generative AI in HCI research and what we should do about it. In *Proceedings of the 2025 CHI Conference on Human Factors in Computing Systems* (CHI '25). New York, USA, Article 206, 1-29. DOI: 10.1145/3706598.3714227

Jones, N. (2018). How to stop data centres from gobbling up the world's electricity. *Nature, 561*(7722), 163–166. DOI: 10.1038/d41586-018-06610-y PMID: 30209383

Kitchin, R. (2014). *The Data Revolution: Big Data, Open Data, Data Infrastructures & Their Consequences*. Sage Publications. DOI: 10.4135/9781473909472

Latour, B. (2004). *Politics of Nature: How to Bring the Sciences into Democracy* (Porter, C., Trans.). Harvard University Press. DOI: 10.4159/9780674039964

Lee-Morrison, L. (2021). Finding pictures in the Sky: Machinic visions of cloudscapes. In *Proceedings of Politics of the Machines- Rogue Research 2021 (POM 2021)* (pp. 344-350). British Computer Society. DOI: 10.14236/ewic/POM2021.46

Malmodin, J., & Lundén, D. (2018). The energy and carbon footprint of the global ICT and entertainment & media sectors 2010-2015. *Sustainability, 10*(9), 3027. DOI: 10.3390/su10093027

Maxwell, R., & Miller, T. (2012). *Greening the Media*. Oxford University Press.

Mbembe, A. (2020). *The Universal Right to Breathe* (C. Shread, trans.), Critical Enquiry. Retrieved January 22, 2026, from https://critinq.wordpress.com/2020/04/13/the-universal-right-to-breathe/

Meier, A. (2015). A Digital Waterfall That Illuminates the Threat of Air Pollution, *Hyperallergic*. Retrieved from https://hyperallergic.com/a-digital-waterfall-that-illuminates-the-threat-of-air-pollution/

Miles, M. (2014). *Eco-aesthetics: Art, Literature and Architecture in a Period of Climate Change*. Bloomsbury Academic.

Moll, J. (2018). *CO2GLE* [Art project]. Retrieved January 22, 2026, from https://www.janavirgin.com/CO2/

Moll, J. (2019). *The Hidden Life of an Amazon User* Ret [Art project]. Retrieved January 22, 2026, from https://www.janavirgin.com/AMZ/

Moll, J. (2022). *Inanimate Species* [Art project]. Retrieved January 22, 2026, from https://www.janavirgin.com/INANIMATESPECIES/inanimate_works.html

Morozov, E. (2013). *To Save Everything, Click Here: Technology, Solutionism, and the Urge to Fix Problems that Don't Exist*. Public Affairs.

Parikka, J. (2015). *A Geology of Media*. University of Minnesota Press. DOI: 10.5749/minnesota/9780816695515.001.0001

Parikka, J. (2019). *Working for Systems that Do Not Do the Work*. Retrieved January 22, 2026, from https://www.janavirgin.com/AMZ/parikka.html

Paul, C. (2015). *Digital Art* (3rd ed.). Thames & Hudson.

Singh, A., & Tholia, S. (2022). Toward the symbiocene through artificial intelligence. *AI & Society*, *39*(2), 805–806. DOI: 10.1007/s00146-022-01546-4

Solomon, L. H. G., & Baio, C. (2022). When do we stop being human? Prefiguring nonanthropocentric thinking. *Leonardo*, *55*(5), 445–450. DOI: 10.1162/leon_a_02246

Tonkinwise, C. (2014). To save everything, click here: The folly of technological solutionism. *Journal of Design History*, *27*(1), 111–113. DOI: 10.1093/jdh/ept034

Vinuesa, R., Azizpour, H., Leite, I., Balaam, M., Dignum, V., Domisch, S., Felländer, A., Langhans, S. D., Tegmark, M., & Fuso Nerini, F. (2020). The role of artificial intelligence in achieving the sustainable development goals. *Nature Communications*, *11*(1), 233. DOI: 10.1038/s41467-019-14108-y PMID: 31932590

Weizman, E. (2019). *Forensic Architecture: Violence at the Threshold of Detectability*. Zone Books.

Chapter 5
Twitch Culture, Participatory Culture:
Affective Publics and Attention Economy in Elraenn's Streams

İpek Fatma Ertan
http://orcid.org/0000-0003-4917-6675
Faculty of Communication, Istanbul Medipol University, Turkey

İhsan Eken
http://orcid.org/0000-0002-0401-8545
Faculty of Communication, Istanbul Medipol University, Turkey

ABSTRACT

This study examines the social and emotional dimensions of streamer–viewer interaction on Twitch through thematic analysis of viewer comments. As users shift from passive consumers to active participants, interaction practices in live streaming have transformed. Twitch's real-time communication enables collective and interactive experiences while fostering dynamic parasocial relationships. The study applies qualitative thematic content analysis to 3,000 randomly selected comments from gaming, reaction, and chatting streams of a highly viewed Turkish streamer. Using NLP-assisted pre-coding and manual validation, themes were identified as direct address, humor, positive and negative emotion, toxic language, and content reaction. Findings show that behavior varies by stream type: positive emotions dominate gaming (13%), humor reaction streams (10%), and direct address chatting streams (35%), while toxic language remains low (0.3%). Results position Twitch as a digital public space where users engage emotionally, co-produce meaning, and compete for visibility.

DOI: 10.4018/979-8-2600-2711-0.ch005

INTRODUCTION

The development of digital media environments has led to fundamental transformations in traditional mass communication models, resulting in the increasing blurring of boundaries between content production and consumption. Particularly with the advent of Web 2.0 technologies, users have evolved from mere content consumers into active producers and distributors, thereby reshaping the structural dynamics of the media ecosystem. As Henry Jenkins (2006) argues, media users are no longer "passive audiences," but rather participants who actively engage in content production processes. This transformation has paved the way for digital platforms to evolve from mere content delivery tools into social environments centered on user interaction. In this context, live streaming platforms emerge as one of the most visible manifestations of digital media transformation. Platforms such as Twitch enable real-time interaction between viewers and content creators, transforming media experience from a unidirectional transmission process into a multidirectional communication practice. The live chat feature allows viewers not only to consume content but also to actively intervene in the content flow instantaneously. This shift redefines the viewer experience and transforms media consumption into a socially interactive process.

Within the literature, platforms such as Twitch are conceptualized not merely as spaces for the consumption of entertainment content, but also as digital environments where social interaction, community formation, and emotional connections are produced. Katy Hamilton, Oliver Garretson, and Michael Kerne (2014) define Twitch as "a live and interactive social space in which participatory gaming communities are formed." Similarly, Jamie Woodcock and Mark R. Johnson (2019) frame Twitch streaming not merely as a technical broadcasting practice, but as a form of digital labor in which emotional labor and performance are deeply intertwined. Research focusing on viewer behavior in the Twitch environment indicates that users engage with the platform not solely for content consumption, but also for motivations such as establishing social interaction, developing a sense of community belonging, and experiencing emotional engagement. In this regard, Juho Sjöblom and Juho Hamari (2017) demonstrate that users' motivations for watching Twitch are largely associated with social interaction, entertainment, and a sense of community. These findings highlight that Twitch functions not only as a media platform, but also as a digital environment in which social bonds are actively produced.

At this point, explaining viewer behavior on Twitch requires the integration of multiple theoretical frameworks. The participatory culture approach accounts for the active involvement of viewers in content production processes (Jenkins, 2006), while parasocial interaction theory explains how relational bonds are formed between viewers and streamers (Horton & Wohl, 1956). In addition, the concept of affective publics, which emphasizes the collective production of emotions within digital networks, suggests that viewer comments are not merely individual expressions but also constitute shared emotional patterns. Zizi Papacharissi (2015) conceptualizes this phenomenon as "networked structures in which emotions circulate and generate public connections." Moreover, the attention economy and platform governance approaches are critical for understanding the operational logic of digital platforms. Michael H. Goldhaber (1997) highlights that attention has become the most valuable resource in the digital age, defining it as the "currency of the network society." In this context, users' pursuit of visibility and their interaction strategies are shaped not only by individual preferences but also by the algorithmic structures of platforms. Taina Bucher (2012) further argues that algorithmic systems function as mechanisms of power that regulate visibility and shape user behavior.

Within this theoretical framework, Twitch can be conceptualized not merely as a platform for content consumption, but as a multilayered digital ecosystem where emotional interactions, social bonds, and algorithmic governance intersect. However, the existing literature offers limited comparative analyses of the thematic structure of Twitch viewer comments across different broadcast types. In particular, the scarcity of empirical studies conducted in the Turkish context indicates a significant gap in the field.

This study aims to address this gap by examining Twitch viewer comments through thematic content analysis, with the objective of revealing the social and conceptual dimensions of viewer behavior. Within this scope, the research seeks to answer the following questions:

- How does the thematic distribution of viewer comments vary across different types of broadcasts (gaming, reaction, and chatting)?
- Within which theoretical frameworks can Twitch viewer behaviors be explained?
- How are viewers' demands for visibility and their modes of interaction related to the attention economy and algorithmic structures?

Accordingly, this study approaches Twitch not merely as a media tool, but as a digital communication space situated at the intersection of social interaction, emotional production, and algorithmic governance, and analyzes viewer behavior within this environment through a multidimensional perspective.

LITERATURE REVIEW

Explaining viewer behavior and the dynamics of streamer–viewer relationships on interaction-based digital platforms such as Twitch cannot be adequately addressed through a single theoretical framework. Live streaming environments constitute complex communication ecosystems in which multiple dimensions—such as media use, social interaction, emotional engagement, and algorithmic platform structures—operate simultaneously. Therefore, understanding viewer practices within Twitch requires the integration of diverse theoretical perspectives. In this study, Twitch viewer behavior is primarily examined within the framework of the Uses and Gratifications approach, which explains media consumption motivations. In addition, a range of theoretical approaches prominent in the literature are employed to account for the forms of interaction emerging in live streaming environments. In particular, the concepts of participatory culture, parasocial interaction, affective publics, the attention economy, and platform governance provide significant analytical tools for interpreting viewer behavior in interactive digital contexts such as Twitch. These theoretical perspectives demonstrate that viewers are not merely passive consumers of content; rather, they are active participants who establish emotional connections, collectively produce meaning, seek visibility within the attention economy, and are shaped by platform norms and algorithmic structures.

Participatory Culture and Streamer–Viewer Interaction on Twitch

Existing findings indicate that viewers on Twitch are not positioned merely as passive consumers within content interaction practices; rather, they actively participate through the use of emotes, humorous references, and direct engagement via chat. For instance, in chatting-type broadcasts, the fact that direct address to the streamer reaches a notably high rate of 35% demonstrates that viewers do not limit their engagement to the act of watching alone. This finding suggests that viewer practices cannot be reduced solely to content consumption; instead, viewers also contribute indirectly to content production processes.

Within this framework, the concept of participatory culture emphasizes that digital media environments transform audiences from passive recipients into active producers and stakeholders. In the work of Henry Jenkins (2006), participatory culture is defined as a cultural formation that blurs the hierarchy between consumers and producers, enabling users to actively engage in content creation, redistribution, and meaning-making processes. In this sense, participatory culture generates a "convergence" ecology in which media is no longer a one-way transmission channel, but a dynamic environment where audiences directly intervene in content circulation. Here, media consumption and production become intertwined. Through the affordances of digital platforms, users are enabled to transform, share, and reframe content. From a participatory culture perspective, audience practices operate within a continuous cycle of meaning production and reproduction. Therefore, audiences are not merely consumers of content, but are recognized as active cultural agents who contribute to content circulation processes (Jenkins et al., 2013).

In the context of Twitch, viewer interaction strongly supports the conceptualization of participatory culture. The use of emotes and the collective production of humor extend beyond individual expressions of meaning, contributing to the formation of shared cultural norms and linguistic codes within the live streaming environment. This process evolves into a collective cultural practice, facilitated by the platform's technical affordances—such as chat features, clip creation, and subscription symbols—and shared across the entire viewer community.

When this theoretical discussion is evaluated in conjunction with the empirical findings, it becomes evident that viewer behavior on Twitch aligns closely with the core characteristics of participatory culture. The production of interactions such as chat engagement, humor, and protest is not limited to the mere act of writing messages; rather, it functions as a shared mechanism of meaning-making embedded within the platform's social and cultural structures. Accordingly, the data obtained from Elraenn's broadcasts demonstrate that participatory culture is not merely a conceptual framework in media theory, but a practice that is concretely enacted within digital platforms.

Parasocial Interaction and the Viewer–Streamer Relationship

The concept of Parasocial Interaction (PSI), originally defined by Donald Horton and R. Richard Wohl, represents a classical conceptual framework describing the formation of a cognitive relationship between media figures and audiences. This form of interaction refers to a one-sided yet intimate bond in which viewers develop a sense of closeness with a media persona (Horton & Wohl, 1956). Within Twitch environments, viewers do not merely consume content; they actively engage in behaviors such as directly addressing the streamer, seeking recognition through name acknowledgment, and expressing personal requests via chat. The high prevalence of such behaviors indicates that viewers experience streamers not only as content providers but also as relational figures. Expressions such as "Can you see my name?" or "Hey bro, I'm here—give me a shoutout " serve as concrete indicators of viewers' desire to establish a personal connection with the streamer. In this sense, these interactions constitute a vivid manifestation of parasocial engagement. Parasocial interaction can be broadly defined as the development of a sense of intimacy with a media figure without direct face-to-face contact. In traditional media contexts, this bond relies primarily on the audience's perception of familiarity with the persona. However, interactive environments such as Twitch extend beyond these limitations. Through live chat and real-time response mechanisms, viewers gain the possibility of receiving individualized feedback from streamers. This dynamic reconfigures the traditionally one-sided nature of PSI, pushing it toward a potentially more reciprocal form of interaction (Wulf, Schneider & Queck, 2025).

Contemporary research indicates that parasocial interaction is no longer confined to traditional one-sided relationships (Kowert & Daniel, 2021). This perspective suggests that the viewer–streamer bond can be further strengthened when viewers receive interactive rewards such as responses from the streamer, acknowledgment of their names, or recognition through donations. In this way, viewers do not merely watch the streamer; they also engage, albeit in a limited and mediated form, in a relational practice with them.

Parasocial interaction is not limited to the viewer's one-sided emotional attachment; it also encompasses the development of adherence to social norms in relation to the streamer. Experimental studies by Wulf et al. on the Twitch environment demonstrate that streamers' direct and individualized addressing of viewers significantly enhances the PSI experience. This finding indicates that PSI, within live streaming practices, is not merely a theoretical construct but also a phenomenon with measurable effects on viewer behavior. In other words, the possibility of receiving direct responses reinforces the classical definition of PSI while simultaneously strengthening viewers' sense of belonging to the community. Accordingly, viewers' tendencies toward direct address and visibility-seeking behaviors on Twitch cannot be explained solely by individual motivations; rather, they reflect a dynamic and mediated form of parasocial interaction. The relationship established with the streamer through chat is experienced by viewers as a form of personal connection and may evolve into a social practice that enhances user engagement with the platform. Therefore, in live streaming environments such as Twitch, PSI should not be understood merely as a passive media consumption experience, but as an organizing dynamic of digital interaction.

Affective Publics and Networked Emotions

Viewer comments on Twitch do not merely respond to content; they also demonstrate the collective production of emotional expressions. The prominence of humor in reaction streams and the relatively high frequency of positive emotional expressions in gaming streams indicate that individual emotions are organized within a shared rhythm. With technological developments, emotions can no longer be understood solely as individual psychological states, but rather as components of collectively structured emotional patterns. The concept of affective publics, developed by Zizi Papacharissi (2015), emphasizes that emotions and affective connections shared across digital networks should be understood not only as individual experiences but also as the foundation of collective public practices. According to this perspective, emotions emerge through processes in which individuals connect with one another and produce shared meanings within social media and networked communication environments. Affective publics thus refer to networked publics in which emotions are organized not as purely subjective expressions, but as forms of collective storytelling and emotional synchronization. These publics are not fixed or hierarchical; rather, they are fluid and shaped dynamically in relation to specific events (Papacharissi, 2015).

Affective publics, as conceptualized by Zizi Papacharissi, emerge as public spaces in which community members share their emotional repertoires, thereby generating a sense of collective emotional connection and belonging. In this context, emotions are understood not merely as individual reactions, but as social connections organized through affective expressions circulating within the everyday rhythms of digital networks. The circulation of emotions in digital public spaces is therefore not simply the aggregate of momentary individual responses; rather, it constitutes an integral part of a shared repertoire of meaning.

In the context of Twitch, the findings derived from this conceptual framework indicate that the use of humor and emotes in reaction streams contributes to the production of shared emotional rhythms and collective norms among viewers within networked communication environments. Through shared humor and expressions of positive affect, viewers not only respond to content but also create a space in which emotions are collectively experienced and amplified. This process aligns with the notion of "the networked production and circulation of emotions" emphasized in Zizi Papacharissi's concept of affective publics: digital networks transform individual expressions into a shared repertoire of collective meaning, thereby establishing a common ground for interaction (Papacharissi, 2015). Accordingly, viewer behavior on Twitch, in terms of emotional expression, cannot be understood solely as the transmission of individual feelings; rather, it reflects the emergence of shared affective publics. The prominent use of humor and positive emotions demonstrates that viewers actively share their emotional repertoires through the platform, generating a collective emotional experience within the digital network. This further indicates that emotions in digital media environments are not merely individual experiences, but are shaped as a dynamic component of a collective public sphere.

Attention Economy and Viewer Behavior on Twitch

The concept of the attention economy is grounded in the argument of classical information theorist Herbert A. Simon, who posited that attention becomes a scarce resource in the face of information abundance. Within this framework, human attention is conceptualized as an economic commodity that must be managed and allocated. In contemporary digital media environments, the notion of the "attention economy" similarly explains how users' temporal and cognitive attention is targeted by platforms as a competitive resource amid an overabundance of information and content. This perspective emphasizes that, due to the limited nature of attention resources, media systems and digital platforms develop strategic design features and algorithmic mechanisms to capture and sustain user attention. Conceptualizing attention as an economic resource at this level allows for a redefinition of the relationships between information, attention, and visibility within media theory.

A substantial body of research demonstrates that digital platforms employ design features and algorithmic mechanisms to increase user engagement within the framework of the attention economy. In this context, social media and live streaming platforms such as Twitch aim to retain user attention for as long as possible, thereby transforming attention-related metrics—such as visibility, watch time, and interaction—into economic value. Mechanisms such as continuously refreshed content feeds and autoplay functions are optimized to sustain user attention within the platform. As a result, attention becomes both an algorithmic and a commercial commodity. This commodification of attention suggests that viewer behavior cannot be explained solely by content preferences, but must also be understood in terms of how and where users allocate their attention within digital environments.

Viewers on Twitch do not merely consume content; they also engage in attention-oriented behaviors such as seeking visibility, eliciting responses from streamers, and actively positioning themselves within the attention economy. In particular, the high rate of direct address observed in chat-based broadcasts indicates that viewers move beyond a passive spectator role and develop strategic practices aimed at attracting attention. This suggests that streamer–viewer interaction on the platform must be understood within a context in which attention is produced, distributed, and negotiated as a commodity.

Direct address and the pursuit of visibility in chat interactions can be interpreted as efforts by viewers to direct their attention not only toward the content itself but also toward the algorithmically structured field of visibility. This indicates that viewer behavior carries economic value and is processed by the platform as a strategic, interaction-based commodity within the control of attention resources. The in-community practices of Twitch viewers are thus shaped not only by individual interaction, but also by economically driven practices centered on the demand for attention. From this perspective, the viewer can be reconceptualized as an "attention actor" who positions their attention within the platform and transforms visibility into economic value. This framing provides a robust analytical lens for understanding the operation of the attention economy within digital platforms.

Platform Governance and Algorithmic Norms

The concept of platform governance is defined as a model that organizes content visibility, interaction rules, and user norms in digital media environments through algorithmic and managerial mechanisms. Within this framework, platforms do not regulate user behavior solely through content policies; they also shape interactions normatively via visibility algorithms, moderation systems, and community governance rules. This mode of regulation can be understood not as a traditional public sphere, but as a form of algorithmic public order structured by platform logics. In the theoretical perspective of Taina Bucher (2012), algorithms are conceptualized as systems that sort data, make decisions, and render content "meaningfully visible." These systems are not merely technical tools; they also function as mechanisms of power that shape users' social behaviors. Through algorithmic processes that prioritize certain content while marginalizing others, platforms directly influence behavioral patterns and guide users' understanding of what is valuable or visible. This process extends beyond simple content classification; it encompasses the production of norms and the structuring of visibility struggles. In this sense, platform governance continuously generates an algorithmic decision-making system that determines which expressions, behaviors, and users become visible within the platform ecosystem.

Contemporary media and platform studies emphasize that this form of governance is not limited to algorithmic decision-making alone, but is also reinforced by human-defined rules, moderation policies, and content regulation practices. In their quantitative and qualitative research, Brooke Erin Duffy and Marcus Meisner demonstrate that the dynamics of visibility and invisibility produced by algorithmic platform governance can exacerbate inequalities and lead to forms of discrimination associated with content creators' social identities. These findings reveal the broader social, cultural, and economic implications of platform governance.

In live streaming environments, moderation practices also emerge as a key component of platform governance. Attacks such as "hate raids" trigger moderation responses aimed at maintaining community safety, while simultaneously reshaping the interaction patterns of targeted groups and the production of norms within the community. Such interventions do not merely function to prevent malicious behavior; they also reveal how platform governance actively organizes community norms and behavioral expectations.

The multilayered nature of platform governance produces both explicit and implicit effects on viewer and streamer behavior. Visibility algorithms reward user behavior in accordance with normative patterns, while moderation mechanisms shape community expectations and acceptable forms of communication. Together, these mechanisms generate an internal normative order that extends beyond the platform's formal rules.

This order evolves into a form of algorithmic community sensibility through which users learn what is acceptable, what is rewarded, and what is deemed worthy of visibility.

It can be argued that moderation practices and chat norms on Twitch do not shape viewer interaction solely through individual preferences; rather, they construct a behavioral order structured by an algorithmically governed "visibility regime." The relatively low prevalence of toxic language and the high frequency of normatively accepted practices such as humor and donations reflect how this governance structure is manifested in viewer behavior. In this sense, Twitch should not be understood merely as a technical infrastructure. Instead, it must be conceptualized as a governance system that, through algorithmic and managerial mechanisms, defines viewer and streamer behavior, produces norms, and regulates visibility. Such an approach enables a deeper and more conceptual understanding of the relationships between visibility, norms, and social behavior within digital platforms.

Uses and Gratifications (UGT) Perspective

The Uses and Gratifications Theory (UGT) is a communication framework developed to explain media choices and the gratifications individuals derive from media use, positioning the audience not as passive recipients but as active users. UGT is based on the assumption that media audiences make choices according to their needs and expectations of gratification. According to this perspective, users consciously select media platforms and expect to obtain various forms of gratification, such as socialization, entertainment, information acquisition, relaxation, and identity fulfillment.

In the context of Twitch, it has been demonstrated that users engage in viewing behavior driven by diverse motivations. The study by Juho Sjöblom and Juho Hamari reveals that viewers use Twitch for cognitive (information acquisition), affective (entertainment), socialization, and tension release purposes, and that these motivations show significant relationships with behavioral outcomes such as viewing duration. Within the Turkish context, findings indicate that entertainment gratification is the most prominent motivation among Twitch users, followed by needs related to socialization and information. These results support the core assumptions of Uses and Gratifications Theory, which conceptualizes media choice as being driven by users' needs and expected gratifications, specifically within the context of Twitch.

From a Uses and Gratifications perspective, engagement with Twitch cannot be reduced to the mere act of spending time on content. Rather, it represents a means through which viewers satisfy psychological and social needs such as forming social connections, achieving emotional gratification, and enhancing self-expression. The tendency of viewers to directly address streamers in chat may be driven not only by a desire for visibility, but also by motivations such as belonging to a community, establishing social bonds with other viewers, and attaining affective gratification. In this regard, UGT can be effectively adapted to interactive platforms like Twitch: users engage with the platform in ways that align with their communicative, psychological, and social expectations of gratification. Understanding Twitch viewer behavior, therefore, requires an analysis of the specific gratifications that underlie their media use motivations. This perspective moves beyond a narrow view of media consumption and reveals the psychosocial functions embedded within user practices.

Platform Economy and Digital Labor

In addition to the social and emotional dimensions discussed above, Twitch should also be understood within the broader framework of platform economy and digital labor. Digital platforms increasingly transform user interaction into economic value, where attention, visibility, and engagement function as commodified resources (Srnicek, 2017). In this context, Twitch operates not only as a communication environment but also as an economic system structured around monetization mechanisms such as subscriptions, donations, and bits. These mechanisms reshape the nature of streamer–viewer interaction. Streamers are not merely content producers but also performers engaged in continuous emotional labor to sustain audience engagement and loyalty (Woodcock & Johnson, 2019). Similarly, viewers' interaction practices—such as sending messages, seeking recognition, or donating—can be interpreted not only as communicative acts but also as participation in an attention-driven economy. Research on influencer and creator economies further demonstrates that visibility and engagement are directly linked to economic outcomes within digital platforms (Cunningham & Craig, 2019; Abidin, 2021). Therefore, understanding Twitch viewer behavior requires not only social and psychological perspectives but also an economic analysis of how interaction is incentivized and monetized within platform structures.

METHOD

This study was conducted using a qualitative thematic content analysis approach in order to reveal the social and conceptual patterns present in viewer comments on Twitch. Qualitative content analysis is a methodological approach that systematically examines meaning structures within communicative texts, aiming to identify recurring motifs, patterns of meaning, and conceptual categories. This approach goes beyond the surface-level content of texts and seeks to analyze their contextual and implicit meanings as well (Mayring, 2000).

The concepts of content analysis and thematic analysis are often used in relation to one another. However, thematic analysis specifically refers to an analytical process focused on identifying patterns of meaning within textual data and generating conceptual themes based on these patterns (Braun & Clarke, 2006). In this approach, the researcher does not merely describe the data, but also interprets the social and conceptual dimensions of the phenomenon under investigation through the themes that emerge from the data. For this reason, thematic content analysis provides a suitable methodological framework for examining behavioral patterns and interaction forms within large textual datasets, such as social media content. Within qualitative content analysis, data are systematically coded through verbal expressions, and these codes are subsequently transformed into conceptual categories. The coding process is not a superficial procedure limited to identifying word frequencies; rather, it aims to detect units of meaning within the text and reorganize them under conceptual categories (Mayring, 2000). In this study, thematic content analysis is employed to identify recurring patterns of social interaction in Twitch viewer comments and to interpret these patterns within a theoretical framework.

Research Design and Paradigm

The study is structured within a qualitative research paradigm. Qualitative research aims to examine not only the measurable aspects of social phenomena but also their contextual dimensions and meaning-making processes. Accordingly, this approach seeks to answer "why" and "how" questions rather than focusing solely on "how much." For this reason, qualitative methods are widely recognized as essential methodological tools for analyzing complex communication processes such as social media interactions (Creswell, 2014). Thematic content analysis is considered a particularly suitable method for systematically examining patterns of meaning within large textual datasets, such as social media comments. This approach enables the researcher to transform data into conceptual themes and to interpret social behavior patterns through these themes (Braun & Clarke, 2006). The primary reason for employing thematic content analysis in the examination of viewer interactions on Twitch is that the social and cultural meanings embedded in user comments can be explored more deeply through a qualitative analytical process.

Sample and Data Source

In qualitative research, sample size is not determined based on statistical representativeness, as in quantitative studies, but rather on the scope of the research question and the thematic diversity emerging within the dataset. In thematic analysis studies, sample size may vary depending on factors such as the complexity of the research questions, the diversity of the data, and the scope of the texts to be analyzed (Braun & Clarke, 2006). Therefore, instead of adhering to a fixed sample size, qualitative data analysis aims to reach a sufficient volume of data that adequately captures the analytical scope of the study.

Methodological studies on qualitative data analysis indicate that sample size in thematic analysis varies according to criteria such as the breadth of the research question, data diversity, and thematic saturation (Braun & Clarke, 2021). Particularly in social media research involving large textual datasets, samples comprising hundreds or thousands of data units are considered methodologically appropriate for capturing thematic diversity.

The sample of the study consists of viewer comments obtained from broadcasts of Elraenn, one of the most-watched Twitch streamers in Türkiye, across different content types. The dataset used in this research comprises 3,000 viewer comments, providing sufficient data diversity to enable a comparative analysis of viewer behavior across various broadcast categories (chatting, gaming, and reaction streams) on Twitch. In thematic analyses of large textual datasets, extensive data samples contribute to the more reliable identification of recurring patterns of meaning (Wutich, Beresford & Bernard, 2024). In this regard, the size of the dataset employed in this study provides a robust methodological foundation for the systematic analysis of the social and conceptual themes emerging in viewer interactions.

Data Collection Process

The research data were obtained using the official API infrastructure of YouTube. During the data collection process, the Python programming language and data processing libraries were employed. Through these tools, viewer comments associated with the selected broadcasts were systematically retrieved and transferred into the research dataset. Each comment was recorded while preserving its original textual content, and contextual metadata (such as comment date and broadcast type) were incorporated into the dataset. As a result of this process, a structured textual database was established for analysis.

Analysis Process

The data analysis process consists of three main stages.

Coding Process: In the first stage, the dataset was preprocessed using natural language processing techniques. During this phase, textual data were cleaned, recurring words and expressions were identified, and the data were transformed into a standardized format for analysis. This preliminary step provided the foundation for thematic coding. Subsequently, the dataset was manually examined, and the comments were segmented into smaller units of meaning and coded accordingly.

Theme Development: The coded data segments were grouped according to similar patterns of meaning and consolidated under broader thematic categories. This process aligns with the data-driven theme development phase defined in the thematic analysis approach of Braun and Clarke (2006). In this approach, themes are not predetermined by the researcher but are instead derived directly from the data itself.

Validity and Reliability Checks: A two-stage validation procedure was implemented during the analysis process. In the first stage, an initial thematic framework was established through automated coding using natural language processing tools. In the second stage, these themes were re-evaluated through manual coding conducted by the researcher. As a result of the intercoder reliability analysis, a 91% agreement rate was achieved among data segments. This level of agreement is consistent with the accepted reliability standards in qualitative content analysis studies (Mayring, 2000).

Thematic Categories

As a result of the data analysis, the identified themes were classified under the following conceptual categories based on the content characteristics of viewer comments on Twitch:

1. **Direct Address to the Streamer:** This category includes expressions that reflect viewers' intent to communicate directly with the streamer.
2. **Humor and Shared Cultural References:** Interactions involving humor, meme usage, and platform-specific cultural references are grouped under this category.
3. **Positive Emotions:** Comments expressing support, appreciation, and positive emotional reactions are included in this theme.
4. **Negative Emotions:** Expressions reflecting disappointment, discomfort, or critical attitudes are evaluated within this category.
5. **Toxic Language and Negative Behavior:** Instances of insults, aggressive language, or behaviors that violate community norms are analyzed under this thematic category.
6. **Content Response and Feedback:** This category encompasses viewers' evaluations, suggestions, and critical comments regarding the content.

These thematic categories were not developed solely to identify surface-level linguistic patterns, but also to interpret the social and communicative dimensions of viewer behavior on Twitch. Accordingly, the analysis process enabled the interaction patterns emerging in viewer comments to be examined within a broader social and conceptual context.

LIMITATIONS OF THE STUDY AND METHODOLOGICAL REFLEXIVITY

This study examines viewer–streamer interactions on Twitch within the Turkish context through the case of Elraenn, a highly viewed streamer. Although this case represents a prominent figure within the Twitch ecosystem with a broad audience reach and significant influence on platform culture, the reliance on a single-case design introduces certain limitations in terms of generalizability. In case study research, the objective is not statistical generalization, but rather analytical generalization that reveals the theoretical dimensions of a particular phenomenon (Yin, 2018). Accordingly, while the findings provide conceptual insights into the Twitch platform, they are not directly generalizable to all streamer typologies or all Twitch communities.

The second limitation of the study lies in the fact that the dataset consists of archived comments from YouTube. This may not fully capture the real-time dynamics of live chat interactions on Twitch. The message flow during live broadcasts generates distinct interaction patterns, including collective synchronization, high message density, spam behaviors, and moderation interventions. Studies on Twitch moderation practices indicate that live chat environments operate differently from archived comment sections in terms of the formation of community norms (Seering, Kraut & Dabbish, 2017). In this context, the current dataset represents the synchronous and temporal dimensions of viewer interaction only to a limited extent.

The third limitation of the study concerns the inability to access the demographic characteristics of users who generated the comments. Variables such as age, gender, socio-economic status, and levels of digital literacy are not available within the dataset. However, digital participation and platform use are closely related to socio-demographic factors (van Dijk, 2020). Therefore, it is not possible to determine precisely which social groups produced the comments analyzed in this study. Future research may address this limitation by employing methods such as surveys, in-depth interviews, or the integration of platform data with survey data, thereby enabling multi-layered data triangulation.

Another limitation of the study is related to the NLP-assisted thematic coding process used in data analysis. Although the results of automated coding were verified through manual evaluation and an intercoder agreement rate of 91% was achieved—consistent with accepted reliability standards in qualitative content analysis (Mayring, 2000)—the capacity of automated classification algorithms to interpret contextual irony, slang usage, and platform-specific emote culture remains limited. In particular, the semantic interpretation of platform-specific linguistic codes may differ from conventional sentiment analysis models, which may have led to contextual misclassifications in certain comments during thematic categorization.

Fifth, the research design is based on a cross-sectional data analysis. Twitch communities are dynamic structures that continuously evolve over time due to factors such as platform policies, algorithmic updates, and internal community crises. Studies demonstrating that algorithmic visibility mechanisms shape user behavior on digital platforms suggest that changes in platform policies may also transform user interactions (Bucher, 2012). For this reason, longitudinal research designs may provide more comprehensive insights into how platform communities evolve over time.

Finally, the researcher's prior work on Twitch culture, digital participation, and platform interaction has contributed to the development of specific conceptual sensitivities during the data interpretation process. However, it is well acknowledged in qualitative research that the researcher's theoretical positioning may influence the analytical process. For this reason, reflexive notes were maintained throughout the analysis, and particular care was taken to ensure that themes were derived inductively from the data during the coding phase. In qualitative research methodology, reflexivity constitutes a key principle that requires researchers to critically examine their own positionality as an integral part of the analytical process (Creswell & Poth, 2018).

Despite these limitations, the study contributes to the literature as one of the few investigations in the Turkish context that examines Twitch viewer interactions through an NLP-assisted thematic content analysis approach.

Ethical Considerations and Data Use

The use of social media data in research necessitates careful consideration of ethical issues such as user privacy, data anonymization, and researcher responsibility. Although data shared on digital platforms may be publicly accessible, their use for research purposes requires ethical evaluation (Williams, Burnap & Sloan, 2017). Accordingly, anonymization and the protection of user identity constitute fundamental ethical principles in social media research. In this study, all comments were obtained from publicly available platform data, and user identities, usernames, and personal information were removed from the dataset. In this way, the data were anonymized, eliminating the possibility of identifying individual users. Anonymization is widely recognized as a core ethical practice in social media research (Zhang et al., 2024). Furthermore, the data collection process was conducted using the official API infrastructure of YouTube, ensuring compliance with platform terms of service. No analysis targeting individual user identities was conducted; instead, comments were evaluated solely based on their textual content. This approach aligns with recommended ethical practices aimed at safeguarding user privacy in social media research (Golder et al., 2017). In this regard, the research design adheres to the fundamental ethical principles proposed in the literature concerning the use of social media data, prioritizing data anonymity and the protection of user privacy as key methodological commitments.

Limitations Related to Live Interaction Dynamics

An additional limitation concerns the absence of real-time interaction dynamics in the dataset. Twitch chat environments are characterized by high-speed message flows, collective synchronization, and platform-specific communicative practices that differ significantly from archived comment sections. Studies show that Twitch chat operates through rapid, collective meaning-making processes shaped by temporal immediacy and user density (Ford et al., 2017). In this context, the use of archived YouTube comments may not fully capture the intensity and synchronicity of live interaction. Real-time chat Dynamics including message overlap, spam behavior, and moderation interventions play a critical role in shaping communication patterns on Twitch. Future research could address this limitation by incorporating live chat data and time-based interaction analysis to better reflect the platform's communicative structure.

FINDINGS

The thematic structure and interaction patterns of viewer comments on Twitch are presented comparatively across three different broadcast types (gaming, reaction, and chatting). The analysis process is based on a thematic content analysis approach that combines NLP-assisted preliminary coding with manual validation. Thematic analysis is a qualitative method that aims to identify recurring patterns of meaning within textual data and organize these patterns into conceptual themes (Braun & Clarke, 2006). The themes identified in the analysis of viewer comments are primarily concentrated around direct address to the streamer, humor strategies, forms of emotional expression, and practices of content evaluation and feedback. The findings are evaluated through both qualitative interpretations and thematic frequency indicators.

Thematic Distribution by Broadcast Type

The thematic distribution of the 3,000 analyzed viewer comments indicates that different communication patterns emerge depending on the type of broadcast. On interaction-based platforms such as Twitch, viewer behavior is shaped not only by the content type but also by the interaction affordances provided by the broadcast format.

Table 1. Thematic trends by broadcast type

Publication Type	Dominant Thematic Trend	Approximate Ratio
Gaming Streams	Positive emotional expressions and performance evaluations	%13
Reaction Streams	Humor and shared cultural references	%10
Chatting Streams	Direct address to the streamer	%35

As shown in Table 1, different broadcast types produce distinct variations in the content structure of viewer comments. This indicates that viewer interaction is shaped not only by individual preferences but also by the social interaction affordances provided by the broadcast format.

Gaming Streams: Emotional Tone and Performance Evaluations

In gaming-focused broadcasts, a significant portion of the comments consists of performance evaluations and emotional expressions directed toward the player. The analysis reveals that comments containing positive emotions account for approximately 13% of the overall dataset. Comments within this category indicate that viewers express their immediate reactions to the gameplay and their evaluations of the streamer's performance within an emotional framework. Viewer comments frequently include expressions such as:

"This segment was amazing, you're doing really well."

"That was really entertaining, we're looking forward to more streams like this."

This finding indicates that gaming streams are not merely an entertainment-oriented content format, but also constitute a social space that fosters positive emotional interaction within the viewer community. The presence of emotional tone in viewer responses suggests that the interaction between viewers and the streamer extends beyond content consumption, encompassing a dimension of emotional synchronization.

Reaction Streams: Humor and Collective Meaning-Making

In reaction streams, viewer comments are observed to concentrate prominently around humor and platform-specific cultural references. The analysis indicates that comments containing humor account for approximately 10% of the dataset. These comments frequently include emote usage and humorous expressions characteristic of platform-specific jargon. For example:

"LOL this scene was totally EPIC "

"This turned into a complete comedy moment "

Such comments do not merely function as expressions of individual reactions; they also contribute to the formation of a shared cultural language among viewers. The use of humor as a collective interaction strategy can be associated with the mechanisms of collective meaning-making within digital communities. This finding is consistent with studies that highlight the role of emotions and humor in generating collective narratives within networked communication environments (Papacharissi, 2015).

Chatting Streams: Direct Address and Interaction Demand

In chatting-format broadcasts, there is a marked increase in comments in which viewers directly address the streamer. The analysis indicates that comments containing direct address account for approximately 35% of the dataset. These types of comments typically reflect a desire to receive a direct response from the streamer or to gain visibility. For example:

"Can you see my name?"

"Hey bro, I'm here—give me a shoutout "

This tendency indicates that chatting-format broadcasts increase the intensity of interaction between viewers and the streamer. Viewers do not merely consume content; they actively attempt to establish direct communication with the streamer. This suggests that viewer behavior may be associated with motivations related to forming parasocial relationships.

Relative Level of Toxic Language Use

The analysis of the dataset indicates that the proportion of toxic language and aggressive comments constitutes approximately 0.3% of the total comments.

Table 2. Distribution of toxic language use

Category	Approximate Ratio
Toxic language / aggressive expressions	%0,3
Neutral or positive communication	%99,7

This result indicates that the use of toxic language in the dataset is relatively limited. Research on the prevalence of aggressive language in online communities suggests that platform norms and moderation mechanisms can significantly constrain such behaviors (Seering, Kraut & Dabbish, 2017).

Examples of comments containing toxic language include the following expressions:

"Stop talking nonsense already."

"This is boring, I just turned it off."

Such comments were evaluated as being inconsistent with the normative communication practices within the platform.

The findings indicate that viewer behavior on Twitch is not limited to content consumption; rather, viewers actively participate in emotional, social, and cultural interaction processes. The positive emotional expressions observed in gaming streams can be interpreted as indicators of the emotional bonds viewers establish with the content. Humor-oriented interactions in reaction streams demonstrate that humor functions as a collective communication strategy within digital platforms. Meanwhile, the high rate of direct address in chatting streams reveals viewers' tendencies to establish relational connections with the streamer and to seek visibility.

These findings demonstrate that viewer behavior in interactive media environments such as Twitch cannot be explained solely as media consumption. Viewers participate indirectly in content production processes, establish emotional connections, and generate platform-specific social practices.

The collective emergence of emotional expressions is consistent with studies suggesting that emotions constitute a fundamental component of public interaction processes within digital networks (Papacharissi, 2015). Additionally, viewers' direct address to streamers indicates that the audience–media figure relationships emphasized in the parasocial interaction literature are taking on new forms within digital platforms. At the same time, the pursuit of visibility and attention-seeking behaviors can be associated with theoretical approaches that explain how digital platforms operate within the framework of the attention economy.

DISCUSSION

Is Twitch an Affective Public Sphere?: The findings of this study suggest that Twitch is not merely a media environment based on content consumption, but rather functions as a digital public space in which emotions are collectively produced and circulated. The concentration of humor in reaction streams, positive emotions in gaming streams, and direct address in chatting streams indicates that viewer behavior is organized not around individual reactions, but around collective emotional patterns. This observation aligns closely with Zizi Papacharissi's conceptualization of "affective publics." Papacharissi argues that publics emerging within digital networks are shaped not primarily through rational deliberation, but through the circulation of emotions, defining them as "fluid and transient public formations constituted through the networked circulation of affect" (Papacharissi, 2015). In this context, emotions function not merely as individual expressions, but as communicative instruments that enable the construction of collective narratives and social bonds.

The findings further indicate that, particularly in broadcast types where humor and positive emotions are prominent, viewers do not merely consume content but operate within a shared emotional rhythm. These synchronous forms of emotional expression emerging in Twitch chat produce a form of publicness that, as Zizi Papacharissi suggests, "enables dispersed individuals to become emotionally aligned through networked communication" (Papacharissi, 2015). Accordingly, Twitch can be conceptualized, in contrast to traditional models of the public sphere, as a digital affective public space in which emotional synchronization—rather than rational deliberation—serves as the primary organizing principle.

Collective Interaction and Platform Affordances: The findings indicate that viewer interactions on Twitch are not limited to individual behaviors but involve collective practices shaped by the platform's technical affordances. In particular, the use of humor, emotes, and recurring expressions as a shared language among viewers demonstrates that collective meaning-making operates at the platform level. This aligns with the characterization of Twitch as a space of "participatory gaming communities" proposed by Katy Hamilton, Oliver Garretson, and Michael Kerne (2014). Viewers do not merely engage in the act of watching; they actively produce shared norms, symbols, and interaction patterns through the communicative tools provided by the platform. Particularly in reaction streams, the use of humor as a collective linguistic resource enables viewers to generate new meanings by referencing one another's expressions. This process points to a community dynamic in which shared cultural codes emerge beyond individual communication. In this sense, the structure of Twitch chat demonstrates that collective interaction on digital platforms is produced not only around content but also around the forms of interaction themselves.

Algorithmic Power and the Struggle for Visibility: The high rate of direct address observed in chatting streams (35%) indicates that viewers are motivated not only by the desire to communicate, but also by the need to gain visibility and attract attention. This phenomenon can be interpreted through the lens of "algorithmic power," which explains the relationship between attention and visibility on digital platforms such as Twitch. Taina Bucher (2012) conceptualizes algorithms not merely as technical ranking systems, but as "socially regulatory power structures" that determine what users see and who becomes visible. In this sense, algorithmic systems function as normative mechanisms that indirectly shape user behavior and encourage particular forms of interaction.

In the context of Twitch, viewers' use of expressions such as "notice me" or "say my name" indicates that the demand for visibility extends beyond an individual motivation and is shaped within the dynamics of the platform's attention economy. This suggests that algorithmic visibility systems influence not only the distribution of content but also the behavior of users. Accordingly, viewer behavior should be interpreted not solely as a form of social interaction, but also as an attention-oriented strategy embedded within the platform's visibility regime.

Algorithmic Culture and Visibility Regimes: Beyond algorithmic governance, Twitch can also be understood through the concept of algorithmic culture, which emphasizes how user practices are shaped by platform-driven systems of visibility and recommendation (Striphas, 2015). Algorithms do not merely organize content; they actively structure user behavior by defining what becomes visible and valuable within the platform. In this sense, viewers' attempts to gain attention such as repeatedly addressing the streamer or producing noticeable messages can be interpreted as strategies shaped by algorithmic visibility regimes. Platform affordances encourage users to compete for recognition within an environment where visibility is unevenly distributed and algorithmically mediated. This perspective suggests that viewer interaction is not solely driven by individual motivation or social connection, but also by the structural conditions imposed by platform algorithms. Accordingly, Twitch interaction should be analyzed as a socio-technical process where human behavior and algorithmic systems are deeply intertwined.

Emotional Labor and Platform Capitalism: Streaming on Twitch is not merely a practice based on content production; it is also part of a platform economy in which emotional labor is intensively produced. The continuous interaction of streamers with viewers, their responses to individual comments, and their efforts to sustain a sense of community can be understood as processes in which emotional labor is visibly enacted. Jamie Woodcock and Mark R. Johnson (2019) conceptualize Twitch streaming as a form of digital labor shaped by performance and emotional labor. Within this framework, streamers do not only produce content; they also construct emotional bonds through their interactions with viewers and continuously generate performative engagement to maintain these relationships.

The findings indicating a high prevalence of direct address and the expectation of responses from streamers suggest that emotional labor on Twitch evolves into a reciprocal form of interaction. Viewers are not merely content consumers; they are also active participants in this process of emotional exchange. In this context, Twitch can be conceptualized not only as a media platform, but as a domain of platform capitalism where emotional labor, the attention economy, and algorithmic governance intersect.

Platform-Specific Communication and Collective Language: Another important dimension of Twitch interaction is the development of platform-specific communication forms. Viewer interaction is not limited to textual messages but includes emotes, memes, and repetitive symbolic expressions that form a shared communicative repertoire. These elements function as a form of digital vernacular, enabling rapid and collective meaning-making within the chat environment (Wohn & Guo, 2021). Such communicative practices contribute to the formation of a collective identity among viewers. Humor, in particular, operates not only as an individual expression but also as a shared cultural code that reinforces group belonging. Therefore, Twitch communication should be understood not only at the level of semantic content but also as a symbolic system shaped by platform culture.

Cultural Context and Localized Platform Practices: The findings of this study gain additional significance when considered within the Turkish digital context. Digital media practices in Türkiye are often characterized by strong tendencies toward collective interaction, humor production, and informal communication styles. These cultural dynamics may help explain the prominence of humor and direct interaction observed in the dataset. Studies on digital culture in Türkiye indicate that social media platforms are frequently used as spaces for community formation and expressive interaction. Additionally, online humor and meme culture play a central role in shaping communication practices and collective identity. In this regard, Twitch interaction patterns observed in this study should not be interpreted solely as universal platform behaviors but also as culturally embedded practices. Incorporating this perspective allows for a more nuanced understanding of how global platforms are locally appropriated and experienced.

CONCLUSION AND IMPLICATIONS

This study demonstrates that viewer–streamer interaction on Twitch cannot be understood merely as a process of content consumption; rather, it operates as a multilayered form of social, emotional, and platform-based interaction. The findings indicate that different broadcast types significantly shape viewer behavior, with each format producing its own distinct interaction ecology. The prominence of positive emotions in gaming streams (13%) suggests that viewers' engagement with content involves not only cognitive but also emotional dimensions. The dominance of humor in reaction streams (10%) reveals that viewers employ humor as a central strategy for collective meaning-making. Meanwhile, the high rate of direct address in chatting streams (35%) highlights strong motivations related to visibility and relational engagement. Conversely, the low rate of toxic language (0.3%) suggests that platform norms and moderation mechanisms play a significant role in regulating communication practices. Taken together, these findings indicate that Twitch is not merely a broadcasting platform, but a digital environment in which viewers actively participate, form emotional bonds, and develop social interaction practices. The live chat structure, in particular, enables viewers not only to consume content but also to engage directly with streamers and interact with other viewers. This dynamic demonstrates that relationships conceptualized in the literature as parasocial interactions have evolved into more interactive and dynamic forms within live streaming environments. Indeed, recent studies suggest that viewers experience not a purely one-sided relationship, but a partially reciprocal interaction with streamers (Kowert & Daniel, 2021; Wulf et al., 2021).

Furthermore, the interactional structure of Twitch generates a collective experiential space among viewers. Synchronous interactions through live chat foster a sense of community and position the platform as a "digital third place." In this respect, Twitch can be understood not simply as a medium for content consumption, but as a space for community formation and social bonding. The literature similarly emphasizes that Twitch provides a digital social environment in which users develop a sense of community through shared interaction.

Accordingly, the study shows that Twitch viewer behavior is structured along three primary dimensions:

1. **Emotional interaction** (positive emotions and humor)
2. **Relational engagement** (direct address and the pursuit of visibility)
3. **Platform-based behavior** (algorithmic visibility and normative structures)

Therefore, Twitch should be conceptualized not merely as a platform for media consumption, but as a digital interaction ecosystem in which emotional, social, and algorithmic processes intersect.

Discussion

The findings of this study offer several practical implications for Twitch and similar live streaming environments. First, from the perspective of platform designers, given that viewer interaction is largely mediated through chat and visibility mechanisms, it is essential to develop balanced moderation systems that both support user engagement and effectively limit toxic behavior. While the low rate of toxic language suggests that existing moderation mechanisms are functional, ensuring their long-term sustainability remains a critical concern. The findings also indicate that direct interaction with viewers plays a significant role in fostering viewer engagement. Streamers' ability to establish individualized communication with their audiences can strengthen parasocial bonds and enhance viewer loyalty. This suggests that streaming should be understood not only as a practice of content production, but also as one that requires community management and emotional engagement strategies. Furthermore, the role of humor in facilitating collective interaction should be carefully considered by both content creators and platform developers. The prominence of humor in reaction streams highlights its function as a key driver of viewer participation and engagement.

Recommendations for Future Research

While this study provides important insights into viewer interactions on Twitch, it also highlights several directions for future research. First, as the present study is based on a cross-sectional dataset, future studies could employ longitudinal designs to examine how viewer behavior evolves over time. In particular, the impact of platform policies and algorithmic changes on user behavior could be analyzed more comprehensively through long-term data. Second, the absence of demographic variables in this study represents a limitation that future research can address. By integrating survey methods and in-depth interviews, researchers can construct multi-layered datasets that include variables such as age, gender, and levels of digital experience, enabling more nuanced analyses. Third, the direct analysis of live chat data would provide a more accurate understanding of synchronous interaction dynamics. Real-time data analysis, in particular, could offer deeper insights into phenomena such as collective emotional synchronization and interaction intensity. Finally, advancements in natural language processing techniques would enhance the accurate analysis of platform-specific linguistic structures, such as emotes, irony, and slang. In this regard, interdisciplinary approaches hold significant potential for expanding the methodological capacity of digital media research.

REFERENCES

Abidin, C. (2021). Mapping internet celebrity on TikTok. *Social Media + Society*.

Braun, V., & Clarke, V. (2006). Using thematic analysis in psychology. *Qualitative Research in Psychology*, *3*(2), 77–101. DOI: 10.1191/1478088706qp063oa

Braun, V., & Clarke, V. (2021). To saturate or not to saturate? Questioning data saturation as a useful concept for thematic analysis. *Qualitative Research in Sport, Exercise and Health*, *13*(2), 201–216. DOI: 10.1080/2159676X.2019.1704846

Bucher, T. (2012). Want to be on the top? Algorithmic power and the threat of invisibility on Facebook. *New Media & Society*, *14*(7), 1164–1180. DOI: 10.1177/1461444812440159

Creswell, J. W. (2014). *Research design: Qualitative, quantitative, and mixed methods approaches* (4th ed.). SAGE.

Creswell, J. W., & Poth, C. N. (2018). *Qualitative inquiry and research design: Choosing among five approaches* (4th ed.). SAGE.

Cunningham, S., & Craig, D. (2019). *Social media entertainment*. NYU Press.

Ford, C., Gardner, D., Horgan, L. E., Liu, C., Tsaasan, A. M., Nardi, B., & Rickman, J. (2017, May). Chat speed op pogchamp: Practices of coherence in massive twitch chat. In *Proceedings of the 2017 CHI conference extended abstracts on human factors in computing systems* (pp. 858-871). DOI: 10.1145/3027063.3052765

Golder, S., Ahmed, S., Norman, G., & Booth, A. (2017). Attitudes toward the ethics of research using social media data. *Social Science & Medicine*.

Goldhaber, M. H. (1997). The attention economy and the Net. *First Monday*, *2*(4).

Hamilton, W. A., Garretson, O., & Kerne, A. (2014). Streaming on Twitch: Fostering participatory communities of play. In *Proceedings of the SIGCHI Conference on Human Factors in Computing Systems*. DOI: 10.1145/2556288.2557048

Horton, D., & Wohl, R. R. (1956). Mass communication and para-social interaction. *Psychiatry*, *19*(3), 215–229. DOI: 10.1080/00332747.1956.11023049 PMID: 13359569

Jenkins, H. (2006). *Convergence culture: Where old and new media collide*. NYU Press.

Jenkins, H., Ford, S., & Green, J. (2013). *Spreadable media: Creating value and meaning in a networked culture*. NYU Press.

Kowert, R., & Daniel, A. J. (2021). The one-and-a-half sided parasocial relationship. *Journal of Gaming & Virtual Worlds, 13*(2), 121–143.

Mayring, P. (2000). Qualitative content analysis. *Forum Qualitative Sozialforschung / Forum: Qualitative. Social Research, 1*(2), 20.

Papacharissi, Z. (2015). *Affective publics: Sentiment, technology, and politics.* Oxford University Press.

Seering, J., Kraut, R. E., & Dabbish, L. (2017). Shaping pro and anti-social behavior on Twitch through moderation and example-setting. In *Proceedings of the ACM on Human-Computer Interaction.* DOI: 10.1145/2998181.2998277

Sjöblom, M., & Hamari, J. (2017). Why do people watch others play video games? *Computers in Human Behavior, 75*, 985–996. DOI: 10.1016/j.chb.2016.10.019

Srnicek, N. (2017). Platform Capitalism. *Polity.*

Striphas, T. (2015). Algorithmic culture. *European Journal of Cultural Studies, 18*(4-5), 395–412. DOI: 10.1177/1367549415577392

van Dijk, J. (2020). *The digital divide.* Polity Press.

Williams, M. L., Burnap, P., & Sloan, L. (2017). Towards an ethical framework for publishing Twitter data in social research. *Sociological Research Online.* PMID: 29276313

Wohn, D. Y., & Guo, M. (2021). Understanding digital audiences in livestreaming. *Journal of Computer-Mediated Communication.*

Woodcock, J., & Johnson, M. R. (2019). The affective labor of live streaming on Twitch. *Television & New Media, 20*(8), 813–823. DOI: 10.1177/1527476419851077

Wulf, T., Schneider, F., & Beckert, S. (2021). Exploring parasocial interaction with streamers.

Wutich, A., Beresford, M., & Bernard, H. R. (2024). Sample sizes for 10 types of qualitative data analysis: An integrative review. *Qualitative Research.*

Yin, R. K. (2018). *Case study research and applications: Design and methods* (6th ed.). SAGE.

Zhang, Y., Fu, J., Lai, J., Deng, S., Guo, Z., Zhong, C., Tang, J., Cao, W., & Wu, Y. (2024). Reporting of ethical considerations in qualitative research utilizing social media data. *Journal of Medical Internet Research.* PMID: 38758590

Chapter 6
Artificial Intelligence–Based Visual Culture Analysis Using Banana Pro:
A Case Study of Turkiye

Tamer Bayrak
http://orcid.org/0000-0003-0776-1606
Çanakkale Onsekiz Mart University, Turkey

Mehmet Emin Arkcı
http://orcid.org/0009-0005-2800-901X
School of Graduate Studies, Çanakkale Onsekiz Mart University, Turkey

ABSTRACT

This study critically examines Google Gemini 3 Pro as an AI-based visual production system, analyzing how it constructs cultural representations of urban space through the lenses of Nicholas Mirzoeff's Visual Culture Theory and Stuart Hall's Representation Theory. Rather than treating AI-generated images as neutral outputs, the research positions them as culturally mediated representations shaped by dominant ideological structures. Using visual content and frequency analysis across all 81 provinces of Turkey, findings reveal that AI-generated visuals rely on Western-centric aesthetic codes and generalized cultural markers, simplifying local identities. These results demonstrate that AI-based visual production actively participates in reproducing cultural meaning, positioning artificial intelligence as a cultural agent that reshapes the relationships between space, identity, and visual representation in digital environments.

DOI: 10.4018/979-8-2600-2711-0.ch006

INTRODUCTION

Systems that acquire a "thinking system" as a result of specific codings and algorithmic structuring are referred to as artificial intelligence. As a consequence of the rapid acceleration of technological advancement, artificial intelligence contributes to technology in a self-reinforcing cyclical manner. The ability of machines to be programmed to exhibit behaviors that can be described as intelligent is defined as weak artificial intelligence, whereas the manifestation of their intelligence as conscious machines is accepted as strong artificial intelligence (Pirim, 2006: 85). The most significant obstacle to artificial intelligence being described as strong is considered to be its insufficient ability to "feel" aesthetic concerns and emotions in the way humans do. Artificial intelligence manifests itself in various fields. When the areas in which it is used are examined, it is frequently employed in fields such as tourism, law, environment, sports, biology, mathematics, and health (Göktaş, 2023: 894), as well as for activities such as article writing, website updating, and news analysis (Mich & Garigliano, 2023: 4). Artificial intelligence, which is expected to take part in artistic activities, also finds a place for itself in this context.

Figure 1. AI-art-creative-process (Elgammal, 2018)

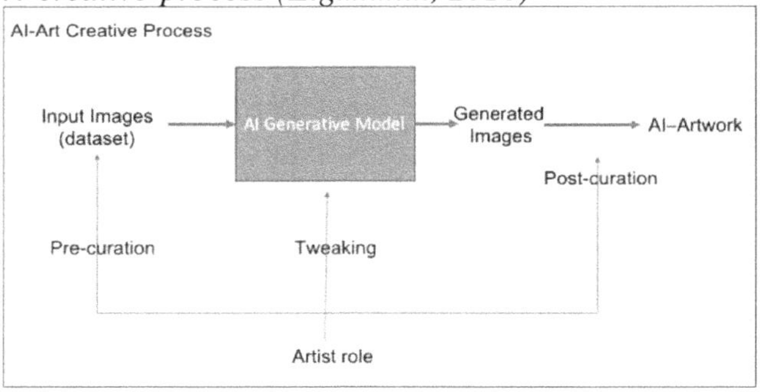

When Figure 1, which is the graph of Elgammal's depiction of the creative cycle in artificial intelligence, is examined, it demonstrates the progression between the algorithm of the artificial intelligence being addressed and the role of the artist (machine–human collaboration) (Aslan, 2019: 232). Hybrid art is described as a new form of art. This form can also be defined from a process-monitoring perspective as how the artist should write a prompt for artificial intelligence and how input images should be presented. In this respect, artificial intelligence models such as "ChatGPT," "Grok AI," and "Google Gemini" stand out. "ChatGPT" is developed by the company "OpenAI." It operates in line with its abilities to produce text and to interpret text with outputs similar to human elements. It can interact with users in natural language, respond to textual questions, generate text, and assist with many language-processing activities. Grok AI, on the other hand, is developed by the company xAI. It is known for its real-time data analysis and response outputs, as it is integrated into the "X" platform.

Figure 2. Google Gemini artificial ıntelligence model (Google Gemini Artificial Intelligence Model, 2023)

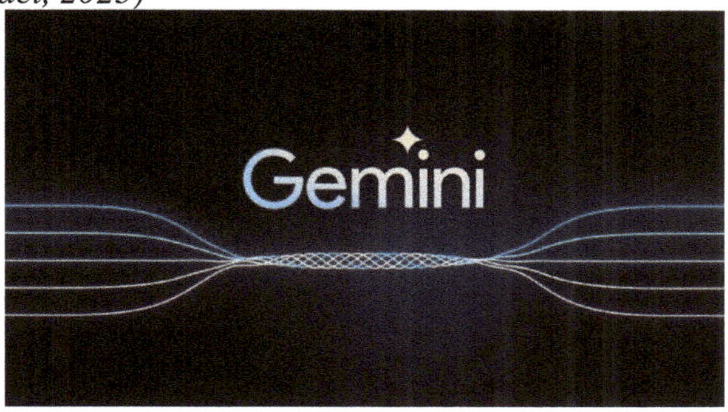

The artificial intelligence model shaped by an algorithm supported by Google PaLM 2, known as "Gemini," has been developed by Google AI (Figure 2). The artificial intelligence model that entered the market under the name "Bard" was renamed "Gemini" as of March 2024 (Sağır, Güdül, & Taştekin, 2025: 2). This model is also currently known, in terms of digital visualization, as "Google Gemini 3 Pro (Nano Banana Pro)" as of 29 November 2025. The most fundamental distinction of many artificial intelligence models lies in their ability to process and interpret various types of data such as visuals, text, source code, and audio (de Carvalho Souza & Weigang, 2025: 3). In this respect, it is emphasized that the Gemini artificial intelligence model produces more effective outputs in dimensions such as aesthetics, visual quality, and accuracy compared to other visually generative artificial intelligence models such as DALL·E, Microsoft Copilot, and Midjourney, according to evaluations by human assessors, as highlighted in the study titled "A multi-stage systematic review comparing text-to-image artificial intelligence models used in the generation of medical images in brain surgery" (Davis et al., 2025). In this study, the "Nano Banana Pro" artificial intelligence model is examined in terms of the consistency of aesthetics, visual quality, and accuracy based on socio-cultural elements, within the context of visual culture and representation theories.

ARTIFICIAL INTELLIGENCE PRODUCTIONS IN THE CONTEXT OF HYBRID ART

Technology does not carry significance on its own in terms of cultural determinism. It is nourished by certain elements and shaped through them. Technology situated within a cultural environment prioritizes and mediates the coexistence of art and science (Candemir, 2006). In this respect, production forms sustained through artificial intelligence are not independent of cultural elements; rather, they can be expressed as phenomena that emerge through the reconfiguration of cultural indicators. Urban images, which are among these cultural codes, are shaped as structures from which technology is nourished.

Art and the understanding of art, which have undergone transformation over the past half century, embody a structure so multi-layered that it cannot be explained solely through technological revolutions. This situation can be explained by the convergence of different disciplines and by the emergence of new technical tools resulting from changes in artists' modes of production. In this context, a hybrid understanding of art emerges through disciplines whose boundaries are gradually dissolving (Kaya, 2017: 169). From this perspective, it can be inferred that production processes in artificial intelligence draw upon multiple disciplines, as artificial intelligence models such as Nano Banana Pro are nourished by the complex nature of contemporary art and benefit from architectural elements or cumulative social components.

Another notable element in artistic practices is that contemporary art forms already take interdisciplinary sources of knowledge as their foundation. The hybrid coexistence reflected in the names of many modern modes of production, such as street art and digital art, emerges as a result of the integration of various fields of knowledge (Kara, 2003). In this respect, symbols originating from different disciplines serve as sources for artificial intelligence, which not only performs data calculations but also brings together aesthetic codes. Artificial intelligence thus becomes a new production tool that concretizes the multi-layered structure of contemporary art.

NANO BANANA IN THE CONTEXT OF VISUAL CULTURE THEORY AND REPRESENTATION THEORY

According to Hall, the concept of representation occupies a significant place in the field of cultural studies. He defines representation as an individual's way of making sense of the world and conveying the world that emerges from this meaning to others through language (1997a: 15). In this context, representation ensures the unity of meaning between culture and language and draws attention to discourse.

Emphasizing the notion of a shared language, Hall also argues that such a common language results in a shared understanding of cultural representation. Words, images, or sounds that signify cultural meaning are defined as "signs" (Güçlüer, 2024: 677). These signs represent the concepts constructed in our minds and the relationships between these concepts, and through their intermingling they form the unity of meaning of culture (Hall, 1997b). According to Hall (1997, as cited in Yurtseven, 2023: 15), popular culture exists as a kind of arena in which we comprehend reality and assume roles in relation to our sense of self and experiences due to the elements constructed in our minds. Language occupies a position as one of the representations of the self within this arena. Alongside written art as a product of language, visual art is examined as an indicator of signs and is addressed from the perspective of cultural representation in terms of the mind's unity of meaning.

According to Başak, the concept of visual culture can be defined as the process by which visual forms that find a place within culture gradually become integrated into the cultural phenomenon itself (Başak, 2021: 201). According to Mirzoeff, who defines the twenty-first century as a "network society," this culture enables everything programmed through technology to establish connections with one another, and this "network" reveals new orders and models not only in computer systems but also in social terms (Aykut, 2013: 707; Mirzoeff, 2015). Thus, this system plays a significant role in understanding the socio-cultural concepts and phenomena of the period in which it exists. The culture of the twenty-first century spreads as visual culture. Mirzoeff's definition of the concept of "visual technology" refers to all tools that engage in visual activity—such as painting, oil painting, the internet, and television—that require visuality or ultimately aim to achieve a natural image (Akay, 2007: 22). In this context, artificial intelligence technology is characterized, from the perspectives of both visual culture theory and representation theory, as the "new visual technology" and a form of "socio-cultural representation" of the twenty-first century.

Artificial intelligence learns while producing a work related to art. By imitating the human mind, artificial intelligence can also develop changes in its behavioral schema depending on its learning capacity based on this mental structure (Canan & Acungil, 2018: 30). In this context, artificial intelligence can develop a schema that enables it to learn the concept of culture, as well as the elements through which this culture is represented in humans, just as it can learn every element related to humans. Alongside this, according to Güney and Yavuz (2020: 435), artificial intelligence learning may lead to algorithmic distortions that the artist cannot foresee. This study is characterized as one of the first to examine artificial intelligence–supported visual production tools through a systematic and comparative analysis from the perspective of cultural representation, using the case of Türkiye. In the existing literature, the production dynamics of artificial intelligence are mostly discussed in terms of aesthetic quality, technical performance, and ethical debates; however, studies that experimentally analyze regional representations within the context of visual culture and representation theories remain limited. Within this scope, the study aims to reveal which social symbols, cultural signs, and color palettes are used by the Google Gemini Pro (Nano Banana Pro) model during the visual production of Türkiye's 81 provinces and selected districts, as well as which codes associated with these themes are systematically reconfigured. In this respect, the study opens up for discussion, through empirical findings, the idea that artificial intelligence–based visualization processes constitute not only a technical field but also an ideological and cultural field of representation.

In line with representation theory and visual culture theory addressed in the study, the manner in which the artificial intelligence model reconstructs and visualizes regional images is problematized. Accordingly, in order to resolve the main problem, two research questions are formulated, and answers to this problem are sought:

RESEARCH QUESTIONS

RQ1: Through which cultural symbols and visual indicators does the Nano Banana Pro artificial intelligence model represent cities in Türkiye?

RQ2: To what extent do social symbols and color preferences in city images generated by artificial intelligence reflect regional differences?

METHOD

Within the scope of the research universe, the 81 provinces of the Republic of Türkiye and the districts representing the socio-cultural differences of these provinces are taken as the basis. This study aims to examine how the broad spatial and cultural representations of Türkiye's geography are shaped by artificial intelligence. By defining the universe comprehensively, the study allows for a comparative analysis of representations.

In the selection of the sample, in order to introduce a limitation beyond provinces and focus on districts, those districts that fall into the first and second development tiers according to the results of the 2022 Socio-Economic Development Index (SEGE) Report (2025) published by the Ministry of Industry and Technology of the Republic of Türkiye are taken as the basis. The reason for determining the sample limitation in this way is that the selected districts provide sufficient socio-economic adequacy in the top two tiers and, accordingly, are observed to lead to data saturation.

As a result of including the names of all provinces in the study, the representational power of cultural differences across the country is enhanced.

During the data collection process, a fixed prompt template is presented to the Nano Banana Pro artificial intelligence model; each province and district is inserted into this fixed template, and outputs are requested from the artificial intelligence model. The main reason for determining a fixed prompt is to ensure that the visuals are generated by the artificial intelligence model under the same conditions.

Within the scope of the analysis methods, both qualitative and quantitative approaches are used together in the study. In this respect, a multi-layered analytical process is ensured in the artificial intelligence model. In the qualitative analysis process, the visual content analysis method is employed. This method enables the systematic examination of visual elements, and the visuals are subjected to classification (Aziz, 2015: 133). Accordingly, each visual is evaluated within the framework of the themes of cultural symbols, social images, and color preferences. Along with this analysis, elements of visual culture can be examined within the context of visual culture theory.

Following the qualitative analysis process, all themes are evaluated using the quantitative analysis method of frequency analysis. Frequency analysis is included within content analysis and contributes to measuring the intensity of themes by revealing how often visual indicators are repeated (Bilgin, 2006). In this respect, it is determined how many times each coded thematic element appears in the visuals, and the cultural elements from which Nano Banana draws are identified. The frequency analysis and percentage intensity methods used in the quantification of qualitative findings provide a comprehensive analysis and enable a multidimensional examination of Nano Banana's use of cultural elements during visual production.

Within the limitations of the study, the lack of transparency regarding the dataset used to train Nano Banana Pro, the possibility of biased behavior due to the model's algorithm, and the potential inconsistency of the model's responses to a fixed prompt are noted. The visualization of cultural representations by Nano Banana Pro through artificial interpretations constitutes another limitation.

The themes of cultural symbols, social images, and color preferences are constructed deductively based on visual culture and representation studies in the literature. Each visual is coded according to predefined subcategories within these themes. The coding process is conducted by the researchers, and due to the exploratory nature of the study, a descriptive content analysis approach is adopted.

FINDINGS

Within the scope of the study, Table 1 lists the 81 provinces of the Republic of Türkiye in alphabetical order and the first- and second-tier districts included in the SEGE Report (2025) according to their scores. In line with this classification, a total of 321 regions—comprising 81 provinces and 240 districts—are accepted as the sample. The Nano Banana Pro artificial intelligence model is provided with the following fixed prompt: "Produce a realistic city image for [...] that includes culturally, socially, and spatially accurate representations; reflects local architecture, cultural symbols, social icons, and the regional color palette. Do not add any elements that do not belong to the region. Ensure that the name of the region is clearly visible in the image." The outputs of the visuals are requested accordingly.

Table 1. Thematic analysis example of the visuals generated for the 81 provinces

Visual No.	Province	Generated Visual	Cultural Symbols (Visual Culture Theory)	Social Symbols (Representation Theory)	Color Preferences
1	Adana		Stone Bridge, grand mosque, and agricultural elements are observed as cultural symbols.	Street food and outdoor eating–drinking culture are observed as social symbols.	Orange, green, and white colors are observed.
2	Adıyaman		Ancient mountain statues and handwoven carpets are observed as cultural symbols.	Traditional bazaar environment and communal dining culture are observed as social symbols.	Yellow and brown colors are observed.
3	Afyonkarahisar		High fortress silhouette, cultivated fields, and historic mansions are observed as cultural symbols.	Market shopping and local food production are observed as social symbols.	Red, brown, and gray colors are observed.
4	Ağrı		Snow-covered high mountain and historic palace structure are observed as cultural symbols.	People in traditional clothing and conversations in front of shops are observed as social symbols.	White, gray, and brown colors are observed.
5	Aksaray		Religious architectural structures, mountain landscape, and carpet looms are observed as cultural symbols.	Use of public squares and interaction of people in public spaces are observed as social symbols.	Light brown and blue colors are observed.

The obtained visuals are tabulated through thematic analysis in terms of social symbols and cultural symbols, as specified in the fixed prompt, corresponding respectively to representation theory and visual culture theory. Through the theme of color preferences, the study aims to determine according to which understanding the Nano Banana Pro artificial intelligence model colors regions within its dataset.

Table 2. Dominant representation patterns in AI-generated provincial ımages

Theme	Dominant Indicators	Observed Trend
Cultural Symbols	Historical structures, religious architecture, monumental elements	AI represents cities through a framework of historical continuity
Social Symbols	Use of public squares, markets/bazaars, street lifen	Everyday public practices are brought to the foreground
Color Palette	Brown, blue, gray	An atmosphere grounded in geography and history is emphasized

In Table 1, within the theme of cultural symbols, cultural elements stand out in the majority of the cities. In provinces with a deep historical background such as İstanbul, İzmir, and Bursa, structures resembling mosques, bridges, fortresses, and caravanserais strongly represent traditional architectural elements. Together with this finding, it is observed that artificial intelligence prioritizes symbols based on historical continuity when defining provinces.

Within the theme of social symbols, distinct diversities emerge among cities. In provinces such as Gaziantep, Hatay, and Diyarbakır, which are prominent for culinary differences, elements related to food culture are noticeable. In coastal provinces such as Antalya, Mersin, and İzmir, coastal life, sea-related activities, and touristic social spaces are observed. In the Black Sea provinces, tea-drinking culture, fishing, and natural landscapes draw attention. In Central Anatolia and Eastern Anatolia provinces, elements such as square culture, plain street life, and traditional tradespeople appear in a limited manner. The visuals obtained indicate that artificial intelligence tends to interpret social representation practices through region-specific lifestyles.

According to the theme of color preferences, a pattern emerges indicating that provinces are rendered with palettes that align with their geographical characteristics. While blue, white, and light yellow tones predominate along the Mediterranean and Aegean coasts, green and gray tones become more prominent in the Black Sea region. In Central Anatolia, earth-toned colors stand out, whereas in Eastern and Southeastern Anatolia provinces, dominant hues such as orange and red are observed. Within the context of these color preferences, artificial intelligence develops representations in accordance with atmosphere. The extent to which the color palette reflects regional accuracy reveals that the artificial intelligence model possesses a strong capacity for atmospheric construction.

Table 1 can be explained within the framework of Hall's theory of representation through the concept of "stereotyping." According to Hall, stereotyping involves defining a complex entity through a limited number of simplified or exaggerated characteristics, thereby creating an entirely essentialist identity. Within the context of Mirzoeff's visual culture theory, the visuals in Table 1 become "images" that are reconfigured in a digital environment and distanced from reality itself. Within visual culture, they gain apparent visibility through touristic and historical figures.

In a general evaluation, the city representations and visual culture reflections presented in Table 1 can be grouped under three main tendencies. According to the first tendency, cultural symbols largely offer consistent representations. This tendency indicates that artificial intelligence performs strong cultural readings. According to the second tendency, social symbols vary across cities. In this respect, artificial intelligence employs a representational approach that is tied to local culture by dynamically following contemporary life. The third tendency is identified as regional coherence in color preferences. Accordingly, artificial intelligence produces visuals by reshaping them within a holistic framework in terms of atmospheric interpretation.

Table 3. Frequency and percentage density analysis of Table 1

Theme	Indicators	Frequency (f)	Percentage (%)
Cultural Symbols (Cultural Representation Theory)	Geographical and Natural Elements (Mountain, River, etc.)	26	32.10
	Traditional Civil Architecture (Mansion, House, Caravanserai)	24	29.63
	Religious Structures (Mosque, Minaret, etc.)	22	27.16
	Statues and Monuments	22	27.16
	Fortresses and City Walls	19	23.46
	Clock Towers	19	23.46
	Handicrafts and Production (Carpet, Industry, etc.)	15	18.52
	Historic Bridges and Arches	13	16.05
Social Symbols (Representation Theory)	Use of Public Space (Square, Street)	47	58.02
	Commercial Life (Market, Bazaar, Shopping)	42	51.85
	Food Culture and Socialization	25	30.86
	Coastal and Maritime Life	18	22.22
	Transportation (Tram, Ferry, etc.)	6	7.41

continued on following page

Table 3. Continued

Theme	Indicators	Frequency (f)	Percentage (%)
Color Preferences	Brown	58	71.60
	Blue / Turquoise	33	40.74
	Gray	32	39.51
	Green	31	38.27
	White	22	27.16
	Yellow	13	16.05
	Red / Brick	9	11.11
	Orange	7	8.64
	Black	5	6.17

Note: Since a single visual may include more than one category, the total percentages may exceed 100%.

Table 4. Thematic analysis example of the visuals generated for first-tier districts according to the SEGE (2025) report

Visual No.	Province - District	Generated Visual	Cultural Symbols (Visual Culture Theory)	Social Symbols (Representation Theory)	Color Preferences
6	İstanbul - Şişli		Museums, mosques, and skyscrapers in the background are observed as cultural symbols	The density of yellow taxis, the rush of business life, and shopping are observed as social symbols.	Yellow, gray, and red colors are observed.
7	Ankara - Çankaya		Atakule, Anıtkabir in the background, and modern state buildings are observed as cultural symbols.	Heavy urban traffic and the life of capital bureaucracy are observed as social symbols.	Orange, gray, and blue colors are observed.
8	İstanbul - Beşiktaş		Bridge, statue, and team flags are observed as cultural symbols.	Ferry pier density, supporter culture, and seaside cafés are observed as social symbols.	Black, white, and blue colors are observed.
9	İstanbul - Kadıköy		Bull statue, team flags, and ferries are observed as cultural symbols.	Meeting at the bull statue, ferry journeys, and bazaar crowds are observed as social symbols.	Yellow, blue, and orange colors are observed.
10	Ankara - Yenimahalle		Metro line, overpasses, and orderly apartment blocks are observed as cultural symbols.	Neighborhood market shopping and the use of public transportation are observed as social symbols.	Yellow, gray, and white colors are observed.

When Table 3 is examined, the Nano Banana Pro artificial intelligence model most frequently draws on natural elements (32.10%) and architectural elements (29.63%) within the context of visual culture theory when constructing provincial indicators. Within the framework of representation theory, the artificial intelligence model uses indicators such as the use of public space (58.02%) and commercial activity (51.85%), which are part of everyday life representation dynamics. In terms of color preferences, the dominance of brown tones indicates that the artificial intelligence model relies on a dataset that predominantly associates the provinces of Türkiye with historical or earth-related elements.

Within the context of Hall's representation theory, Table 3 demonstrates that representation is not carried out through mere reflection but rather resembles a process of construction. Instead of reflecting the existing perception of the modern city, the artificial intelligence model constructs a new urban reality by emphasizing traditional codes. Within the framework of Mirzoeff's visual culture theory, this situation indicates that technology creates a new cultural perception by deciding what is to be seen and what is not.

Table 5. Representation tendencies in first-tier (SEGE) districts

Dimension	Dominant Representatio
Cultural Code	Modern architecture, skyscrapers, transportation infrastructure
Social Life	Consumption, mobility, leisure practices
Visual Language	Global / metropolitan aesthetics
Color Palette	Gray – Blue – Yellow

When the theme of cultural symbols in Table 3, which primarily focuses on Türkiye's western regions, is examined, it is seen that—alongside elements such as mosques and fortresses found in the province-based analyses in Table 1—structures such as skyscrapers and marinas are also encountered. In the context of Hall's theory of representation, this indicates that the concept of the "metropolis," as provided by provinces such as İstanbul, Ankara, and İzmir, exists within the artificial intelligence dataset in association with an understanding of "Western" provincial aesthetics. Within the framework of Mirzoeff's visual culture theory, this situation may suggest that the artificial intelligence's perception of development progresses in parallel with vertical architecture and reinforced-concrete structures. While visualizing "developed" districts, Nano Banana Pro renders local cultural elements less salient and instead includes elements dominated by a globalized perception of development, such as skyscraper silhouettes. This is particularly observed in the Şişli and Çankaya districts of İstanbul and Ankara.

When the theme of social symbols is examined, districts are visualized in terms of lifestyle through representations centered on traditional socialization, the creation of public spaces, and production–consumption dynamics. Within the context of Hall's theory, Nano Banana Pro draws on representations of mobility and consumer society, defining places such as shopping malls and metro lines as "spaces of speed." In districts such as Beşiktaş, Kadıköy, and Karşıyaka, elements such as supporter culture, ferry piers, and seaside cafés are observed. This indicates, within the framework of Mirzoeff's visual culture theory, the presence of a culture oriented toward perceptions of leisure time; according to Hall, it also reveals the visualization of a secular lifestyle representation. In the case of the Esenyurt district in İstanbul, the emphasis on "Syrian cuisine" demonstrates that the model codes the concept of "multiculturalism" in relation to migration as interpreted by Nano Banana Pro.

When the theme of color preferences is examined, Nano Banana Pro shifts from the dominance of brown palettes used in Table 1 to a color palette in Table 3 dominated by blue and gray tones. To visualize representations such as concrete, asphalt, and roadways and to reflect urbanization culture, gray tones are used in districts such as Gebze, Güngören, and Ataşehir. In particular, blue tones are employed by the Nano Banana Pro artificial intelligence model to represent maritime tourism and marina culture in coastal districts such as Bodrum, Kadıköy, and Alanya. Yellow and red tones are used by the artificial intelligence model to visualize vehicle headlights and solar angles and to indicate the districts' alignment with the concept of the "city that never sleeps."

When Table 3 is examined within the context of representation theory, the artificial intelligence model defines the top-ranked districts with modern codes while classifying other districts with traditional codes. This creates a visual contrast. From the perspective of Mirzoeff's visual culture theory, the top-ranked districts embody a more globalized visual culture perception and, by shedding local characteristics, represent a standardized metropolitan image.

It is observed that Nano Banana Pro visualizes districts with first-tier socio-economic development levels by distancing them from Türkiye's "Eastern" identity and by using elements that represent the visual language of capitalism. Rather than emphasizing the continuity of cultural elements, the model appears to produce visuals dominated by an understanding aligned with global standards.

Table 6. Frequency and percentage density analysis of Table 3

Theme	**Indicators**	**Frequency (f)**	**Percentage (%)**
Cultural Symbols (Visual Culture Theory)	Historical and Religious Structures (Fortress, Mosque, Historic Monument)	39	58.21
	Urban Icons and Monuments (Clock Tower, Statue)	27	40.30
	Transportation Infrastructure (Metro, Tram, Bridge)	25	37.31
	Coastal and Maritime Elements (Marina, Harbor, Coastline)	23	34.33
	Modern Architecture and Urbanization (Skyscraper, Plaza, Apartment)	18	26.87
	Nature and Landscape (Park, Trees, Lake)	14	20.90
	Industrial and Production Structures	8	11.94
Social Symbols (Representation Theory)	Leisure, Food & Beverage, and Socialization (Café, Restaurant, Walking)	46	68.66

continued on following page

Table 6. Continued

Theme	Indicators	Frequency (f)	Percentage (%)
	Consumption and Shopping Culture (Shopping Mall, Bazaar)	31	46.27
	Urban Mobility and Transportation (Traffic, Public Transport)	20	29.85
	Tourism and Holiday Activities	17	25.37
	Distinct Social Groups (Students, Supporters, Workers)	7	10.45
Color Preferences	Gray	39	58.21
	Blue	38	56.72
	Yellow	22	32.84
	Red	20	29.85
	Orange	19	28.36
	White	19	28.36
	Green	18	26.87
	Brown	11	16.42
	Black	1	1.49

Note: Since a single visual may include more than one category, the total percentages may exceed 100%.

Table 7. Thematic analysis example of the visuals generated for second-tier districts according to the SEGE (2025) report

Visual No.	Province - District	Generated Visual	Cultural Symbols (Visual Culture Theory)	Social Symbols (Representation Theory)	Color Preferences
11	Manisa - Yunusemre		Tulip sculpture, mountain landscape, mansions, and mesir paste carts are observed as cultural symbols	Mesir paste, the municipal square, and the use of public transportation are observed as social symbols.	Green, yellow, and red colors are observed.
12	Tekirdağ - Çorlu		The historic clock tower, industrial chimneys, sunflower motifs, and "Çorlu Köftecisi" signs are observed as cultural symbols.	Meatball-eating culture, square traffic, and industrial city life are observed as social symbols.	Yellow, gray, and red colors are observed.
13	Kocaeli - Başiskele		Port cranes, industrial facilities, fishing boats, and mountains in the background are observed as cultural symbols.	Fishermen, walking along the coastal band, and industrial life are observed as social symbols.	Blue, gray, and orange colors are observed.
14	Kayseri - Kocasinan		A statue, mountain silhouette, külliye, and tram line are observed as cultural symbols.	Pastırma and sucuk shopping, modern transportation by tram, and the use of the historic square are observed as social symbols.	Yellow, gray, and white colors are observed.
15	Muğla - Menteşe		Whitewashed houses and a "Muğla Köftesi" shop are observed as cultural symbols.	Street-side restaurant culture and conversations among local residents are observed as social symbols.	White, brown, and blue colors are observed.

When Table 4 is examined, it is observed that while visualizing developed districts, artificial intelligence employs modern transportation infrastructure (37.31%) and vertical architecture (26.87%) as cultural references. In representations of social life, the high rate of traditional public square usage observed in Table 2 is replaced by elements related to leisure and food–beverage habits (68.66%) and consumer culture (46.27%). In color palettes, a shift is also observed: the dominance of brown tones in Table 2 gives way to an increase in gray (58.21%) and blue (56.72%) tones in Table 4, which emphasize urban symbols.

When Table 4 is analyzed within the framework of Hall's theory of representation, meanings are shaped and fixed through specific indicators. As a result of these indicators, the concept of development is associated with material signs. From the perspective of visual culture theory, Table 4 contains visuals that convey a perception of modernity and includes representations indicating that spaces of consumer culture have transformed into sites of spectacle.

Table 8. Representation tendencies in second-tier (SEGE) districts

Dimension	Dominant Representatio
Cultural Code	Traditional architecture, local production
Social Life	Public square, local market, everyday sociality
Logic of Representation	Emphasis on "locality" and tradition
Color Palette	Brown – Green – Yellow

Within the scope of Table 7, the visuals generated by Nano Banana 3 Pro for the second-tier districts examined and derived from the SEGE Report (2025) data move away from a metropolitan lifestyle identity compared to Table 4 and contain more local elements. The visuals analyzed between 149 and 321 abandon the global city image of the first-tier districts presented in Table 4 and instead feature agriculture, industry, and local food elements. In this context, an emphasis on "Anatolia" becomes prominent.

When examined within the framework of visual culture theory, the visuals provide a basis for the concept of "identification." In this regard, districts such as Manisa–Akhisar and Balıkesir–Ayvalık can be cited as examples of the AI model identifying regions through agriculture and food products and the notions for which these regions are known. The placement of elements such as "cotton" in Aydın–Söke, "grapes" in Manisa–Salihli, and "olives" in Balıkesir–Burhaniye at the main focal point of the visual indicates that the AI model presents local identity elements as commodities. This also exemplifies the reduction of the complex structure of districts to a single product; notably, the presence of this reductionist representational pattern in the texts is observed through fictional signs added by the AI to the visuals, such as "Capital of Olives" or "Capital of Grapes."

From the perspective of representation theory, town squares and bazaars replace the concept of shopping malls observed in Table 4 as elements of social life representation. In districts such as Yozgat–Merkez, Tokat–Merkez, and Bilecik–Bozüyük included in the data of Table 5, social symbols are seen to be shaped around "market squares," "local product sales," and "tea garden culture." The AI model draws attention to traditional communal life representations that are distant from individualization and emphasizes a calm lifestyle through visualizations of people waiting at market stalls.

Industrial representation constitutes one of the most striking themes of Table 5. In industrially intensive districts such as Kocaeli–Dilovası, Tekirdağ–Çerkezköy, Manisa–Soma, and Zonguldak–Ereğli, cultural symbols are identified as being coded through "factory chimneys," "mining towers," and "people in workers' overalls." The AI model approaches these districts through representations of industrial production zones and produces visuals that emphasize the identity of worker individuals.

In spatial representations, a hybrid structure that intertwines rural and urban forms is observed. In districts such as Antalya–Kumluca and Mersin–Silifke, the integration of agricultural representations with the city center indicates that nature is characterized by the AI not merely as a background element but as a representation of economic life.

Hall emphasizes representation through its constitutive role. In this context, the visuals of the districts in Table 7 are reconstructed using easily recognizable and consumable symbols rather than culturally deep elements. Within the framework of Mirzoeff's visual culture theory, districts are transformed into commodities, being processed as marketable objects within visual culture.

According to the theme of color preferences, warm color tones are observed to be dominant. Yellow and green tones, which represent agriculture, are used in these districts. In preferences for house and road colors, white paint and stone-colored gray tones stand out. Red tones, associated with roof tiles, are used on the roofs of historical buildings, while shades of yellow are observed to convey the theme of daylight. The colors of local products are prominent within the palette; in particular, districts featuring representations of "coppersmiths," commonly associated with eastern regions, can be exemplified by Adıyaman–Merkez and Kahramanmaraş–Dulkadiroğlu.

Table 9. Frequency and percentage density analysis of Table 5

Theme	Indicators	Frequency (f)	Percentage (%)
Cultural Symbols (Visual Culture Theory)	Traditional Architecture and Historical Structures (Mosque, Mansion, Castle)	131	75.72
	City Identity Signs and Slogans ("Capital of Olives," etc	72	41.62
	Agricultural Production and Local Products (Cotton, Olives, Grapes)	71	41.04
	Natural Geography (Mountain, River, Lake)	59	34.10
	City Square Statues (Atatürk, Efe, Product Statues)	47	27.17
	Industrial and Mining Elements (Factory Chimneys, Mining)	22	12.72
Social Symbols (Representation Theory)	Local Trade and Market Culture (Neighborhood Market, Tradespeople)	112	64.74

continued on following page

Table 9. Continued

Theme	Indicators	Frequency (f)	Percentage (%)
	Traditional Socialization (Tea Gardens, Coffeehouses)	57	32.95
	Production-Oriented Life (Agricultural Labor, Industrial Shifts)	44	25.43
	Coastal and Seaside Life	40	23.12
	Local Gastronomy and Street Food (Meatballs, Toast)	26	15.03
Color Preferences	Yellow	86	49.71
	Brown	78	45.09
	Green	72	41.62
	Red	69	39.88
	Gray	65	37.57
	Blue	65	37.57
	White	34	19.65
	Orange	22	12.72
	Black	4	2.31

Note: Since a single visual may include more than one category, the total percentages may exceed 100%.

The data in Table 6 indicate that when constructing second-tier districts, artificial intelligence moves away from a global city aesthetic (skyscrapers, shopping malls) and instead turns toward traditional architecture (75.72%) and a local production-oriented identity. In particular, the high use of agricultural production (41.04%) and city identity signs emphasizing this production (41.62%) (e.g., "Capital of Olives") demonstrates that the AI encodes these districts with the identity of "producing Anatolia." In social life, shopping mall culture is overwhelmingly replaced by local trade and market culture (64.74%), while in the color palette, tones symbolizing agriculture—yellow (49.71%) and green (41.62%)—along with brown (45.09%), which signifies historical texture, once again become dominant. This table reveals that AI algorithms construct the image of the "periphery" or the "developing city" through production, marketplaces, and traditional socialization practices.

The use of signs, within the framework of representation theory, functions to fix meaning—that is, by classifying the polysemous structure of the visuals, it defines exactly what the district is for the viewer. From the perspective of visual culture theory, this demonstrates that culture is not only about seeing but also about how the symbols identified in a district carry meaning through written language.

DISCUSSION

The data from Tables 1 and 2 indicate that when representing Turkey's 81 provinces, artificial intelligence shapes the cities from a traditionalist perspective rooted in the past rather than through modern urbanization dynamics. Even in metropolitan provinces such as Adana, Erzurum, and Diyarbakır, elements such as historical city walls, stone bridges, and figures in traditional clothing are employed. This situation is directly associated with the concept of stereotyping. By distancing the provinces from their industrial or sociological realities, Nano Banana Pro reiterates Mirzoeff's argument that the visual is not merely a physical element but also concerns "what is made visible." The model visualizes the modern life dynamics of local populations as "pre-modern," while simultaneously imposing an external, tourist-oriented gaze.

The second point of discussion concerns the representation of "development" that emerges in Tables 3 and 4. In the visuals of socio-economically advanced districts ranked at the top, such as Şişli, Çankaya, and Kadıköy, historical elements are replaced by skyscrapers, office towers, and traffic lights. The human figures in these districts correspond not to calm individuals drinking tea, but to representations of modern individuals rushing through business life. This situation reflects, within the national context, Hall's notion of "the West and the rest," in which what is developed is associated with a Western urban form, while the remaining regions are reflected through a traditional urban form. Within the framework of Mirzoeff's critique of global visual culture, these visuals define and reshape images in which "capital equals the global city."

Third, the data in Tables 5 and 6 show that cities cease to be living spaces and instead become "commodified" contents that are easily consumable and able to find a place in the market. Districts turn into brands presented outward rather than spaces lived in by local communities. From the perspective of representation theory, this indicates a weakening of the cultural depth of space and the creation of a perception of the "presented space." Mirzoeff's idea that visual culture is a process of constructing a worldview demonstrates that artificial intelligence reveals this process by simplifying reality. The produced visuals do not reflect the actual realities of regions in Türkiye; instead, they recirculate accumulated "ideal" and "standardized" representations within digital memory. In this respect, Nano Banana Pro emerges not only as a technological innovation but also as a critical visual culture issue concerning how social memory and cultural identity are transformed in the digital environment.

CONCLUSION AND RECOMMENDATIONS

With the integration of artificial intelligence technologies into visual production processes, a fundamental transformation is being observed in the stages through which cultural representations are constructed and circulated. This study, which examines regional images of Türkiye through the Nano Banana Pro artificial intelligence model, aims to demonstrate that artificial intelligence is not merely a technical visualization tool but also an agent that reconstructs social memory. In this context, the research analyzes the symbolic representations employed by digital algorithms when visualizing regions and the codes underlying these representations within the framework of Stuart Hall's representation theory and Mirzoeff's visual culture theory. As a primary objective, the study interrogates whether the "Türkiye" image produced by artificial intelligence is derived from physical reality or composed of digitally constructed simulations. The findings reveal that the visual production process of the artificial intelligence model is not objectively neutral; on the contrary, it reproduces existing cultural biases and traditional perspectives within the digital sphere.

In response to the first research question—"Through which cultural symbols and visual indicators does the Nano Banana Pro artificial intelligence model represent cities in Türkiye?"—it is observed that Nano Banana Pro largely constrains provincial images within a historical framework. As a result of analyses covering all 81 provinces, cities are centered not on their modern appearances but on elements belonging to the past, such as mosques, caravanserais, fortifications, and historical bridges. Across a broad geography stretching from Edirne to Kars, the dynamic structures of urban life are disregarded, and instead a collective digital spatial memory is adopted. Within the artificial intelligence model's database, perceptions of the "Turkish city" and the "historical city" are clearly evident. In this context, the algorithm renders modern and contemporary architecture invisible through visual selectivity, presenting historical elements as the sole visible reality.

In response to the second research question—"To what extent do social symbols and color preferences in AI-generated urban images reflect regional differences?"—the analysis indicates that Nano Banana Pro encodes and visualizes socio-economic development through a Western-centered perception of modernity. Accordingly, in first-tier developed districts, historical texture gives way to vertical architecture. The AI model, which fixes development to vertical architecture and consumer culture, defines second-tier districts through agricultural production and local products. This situation is observed as a reduction of regional identity to commodities, once again disregarding dynamic urban life.

According to the artificial intelligence model, blue and gray tones are used as the dominant color palette in districts and provinces classified as developed. In contrast, regions defined by the same model as developing districts and provinces are confined to a "provincial" identity through yellow and earth-toned color palettes. At the same time, Nano Banana Pro provides written narration through signboards in order to limit the multiple meanings of regional structures.

The theoretical contribution of the study can be summarized as demonstrating that AI-supported visual production tools draw not only on aesthetic elements but also on cultural and ideological representations, and that these elements reopen visual culture theory and representation theory to discussion within a digital artificial intelligence context. In this framework, representations maintain their validity as they shift from human perception to machine production and through media transition. This situation, which can also be described as an artificial transition, introduces a new stage to the culture of visuality shaped by an artificial perception of reality. Artificial intelligence does not engage in creative action; instead, it relies on dominant codes within its database, exhibiting an imitative and status-quo-preserving orientation. Accordingly, a critical perspective is offered to visual culture studies, as digital consumption produces new identity images that function not as a democratic act but as a global visual marketplace. This structure poses a threat to local originality.

There are certain limitations to the study in terms of its scope and methodology. The research is limited to the use of the Nano Banana Pro artificial intelligence model only. Visuals produced by other popular AI models may potentially contain different aesthetic codes and representations, as each model has its own distinct training data and algorithmic architecture. Therefore, the findings obtained cannot be generalized to all generative AI models.

As a second limitation, the study focuses on urban images and socio-economic development variables and does not address demographic structures—such as gender or age—that artificial intelligence might employ when visualizing representations. The fact that the analyzed visuals may be generated differently by the AI in each iteration constitutes a limitation regarding the stability of the findings; however, the study attempts to overcome this limitation by identifying recurring motifs. Finally, the research is confined to visual content analysis and does not include an analysis that measures audience perceptions of the visuals.

The recommendations that can be offered for future studies are aimed at overcoming these limitations and deepening the research. In subsequent studies, it is anticipated that new research may be conducted comparing how different artificial intelligence models represent Türkiye. Such comparisons would enable a clearer understanding of the training data of these algorithms and the cultural predispositions embedded within different AI models.

Research examining how AI-generated urban visuals are perceived by local residents and tourists would provide an experimental pathway and shed light on the measurement of visual perception. Another important issue concerns how artificial intelligence addresses the concept of cultural heritage and to what extent it preserves historical authenticity in digital restoration projects. Finally, it is recommended that local governments develop AI literacy strategies to manage digital representations of regions and that these initiatives be supported by academic research. In the age of artificial intelligence, questioning visual perception depends on the ability to critically evaluate what algorithms present to us.

REFERENCES

Akay, A. (2007). Toplumbilim, görsel kültür özel sayısı. *Toplum ve Bilim*, •••, 22.

Aslan, E. (2019). Yapay zekâ resimleri ve sanatın başkalaşan mecrası üzerine. *Güzel Sanatlar Enstitüsü Dergisi*, (42), 231–242. DOI: 10.32547/ataunigsed.516382

Aykut, A. (2013). Güncel sistemden estetik eğitimine bir öneri: Görsel kültür kuramı. *Electronic Turkish Studies*, *8*(9), 705–714. DOI: 10.7827/TurkishStudies.5280

Aziz, A. (2015). *Sosyal bilimlerde araştırma ve yöntem teknikleri*. Nobel Akademik Yayıncılık Eğitim Danışmanlık.

Başak, R. (2021). Görsel sanatlar eğitiminde ideoloji tartışmaları temelinde görsel kültür kuramı ve materyal kültürü. *E-Kafkas Journal of Educational Research*, *8*(2), 198–221. DOI: 10.30900/kafkasegt.957360

Bilgin, N. (2006). *Sosyal bilimlerde içerik analizi: Teknikler ve örnek çalışmalar*. Siyasal Kitabevi.

Canan, S., & Acungil, M. (2018). *Dijital gelecekte insan kalmak*. Nefes Yayıncılık.

Candemir, T. (2006). *"Çağdaş Teknolojinin Sanat Dallarına Etkileri Ve Yardımcı Yazılımlarla Bilgisayarda Resim Yapmak"*. 6 th International Educational Technology Conference, (pp.357-365).

Davis, P., Napole, A., Reddy, C., Palepu, S. K., Wu, A. Q., Mannam, S. S., Gajjar, A. A., Jabarkheel, R., Ajmera, S., Ahmad, H., Scott, K. W., Sioutas, G., Shekhtman, O., Kandregula, S., Rahmani, R., Catapano, J. S., Burkhardt, J. K., & Srinivasan, V. M. (2025). Systematic evaluation of AI-based text-to-image models for generating medical illustrations in neurosurgery: A multi-stage comparative study. *Clinical Neurology and Neurosurgery*, *257*, 109039. DOI: 10.1016/j.clineuro.2025.109039 PMID: 40614319

de Carvalho Souza, M. E., & Weigang, L. (2025). Grok, Gemini, ChatGPT and DeepSeek: Comparison and applications in conversational artificial intelligence. *Inteligencia Artificial*, *2*(1). Advance online publication. DOI: 10.5281/zenodo.14885243

Elgammal, A. (2018, October 26). *AI-Art-Creative-Process* [Graph]. The Conversation. Retrieved February 15, 2026 https://theconversation.com/when-the-line-between-machine-and-artist-becomes-blurred-103149

Göktaş, L. S. (2023). ChatGPT uzaktan eğitim sınavlarında başarılı olabilir mi? Turizm alanında doğruluk ve doğrulama üzerine bir araştırma. *Journal of Tourism and Gastronomy Studies*, *11*(2), 892–905. DOI: 10.21325/jotags.2023.1224

Google Gemini Artificial Intelligence Model. (2023, December 06). [Screenshot]. Retrieved February 15, 2026 https://blog.google/technology/ai/google-gemini-ai/?utm_source=tldrai#sundar-note

Güçlüer, S. B. (2024). Stuart Hall'un yaklaşımıyla: Medyanın etkisinde Ciguli'nin temsili ve kimliği. *Online Journal of Music Sciences*, *9*(2), 676–687. DOI: 10.31811/ojomus.1522355

Güney, E., & Yavuz, H. (2020). Yapay Zekâ ile Sanatsal Üretim Pratiğinde Sanatçının Rolü ve Değişen Sanat Olgusu. *Sanat ve Tasarım Dergisi*, (26), 415–439.

Hall, S. (1997a). Introduction. In Hall, S. (Ed.), *Representation: Cultural representations and signifying practices* (pp. 1–12). Sage Publications.

Hall, S. (1997b). The work of representation. In Hall, S. (Ed.), *Representation: Cultural representations and signifying practices* (pp. 13–74). Sage Publications.

Kara, D. (2003). Sanat Eğitiminde Disiplinlerarası Sanat. *Yapı Mimarlık Tasarım Kültür Sanat*, 108-112.

Kaya, Y. (2017). Güncel Sanatta Yeni Bir Yaklaşım Olarak "Melezlik". *Sanat ve Tasarım Dergisi*, (20), 165–182. DOI: 10.18603/sanatvetasarim.370751

Mich, L., & Garigliano, R. (2023). ChatGPT for e-tourism: A technological perspective. *Information Technology & Tourism*, *25*(1), 1–12. DOI: 10.1007/s40558-023-00248-x

Mirzoeff, N. (2015). *How to see the world.* Pelican Books.

Pirim, A. G. H. (2006). Yapay zekâ. *Yaşar Üniversitesi E-Dergisi*, *1*(1), 81–93.

Sağır, M., Güdül, A., & Taştekin, A. U. A. (2025). Tur rotası oluşturmada yapay zekâ uygulamalarının karşılaştırılması: ChatGPT ve Gemini örneği. *Selçuk Üniversitesi Akşehir Meslek Yüksekokulu Sosyal Bilimler Dergisi*, (19), 1–12.

Socio-Economic Development Index (SEGE). (2025). *T.C. Sanayi ve Teknoloji Bakanlığı*. Retrieved February 15, 2026 https://www.sanayi.gov.tr/merkez-birimi/b94224510b7b/sege

Yurtseven, N. B. (2023). Wakandalının Kültürel Kimliği: Black Panther Filmi Üzerine Bir Temsil İncelemesi. *4. BOYUT Medya ve Kültürel Çalışmalar Dergisi*, *0*(23), 1–21. DOI: 10.26650/4boyut.2023.1340900

Chapter 7
Speculative Design in the Age of AI: A Comparative Visual Rhetorical Analysis

Yasemin Kayabaşı
http://orcid.org/0000-0002-6647-778X
Faculty of Art and Design, Department of Digital Game Design, Burdur Mehmet Akif Ersoy University, Turkey

ABSTRACT

Speculative design is a critical design approach that aims to question existing social and technological orders through images of alternative futures. The integration of generative AI tools into design practices is opening up a new arena of discussion regarding the visual strategies of this critical practice. This study aims to make this transformation visible by examining speculative design projects produced before and after the era of generative AI through a comparative visual rhetorical analysis. The analysis is based on a framework that combines Barthes' concepts of denotation, connotation, and myth with Aristotle's concept of pathos and Auger's perceptual bridge approach. The findings indicate that generative AI tools can, in some cases, reproduce dominant visual aesthetics, thereby creating tendencies toward aesthetic convergence. It has been observed, however, that projects that position AI as a critical design object can preserve the critical potential of speculative design.

INTRODUCTION

Imagine a designer entering the following command into an AI-powered visual generation tool: *'Visualize the daily lives of people living in a city grappling with the*

DOI: 10.4018/979-8-2600-2711-0.ch007

climate crisis in 2047 from a critical perspective.' Within seconds, dozens of images appear on the screen, all featuring a sky in muted tones, figures wearing plastic masks, and crumbling urban skylines. These images appear technically impressive, aesthetically consistent, and compositionally strong. However, closer inspection reveals that the outputs in question are merely variations of one another. Artificial intelligence tools operate by learning the most common patterns of contemporary visual culture. In an experimental study by Hintze et al. (2025), image-generation systems interacting without human intervention were observed to converge rapidly on a narrow set of visual motifs, regardless of their initial inputs. Researchers refer to this phenomenon as 'visual elevator music': just as elevator music converges on the safest and most mundane sound, AI systems drift towards the most dominant visual motifs in their datasets during iterative generation cycles. Consequently, the issue is not merely a matter of visual generation speed. The real question is: are AI tools truly expanding our capacity to imagine the future, or are they limiting this imagination by reproducing it within the statistical averages of past datasets?

This question opens a critical debate over design's capacity to generate social critique. Speculative design, as defined by Dunne and Raby (2013), is a practice that questions rather than validates existing reality, unsettling the viewer and inviting them to contemplate alternative futures. In this practice, meaning is produced through a visual rhetorical strategy that breaks, refills, or reverses familiar visual codes. The concept of the 'perceptual bridge' developed by Auger (2013) explains how this strategy operates: speculative design triggers critical thinking by deliberately subverting the viewer's familiar visual expectations. Generative AI tools, however, tend to reinforce dominant visual expectations because they are trained on large datasets. In other words, AI tools may reconstruct the very thing speculative design seeks to subvert. This structural tension has not yet been sufficiently addressed in the literature (Østvold et al., 2024). The visual rhetorical function of speculative design becomes clearer when examined through Barthes's (1977) framework of denotation, connotation, and myth. According to Barthes (1977), visual messages contain multiple layers of meaning; at the mythical level, dominant cultural values are presented as 'natural' and 'normal', thereby serving an ideological function. It is precisely at this point that the critical potential of speculative design comes to the fore: by subverting the visual codes of the prevailing myth, it compels the viewer to step outside the familiar. Artificial intelligence tools, however, tend to reproduce what they have learned through statistical dominance and, by operating in the opposite direction to this process, risk reinforcing the very myth that speculative design seeks to challenge (Hintze et al., 2025).

This study aims to fill this gap by examining six speculative design projects produced before (2007–2015) and after (2024–2026) the widespread adoption of generative AI tools through a comparative visual rhetoric analysis. From the pre-generative AI era, the selected works include Technological Dreams Series (Dunne & Raby, 2007), Facestate (Metahaven, 2011), and TBD Catalog (Near Future Laboratory, 2012). From the post-generative AI era, the projects AI Newspaper (Near Future Laboratory, 2024), Design Against the Machine (Müller, 2024), and Latent Spacecraft (Beguš et al., 2026) are included in the analysis. The central research question is: How does the proliferation of generative AI tools transform the visual rhetorical strategies of speculative design and, consequently, its critical potential?

In the literature, speculative design theory, visual rhetoric analysis, and the impact of artificial intelligence on creative practices have largely progressed as separate strands. Studies addressing speculative design at a theoretical level do not incorporate the dimension of artificial intelligence; conversely, research examining the impact of artificial intelligence on design does not center on visual rhetoric and critical potential. The intersection of these three strands has not been directly addressed, and this study aims to fill this gap. The study is structured as follows: the second chapter presents the theoretical framework, the third chapter outlines the methodology, the fourth chapter presents the findings and discussion, and the fifth chapter presents the conclusions.

THEORETICAL FRAMEWORK

Speculative and Critical Design

Speculative design began to take shape in the mid-1990s at the Royal College of Art (RCA) in London, developed by Anthony Dunne and Fiona Raby. The concept of critical design was first introduced in Dunne's (1999) book *Hertzian Tales* and subsequently developed within a broader framework in *Design Noir* (Dunne and Raby, 2001). Dunne and Raby (2013) clearly articulated that speculative design does not aim to "predict the future," but rather to suggest that it is possible to reimagine the present through "what if?" questions. Dunne and Raby developed the A/B Manifesto to make the distinction between speculative and traditional design visible. In this manifesto, while traditional design reinforces the existing system, speculative design questions it (Dunne and Raby, 2013). Johannessen, Keitsch, and Pettersen (2019) conceptualize this distinction through three core functions. Reshaping existing perceptions, opening up a platform for social debate, and shifting the designer's role from problem-solving to problem-finding. In this context, speculative design is defined not only as a practice but also as a normative stance. Speculative design intersects with a series of related yet distinct conceptual fields. Among these fields, design fiction, adversarial design, and transition design stand out. Bleecker (2022) defines design fiction as a practice in which design, scientific fact, and science fiction converge. In design fiction, design objects transform into carriers of narratives about a possible future rather than merely offering functional solutions. DiSalvo's (2012) concept of adversarial design, on the other hand, explores how design can be positioned as a tool for political intervention. This approach emphasizes design's capacity to make existing power relations visible and open them up for debate, aligning directly with the critical function of speculative design. Irwin's (2015) "transition design," on the other hand, combines this critical practice with the goals of sustainability-focused social transformation. It shifts the designer's role from immediate problem-solver to architect of long-term systemic change. These three approaches sustain the critical and transformative potential of speculative design across different contexts and through various tools. Auger (2013) conducted an in-depth examination of the theoretical foundations of speculative design and developed the concept of the "perceptual bridge." According to this concept, the success of a speculative design proposal depends on the connection it establishes with the viewer being both sufficiently familiar and sufficiently unsettling. Without this tension, the critical potential of speculative design cannot be realized. Auger's framework has become a defining reference point for subsequent researchers. Cardenas Cordova et al. (2025), in a systematic literature review examining the speculative design process, demonstrated that this field has found applications in numerous disciplines, including human-computer interaction, urban planning, fashion, and health. In the context of graphic design and speculative practice, Skjulstad and Rynning (2015) presented a pioneering study that approaches visual identity design education within a speculative framework. Rynning (2017), meanwhile, demonstrated how speculative graphic design can serve as a tool for interpreting issues in Western societies through three student projects. It demonstrates that speculative graphic design can generate social critique by consciously transforming the codes of visual identity. This approach paves the way for the practice of deliberately appropriating and reinterpreting the dominant corporate visual language, as seen in Metahaven's Facestate project.

Visual Rhetoric: Barthes and Aristotle

Speculative design is defined not only as a conceptual practice but also as a discipline that employs visual tools to render abstract ideas concrete and perceptible (Auger, 2013). Roland Barthes (1977) demonstrates that images are never independent of the signifier. He explains how denotation and connotation encompass one another through a structural analysis. According to Barthes, a visual carries three layers of meaning: the linguistic message, the encoded iconic message (connotation), and the unencoded iconic message (denotation). At the level of myth, cultural values are presented as "natural" and "normal," thereby serving an ideological function of naturalization. The critical potential of speculative design comes into play precisely at this point: by breaking the visual myth, it transports the viewer beyond the familiar. Mitchell (1994) extends Barthes' structural framework to a cultural and historical dimension through the concept of the "pictorial turn" in the field of visual representation. According to Mitchell, it is emphasized that visual representation must be read not only through language but also through its own unique logic, and that the discursive power of the visual is gaining increasing importance. This perspective enables evaluation of the visual strategy of speculative design not merely in formal terms but also within the context of cultural power relations. Aristotle (2006) identified three fundamental strategies in persuasion: ethos (character), pathos (emotion), and logos (reason). He noted that these elements form the foundation of rhetoric. Over time, this classical approach has not been limited to spoken and written discourse but has also become a defining framework in visual representations. As images increasingly replace words in modern communication environments, visual rhetoric has emerged as a distinct field of study (Foss, 2005, p. 146). According to Foss (2005), visual rhetoric is an interdisciplinary approach that examines how visual messages intended to persuade audiences are structured and the formal and semantic strategies employed in their creation.

Barthes's semiotic framework and Aristotle's rhetorical approach serve as complementary analytical layers in this study. While Barthes explains the mechanisms of meaning production in a visual through the levels of denotation, connotation, and myth, Aristotle's concept of pathos addresses the emotional impact of this meaning production on the audience. The critical power of speculative design is not limited to deconstructing the visual myth. It is also directly related to the sense of unease and questioning that this deconstruction creates in the viewer. For this reason, pathos is treated as a separate analytical category in this study.

Generative AI and Aesthetic Normalization

The incorporation of generative AI tools into design practice carries the risk of narrowing visual diversity while expanding visual production capacity. Because AI tools rely on built-in datasets and algorithms, they tend to produce repetitive and homogeneous stylistic solutions. This convergence phenomenon, experimentally demonstrated by Hintze et al. (2025) (a trend researchers refer to as "visual elevator music"), can be situated within a theoretical framework through the concept of aesthetic normalization. Aesthetic normalization refers to the process by which a tool's structural logic reinforces dominant visual patterns, thereby hindering the production of alternative visual strategies. The origins of this trend point to a deeper cultural-critical issue that goes beyond a mere technical problem. Adorno & Horkheimer (2002) have demonstrated, within the framework of the concept of the culture industry, how cultural practices based on mass production converge toward standardized forms and how this process erodes critical thinking. Generative AI tools can be interpreted as an algorithmic continuation of this process. Operating according to the principle of statistical dominance, these systems automatically reproduce dominant visual patterns in datasets and carry the homogenizing logic of the culture industry into the digital production environment. Crawford (2021) argues that artificial intelligence is not a neutral tool but operates by internalizing specific social and cultural power relations. Bender et al. (2021), meanwhile, have documented that large language models tend to statistically reproduce dominant cultural patterns and that this process can yield homogenizing results. A similar structural logic applies to visual production systems as well.

The integration of generative artificial intelligence tools into design practice carries the risk of narrowing visual diversity while simultaneously expanding visual production capacity. Since AI tools rely on embedded datasets and algorithms, they tend to produce repetitive and homogeneous stylistic solutions. This convergence phenomenon, experimentally demonstrated by Hintze et al. (2025) (a trend the researchers refer to as "visual elevator music"), can be situated within a theoretical framework through the concept of aesthetic normalization. Aesthetic normalization refers to the process by which a tool's structural logic reinforces dominant visual patterns, thereby hindering the generation of alternative visual strategies. This structural tension between speculative design and AI tools has not yet been sufficiently addressed in the literature. Østvold et al. (2024) demonstrate that while AI in speculative design offers opportunities, the resulting visuals are often devoid of context and fail to inspire. This finding indicates that AI is in a structural conflict with the fundamental strategy of speculative design.

Based on this, the study's central argument is formulated as follows: The visual rhetorical strategy is the foundation of speculative design's critical potential. In the pre-generative AI era, this strategy was the direct product of the designer's conscious choice. In the post-generative AI era, however, the structural logic of the tools risks transforming this conscious choice into an automatic tendency. This transformation also fundamentally alters who decides what is made visible and how it is questioned (Østvold et al., 2024).

METHODOLOGY

This study adopts a qualitative comparative visual rhetoric analysis method structured around Barthes's (1977) theory of visual rhetoric. A qualitative approach constitutes the most appropriate methodological option for revealing the critical potential of visual design practices through an interpretive reading grounded in theoretical frameworks rather than quantitative criteria. The analysis categories were deductively derived from the theoretical background in accordance with Mayring's (2015) guidelines, and each project was examined across four categories: visual content at the denotative level, visual strategy at the connotative level, ideological function at the mythical level, and the targeted emotional response in the viewer.

The scope of the study consists of speculative design projects produced from the early 2000s to the present, as well as the academic literature, institutional archives, and design publications in which these projects appear. The interdisciplinary nature of speculative design and its broad range of applications make it difficult to define a homogeneous scope with clear boundaries. Indeed, Østvold et al. (2024) emphasize that the terminological diversity in the field of speculative design structurally complicates researchers' efforts to define the population. For this reason, the study's population has been broadly defined, while the sample has been narrowed down based on specific and justifiable criteria.

In qualitative research, sample quality is assessed based on the degree of strategic alignment with the research question, independent of numerical size. In this study, a total of six projects—three from each period—are examined. The sample was determined using purposive sampling (Palinkas et al., 2015). From the pre-generative AI era, the following works have been selected: *Technological Dreams Series* (Dunne & Raby, 2007), *Facestate* (Metahaven, 2011), and *TBD Catalog* (Near Future Laboratory, 2012). From the post-generative AI era, the projects AI Newspaper (Near Future Laboratory, 2024), Design Against the Machine (Müller, 2024), and Latent Spacecraft (Beguš et al., 2026) have been included. Projects were selected based on three key criteria. In terms of field representation and legitimacy, all projects come from practitioners who have been cited in academic literature on speculative design, featured in institutional exhibitions, or published in recognized platforms. In terms of temporal representation, the sample consists of two historical periods: the pre-generative AI era (2007–2015), when generative AI tools had not yet been integrated into design practice, and the post-generative AI era (2024–2026), marked by the widespread adoption of platforms such as Midjourney, DALL-E, and Stable Diffusion. This historical turning point is also recognized in the academic literature as occurring in 2022 (Østvold et al., 2024). In terms of visual diversity, the selected projects encompass a range of practices, including speculative object design, corporate identity critique, speculative product catalogs, AI-assisted newspaper design, pedagogical web design, and neuroscience-based installations.

In qualitative research, selecting only examples that support the research creates methodological weaknesses, whereas including counter-examples enhances the reliability of the findings (Patton, 2015). In this study, two projects selected from the post-generative AI era, *Design Against the Machine and Latent Spacecraft* have been included as counter-examples in which artificial intelligence is positioned as an object of critical dialogue. One project in the post-generative AI sample, Design Against the Machine (Müller, 2024), is documented on a public professional platform rather than in a peer-reviewed publication. This source is treated as a primary practitioner document: the object of analysis is not the written text itself but the visual output and pedagogical practice it records. The methodological limitation posed by the source's non-peer-reviewed status is acknowledged accordingly. AI Newspaper, on the other hand, is evaluated as a concrete example of the tendency toward aesthetic normalization. Latent Spacecraft, the sixth project in the sample, differs methodologically from the other five projects. Unlike the other projects, which use familiar visual communication formats, Latent Spacecraft positions the visual experience as the research itself. This project has been included in the sample as an outlier case due to its interdisciplinary structure, which brings together computational linguistics, neuroscience, and literary analysis. The outlier strategy is consciously adopted to test the boundaries of the analytical framework and evaluate findings within a broader context (Patton, 2015). In this context, Latent Spacecraft serves as an example that questions what visual rhetorical analysis can and cannot encompass.

The analyses were conducted in four stages. In the first stage, the visual material of each project was described at the denotative level to identify objective visual content. In the second stage, an interpretive analysis at the connotative level examined which visual codes were used, broken, or transformed. In the third stage, the ideological function at the mythical level was examined; the analysis focused on how dominant cultural values are naturalized or questioned at the visual level. In the fourth stage, the intended emotional response in the viewer was evaluated, and the projects' critical potential was discussed comparatively. Deriving the categories deductively from the theoretical framework ensures that the analysis process is systematic and reproducible (Mayring, 2015).

FINDINGS

In this section, six speculative design projects are examined using a comparative visual rhetorical analysis method based on the categories of denotation, connotation, myth, and pathos.

Technological Dreams Series: No.1, Robots - Dunne & Raby

Designed by Dunne and Raby (2007), this project reimagines the human-robot relationship within the context of everyday life. By systematically subverting the myth of the powerful, obedient robot, the project presents prototypes that are dependent, fragile, and even in need of care. The design objects are intended to create a platform for discussion and invite the viewer to question technology's social role. The project is part of MoMA's permanent collection and is recognized as one of the works that most clearly employs the visual rhetorical tools of speculative design.

Figure 1. All the Robots (a), All the Robots 2 (b), Robot 4 Needy One (c), and Stomach: Microbial Fuel Cell (d), from Technological Dreams Series: No. 1, Robots, by Dunne & Raby, 2007. (From left to right)

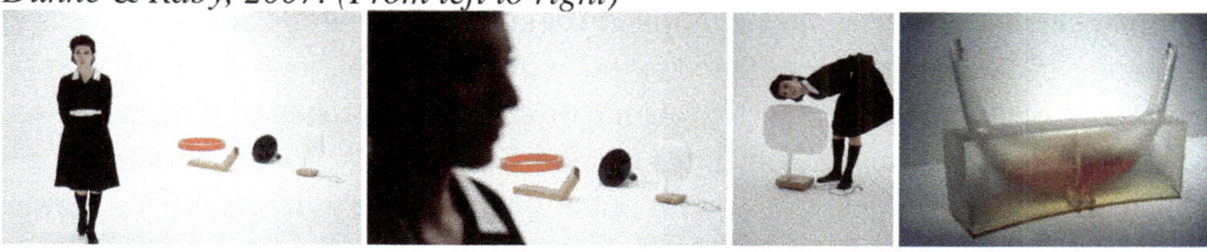

Denotative Level: Visual Content

The four images feature objects against a white, neutral studio background. In Figure 1a, a female figure dressed in black stands on the left side, while on the right are three small objects: a red ring, a wooden corner piece, and a black round object. In Figure 1b, the female figure's face is in close-up and appears faint in the background, while the objects stand out clearly in the foreground. In Figure 1c, the female figure in black clothing is leaning toward a large white square object and aligning her head with it. In Figure 1d, a pink-red, organic-looking liquid is contained within a transparent rectangular container, with two plastic tubes extending upward from the container.

Connotative Level: Coded Meaning

The series' visual strategy is based on a gradual convergence and shift in power across four images. In Figure 1a, the distance between the human figure and the objects is maintained, keeping the viewer at a safe distance. In Figure 1b, this balance begins to shift. While the woman's face remains blurred and, in the background, the objects stand out with crystal clarity, the shift of focus from the human to the object reverses the conventional visual hierarchy. In Figure 1c, the transformation becomes concrete. The human figure leans toward the object, bringing her head to the same level as it. In the traditional human-object relationship, the object serves the human. In this image, however, the human is compelled to approach the object and contact it; the scene simultaneously evokes concepts of dependency, care, and fragility. Figure 1d represents the most radical visual step in the series. Composed of organic fluid and plastic tubes, this object erases the boundary between the biological and the technological. The object is no longer a tool but is positioned almost as a living entity.

Mythical Level: Ideological Function

Viewed through the framework of Barthes's (1977) concept of myth, this series systematically deconstructs the dominant robot myth. In Western visual culture, the image of the robot is positioned as powerful, obedient, and at the service of humans. Dunne and Raby (2007) dismantle this myth in four stages. First, reassures the viewer by presenting the object as small and familiar; then, it disrupts the established hierarchy by pushing humans out of the frame; next, it reverses the power dynamic by portraying humans as dependent on the object; and finally, it questions the ontological boundary between human and machine by biologizing the object. This deconstruction constitutes a visual rejection of the myth that "technology is always good and liberates humanity."

Pathos: Emotional Strategy

Auger's (2013) concept of the "perceptual bridge" serves as a key analytical tool here. The series gradually builds unease in the viewer. Since Figure 1a is familiar and safe, the viewer feels at ease. Figure 1b creates a slight sense of alienation. Figure 1c concretizes the discomfort. The human figure leaning toward the object establishes a tension that is both comical and unsettling. Figure 1d, meanwhile, elevates this discomfort to a piercing intensity. This gradual structure is a deliberate rhetorical choice that compels the viewer to engage in critical thinking.

Facestate - Metahaven

Facestate is a graphic design installation that envisions a speculative world where Facebook and the state merge. Metahaven (2011) designed the identity system for a fictional institution called "Facestate." Passport Phone instead of a passport, a PASSWORD card instead of an ID, and fface recognition instead of facial recognition. The project, created in 2011, poses the speculative question: "If Facebook were to function like a state, what would the visual language of that power look like?" It was featured in the exhibition "Graphic Design: Now in Production" at the Walker Art Center.

Figure 2. Face Recognition (a), Password / Passport (b), View of installed devices under cases (c), and Phone with "tantalum powder" under case (d), from Facestate - Metahaven, 2011. (From left to right)

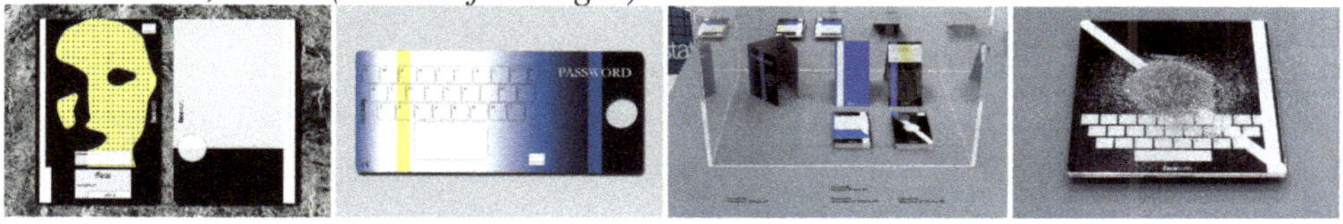

Denotative Level: Visual Content

Four images document the design elements that make up the identity system of a fictional organization called "Facestate." Figure 2a shows the front and back sides of two cards featuring a silhouette of a face mask with yellow dots on a dark background and the text "face recognition. submit." Figure 2b features a card in credit card format with a blue-yellow-white gradient, displaying a QWERTY keyboard layout and the text "PASSWORD" written in reverse. The "CE" mark is visible in the upper left corner, and the "facestate." logo is visible at the bottom. Figure 2c shows numerous identity documents and phone designs labeled "Facestate Passport Phone," "Facestate Folded Phone," and "Facestate Blackberry" displayed together inside a transparent display case. In the background, the address "www.govface" and the phrase "we are a Patriot Act protected government business" are visible. In Figure 2d, a square object composed of white keyboard keys on a dark background is covered with a pile of crystal dust, featuring diagonal lines and the "facestate." logo.

Connotative Level: Coded Meaning

Facestate's visual strategy is based on transforming the visual codes of state and technology institutions into a hybrid identity system. Each object simultaneously evokes two distinct visual repertoires familiar to the viewer: state identification documents and digital platform interfaces.

The "fface recognition" card in Figure 2a presents the most intense example of this hybridization. The silhouette of a face mask with yellow dots directly references both the visual language of biometric data collection technology and Facebook's facial recognition feature. The double "f" in the spelling of "fface" is a deliberate typographic intervention. Facebook's "f" and the government's facial recognition practice are fused into a single sign. The "PASSWORD" card in Figure 2b combines the format of a bank card with that of an ID document. Placing the word "PASSWORD" in reverse on an ID card concretizes the merging of digital and physical identity at the visual level. While Figure 2c presents the entire identity system as an exhibition layout, the phrase "patriot act protected government business" anchors this hybridity within an ideological framework. Facestate positions itself not merely as a platform but as a state institution with legal safeguards. In Figure 2d, the accumulation of crystal dust on the keyboard keys constitutes the most abstract and poetic visual gesture. The tension between digital data and physical traces, and between surveillance and transparency, converges on a single object.

Mythical Level: Ideological Function

Viewed through the framework of Barthes's (1977) concept of myth, Facestate simultaneously reveals and questions two dominant myths. The first is the myth that "state identity is secure and neutral." Passports, ID cards, and official documents have been naturalized in visual culture as symbols of a neutral, protective, and legitimate authority. Metahaven (2011) debunks this claim of neutrality by combining this visual code with Facebook's corporate identity. The institution that determines who you are is now also the platform that collects your data. The second is the myth that "digital platforms are liberating." Facebook and similar platforms have been equated in visual culture with connection, freedom, and individual expression. Facestate shatters this myth as well. When the platform's visual language aligns with the state's identity system, the image of the liberating platform becomes a tool of control.

Pathos: Emotional Strategy

Facestate's emotional strategy transforms the tension between familiarity and discomfort into a visual provocation. Auger's (2013) concept of the "perceptual bridge" is explored here in a multi-layered manner. The design objects are sufficiently familiar because they utilize the visual codes of real government documents and digital interfaces; yet they are sufficiently unsettling because these codes merge contexts that should never coexist onto a single object. The project's most powerful emotional impact stems from the phrase "we are a Patriot Act protected government business" in Figure 2c. This sentence keeps the viewer on the edge of the speculative. While this statement appeared dystopian and exaggerated in 2011, today it can almost be read as a factual statement. This temporality positions Facestate as much a prophecy as it is a critique.

TBD Catalog - Near Future Laboratory

This project, which emerged from an interdisciplinary workshop conducted by Near Future Laboratory (2012) in Detroit, is designed as a 112-page speculative product catalog. By directly adopting the format of a standard consumer catalog, the project presents possible futures—such as wearable technology, cryptocurrency, and surveillance—in an ordinary manner. In the words of Near Future Laboratory, the project presents "extraordinary ideas in a completely ordinary way." The deliberate use of a familiar format forms the core of the project's visual rhetorical strategy.

Figure 3. Tbd catalog image (a), and tbd catalog image (b), from TBD Catalog Near Future Laboratory 2012. (From left to right)

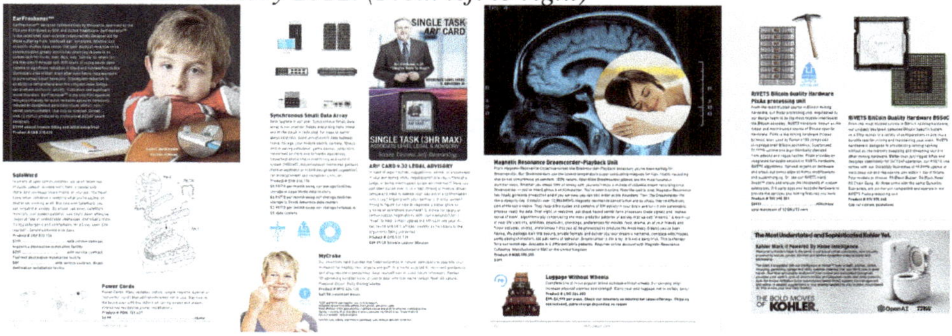

Denotative Level: Visual Content

Two images document double-page catalog layouts that fully utilize the typographic and visual codes of an actual consumer catalog. Each product is presented with its product name, description, product number, and price information. The address "tbdcatalog.com" appears at the bottom of the page. In Figure 3a, on the left are the EarFreshener™ wearable device, the SafeWord surveillance product, and the Power Cords advertisement; in the center are the Single Task ARI Card and Synchronous Small Data Array products; and on the right is the MyCrobe biological product. In Figure 3b, on the left are the Magnetic Resonance Dreamcorder-Playback Unit, in the center are the Luggage Without Wheels and RIVETS Bitcoin Quality Hardware products, and on the right is the Kohler Mark II advertisement titled "The Bold Moves of Kohler." The OpenAI and TRW logos are visible in the lower corner of the Kohler advertisement.

Connotative Level: Coded Meaning

The visual strategy of the TBD Catalog is based on a single, radical choice: presenting extraordinary ideas in an ordinary way. The catalog format serves as the vehicle for this strategy. When the viewer looks at the page, they first see a Sharper

Image or Brookstone catalog; the typography, product numbers, pricing structure, and ad layout are entirely authentic. The sense of unease gradually sets in as they begin to read the product descriptions. This strategy operates differently for each product. EarFreshener™ employs the language codes of the healthcare industry by legitimizing a fictional medical diagnosis called "confused ear syndrome" with FDA approval; the product is not a therapeutic tool, but a means of normalizing screen addiction. SafeWord presents surveillance technology through the lens of hygiene discourse. This device, which monitors speech and blocks inappropriate expressions, subverts the myth of "free communication" by transforming self-censorship into a comfort product. The Single Task ARI Card is described as an AI lawyer that whispers in your ear; the phrase "Ari Birnbaum v.32" presents the AI not as a software version but as a personal assistant. The Magnetic Resonance Dreamcorder, however, makes the most speculative move. This device, which records dreams and processes them on cloud servers, frames the unconscious as a data source. The Kohler Mark II ad carries the sharpest irony of the series. The OpenAI logo appears directly beneath the headline "The Bold Moves of Kohler," transforming the smart toilet into a technological product within the ad's linguistic and visual hierarchy.

Mythical Level: Ideological Function

Viewed through the framework of Barthes's (1977) concept of myth, the TBD Catalog deconstructs the most fundamental myth of consumer culture, "there is a product solution for every problem," within its own format. The catalog format is one of the primary visual tools that naturalizes this myth. In a world where everything has a product number and a price, problems are not solved—they are consumed. Near Future Laboratory (2012) uses this format directly to transform surveillance, data collection, dependence on artificial intelligence, and the commodification of the unconscious into ordinary consumer objects. The catalog thus both mimics what it critiques and renders it visible.

Pathos: Emotional Strategy

The TBD Catalog's emotional strategy is situated on the fine line between the ridiculous and the terrifying. Auger's (2013) concept of the "perceptual bridge" is explored here in its sharpest form. The viewer laughs at first, because the products appear familiar and absurd. Then, the screen addiction defined by EarFreshener, the self-censorship implied by SafeWord, the data trade framed by Dreamcorder, and the home AI integration presented by Kohler—things that were speculative in 2012 are no longer speculative today. This sense of timeliness is TBD Catalog's most powerful rhetorical weapon. The catalog has transformed into an archive that documents not an unrealized future, but a present being lived out unnoticed.

The TBD Catalog stands out among the three projects of the pre-AI era as the one that most radically concentrates its visual rhetorical strategy into a single choice: transforming the format itself into the vehicle of criticism. The Technological Dreams Series established this strategy through the relationship between object and human, while Facestate did so through a hybridization of corporate identity. The TBD Catalog, however, produces criticism not at the visual level, but at the structural level. The complete and exact replication of the consumer catalog format exponentially amplifies the unsettling nature of the content. Because the viewer recognizes the format, they believe the content; and because they believe it, they feel unsettled.

A Newspaper From An Artificially Intelligent Future - Near Future Laboratory

This project by Near Future Laboratory (2024) is a speculative newspaper design that simulates a possible future in which artificial intelligence is seamlessly integrated into everyday life. Using the familiar newspaper format, the project presents news, advertisements, and opinion pieces from an AI-driven world. AI tools were actively used in creating the content. This choice makes the project comparable to the deliberate visual rhetoric of the pre-AI era.

Figure 4. Interview page and film poster on the left (a), inner news pages (b), and front page (c), A Newspaper from an Artificially Intelligent (Near) Future, Near Future Laboratory, 2024. (From left to right.)

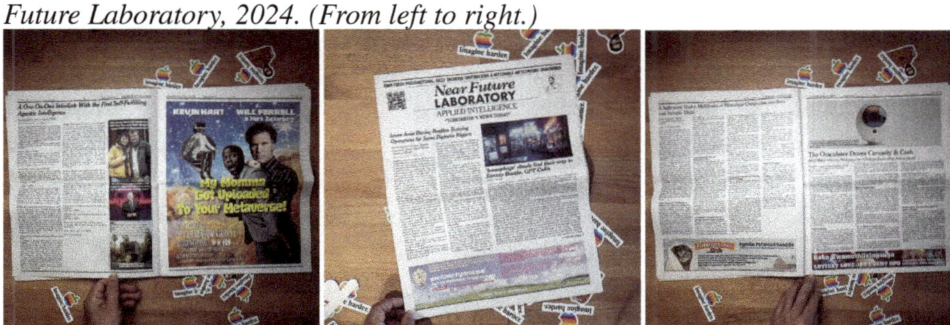

Denotative Level: Visual Content

Three images document different pages of a speculative newspaper titled "Near Future Laboratory Applied Intelligence — Tomorrow's News Today." In all images, rainbow-colored Apple stickers reading "Imagine harder" are scattered around the wooden floor on which the newspaper is displayed. Figure 4a shows a newspaper spread held upside down. On the left page is a movie poster titled "My Momma Got Uploaded To Your Metaverse!" featuring Kevin Hart and Will Ferrell; the poster reads "Will Ferrell is Mark Zuckerberg." The right page contains interview and news content. Figure 4b shows the newspaper's front page. Headlines set in traditional newspaper typography include "Issues Arise During Routine Training Operations for Some Digitwin Riggers" and "'Iconophage' rituals find their way to Sorcery Booths, GPT Cafés." At the bottom of the page is an advertisement for a speculative product called "profasic hydrolase." Figure 4c shows the inside pages. The left page features a news article titled "A Splintered World: Multitudes of Microlocal Companion Intellects and Portable Ubiks," and the right page features a news article titled "The Oraculator Draws Curiosity and Cash." The bottom banner ads include advertisements for "Agentic Pet Mood Swaddle" by Pepperidge Farm and "Baba Kwamuthiizinyanga Lottery Love Job Enemy GPU."

Connotative Level: Coded Meaning

At first glance, AI Newspaper's visual strategy appears similar to that of TBD Catalog. Unconventional content is presented within a familiar format. However, there is a fundamental difference between the two projects. In TBD Catalog, the tension between format and content is deliberate and controlled. Although each product is speculative at the textual level, the typographic and visual language remains consistent and intentional. In AI Newspaper, however, this tension manifests differently.

The visual language used on the newspaper pages is functional. The column layout, news hierarchy, and typography resemble a real newspaper. At the level of connotation, however, the visual codes present a contradictory picture. While headlines like "Digitwin Riggers" and "Iconophage rituals" carry strong critical potential, this potential is not reflected in the visuals. The visual code of the advertisements (conventional lighting, standard typographic hierarchy, familiar product image layout) amounts to nothing more than a superficial modification of existing design templates. This gap between the speculative content and the visual code indicates that the critical tension at the level of connotation has not been established. The Apple stickers bearing the phrase "Imagine harder" reinforce this inconsistency, serving merely as decorative elements without establishing a meaningful connection to the newspaper.

Mythical Level: Ideological Function

Viewed through the lens of Barthes's (1977) concept of myth, the AI Newspaper risks reproducing the myth that "artificial intelligence will transform everything" rather than questioning it. The newspaper format has historically served to document reality and shape public opinion. Combining this format with speculative content can legitimize and normalize it. However, this potential fails to transform into a critical function where visual rhetorical strategies fall short. The movie poster featuring Kevin Hart and Will Ferrell with the caption "Will Ferrell is Mark Zuckerberg" concretizes this issue. Hollywood's language domesticates metaverse criticism and reduces dystopian content to an entertainment format.

Pathos: Emotional Strategy

AI Newspaper evokes a sense of familiarity rather than discomfort in the viewer. Auger's (2013) concept of the "perceptual bridge" fails to function here. The viewer is not sufficiently unsettled because the speculative content is too closely aligned with existing cultural patterns on a visual level. The finding by Hintze et al. (2025) that AI production cycles converge on common visual motifs finds a concrete counterpart here. The visuals and text blocks produced by AI reproduce the most familiar patterns of existing visual culture rather than expanding the imagination. This becomes particularly evident when compared to the TBD Catalog. The critical distance established in 2012 with a handcrafted catalog now faces the risk of being lost in a newspaper produced with AI tools in 2024. The AI Newspaper positions itself as a project directly comparable to the powerful visual rhetorical strategies of the pre-AI era, standing at the forefront of post-AI era projects. The critical distance established by Near Future Laboratory in the TBD Catalog in 2012 through a handmade catalog cannot be reproduced with the same force in a newspaper produced using AI tools in 2024. This comparison concretizes the work's fundamental tension.

Design Against the Machine - Boris Müller

This project, led by design educator Boris Müller (2024), is designed as a pedagogical experiment that makes AI tools mandatory in a speculative design course rather than banning them. Students were asked to work alongside AI without submitting to it, and to transform the tools' structural logic from a critical perspective. The project serves as one of the counter-examples in this study, concretely demonstrating how artificial intelligence can be positioned as an object of critical dialogue.

Figure 5. AI-generated image collage (2×6 grid) visualizing the concept of "clothing and machine", from Design Against the Machine - Boris Müller 2024

Denotative Level: Visual Content

The visual is an AI-generated collage consisting of twelve squares arranged in a 2×6 grid. All squares visualize the same conceptual question in different forms, such as a machine or a mechanism interacting with clothing and textile materials. The left two squares of the top row feature organic and chaotic-looking structures covered with colorful fabric pieces. The third and fourth squares of the top row depict industrial-style machines with glass panels and human figures standing in front of them. The right two squares of the top row feature spaces resembling MRI machines situated in a sterile and bright interior, along with figures interacting with them. The bottom row follows a similar pattern. The left two squares depict chaotic, industrial-looking warehouse-like structures; the middle squares show figures interacting with textile products in store environments with glass display cases; and the right two squares document machines resembling MRI devices in a sterile, commercial setting. The visual language evokes an Apple Store or a luxury retail store.

Connotative Level: Coded Meaning

When viewed from left to right, a narrative of transformation emerges. This transformation occurs independently of the designer's control, guided by the structural logic of artificial intelligence. The chaotic and raw images in the left column reflect the research and inquiry phase. The machines are undefined, the accumulation of materials is disorderly, and the space is ambiguous. However, as one moves to the right, the dominant patterns in the AI's training data become more pronounced. The machines gradually transform into an MRI machine, an automated clothing machine, or retail store equipment. Human figures stand in a uniform posture in front of the machine, the lighting mimics commercial product photography, and the space evolves into a familiar consumer environment. The AI responds to the concept of "clothing and machine" with the images it statistically encounters most frequently together. Consequently, the twelve images generated independently of one another converge toward similar visual focal points, such as sterile spaces, commercial lighting, and familiar machine forms. The result is the product of a structural tendency.

Mythical Level: Ideological Function

Viewed through the lens of Barthes's (1977) concept of myth, this collage reveals the dominant myth within which artificial intelligence operates. Good design is clean, sterile, and commercial. This visual myth, which dominates the training data of artificial intelligence, quietly guides the production process and erodes the designer's critical intent. This trend is not accidental but structural. The datasets used to train AI models consist of the most widespread and accessible content within digital visual culture. Within this content, commercial photography, product imagery, and corporate design language have historically been dominant. As Crawford (2021) demonstrates, AI systems are not neutral; they operate by internalizing specific visual cultural norms and power dynamics. In the "Design Against the Machine" collage, this algorithmic bias becomes visibly apparent. Müller (2024) asked his students to work with AI but not to submit to it. This collage visually demonstrates just how challenging a methodological problem this request entails. The tool tends to pull the designer into its own structural logic.

Pathos: Emotional Strategy

The emotional strategy of *Design Against the Machine* extends beyond its content to unsettle the viewer. It constructs this unease through the visible contradictions of the production process. Auger's (2013) concept of the "perceptual bridge" operates differently here. The viewer encounters neither dystopian content nor the disruption of a familiar format. The discomfort arises from recognizing the pattern formed when the twelve visuals are placed side by side. The findings by Hintze et al. (2025), which show that autonomous production cycles converge on a narrow set of visual motifs, are clearly confirmed in this collage. The viewer directly experiences that artificial intelligence does not expand the imagination but, on the contrary, narrows it by confining it to familiar patterns.

As one of the projects of the post-AI era, *Design Against the Machine* stands in direct contrast to *AI Newspaper*. Both projects utilize AI tools for content production. The difference in approach between the two projects (using AI passively versus transforming it into an object of critical dialogue) exerts a decisive influence on the visual rhetorical strategy.

Latent Spacecraft: Brains, GANs, Finnegans - Beguš, N., Metahaven and Beguš, G.

This interdisciplinary project, published by Beguš et al. (2026) in *Antikythera: Journal for the Philosophy of Planetary Computation*, brings together computational linguistics, neuroscience, and literary analysis to investigate the hidden internal structure of artificial neural networks—that is, the "latent space." Centered on a GAN model trained on James Joyce's novel *Finnegans Wake*, the project visualizes the structural similarities between human and machine language generation. Rather than relying on familiar formats of visual communication, this project positions the visual experience itself as the research and is treated as an outlier in the sample.

Figure 6. Latent space for FinneGANs output: Right, we inhabit a locked hole, but can we use it? The figure shows 100 numbers as values that generate this specific utterance (a), Finnegans Wake Screenshot from ConcatenationGAN Latent Space (b), from Latent Spacecraft: Brains, GANs, Finnegans - Beguš, N., Metahaven ve Beguš, G. 2026

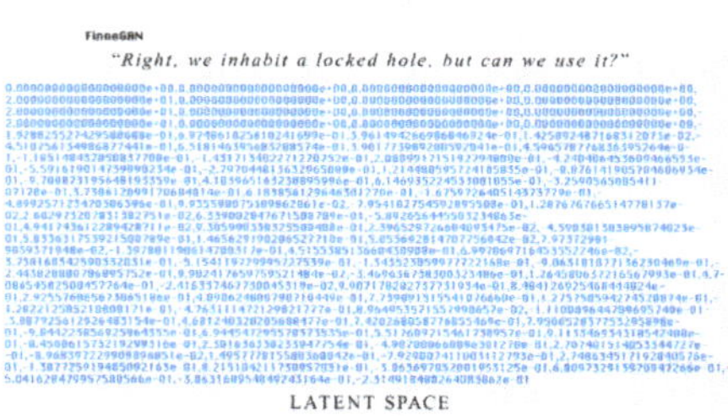

Denotative Level: Visual Content

Two images document different layers of the project. In Figure 6a, the title "FinneGAN" appears on a white background, and beneath the italicized quote "Right, we inhabit a locked hole, but can we use it?" lies a dense sequence of numerical vectors in blue. The sequence consists of decimal values written in scientific notation, and the text "LATENT SPACE" is positioned in large font at the bottom of the page. Figure 6b features an abstract image created using a black-and-white glitch aesthetic. Horizontal band patterns, pixel distortions, and layers of noise converge around a large black circle in the center. At the bottom of the image, the phrase "water, water, under." is written in thick yellow text.

Connotative Level: Coded Meaning

When viewed together, the two images reveal an input-output relationship. Figure 6a depicts the latent space through its raw mathematical representation. The sequences of numbers convey information without communication, making visible the mathematical structure that precedes the production of meaning. The project's methodological process is built upon this image. Audio recordings derived from Joyce's novel *Finnegans Wake* were used as training data for a GAN model, and the numerical vectors within the model's latent space were visualized. The question "Right, we inhabit a locked hole, but can we use it?" summarizes the epistemological status of this layer. Figure 6b shows the output side of the same process. The audio outputs generated by the GAN model have been visualized, with the phrase "water, water, under" presented as the output closest to the linguistic level. The meaning is fragmented, the syntax is broken, and the context is ambiguous. The glitch aesthetic and pixel noise visually capture that threshold where language has not yet been established.

Mythical Level: Ideological Function and the Limits of the Framework

Barthes's (1977) concept of myth encounters an analytical tension at this point. Barthes's framework assumes that visual messages always carry an intention to communicate, that codes are shared within a cultural context, and that viewers can decipher these codes. Latent Spacecraft, however, challenges precisely these assumptions.

The number sequences in Figure 6a do not carry a myth. The phrase "water, water, under" in Figure 6b appears to carry connotations. However, these meanings reflect the viewer; they are not the product of a deliberate rhetorical strategy within the visual. This is precisely the argument of Beguš et al. (2026). Latent space is first and foremost categorical; that is, it is a structure that exists prior to the establishment of meaning categories. Representing this structure through visual communication tools will inevitably fall short. Latent Spacecraft goes beyond the dominant myth-breaking strategy focused on by the other five projects to investigate how myth production itself operates. This epistemological stance firmly establishes the project as an outlier within the sample.

Pathos: Emotional Strategy and the Transformation of the Framework

Latent Spacecraft induces a conceptual disorientation in the viewer that goes beyond mere discomfort. Auger's (2013) concept of the "perceptual bridge" becomes inoperative here. The viewer encounters something that is neither sufficiently familiar nor sufficiently unsettling. What they encounter is indefinable. The placement of the phrase "water, water, under" in yellow beneath the glitch image directs the viewer to seek meaning, yet this quest remains unsatisfied. This dissatisfaction should be read not as a rhetorical failure but as the design itself. At this point, it becomes evident that the four analytical categories (denotation, connotation, myth, and pathos) cannot fully capture Latent Spacecraft. The project employs visual rhetoric as the research itself. This distinction also brings to the fore the fundamental methodological question addressed in the study's findings section. In the age of artificial intelligence, speculative design does not remain limited to visual rhetorical strategies but generates meaning through multi-sensory and algorithmic layers. Among the six projects in the sample, Latent Spacecraft stands out as the study that most radically transforms the visual rhetorical strategy.

The findings reveal four key trends. First, during the pre-AI era, speculative design projects consciously and creatively devised visual rhetorical strategies. The Technological Dreams Series, Facestate, and TBD Catalog stand out as works that deliberately employ, subvert, and reinterpret familiar visual codes. A common feature of these projects is their construction of visual rhetorical strategies that consciously subvert the viewer's customary visual expectations and trigger critical thinking at the moment of this disruption. Second, in post-generative AI projects that passively use generative AI tools, visual rhetorical strategies are at risk of weakening. The AI Newspaper analysis demonstrates that AI's structural tendency to reinforce the dominant trends of current visual culture corresponds to the phenomenon of "convergence" experimentally demonstrated in Hintze et al.'s (2025) research on autonomous production cycles within speculative design practice. Third, projects that position artificial intelligence as an object of critical dialogue can preserve their critical potential. Design Against the Machine and Latent Spacecraft demonstrate that artificial intelligence can serve as a basis for critical inquiry rather than merely as a passive production tool. Finally, Latent Spacecraft reveals that Barthes's (1977) categories of visual rhetoric do not fully capture the new form that speculative design has taken in the age of artificial intelligence.

DISCUSSION

The findings of this study reveal that the critical potential of speculative design is directly related not only to the content of the future scenarios produced but also to the visual rhetorical strategies through which these scenarios are presented. The analysis of visual rhetoric shows that, prior to the widespread adoption of generative AI tools, visual rhetorical strategies were consciously and creatively constructed in speculative design projects. Dunne and Raby's Technological Dreams series, Metahaven's Facestate project, and Near Future Laboratory's TBD Catalog generate cognitive tension in the viewer through the strategic reinterpretation of familiar visual codes. This tension between the levels of denotation, connotation, and myth—as conceptualized by Barthes (1977)—emerges as the fundamental rhetorical mechanism enabling the critical function of speculative design. Aristotle's (2006) concept of pathos completes the emotional dimension of this mechanism. The visual strategies employed in these projects align with the concept of the "perceptual bridge" as defined by Auger (2013). While the use of familiar visual forms allows the viewer to relate the speculative scenario to the realm of reality, the subversion of this familiarity at the level of content establishes critical distance. The critical power of speculative design stems not so much from its ability to imagine the future as from the tension it creates by framing that imagination through familiar visual-cultural codes. In the pre-generative AI era, this strategy was a conscious choice by the designer.

A distinct trend has emerged in speculative design projects following the widespread adoption of generative AI tools. The learning processes of AI tools, which rely on large datasets, tend to reproduce the stylistic trends dominant in current visual culture. This phenomenon, experimentally defined by Hintze et al. (2025) and referred to by researchers as "visual elevator music," is interpreted in this study within the framework of aesthetic normalization. Aesthetic normalization refers to the process by which generative AI systems, through data-driven learning processes, reinforce dominant visual aesthetics, thereby hindering the production of alternative visual strategies. This situation can hinder the establishment of critical distance, a fundamental function of speculative design. Since the critical impact of speculative design emerges through the deliberate disruption of the viewer's familiar visual order, it cannot be expected that these tools will automatically produce such a disruption.

The "Design Against the Machine" collage visualizes this phenomenon. Although the twelve images were created from different starting points, they all converge toward a similar visual focal point: a sterile space, commercial lighting, and familiar machine forms. This convergence aligns with the findings of Østvold et al. (2024) on the use of AI in speculative design. While AI tools are seen as useful for generating speculative scenarios, the visuals they produce mostly reproduce the dominant trends of current visual culture. This finding becomes particularly evident when compared to the TBD Catalog. Near Future Laboratory has been unable to maintain the critical distance it established in 2012 with a handcrafted catalog with the same force in a newspaper produced using generative AI tools in 2024.

At this point, it is necessary to explicitly acknowledge a methodological limitation regarding the binary periodization framework adopted by this study. The distinction between the pre-generative AI period (2007–2015) and the post-generative AI period (2024–2026) is a framework deliberately constructed to ensure analytical clarity. However, this binary structure may give the impression that the transition between the two periods is abrupt. In reality, the influence of GANs, DeepDream, and similar computational visual production tools on design practices extends back to before 2022. The dominance of generative AI in the design field is the result of a gradual transformation. The periodization adopted in this study enhances the reliability of the comparative analysis rather than fully reflecting the complexity of this transition. Future research examining this transition process with finer time intervals and broader samples will deepen our understanding of the field.

However, it is noteworthy that not all of the analyzed AI-driven projects exhibit the same trend. In projects that position AI as an object of critical discourse, the tendency toward aesthetic convergence appears to be weaker. In *Design Against the Machine*, the structural pull of AI has been recognized and transformed into an object of pedagogical critique. In "Latent Spacecraft," however, the AI output is positioned as the research itself. In both projects, the tool itself has been incorporated into a speculative narrative, a choice that has enabled it to preserve its critical potential. This strongly supports Müller's (2024) pedagogical approach.

Latent Spacecraft also extends the discussion to a methodological dimension. Barthes' (1977) categories of visual rhetoric do not fully capture this project. According to the argument put forward by Beguš et al. (2026), latent space is first and foremost a categorical structure, and its representation through visual communication tools will necessarily fall short. This observation clearly highlights the need for new analytical frameworks that go beyond visual rhetorical analysis to encompass algorithmic, auditory, and interdisciplinary layers.

These findings fill a significant gap in the literature. Speculative design theory, visual rhetoric analysis, and the impact of generative artificial intelligence on creative practices have largely been treated as independent fields of research. By directly addressing the intersection of these three areas, this study concretizes the impact of artificial intelligence on the visual rhetorical strategies of speculative design through a comparative analysis. The primary determining factor is how the designer positions the tool and constructs visual rhetorical strategies. The issue goes beyond being merely a matter of a technological tool; it is an epistemic issue tied to the designer's attitude. This observation points to the need to rethink the designer's role and the practice of speculative design in the age of generative artificial intelligence.

CONCLUSION

This study examines how the proliferation of generative AI tools has transformed the visual rhetorical strategies and critical potential of speculative design. A comparative analysis of six projects spanning two historical periods reveals a finding that goes beyond a simple before-and-after narrative. The critical potential of speculative design is determined not by the tools used, but by the designer's conscious intervention in visual rhetorical strategies.

The concept of aesthetic normalization proposed in this study offers a theoretical framework for understanding the structural risk that generative AI tools pose to speculative design practice. When positioned as a passive production tool, AI tends to reproduce dominant visual patterns through its data-driven structural logic, thereby weakening the critical distance that speculative design aims to achieve. The "Design Against the Machine" visual directly highlights this tendency. Twelve images generated from different starting points converge around sterile spaces and commercial lighting patterns without the designer's intervention. This situation goes beyond a mere technological failure; it is a direct consequence of the tool's positioning. The contrast between AI Newspaper and Design Against the Machine brings this distinction into sharp relief. When placed in different pedagogical contexts and guided by distinct critical orientations, the same set of tools produces fundamentally different rhetorical outcomes.

The Latent Spacecraft analysis shifts the discussion to a methodological dimension. Barthes's visual rhetoric framework functions productively in five of the six projects; however, it reaches its analytical limits when confronted with works that position the algorithmic process as the research itself. This situation should be interpreted not only as a limitation of the framework but also as an indicator of the new territory that speculative design has entered. Future research must go beyond visual rhetoric analysis to develop integrated analytical frameworks that encompass auditory and algorithmic layers of meaning production.

Three key conclusions can be drawn from these findings. From the perspective of design practice, the critical function of speculative design can be preserved in the age of generative artificial intelligence; however, this requires establishing a conscious and critical relationship with the tool's underlying logic, rather than passively relying on its outputs. From the perspective of design education, Müller's (2024) pedagogical approach stands out as an example deserving of a broader scope of application. From a research perspective, however, the limited scope of this study—restricted to six projects and a single analytical framework—needs to be expanded. Larger datasets, user engagement studies, and analyses of the production process would significantly strengthen the claims put forward here.

Speculative design's capacity to question current reality and imagine alternative futures always relies on the designer's will to make visible what the dominant visual culture conceals. Generative AI does not eliminate this responsibility; rather, it deepens it.

REFERENCES

Adorno, T. W., & Horkheimer, M. (2002). *Dialectic of enlightenment: Philosophical fragments* (Jephcott, E., Trans.). Stanford University Press. (Original work published 1947)

Aristotle. (2006). Retorik (M. Çiftkaya, Çev.). İmge Kitabevi Yayınları. (Original work published ca. 350 B.C.E.)

Auger, J. (2013). Speculative design: Crafting the speculation. *Digital Creativity (Exeter)*, *24*(1), 11–35. DOI: 10.1080/14626268.2013.767276

Barthes, R. (1977). *Image, music, text.* Hill and Wang.

Beguš, N., Metahaven, & Beguš, G. (2026). Latent spacecraft: Brains, GANs, Finnegans. Antikythera: Journal for the Philosophy of Planetary Computation. DOI: 10.1162/ANTI.5KP1

Bender, E. M., Gebru, T., McMillan-Major, A., & Shmitchell, S. (2021). On the dangers of stochastic parrots: Can language models be too big? In *Proceedings of the 2021 ACM Conference on Fairness, Accountability, and Transparency* (pp. 610–623). Association for Computing Machinery. DOI: 10.1145/3442188.3445922

Bleecker, J. (2022). Design Fiction. In Carta, S. (Ed.), *Machine Learning and the City*. DOI: 10.1002/9781119815075.ch47

Cardenas Cordova, D., Kelly, N., & Rezayan, L. (2025). A systematic literature review of the speculative design process and a proposed framework for speculative design. *Design Science*, *11*, e38. DOI: 10.1017/dsj.2025.10030

Crawford, K. (2021). *Atlas of AI: Power, politics, and the planetary costs of artificial intelligence*. Yale University Press. DOI: 10.2307/j.ctv1ghv45t

DiSalvo, C. (2012). *Adversarial design.* MIT Press. DOI: 10.7551/mitpress/8732.001.0001

Dunne, A. (1999). *Hertzian tales: An investigation into the critical and aesthetic potential of the electronic product as a post-optimal object*. RCA CRD Research Publications.

Dunne, A., & Raby, F. (2001). *Design noir: The secret life of electronic objects.* Birkhäuser.

Dunne, A., & Raby, F. (2007). Technological dreams series: No.1, robots. Kunstmuseen Krefeld; MoMA permanent collection. https://dunneandraby.co.uk/content/projects/10/0

Dunne, A., & Raby, F. (2013). *Speculative everything: Design, fiction, and social dreaming*. MIT Press.

Foss, S. K. (2005). Theory of visual rhetoric. In Smith, K., Moriarty, S., Barbatsis, G., & Kenney, K. (Eds.), *Handbook of visual communication: Theory, methods, and media* (pp. 141–152). Lawrence Erlbaum.

Hintze, A., Proschinger Åström, F., & Schossau, J. (2025). Autonomous language-image generation loops converge to generic visual motifs. *Patterns*, *7*(1), 101451. DOI: 10.1016/j.patter.2025.101451 PMID: 41583980

Irwin, T. (2015). Transition Design: A Proposal for a New Area of Design Practice, Study, and Research. *Design and Culture*, *7*(2), 229–246. DOI: 10.1080/17547075.2015.1051829

Johannessen, L. K., Keitsch, M. M., & Pettersen, I. N. (2019). Speculative and critical design — Features, methods, and practices. *Proceedings of the 22nd International Conference on Engineering Design (ICED19)* (pp. 1623–1632). Cambridge University Press. DOI: 10.1017/dsi.2019.168

Mayring, P. (2015). Qualitative content analysis: Theoretical background and procedures. In Bikner-Ahsbahs, A., Knipping, C., & Presmeg, N. (Eds.), *Approaches to qualitative research in mathematics education (ss* (pp. 365–380). Springer. DOI: 10.1007/978-94-017-9181-6_13

Metahaven [Kruk, V., & van der Velden, D.]. (2011). Facestate. Walker Art Center; Graphic Design: Now in Production exhibition. https://walkerart.org/magazine/metahavens-facestate

Mitchell, W. J. T. (1994). *Picture theory: Essays on verbal and visual representation*. University of Chicago Press.

Müller, B. (2024). Design against the machine: The role of generative AI tools in design education [Practitioner report]. https://borism.medium.com/design-against-the-machine-72648374aec1

Near Future Laboratory [Bleecker, J.]. (2024). A newspaper from an artificially intelligent (near) future. Near Future Laboratory.

Near Future Laboratory [Bleecker, J., Girardin, F., Byrne, E., & Foster, N.]. (2012). TBD catalog: The design fiction product catalog for the normal ordinary everyday near future. Near Future Laboratory.

Østvold, M., Paulsen, M., & Trondsen, J. K. (2024). Speculative design through the lens of AI. *Proceedings of the 26th International Conference on Engineering and Product Design Education (EPDE2024)* (pp. 627–632). Aston University. DOI: 10.35199/EPDE.2024.106

Palinkas, L. A., Horwitz, S. M., Green, C. A., Wisdom, J. P., Duan, N., & Hoagwood, K. (2015). Purposeful sampling for qualitative data collection and analysis in mixed method implementation research. *Administration and Policy in Mental Health*, *42*(5), 533–544. DOI: 10.1007/s10488-013-0528-y PMID: 24193818

Patton, M. Q. (2015). *Qualitative research & evaluation methods: Integrating theory and practice* (4th ed.). SAGE.

Rynning, M. (2017). Speculative graphic design: Visual identity branding as a catalyst for change. Nordes 2017: Design + Power. DOI: 10.21606/nordes.2017.042

Skjulstad, S., & Rynning, M. (2015). Graphic design speculations: Teaching visual identity for water sustainability within a speculative design framework. Cumulus Mumbai 2015 Conference Proceedings. https://www.researchgate.net/publication/286040232

Chapter 8
The Aesthetics of Artificial Intelligence and the Search for a New Agent:
A Research on Aesthetic and Technological Orientations

Özge Kaya
http://orcid.org/0000-0001-7870-2596
Uskudar University, Turkey

Kader Sürmeli
http://orcid.org/0000-0001-5175-4847
Yıldız Technical University, Turkey

ABSTRACT

Artificial intelligence stands out as a central technological paradigm transforming the current design ecosystem. The discussion revolves around computer systems moving beyond passive tools to become creative agents that organically partner with designers and incorporate their aesthetic preferences into the process. This study analyzes how artificial intelligence transforms design practices within the framework of Lev Manovich's new media approach, encompassing epistemology, phenomenology, and ontology. Adopting a mixed-methods approach, the research combines quantitative data with expert opinions. The findings demonstrate that artificial intelligence is positioned as an agent in the design process, while users are transformed from technical implementers into curators/selectors managing the

DOI: 10.4018/979-8-2600-2711-0.ch008

process. Consequently, a hybrid subjectivity model is proposed, where agency in design is distributed between humans and algorithms; and the necessity of a human-centered transformation in design education is argued.

INTRODUCTION

In order to discuss the relationship between artificial intelligence (AI) and art, it is first necessary to define what is meant by art. A review of the literature, however, reveals the inherent ambiguity of the term. This study does not claim to provide a universal, immutable, or binding answer to the question "What is art?" Rather, it aims to explore how artists, designers, and audiences interpret this new mode of production introduced by AI technologies. In other words, the research focuses less on the question of what art is and more on "how it is experienced," "how it acquires meaning," and "under which contexts it is recognized as art." This approach forms a fundamental rationale for situating the study within an interpretive paradigm.

Art is characterized by a fundamental indeterminacy, making its definition difficult to fix. Defining art is logically impossible because art is inherently creative and innovative. If art is defined solely by its current characteristics, any new technique emerging in the future would be prematurely excluded (Weitz, 1956), which contradicts the principle of creativity inherent in art. The design discipline, historically, has always maintained an organic relationship with the technological paradigms of its time. From the mechanical production of the Industrial Revolution to the digital revolution, design has manifested as an aesthetic expression of technological possibilities in tandem with formal exploration (Özselçuk, 2023: 3). Today, AI represents the most radical link in this evolutionary chain. This paradigm shift transforms both art and design from distinct perspectives.

AI has evolved beyond being a mere tool in the art and design domains, assuming the role of an active participant in the production process. In this context, the human–machine relationship has shifted from a unidirectional command-output dynamic to an interactive, reciprocal engagement. While AI extends the cognitive boundaries of the designer (Shen & Yu, 2021:1), the designer assumes the role of a selector/curator, guiding the algorithm with aesthetic and ethical considerations. This study treats AI not merely as a technical tool, but as an ontological phenomenon positioned at the intersection of technology, philosophy, and art.

This rapid transformation in art and design introduces both aesthetic and technical uncertainties. The speed of AI-driven production often surpasses the capacity of academic literature and professional practice to fully comprehend these changes. Accordingly, this study seeks to analyze how AI is transforming contemporary design practices and to evaluate emerging aesthetic and technological tendencies in the near future. The research examines the relationship established by artists, designers, academics, and students with AI, the transformations they experience in their production processes, the new aesthetic and technical opportunities they encounter, and the challenges that arise. Specifically, the study assesses how AI-assisted production practices influence perceptions of creativity, decision-making mechanisms in the design process, and the formation of visual language. Furthermore, it discusses potential new aesthetic approaches, production models, and modes of perception in the visual arts and design, drawing upon the perspectives of domain experts and design students. The findings are expected to contribute to current debates on AI and design and to foster an interdisciplinary perspective.

The scope of the research is structured around the role of AI as an agent, the strategic curation it prompts in designers, and the ontological transformation of the produced works. The study addresses this transformation through a combination of theoretical analysis and empirical investigation based on practitioners' experiences. To this end, the interdisciplinary research process is built on the following structure:

- Qualitative Data: Descriptive analysis was conducted through semi-structured interviews with artists, designers, and academics.
- Quantitative Data: Descriptive statistics were derived from a survey administered to a larger participant group to identify general trends.

The research discussed through the concepts of artist-subject agency, hybrid production models, and the role of the designer as a selector/curator. The study is framed around the following hypotheses:

Hypothesis 1: AI functions as an active agent in the design process, influencing designers' decisions, sometimes resisting them, interpreting the process, and ascending to a position of creative co-agency, beyond merely serving as a passive tool.

Hypothesis 2: The ontological center of design shifts from merely shaping forms to selecting and interpreting possibilities from a pool of options.

Hypothesis 3: Design education should evolve from imparting technical skills toward fostering algorithmic literacy competencies capable of managing AI.

Hypothesis 4: While the acceptance of AI agency is legitimized through functionality in design, it encounters greater resistance in the arts due to the necessity of human presence and ethical considerations.

The following research questions have been formulated to systematically assess these hypotheses:

1. How do AI tools transform the balance of agency in the designer's creative process, and how is this transformation interpreted by designers?

2. How does the transition from the designer's role as a technical producer to that of a strategic curator affect professional identity and perceptions of originality?
3. In design education, what paradigm shifts emerge along the axes of skill and technology when AI support is integrated?
4. How do the art and design disciplines diverge in terms of the artistic status and ethical legitimacy of AI-generated outputs?

This research stands out by going beyond a mere technical evaluation of artificial intelligence; it situates it within a solid ontological and aesthetic framework. By synthesizing theoretical approaches from Manovich(2001), Heidegger (2011), Danto(1964), Dickie (1969), and Weitz (1956) with empirical data collected from experts and students, the study offers a comprehensive perspective on the evolving boundaries of creativity. The findings are expected to serve as a fundamental reference for redefining professional identity in the age of algorithmic production and to provide strategic recommendations for the future of design education.

THEORETICAL AND PHILOSOPHICAL APPROACHES: WHAT IS ART? FROM NEW MEDIA TO ARTIFICIAL INTELLIGENCE

This section discusses how artificial intelligence represents a new paradigm in the evolution of art, extending beyond its role as a mere tool. This paradigm is examined through technological and philosophical interpretations of art and design, tracing the trajectory from the new media era to the age of artificial intelligence.

Throughout history, art has remained an open-ended concept, continuously redefined in response to evolving cultural and technological contexts. Traditional definitions of art began to be challenged in the latter half of the 20th century, particularly with the rise of digital technologies (Dickie, 2001). The concept of new media emerged not merely as a change in artistic tools but as a paradigm questioning the ontological, epistemological, and phenomenological foundations of art itself. At its core, a new understanding of art has emerged that challenges the established conventions of traditional art in both practice and content. In this regard, the first noticeable distinction is the separation between art and design.

The question of what constitutes art has never yielded a universally agreed-upon definition within the history of aesthetics and the philosophy of art. Art acquires meaning according to historical and cultural contexts and is continuously reinterpreted through each new form and mode of production (Dickie, 2001: 7). While classical approaches have treated art as a representation of nature, an expression of beauty, or a product of skilled craftsmanship, contemporary theories focus on the processes of meaning-making, experiential engagement, and contextual interpretation.

This diversity underscores the difficulty of framing art through a fixed, essentialist definition (Deleuze & Guattari, 1993: 172). The transformation and shift in the production of artworks has evolved from a fixed definition towards indeterminacy.

Since the last quarter of the 20th century, the acceleration of digitalization has redefined the relationship between art and technology through new media art. The proliferation of computer-assisted production has shifted artists from being subjective agents making aesthetic decisions to becoming designers and system developers collaborating with algorithms. This transformation has progressively blurred the boundaries between human and machine in artistic production (Johnson & Shaw, 2005:10). Artificial intelligence technologies play a decisive role in this ongoing transformation of new media art. Through machine learning, deep learning, and generative models, art production has evolved from a human creativity-centered process into a hybrid domain shaped by datasets, algorithms, and statistical probabilities. AI-supported systems offer artists new opportunities for the automatic generation, transformation, and diversification of aesthetic forms (Wands, 2006: 14). In this context, AI functions both as a tool and as a co-creator within new media art. Artists guide the production process through their interactions with AI; however, the outcomes often exhibit unpredictable and variable characteristics. This dynamic challenges traditional concepts of control, authenticity, and authorship in art.

In contemporary new media practices, AI-supported productions frequently take the form of data-driven visualizations, generative aesthetic applications, and interactive installations. Algorithms fueled by large datasets generate visual and auditory outputs, which are continuously reshaped through interaction with audiences (Özselçuk, 2023). Consequently, the artwork emerges not as a finished object but as a living, evolving process. According to Lewis (2014), AI was first formally defined in 1956 at Dartmouth College in Hanover, New Hampshire (Lewis, 2014). In the 1960s, pioneers such as Frieder Nake, Georg Nees, and Vera Molnár initiated computer art, marking the first experimental application of Manovich's (2001) principle of automation as an artistic agency. During this period, the artist acted less as the producer of the final visual and more as the designer of a pool of probabilistic possibilities from which the visual would emerge. At this point, it can be stated that the artist occupies the position of an aesthetic decision-maker, with the activation of their consciousness and decision-making mechanism.

A landmark in AI and art is Harold Cohen's AARON program, developed in the 1970s. AARON went beyond being a simple tool to become one of the first AI agents capable of making autonomous decisions within rules taught by the artist (Çelebi, 2021:88; Güney & Yavuz, 2020: 425; Al, 2019:83). This historical milestone forms the foundation for the concept of hybrid subjectivity underpinning this study.

By the 2010s, with the advancement of deep learning and neural networks, the process shifted from rule-based formalism to data-driven production. One prominent example is Google's DeepDream program, which uses data collected from Google's visual search engine to transform uploaded images into content that can be considered artistic. Alex Rayner, writing for The Guardian, notes that while the program sometimes produces impressive results, it can also fail to meet expectations. Rayner explains that DeepDream began development in 2014 at Google's Zurich office and that the algorithm was designed to amplify features based on perceived patterns, such as clouds resembling birds (Rayner, 2016). This example demonstrates how algorithms have increasingly become an active agent in the creative process.

Digitalization has caused profound transformations in artistic production processes, reshaping both the form and content of aesthetic experience. Digitally produced artworks transcend material limitations, becoming reproducible, modifiable, and interactive. In this context, algorithms evolve from technical tools into active systems generating aesthetic decisions. Algorithmic aesthetics allows for unforeseen visual and auditory outcomes within parameters set by the artist. These unpredictable infinite combinations require strategic selection. At this stage of the process, there is a need for selective curators who not only possess intellectual expertise but also have the capacity to develop original perspectives.

In new media art, AI treats data as a raw material. For artists, the role of brushstrokes has been replaced by the training of vast datasets and the discovery of hidden patterns within them. AI-focused artworks are often understood less as visualizations of data than as reinterpretations of data. The artist assumes the role of curator, training the algorithm, setting parameters, and selecting outcomes from the results produced.

Lev Manovich and Software Culture

Lev Manovich identifies the defining characteristics that distinguish new media from traditional forms of media as numerical representation, modularity, automation, variability, and the separation between code and interface. While specific content exists in digital environments, Manovich asserts that new media fundamentally relies on a software-based logic of production and representation (Winegard, 2019: 74). In this context, digital art practices transform into dynamic structures generated through code, data, and algorithms (Wands, 2006: 14-21). From the perspective of artificial intelligence, it can be observed that new media approaches and digital art practices have evolved into a more advanced and productive model within the creative process.

Manovich's concept of software culture emphasizes that contemporary aesthetic production largely occurs within software environments. New media objects are represented through digital code, can be mathematically defined, and processed algorithmically. While software serves as the technical language in which content is produced, it also functions as an environment in which aesthetic decisions are made, shaped, and constrained (Güney & Yavuz, 2020: 434). Artists produce works within the tools, interfaces, and algorithmic possibilities offered by software, which indirectly guides their aesthetic choices. Similarly, McLuhan's dictum, "the medium is the message" (McLuhan, 1965), suggests that works created within software-mediated environments can also be understood as a new form of communication.

In software-based production, the artist assumes a position not of directly producing objects but of designing rules, parameters, and systems. This approach frames artistic creativity not as a singular act but as a process-oriented design activity. According to Manovich, software constitutes the new infrastructure of cultural production, becoming a fundamental layer that shapes how aesthetic forms emerge (Manovich, 2001). In this regard, software culture provides a theoretical framework for understanding AI-supported artistic production and makes visible the decisive role of algorithms in aesthetic processes.

New media, with its characteristics of digital codability, modularity, automation, variability, and cultural transmission (Manovich, 2001), has fundamentally transformed the production, distribution, and consumption of art. This transformation shifts art from a traditional object-centered understanding to a process-, interaction-, and data-centered perspective. Consequently, new media art relocates the question "What is art?" into a technological and philosophical inquiry alongside aesthetic considerations. In the understanding of art that emerged with new media and beyond, the artist and the artwork are complemented by the inclusion of the viewer/audience. Due to the interactive nature of this art, the viewer/audience assumes a participatory role in the subsequent process.

Manovich foresaw, through the principles of automation and variability, that new media could generate objects without human intervention. Generative AI maximizes the principle of variability, producing thousands of variations from a single prompt within seconds. Furthermore, regarding database aesthetics, Manovich posits that new media is not a narrative but a database (Pepi, 2020). AI design functions as an algorithmic selection and synthesis within this vast pool of data.

Philosophical Paradigm in the Context of Art Theories and Artificial Intelligence

The legitimacy of AI-supported productions as artworks is less a matter of technological proficiency than a philosophical problem of definition. Because of the changes brought about by artificial intelligence, there has been a shift in the ontological and epistemological nature of art. Furthermore, considering the way an artwork is received by the participant, there has been a need for different evaluative perspectives. This section examines AI objects through the layers of ontological status, epistemological knowledge production, and phenomenological experience, synthesizing them with foundational art theories.

Ludwig Wittgenstein's later work Philosophical Investigations (1953/2007) introduces the concept of family resemblance, which constitutes a cornerstone of art philosophy. According to Wittgenstein, when we consider the concept of "game," it is impossible to identify a single common feature that encompasses all games. Some games involve competition, others rely on amusement; some are governed by rules, others allow improvisation. Yet, despite these differences, what allows all these activities to be called "games" is a network of overlapping and crisscrossing similarities. Just as family resemblance emerges through the intergenerational transmission of varied traits such as eye color, nose shape, and gestures- even when no single physical feature is shared- concepts cohere through networks of resemblance (Wittgenstein, 1953/2007). When Wittgenstein's approach is applied to art, the multiplicity and diversity of definitions come to the forefront. Art encompasses a variety of practices, forms, and meanings that cannot be defined through a single essence. Therefore, the answer to the question 'what art is' should be sought not in a fixed definition, but within a network of overlapping and intersecting similarities.

Wittgenstein's concept laid the foundation for Morris Weitz's major contribution to the philosophy of art. In The Role of Theory in Aesthetics (1956), Weitz applied Wittgenstein's analysis of games to the concept of art, arguing that art, like games, cannot be defined through necessary and sufficient conditions and is instead an open concept. According to Weitz, art is a concept family that has historically expanded through new forms, techniques, and semantic domains, its boundaries inherently indeterminate (Weitz, 1956). This approach offers a paradigm for understanding and conceptualizing the evolving notion of art. The evaluation of art, the artwork, and the artist is a system of values that can be measured by the dominant paradigm of the period. Each era defines its own aesthetic criteria, taste judgments, and conditions for artistic legitimacy; within this framework, the meanings attributed to art, the artist, and the artwork also undergo transformations.

AI-supported productions provide contemporary examples that reaffirm Weitz's thesis of the open concept. A visual generated by an AI algorithm shares family resemblances with traditional artworks: it may exhibit composition like a painting, realism like a photograph, assemblage like a collage, or provoke conceptual inquiry like conceptual art. Yet, it does not share identical properties with any conventional artwork: it has no human hand, its intentionality is debatable, and its originality depends on its dataset. What qualifies it as art is the overlapping and crisscrossing network of resemblances it shares with traditional artworks. In this sense, an AI-generated visual adds a novel family resemblance to the art family, one characterized by algorithmic production. Just as photography or digital techniques historically expanded the art family, AI similarly redefines the boundaries of art (Özselçuk,

2023). Following Weitz, the concept of art expands to include this new member; during this expansion, boundaries are negotiated, and new resemblances transform previous definitions. In this context, Weitz's approach provides the legitimacy of the artwork produced with artificial intelligence as a work of art.

Another consequence of Weitz's (1956) open-concept thesis is that attempts to define art contradict its creative nature. AI exemplifies this claim: criteria such as human creation, conscious intention, and originality would have excluded AI outputs a decade ago. Today, however, AI-generated works fetch millions at auctions, demonstrating that the art world recognizes these outputs as legitimate members. This recognition is the product of historical and contextual consensus rather than a universal definition (Dickie, 2001; Weitz, 1956). Consequently, cultural approaches to the nature of art remain indispensable.

Paradigmatic shifts have led to new definitional explorations beyond closed definitions of art. Traditional definitions- mimetic, expressive, formalist- have proven inadequate in certain contexts, emphasizing anthropocentric perspectives focused on the artist. As Weitz (1956) notes, each closed definition elevates one aspect of art while excluding others. Similarly, Arthur C. Danto emphasizes that what makes an object an artwork is not its physical properties but its theoretical and historical context (Danto, 2013). Taken together, these approaches suggest that AI-supported productions should not be regarded as threats to the art concept but as reflections of its evolving, contextual nature, indicating an ontological transformation of the artwork.

Discussions of the ontological status of art trace back to Ancient Greece. In *The Republic* (c. 380 BCE/2022), Plato positions art as a passive reflection of reality and a flawed imitation. A carpenter's bed copies the idea of a bed, while a painter's depiction of the bed is a copy of a copy, distancing art from truth. In this hierarchy, the artist lacks true knowledge of the subject and is primarily an imitator, marginalized socially (Plato, c. 380 BCE/2022). At this point, the object, representation, and function have been evaluated separately.

The question "What is an artwork?" may seem straightforward but is highly complex; no universally satisfying answer has been found (Carey, 2005: 15). Traditionally, the artwork is conceived as a physical, singular object (Heidegger, 2011). AI complicates this ontological inquiry, raising questions such as whether an algorithmic collage composed of thousands of data fragments can be considered ontologically original. Co-creativity- artistic production in collaboration with machines- further challenges traditional notions of authorship. This necessitates reconsideration of the question "What is art?" through the lens of historical and contemporary art theory.

Weitz, following Wittgenstein, argues that art cannot be captured by a single concept but is instead defined by resemblances, relations, and their networks. George Dickie extends this perspective through his Institutional Theory of Art, asserting that art's definition is socially mediated. For Dickie (1969), an artwork is: (1) human-made, (2) a candidate, (3) presented to the art world, and (4) recognized within that institutional context. Art thus gains status not from inherent properties but from institutional recognition. According to this definition, the status of an object as a work of art is determined by the space in which it is exhibited and the individuals associated with that space. In this context, what is defined and named by the art world is considered to be a work of art. In other words, to be a work of art is not an intrinsic characteristic of the object, but rather a status attributed to it within a specific institutional framework.

Contrastingly, Plato's mimetic view situates art ontologically distant from truth, whereas Danto (1964) contends that art is liberated from visual imitation and acquires meaning within a theoretical context. AI output exemplifies this ontological threshold: technical proficiency may perfect mimetic aspects, but artistic status depends on interpretive and theoretical framing. Warhol's Brillo Boxes (1964) illustrate this: physically identical objects differ ontologically due to their placement within the art world and theoretical discourse (Lenoir, 2005). AI outputs similarly derive ontological legitimacy not from production alone but from their contextual embedding.

Epistemologically, the artwork's status entails questions of recognition and understanding. With AI, the query extends to "How do I know this is art?" Who produced it- human, machine, or both? Which knowledge frameworks are operative? This shifts knowledge production from direct human creation to interaction between linguistic prompts and algorithmic data spaces, positioning the designer as an epistemic curator rather than a craftsman (Purves, 2005). The work created through linguistic inputs and algorithmic guidance requires a layer of information, or in other words, human selection, during the evaluation phase at the end of the production process. In this context, while artificial intelligence actively participates in the production process, the final decision and interpretation remain with the human.

AI is no longer merely a tool but a collaborative partner in hybrid production, combining human intuition with probabilistic computation to produce novel visual languages. Meaning emerges through interaction, not solely from the designer or the algorithm. The Institutional Theory supports this view, highlighting that art status arises from recognition and positioning within the art world rather than inherent properties. AI-supported production thus challenges traditional conceptions of artistic agency, distributing authorship between human and machine. Historically, institutions such as religion, state, and private sectors have mediated art's value, aligning with Danto's concept of the art world (Gültekin, 2014). The interactive collaboration between humans and artificial intelligence is transforming not only the production process but also the positioning of the artwork within the art world. The artworks exhibited in the art world are becoming interactive structures that are reshaped through the audience's participation. This situation necessitates a re-examination of how art is experienced. From a phenomenological perspective, the viewer's experience in relation to artificial intelligence production is shaped less by the physical presence of the artwork and more by the theoretical atmosphere surrounding it and the possibilities for interaction.

Finally, phenomenologically, AI complicates experience. Visually indistinguishable objects are experienced differently due to context and theoretical framing (Danto, 1964; Toprak, 2020). Similarly, AI outputs acquire artistic meaning through exhibition, discourse, and audience engagement. New media amplifies these possibilities, positioning the viewer as a participatory actor in the artwork's phenomenological realization.

METHODOLOGY

This study is designed to understand the ontological, epistemological, and phenomenological transformations of AI-supported art and design productions. Rather than seeking an essential definition of art, the research aims to examine how these productions are positioned within the art world and how they are interpreted by relevant actors. Accordingly, the study is structured within an interpretivist paradigm. The interpretivist approach assumes that social reality is not an objectively discoverable structure but a process constructed and interpreted by actors (Neuman, 2014, p. 135). Within this framework, AI-generated art practices are approached not as measurable technical outputs but as cultural constructs shaped through meaning, experience, and context.

To analyze how AI transforms design practices both theoretically and empirically, the study adopts a mixed-methods approach. The research aims to test theoretical claims- developed through Lev Manovich's new media perspective and ontological, epistemological, and phenomenological philosophical frameworks- against the lived experiences of practitioners.

Within the interpretivist paradigm, the study employs a mixed-methods design. Two primary instruments were used for data collection: semi-structured in-depth interviews with artists, designers, and academics actively using AI tools, and a Likert-scale questionnaire to identify broader participant trends. Qualitative data were analyzed using descriptive analysis methods, while quantitative data were evaluated through descriptive statistics.

The study sample was determined using purposive sampling. The participants included artists, designers, and individuals trained in relevant fields who actively use AI-supported design tools. This approach aligns with the theoretical framework of the study, aiming to center the perspectives of key actors within the art world.

FINDINGS AND DISCUSSION

In this section, quantitative data obtained from 76 participants and qualitative findings derived from semi-structured interviews (with Prof. Dr. Selçuk Artut and Asst. Prof. İrem Çoban) are synthesized. The data are structured to test four main hypotheses and address the research questions within the interpretivist paradigm.

A total of 76 individuals (N = 76) participated in the study. Of the participants, 48.6% were aged 25-34, while 31.4% were aged 35- 44. The fact that 57.4% of the sample held postgraduate degrees indicates the academic depth of the perspectives provided. This qualified profile also reflects that the interviewees have firsthand experience with the technological paradigm shifts discussed in the study. During the analysis of the findings, the hypotheses defined within the scope of the study were matched with specific themes. Subsequently, these hypotheses were tested and interpreted using the data obtained.

Hybrid Agency Analysis

The first hypothesis of the study posits that artificial intelligence has evolved from a passive tool into a creative agent.

More than 80% of participants identified AI systems as a creative partner (Figure 1). AI is extensively utilized in areas such as idea generation, draft creation, and final visual production. These findings indicate that AI is recognized not merely as a command-executing tool but as an active contributor within the creative process. Indeed, the outputs produced demonstrate the collaborative agency of both human and AI actors.

Figure 1. Areas of AI utilization by users (n= 76)

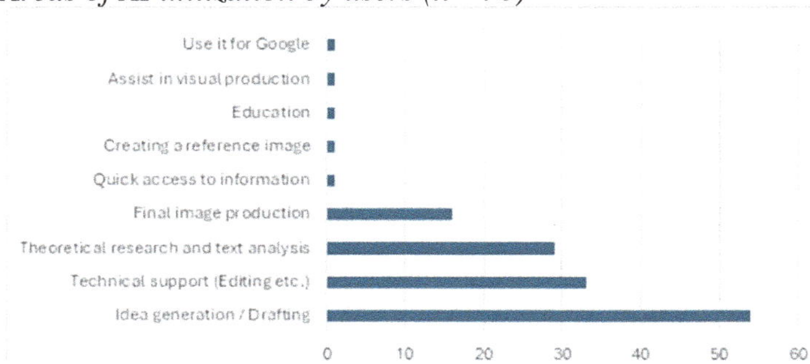

In the interview with Prof. Dr. Selçuk Artut, the role of artificial intelligence in the creative process was characterized not as an autonomous structure independent of the artist's intent, but as an assistant supporting human intellectual capacity. Artut emphasized that the human should always remain at the center of the process, stating:

Prof. Dr. Selçuk Artut's Variable (2017) provides a concrete example of this relationship. The electronic sculpture, composed of nine separate LCD screens, is governed by an algorithm written in the Python programming language, generating a continuously changing, fluid visuality on the screens (Figure 2).

Figure 2. Selçuk Artut, Variable, 2017. 70 × 150 × 20 cm. (Artut, 2017)

Although the system was established by the artist, the algorithm generates its own variations within this system. The resulting visual output cannot be reduced solely to the artist's intention or to the functioning of the algorithm. The outcome of the experience is the product of the interaction between human and machine. This example demonstrates that artificial intelligence has moved beyond being a passive tool and has become an active agent participating in the creative process.

When evaluating the artist's intent, the interactive ontology of the artwork, and the collaborative elements of artificial intelligence alongside both the quantitative and qualitative data of the study, it can be argued that AI-generated artworks transform into a system design. The definition of the artwork can be made at the moment of interaction, and with its characteristics as an engine of possibilities, it offers surprises to the artist while expanding the artist's universe, forming a multi-layered structure. These findings do not undermine the artist's agency over the artwork but reveal a creative process in which the artist shares their dominion with the machine.

Curatorial Transformation and Decision-Making Analysis

The H2 hypothesis suggests that the designer's role extends beyond technical execution, as it involves selecting from a pool of possibilities generated by AI. This process is therefore interpreted as evolving into strategic curatorship. More than 50% of participants reported that they felt like a curator or decision-maker while using AI tools (Figure 3).

Figure 3. Responses to the question on AI users' role as strategic curators

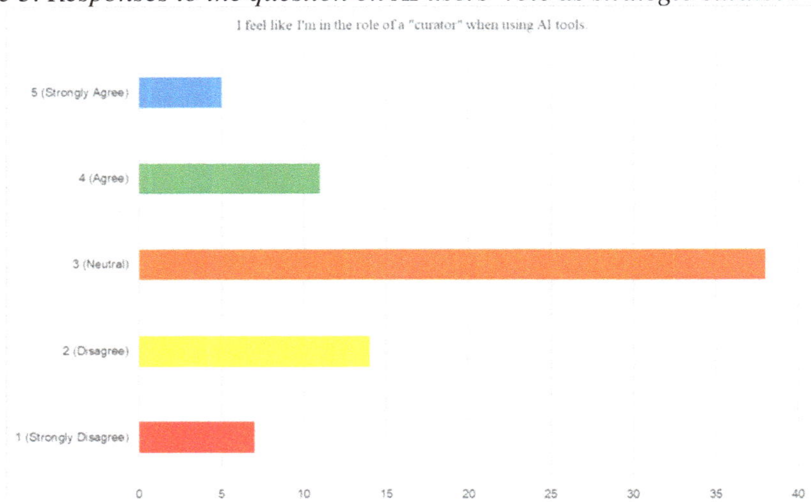

These results suggest that creativity requires the ability to identify the correct choice among thousands of possibilities. This shift has moved the ontological focus of design from the production of objects to the process of selection, interpretation, and meaning-making of objects.

Educational Paradigm Shift and the Talent Paradox Analysis

The H3 hypothesis argues that AI will create a profound rupture in art and design education. Approximately 80% of participants expressed full consensus that AI will fundamentally transform design education and that curricula should be restructured to reflect this new reality (Figure 4).

In the interview, İrem Çoban noted, "My students are more conservative than I am," which can be interpreted as the designer-subject's reflex to protect their craft and skills from the algorithm. On the other hand, students lacking technical drawing skills using AI as a creativity prosthesis demonstrates that education should now focus less on technical tools and more on algorithmic literacy.

The quantitative and qualitative findings obtained in this study suggest that different forms of education may be required. In this context, it is necessary to redefine roles in education, with steps not only for technical updates but also for a shift in perspective to address this dual conflict.

Figure 4. Participants' responses on the future of design education

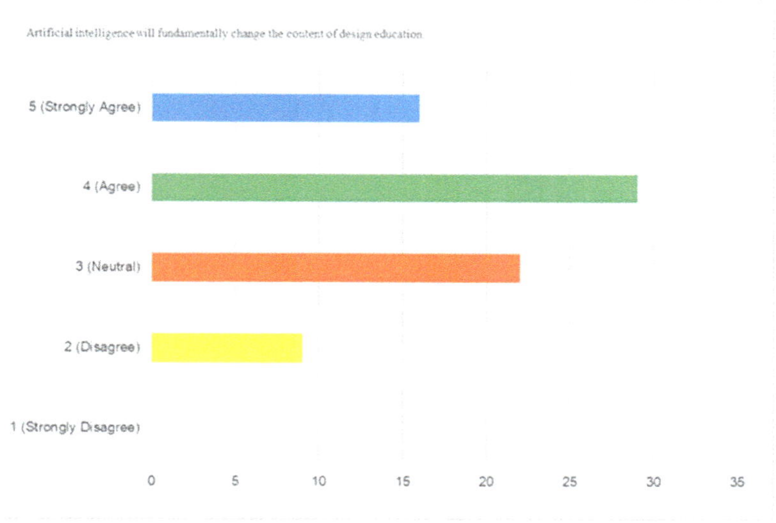

Disciplinary Divergence: Analysis of Design Functionality and Artistic Subjectivity

The H4 hypothesis posits that while AI usage is legitimized in design through functionality, it encounters resistance in the realm of art.

While there was full consensus on the speed and efficiency of AI, opinions on originality and artistic value were more fragmented, concentrating around ratings of 3 and 4 (Figure 5). In design, AI usage does not pose an ethical obstacle as long as it ensures functionality; in art, however, the human presence remains a necessary component.

Figure 5. Responses to questions on AI, originality, and creativity

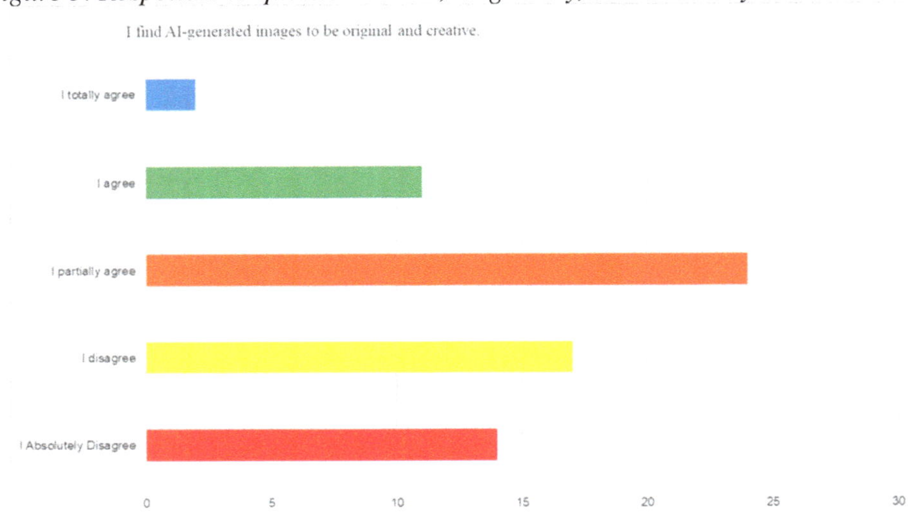

The differing perspectives seen in this hypothesis stem from the fundamental significance of human existence. While artificial intelligence has secured a positive position in terms of functionality, particularly in speed and efficiency, it has shown hesitation in attributing characteristics traditionally associated with the human experience, such as originality and creativity, to a machine (Figure 6).

Figure 6. Responses to the question on AI and art

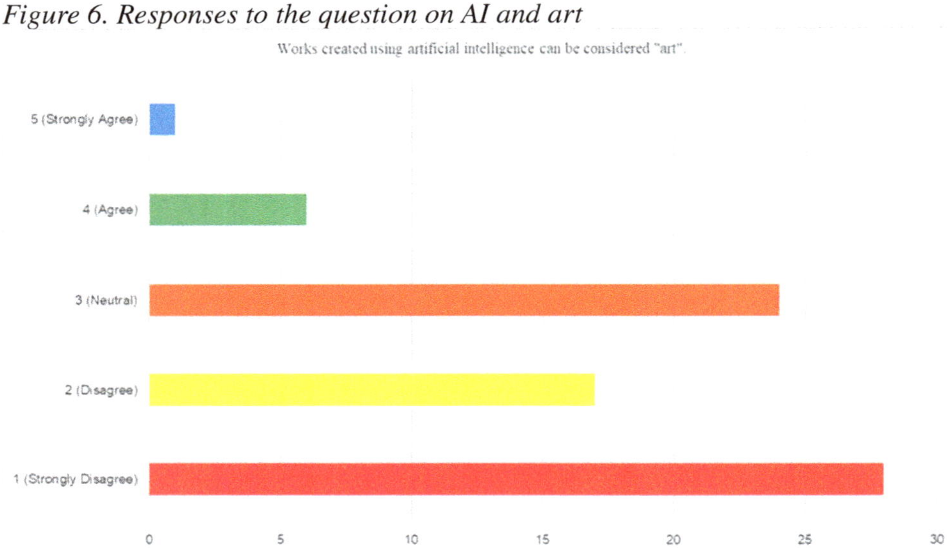

Holistic Synthesis: The Relationship Between Theoretical Framework and Findings

This study approaches the role of artificial intelligence in the design ecosystem not merely as a technological innovation, but as a paradigm shift that challenges and reconfigures the ontological foundations of design. When the quantitative and qualitative findings are integrated with the theoretical framework based on art philosophy, the designer's position as a "New Agent" is synthesized along three main axes.

Table 1. Overall findings and synthesis

Hypothesis	Theoretical Basis	Quantitative Finding (N=76)	Qualitative Evidence (Expert Opinion)
H1: Agency/Hybrid Subjectivity	Manovich / Automation	More than 80% of participants Co-Creator	Dialogue Partner/ Assistant
H2: Curatorial Role	Dickie/Corporate Approval	%50 Curator Sense	The Importance of Human-Centered Choices
H3: Education Paradigm	Algorithmic Literacy	80% Participation	Skills and Prosthetic Skills
H4: Interdisciplinary Differences	Danto/ Theoretical Atmosphere	Indecision in Originality	The Distinction Between Art and Design

This study defines artificial intelligence as a paradigm shift that disrupts the ontological foundations of design, demonstrating the evolution of the designer from a form-giving craftsman to an epistemic curator who governs possibilities. The research reveals that in design, legitimacy is achieved through functional efficiency, whereas in art, human existence remains an indispensable ethical threshold. It emphasizes that education should focus not on technical skills, but on algorithmic literacy and the ability to use machines as creativity prostheses (Table 1).

Human as Approver and Decision-Maker: Dickie and Curatorial Transformation

In the interview with Selçuk Artut, the role of artificial intelligence in the creative process was described not as an autonomous entity independent of the artist's intention, but rather as an "assistant" that supports human intellectual capacity. Artut emphasizes that the human must always remain at the center of the process:

"Artificial intelligence actually presents you with a set of possibilities, but it is still you who decides which of these possibilities is valuable. In other words, the hand that presses the button and the eye that selects the outcome must possess accumulated experience. AI cannot independently say ‘this is beautiful’ or ‘this is a work of art’; the label is always applied by a human.” (Artut, 2026).

This perspective aligns directly with George Dickie’s Institutional Theory of Art. According to Dickie, it is the art world- or an actor acting on its behalf- that grants an object its status as art. Artut’s emphasis on the acts of “making a choice” and “applying a label” corresponds to Dickie’s notion of the authority to determine the “candidate for appreciation” status. While AI, following Manovich’s (2001) principle of variability, can generate an infinite number of candidates, it is ultimately the human or the appreciating institution that elevates these candidates to the level of a “work of art.”

Meaning Construction and Functional Aesthetics: Danto’s Atmosphere and the Boundaries of Design

Arthur Danto’s theoretical concept of the “atmosphere” that distinguishes an ordinary object from an artwork helps explain why and how AI-generated outputs are recognized as “art” or “design.” The “chair” example highlighted by Asst. Prof. İrem Çoban in the interview demonstrates that design is legitimized through functionality, whereas in art the presence of the subject is sought. According to Çoban, AI can technically produce a flawless form, but it is the artist who situates this form within an artistic narrative and imbues it with the atmosphere of meaning described by Danto. By placing the mechanical output of AI into a cultural context, the artist elevates it from a mere dataset to the level of a “work of art.”

Çoban emphasizes the ontological distinction between design and art as follows:

“If AI designs a chair for me with perfect ergonomics and aesthetic appeal, and the chair fulfills its function, it no longer matters who designed it. But when it comes to a painting, I am looking for the human behind the brushstroke, the lived experience. Design is outcome-oriented, while art is subject-oriented.” (Çoban, 2026).

According to Danto, what makes an object a work of art is the narrative that accompanies it. In this context, the production of art requires meaning, and for this meaning, a human subject is necessary. In design, however, AI’s role as the agent is unproblematic as long as functionality is achieved.

The Open Concept and Resistance to the Subject: Weitz and the Uncanny Agent Experience

Morris Weitz’s thesis that art is an ever-expanding open concept provides a foundation for understanding the uncertainties and innovations introduced by artificial intelligence. The struggle experienced by Asst. Prof. İrem Çoban in the AI-generated film scene exemplifies the limits of openness within Weitz’s theory and symbolizes

AI's resistance as an unpredictable agent to the designer. The "cloak continuity" experience, highlighted in the interview with İrem Çoban, demonstrates that AI operates not merely as a tool within the technical production process, but also as an autonomous agent that resists the designer's will.

Çoban describes this process as follows:

"I could never place the cloak exactly where I wanted it (Figure 7). The machine acted according to its own logic; sometimes the cloak remained inside the character, and at other times it hovered in midair. I fought with it for ten days: it would propose something, I would reject it; I would request something, and it would produce an entirely different outcome." (Çoban, 2026). Çoban's struggle with the machine illustrates that the designer is no longer an absolute authority over the process; rather, they engage in a dialogue with an unpredictable agent capable of imagination and interpretation. In this context, the cloak, at the moment it resists the designer and offers a new interpretation, ceases to be merely a software output and becomes an aesthetic co-creator. This situation exemplifies a non-deterministic relationship with a technology that exhibits imaginative agency.

Figure 7. İrem Çoban – Essence, 2025

CONCLUSION

This study analyzed the impact of artificial intelligence technologies on the fields of art and design within an epistemological, ontological, and phenomenological framework, synthesizing both quantitative and qualitative data. The findings confirm that AI is not merely a tool for efficiency, but a central paradigm capable of fundamentally transforming the designer's agency and professional identity.

The main conclusions derived from the research can be summarized as follows:

Redistribution of Agency and Hybrid Subjectivity: The H1 hypothesis proposed at the outset of the study is largely validated. Approximately 80% of participants identified AI as a creative partner, and the inclusion of AI as an agent in the production processes of Prof. Dr. Selçuk Artut and Asst. Prof. İrem Çoban confirms that design operates within a field of hybrid subjectivity. In the produced works, the artwork achieves a new perspective at the ontological level. Despite hybrid subjectivity, human-centered design continues to hold significance. From a phenomenological standpoint, the interaction between the artwork and its perceiver questions the human-centered nature of the work. Human touch and decision-making remain central in the artist's ethical and conscientious approaches.

The Rise of the Curatorial Designer Model: Within the framework of H2, the designer's role is seen to have evolved from a technical executor to a strategic curator who employs AI as a decision-making mechanism. Moreover, it is emphasized that the designer requires not only input commands but also an aesthetic and conscious foundation when selecting data. The artist or designer must select and determine the epistemic qualities of an artwork from among thousands of datasets, making the context of the produced data critically important.

Paradigm Shift in Education and the Talent Paradox: In line with the H3 hypothesis, a fundamental transformation in design education has been identified or is anticipated. Approximately 80% of participants acknowledged this shift, indicating that education should now focus more on algorithmic literacy competencies than on traditional craft skills. In this context, both the ontological and value-based dimensions of an artwork must be re-evaluated, and production processes should be adapted into the curriculum.

Ontological Divergence, Functionality, and Artistic Signature: According to the H4 hypothesis, AI acceptance varies across disciplines. In design, AI use is legitimized through functionality, whereas in art, human presence remains a core value. A design object may allow the producer's perspective to recede if it fulfills its purpose. For an artwork, however, human-centeredness is fundamentally prioritized.

Overall, AI elevates the designer from technical labor to a position of decision-making and meaning-making while providing a technological infrastructure to support these functions. This elevation, however, makes the designer's ethical and intellectual responsibility more critical than ever. The designer of the future must act as a strategic agent, capable of integrating algorithmic data with the intuitive knowledge of human will. At this point, hybrid production models and specific agent experiences should be examined and researched from a human-centered perspective.

The integration of AI into the design ecosystem has also introduced a complex set of unresolved ethical and legal debates. Artut highlights the training of AI on massive datasets and its relationship with the artist's labor, pointing to a future in which design will intersect with legal struggles alongside aesthetic considerations. In light of the findings of this study, the following open-ended questions emerge as crucial for future research:

Algorithmic Ownership and Labor: How can the rights of artists whose data have been used in training AI models be protected in the outputs generated by these models? Does this emerging mode of production necessitate a redefinition of intellectual property?

Ethical Agency and Responsibility: Who is accountable for AI-generated designs that involve ethical violations or copyright infringement?

Democratization and Exploitation of Copyright: Does AI provide equal opportunities for small-scale designers, or does it become a new tool of exploitation for tech corporations controlling large datasets?

These questions demonstrate that AI aesthetics is not merely a matter of tools or instrumentation but fundamentally concerns rights and justice. The study argues that defining the designer as a curator also entails ethical responsibility for the data used alongside aesthetic decisions. Future research should focus on these ethical curation practices and new copyright models in AI-assisted design to ensure the discipline evolves in a healthy and responsible manner.

REFERENCES

Al, B. (2019). The concept of generative art and digital creativity in visual arts. *Design Informatics*, *1*(2), 78–91.

Artut, S. (2017). *Variable* [Electronic sculpture]. Zilberman Gallery.

Carey, J. (2005). *What good is art?* Vakıfbank Cultural Publications.

Çelebi, B. (2021). *The effect of machines on art and the transformation of the artist from the 20th century to the present* (Master's thesis). Sakarya University, Sakarya, Turkey.

Çoban, İ. (2025). *Substance- Essence* [Film]. Istanbul. Retrieved 10.02.2026 https://filmfreeway.com/Essence998

Çoban, İ. (2026, March 10). *Interview on the role of artificial intelligence in art and design* [In-depth interview by the author]. Personal Archive.

Danto, A. (1964). The art world. *The Journal of Philosophy*, *61*(19), 571–584. DOI: 10.2307/2022937

Danto, A. C. (2013). *What is art?* (Baransel, Z., Trans.). Sel Yayıncılık.

Deleuze, G., & Guattari, F. (1993). *What is philosophy?* (Ilgaz, T., Trans.). YKY.

Dickie, G. (1969). Defining art. *American Philosophical Quarterly*, *6*(3), 253–256.

Dickie, G. (2001). *Art and value*. Blackwell Publishers.

Gültekin, A. C. (2014). The institutional structure of art activity in Arthur Danto and George Dickie. *FLSF Journal of Philosophy and Social Sciences, 18*, 115–132. Retrieved: 08.02.2026 https://izlik.org/JA23NT44LF

Güney, E., & Yavuz, H. (2020). The role of the artist and the changing concept of art in AI-assisted artistic production. *Journal of Art and Design*, *26*, 415–439.

Heidegger, M. (2011). *The origin of the work of art* (Tepebaşlı, F., Trans.). Deki Yayınları. (Original work published 1950)

Johnson, H., & Shaw, J. S. (2005). *Glossary of digital art and printmaking*. Digital Art Practices & Terminology Task Force. Retrieved: 05.03.2026 https://www.bermangraphics.com/dapttf/GlosDigArt.pdf

Lenoir, B. (2005). *The work of art* (Derman, A., Trans.). Yapı Kredi Publications.

Lewis, T. (2014, December 4). A brief history of artificial intelligence. *LiveScience*. Retrieved: 20.03.2026 https://www.livescience.com/49007-history-of-artificial-intelligence.html

Manovich, L. (2001). *The language of new media*. MIT Press.

McLuhan, M. (1965). *Understanding media: The extensions of man*. McGraw-Hill.

Neuman, W. L. (2014). *Social research methods: Qualitative and quantitative approaches I*. Yayınodası Yayıncılık.

Özselçuk, S. K. (2023). A critical study on the use of AI algorithms in digital art: Refik Anadol's *Machine Memories: Space*. *International Journal of Economic and Administrative Academic Research*, *3*(1), 1–21.

Pepi, M. (2020). How does a human critique art made by AI? *Art in America*, *108*(4), 26–29. https://www.artnews.com/art-in-america/features/creative-ai-art-criticism-1202686003/

Plato. (2022). Republic (Translated by S. Eyüboğlu and M. A. Cimcoz). Türkiye İş Bankası Cultural Publications. (Original work written around 380 BC)

Purves, T. (2005). *What we want is free*. State University of New York Press.

Rayner, A. (2016, March 28). Can Google's Deep Dream become an art machine? *The Guardian*. Retrieved: 15.01.2026 https://www.theguardian.com/artanddesign/2016/mar/28/google-deep-dream-art

Shen, Y., & Yu, F. (2021). The influence of artificial intelligence on art design in the digital age. *Hindawi Scientific Programming*, Retrieved: 03.01.2026 1–10. DOI: 10.1155/2021/4838957

Toprak, A. (2020). Transformation of AI algorithms into digital installations. *Yeni Düşünceler E-Refereed Journal*, *14*, 47–59.

Wands, B. (2006). *Art of the digital age* (Akınhay, O., Trans.). Akbank Publications.

Warhol, A. (1964). *Brillo Boxes*. Philadelphia Museum of Art. Retrieved April 5, 2026, from https://www.philamuseum.org/objects/89204

Weitz, M. (1956). The role of theory in aesthetics. *The Journal of Aesthetics and Art Criticism*, *15*(1), 27–35. DOI: 10.1111/1540_6245.jaac15.1.0027

Winegard, E. (2019). The role and significance of digital media technologies in the dissemination of art and design. (Master's thesis). Istanbul University, Istanbul, Turkey.

Wittgenstein, L. (2007). *Philosophical Investigations* (Barışcan, H., Trans.). Metis Publishing. (Original work published 1953)

Chapter 9
GEN-AI + VR:
Toward an Experiential Visual Communication Framework in Interior Architecture

Uğur Efe Uçar
http://orcid.org/0000-0002-1080-3080
Istanbul Technical University, Turkey

ABSTRACT

This chapter examines the intersection of generative artificial intelligence and immersive virtual reality as a transformative shift in the communicative structure of architectural representation. It aims to reconceptualize representation not as a linear process of visual production but as a multilayered system of mediation through which spatial meaning is progressively constructed. The chapter outlines how linguistic input, algorithmic interpretation, visual synthesis, volumetric modeling, and immersive experience operate as interconnected stages within a unified framework. Through this perspective, representation is positioned as a dynamic and iterative process shaped by feedback loops between human intention and computational systems. The proposed AI–IVR mediated framework highlights how design knowledge is generated, evaluated, and reformulated across semantic, visual, geometric, and experiential domains, offering a conceptual model for understanding contemporary interior architectural practice.

INTRODUCTION

Architectural representation has never functioned as a passive record of built form; rather, it has operated as a structured communicative regime that renders

DOI: 10.4018/979-8-2600-2711-0.ch009

spatial ideas legible, negotiable, and transferable among designers, users, and other actors. Historically, orthographic drawings, perspectives, and models have served not only as instruments for expressing design intent but also as epistemic interfaces that determine how spatial meaning is produced, organized, and interpreted. In this sense, representation functions not merely as a medium of transmission but as an active system that shapes the conditions under which design knowledge is generated, reproduced, and circulated.

The historical evolution of architectural representation further demonstrates that representational techniques are not neutral carriers of information but operative systems that structure architectural thinking itself. As Evans (1997) argues, architectural drawings do not translate directly into built form but operate through a sequence of transformations in which each stage introduces interpretive shifts. Representation, therefore, must be understood as a process of mediation rather than direct correspondence, linking conceptual intention to material realization through a structured chain of translations.

Within this framework, representation can be described as a processual system in which ideas are progressively transformed into geometric, visual, and spatial constructs. Each stage in this sequence introduces its own conventions, constraints, and modes of interpretation, thereby actively shaping how architectural knowledge is constructed and communicated. This understanding aligns with the argument that design tools and material systems do not merely support action but fundamentally shape the experience and meaning of that action, as the material configuration of tools structures how activities are performed and perceived (Klapperich et al., 2020).

The transition from geometry-based design practices in the early modern period to numerical and computational forms of representation constituted not only a technical shift but also a rupture that redefined how architectural form is measured, produced, and communicated (Carpo, 2003). Within this transformation, representation became an instrument of standardization grounded in measurability and reproducibility. However, as digital technologies emerged, this relationship began to shift. As Kolarevic (2003) suggests, digital processes increasingly collapse the distinction between representation and production, integrating design generation and fabrication into continuous workflows.

In parallel, the paradigm of "identical reproduction," which became central to modern architecture, has gradually dissolved. As Carpo (2011) argues, the principle of mechanical sameness has given way to variable, derivative, and plural modes of production. In digital environments, design no longer operates as the execution of a fixed notation but as an open-ended system capable of generating multiple variations. Projects are no longer singular objects; instead, they evolve into reproducible and modifiable series of outputs. Architectural representation thus functions not only as a means of depicting space but as a fundamental interface through which space is decoded, coded, and re-coded (Carpo, 2003; 2011).

Rather than replacing representation, digital technologies reorganize its internal structure. Representation becomes increasingly processual, distributed, and interactive, extending beyond linear sequences of idea, drawing, model, and render. Computer-aided design, parametric modeling, and real-time rendering technologies have significantly increased the speed, precision, and variability of representation; however, they have largely preserved the underlying logic of a sequential transformation chain. The design process has therefore continued to rely on a relatively linear production logic, extending from idea to geometry and from geometry to visualization. The conventional workflow operates through sequential dependency, where only limited local iteration is possible, while conceptual revisions require full reconstruction of the entire representational chain (Figure 1). The linear structure illustrated in Figure 1 emphasizes the strict dependency between stages, where each representational layer builds upon the previous one, limiting the possibility of incremental revision and reinforcing a reconstruction-based workflow.

Figure 1. Conventional linear architectural representation workflow

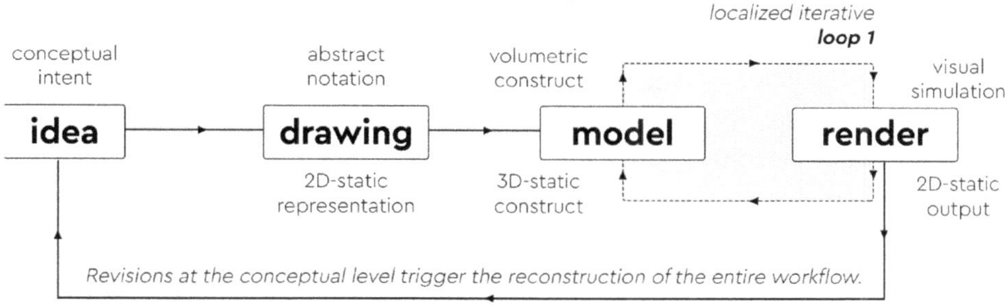

In recent years, the emergence of generative artificial intelligence (Gen-AI) systems has introduced a qualitative and structural rupture within this continuity. Rather than extending the existing representational chain, Gen-AI reconfigures its point of origin. Prompt-based diffusion models, in particular, reposition language from the periphery to the center of the design process by establishing a direct translation mechanism from the linguistic to the visual. A textual expression can be transformed into complex spatial imagery within seconds through text-to-image diffusion models (Rombach et al., 2022). This shift not only accelerates production but also redefines the epistemic structure of design, transforming representation into a dynamic and computational process rather than a fixed mode of depiction (Manovich, 2023; Picon, 2010).

Within this process, Gen-AI ceases to function as a passive tool and instead operates as an interpretive layer embedded within the representational system itself, mediating between human intention and machine interpretation (Suchman, 2007). Production unfolds through two intertwined stages: semantic encoding performed by the designer and probabilistic interpretation executed by the model. The resulting image is neither a direct reflection of the designer's intent nor an entirely autonomous output generated by the machine; rather, it constitutes a hybrid production emerging at the intersection of linguistic expression and data-driven pattern recognition. This condition transforms the nature of authorship in architecture, shifting it toward a distributed and collaborative structure (Elgammal et al., 2017).

However, despite their generative capacity, AI-based systems remain limited in their ability to produce coherent spatial constructs. Inconsistencies in single-perspective generation, disruptions in spatial continuity, and ambiguities in object placement make it difficult to directly employ AI outputs as stable representations of interior space. These limitations are particularly critical in interior architecture, where a single visual frame often contains multiple surfaces, depths, and relational conditions that must remain spatially consistent. As a result, issues of controllability, continuity, and coherence have become central concerns in the integration of Gen-AI into design processes (Lin, 2025).

Despite these advancements, a critical gap remains in the literature. Generative artificial intelligence and immersive virtual reality are predominantly examined as separate domains, focusing respectively on visual generation and experiential simulation. This separation limits the ability to understand how spatial meaning is constructed across successive representational stages, particularly in interior architecture, where visual coherence and experiential validity must operate in tandem. Addressing this gap requires a framework capable of articulating how linguistic, visual, geometric, and experiential layers interact within a unified system of representation.

In response, recent approaches have begun to reconceptualize Gen-AI not as an isolated image-generation tool but as a component within a broader and sequential spatial production system. The integration of low level-of-detail (low-LOD) parametric models with control mechanisms enables AI outputs to align more closely with design intent (Lin, 2025). Similarly, panoramic image generation extends representation beyond single-perspective limitations, enabling a more continuous and immersive perception of space. When coupled with immersive virtual reality (IVR) environments, these developments allow visual outputs to be reinterpreted as spatial experiences rather than static images.

Taken together, these transformations suggest that representation is no longer organized as a linear sequence but as a layered system of mediation in which spatial meaning is progressively constructed across multiple stages, from linguistic encoding to immersive spatial experience (Figure 2). As illustrated in Figure 2, this structure introduces localized iterative loops across multiple representational layers, particularly through linguistic interpretation and generative image production, enabling distributed and incremental refinement across representational layers without requiring full reconstruction of the workflow.

This study makes three primary contributions to the discourse on architectural representation. First, it conceptualizes generative artificial intelligence and immersive virtual reality not as independent tools, but as sequential and interdependent mediation layers within a unified representational system. Second, it reconceptualizes architectural representation as a multilayered, iterative, and feedback-driven process rather than a linear chain of transformations. Third, it situates this transformation within the specific constraints of interior architecture, emphasizing the role of experiential validation in the construction of spatial meaning.

Figure 2. AI-mediated iterative representation workflow

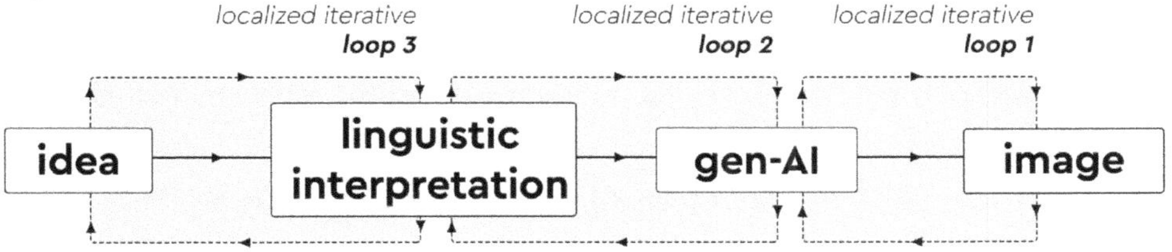

Conceptual revisions can be iteratively processed through localized iterative loops without requiring full reconstruction.

Parallel to the linguistic–visual mediation of artificial intelligence, immersive virtual reality (IVR) introduces a distinct and complementary level of transformation in representation. In traditional visual media, the observer perceives space from an external position, interpreting two-dimensional cues. Immersive environments, by contrast, position the observer within the spatial construct itself, transforming representation into a bodily, situated, and temporal experience. Space is no longer merely an object to be viewed but an environment to be inhabited and navigated.

The literature widely recognizes immersive virtual reality (IVR) as a powerful medium for spatial communication and learning. Immersive environments support multisensory interaction, presence, and experiential learning processes, enabling users to develop a deeper understanding of spatial information (Christou, 2020; Makransky & Petersen, 2021; Radianti et al., 2020). Furthermore, recent studies suggest that VR environments, when integrated with computational systems, can adapt to user behavior and interaction patterns, enabling more responsive and personalized experiences (Makransky & Petersen, 2021). IVR thus operates not only as a representational medium but as an active environment of experiential communication.

Despite these developments, generative artificial intelligence and immersive virtual reality are often addressed within separate research trajectories. The sequential and multilayered mediation processes that emerge at their intersection remain relatively underexplored. While Gen-AI research tends to focus on visual production and generative capacity, IVR studies predominantly emphasize immersion and user experience. As a result, the question of how these systems collectively construct a communicative structure and transform spatial meaning remains fragmented.

When considered together, however, these technologies do not eliminate the representational chain; rather, they expand, stratify, and reorganize it. Spatial meaning is progressively reconfigured through successive transformations, including linguistic articulation, algorithmic interpretation, visual synthesis, volumetric inference, spatial reconstruction, and immersive experience. Representation thus shifts from a singular visual surface to a multilayered communicative sequence that is iterative, feedback-driven, and open to reinterpretation (Figure 3). Figure 3 demonstrates how the integration of immersive virtual reality establishes a closed-loop system, where spatial experience feeds back into conceptual and linguistic stages, enabling continuous, experiential, and cross-layer iteration across the entire representational chain.

Figure 3. AI–IVR mediated representation as a closed iterative system

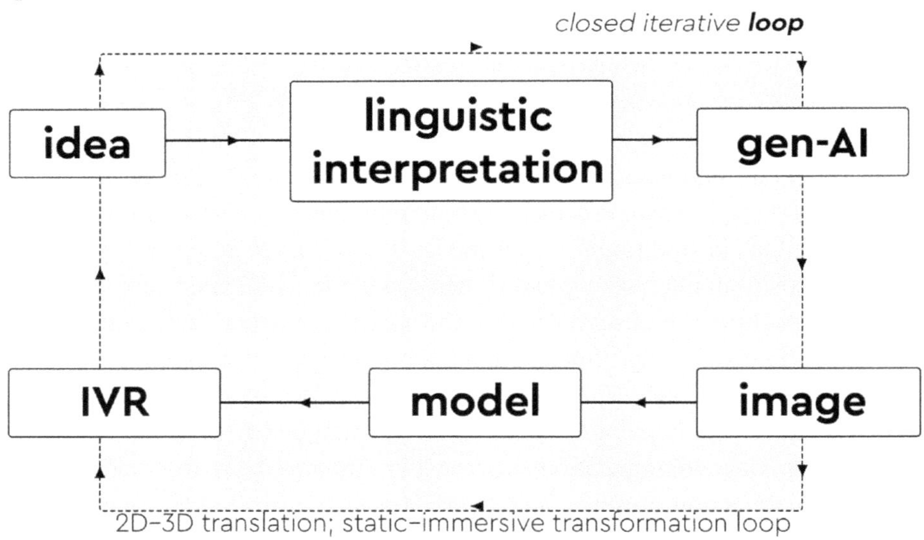

Taken together, Figures 1–3 illustrate a progressive transformation in the structure of architectural representation, from a sequential and reconstruction-based workflow to a distributed iterative system, and ultimately to a closed-loop experiential framework of representation.

In response to this transformation, this study proposes a Gen-AI+IVR mediated framework. This framework reconceptualizes architectural representation not as a static act of depiction but as a cumulative and layered process in which spatial meaning is progressively produced, stabilized, and reinterpreted across technological strata. Methodologically, this study adopts a conceptual and theory-driven approach grounded in the synthesis of existing literature and the interpretive analysis of emerging technological paradigms. Rather than presenting a validated technical workflow or an empirical case study, the study offers a conceptual and interpretive framework for examining how spatial meaning is mediated across linguistic, visual, geometric, and immersive layers. Generative artificial intelligence and immersive virtual reality are therefore approached not in terms of performance or accuracy, but in terms of how they restructure the epistemic conditions of representation. In this sense, the study should be read as a structured inquiry into the evolving nature of representation in interior architecture.

The conceptual framing presented above positions representation as a multilayered and sequential system of mediation. However, such a proposition requires a more detailed examination of the distinct technological layers through which this transformation unfolds. In particular, generative artificial intelligence and immersive virtual reality must be understood not merely as tools, but as fundamentally different modes of mediation operating at separate yet interconnected stages of the representational process. While AI restructures the relationship between language and image through probabilistic interpretation, IVR redefines the relationship between image and space through embodied experience.

Accordingly, the following section examines these two domains in detail, not as isolated technological developments, but as complementary mediation layers that collectively contribute to the reconfiguration of architectural representation. This distinction is essential for establishing the theoretical grounding of the proposed framework.

BACKGROUND

Artificial Intelligence as Linguistic–Visual Mediation

Generative artificial intelligence systems, particularly diffusion-based and prompt-driven models, have fundamentally transformed the conditions of visual production. These systems shift visual generation away from deterministic and rule-based processes toward a logic grounded in learned data distributions and probabilistic synthesis. Studies on generative AI demonstrate that outputs are produced through the modeling of high-dimensional data distributions rather than fixed rules

(Banh & Strobel, 2023). In the context of architecture, this transformation can be understood as repositioning AI-assisted image generation from a representational tool into an active design environment for conceptual exploration, stylistic variation, and rapid iteration.

This shift becomes clearer when situated within the broader evolution of digital design technologies. Early digital systems primarily functioned as tools for representation and documentation, whereas more recent approaches have increasingly positioned computation as an active component of design thinking. Contemporary AI systems extend this trajectory further by enabling iterative and interactive design processes, in which generative systems actively participate in shaping design outcomes rather than functioning solely as passive tools (Horvath & Pouliou, 2024).

One of the most significant transformations identified in recent literature concerns the redefinition of language within the design process. Prompt-based generative systems reposition text as the primary structure through which spatial meaning is encoded, effectively shifting design initiation toward linguistic articulation. In this context, artificial intelligence necessitates the reconceptualization of design tools as linguistic interfaces, where meaning construction precedes and guides visual production (Gökdemir & Kayan, 2025).

This linguistic shift is closely related to broader transformations in how knowledge is encoded and processed within computational environments. Generative AI operates through layered interactions between semantic input, training data, and probabilistic inference, producing outputs that emerge from complex data-driven relationships rather than explicit geometric modeling (Dwivedi et al., 2023). The design process can therefore be understood as a multilayered system operating through semantic encoding, data processing, and probabilistic regeneration.

This transformation has significant implications for mediation and authorship. Research on human–AI interaction in architectural contexts indicates that generative outputs reflect both user input and learned patterns embedded within datasets, resulting in hybrid forms of production shaped by both human intention and algorithmic processes (Horvath & Pouliou, 2024). Recent studies in human–AI interaction further emphasize that this hybrid condition extends beyond a purely technical coupling toward forms of iterative interaction, in which designers and generative systems shape outcomes through prompt exploration, visual feedback, and successive refinement (Brade et al., 2023), reinforcing the notion of distributed agency in human–machine configurations (Suchman, 2007). As a result, authorship becomes distributed across human and computational agencies rather than attributable to a singular designer. Artificial intelligence, in this sense, operates as an interpretive layer mediating between intention and visual output.

Research also highlights the iterative temporality enabled by generative systems. Rapid prompt revisions create a continuous dialogue between textual input and visual feedback, transforming representation from a linear production sequence into a recursive loop. Spatial hypotheses are continuously reformulated through linguistic adjustments and algorithmic regeneration, reframing design as an exploratory field structured by continuous feedback. This recursive cycle has been explicitly described in design studio contexts as an iterative loop of generate–evaluate–select–refine–repeat, where textual prompting and visual assessment operate as coupled phases of design thinking (Kolarevic, 2025).

At the same time, AI-mediated production processes raise critical concerns. Issues such as dataset bias, opacity, and the limitations of generative outputs constitute central debates within contemporary discourse. Generative AI systems are known to reflect biases embedded in training data and to operate through processes that are not fully transparent to users (Floridi & Chiriatti, 2020). While these conditions may constrain design diversity, the same systems also enable expanded exploration through rapid variation and iteration. This dual condition necessitates understanding AI as both a constraining and enabling interface.

From a mediation perspective, artificial intelligence introduces a probabilistic interpretive layer between language and image, fundamentally reorganizing how spatial intent is visually constructed. This layer reveals that representation operates not merely as an output-generating process but as a multilayered communicative system in which meaning circulates between language, data, and algorithmic processes. However, existing literature tends to address this transformation primarily in terms of visual production and creative exploration, without systematically articulating the sequential mediation between linguistic encoding and spatial experience. As a result, the role of AI in architectural representation remains only partially conceptualized.

However, while these studies successfully explain the generative and iterative capacities of AI systems, they tend to remain confined to the domain of visual production. The transition from AI-generated imagery to spatial and experiential representation is rarely addressed as part of a continuous representational process. This limitation restricts the ability to understand how spatial meaning evolves beyond the image, particularly in interior architecture where visual coherence alone is insufficient for spatial validation.

While generative AI redefines the relationship between language and image, it does not inherently resolve how these visual outputs translate into spatial and experiential understanding. This limitation points toward the necessity of complementary systems capable of extending representation beyond the visual domain.

Virtual Reality as Experiential Mediation

Parallel to developments in generative artificial intelligence, immersive virtual reality (IVR) has received increasing attention in architecture, interior architecture, and environmental cognition. Virtual reality can be understood as a multisensory and interactive system that enables users to experience a sense of presence within computer-generated environments (Radianti et al., 2020; Steuer, 1992). Through integrated sensory inputs and real-time interaction, these systems situate the user within a simulated spatial environment, transforming representation from a purely visual transmission into an experiential process.

Recent work in architectural and interior design education further emphasizes that IVR offers an embodied and interactive mode of engagement through which users can explore geometry, spatial relationships, materiality, and design alternatives in real time. In this sense, IVR has been described as a medium capable of bridging the gap between conceptual design and embodied spatial experience, while enhancing students' ability to analyze spatial relationships, proportions, and design alternatives (Cenani et al., 2025; Hou et al., 2024; Kaleja & Kozlovska, 2017; Ritz & Buss, 2016).

One of the key concepts in VR literature is presence, defined as the user's sensation of being located within a virtual environment rather than the physical world (Slater & Wilbur, 1997; Lombard & Ditton, 1997). This condition becomes particularly pronounced in immersive systems such as head-mounted displays, where increased sensory engagement enhances spatial awareness and perceptual involvement (Makransky & Petersen, 2021). In this context, immersion can be understood not only as a technical property of the system but also as a cognitive condition that reshapes how space is perceived and interpreted (Sanchez-Vives & Slater, 2005).

One of the most critical contributions of VR in architectural and interior architectural contexts is the ability to experience space at a 1:1 scale and to incorporate embodied perception into the design process. While traditional representations rely on abstract devices such as perspective and projection, VR environments situate the user within the spatial environment, allowing relationships such as scale, proportion, proximity, and circulation to be experienced through embodied interaction and bodily movement. This demonstrates that spatial cognition is shaped not only visually but also through kinesthetic and sensory processes (Mills & Brown, 2022). In this regard, VR transforms representation from a visualization tool into a cognitive interface through which spatial meaning is constructed experientially.

Empirical findings suggest that immersive environments can approximate real-world spatial perception when perceptual conditions are carefully calibrated. In particular, VR environments can simulate size perception in ways that closely correspond to physical environments, supporting their use as tools for spatial evaluation and validation in design processes (Uçar et al., 2023). However, this perceptual alignment does not emerge automatically; rather, it depends on the interaction between sensory input, cognitive interpretation, and representational structure (Uçar, 2022). From this perspective, VR should be understood not merely as a simulation technology but as a mediated cognitive environment in which spatial perception is actively constructed.

Studies in environmental psychology and design education further demonstrate that this experiential condition has significant effects on cognition and decision-making. Immersive environments enhance spatial awareness, support more intuitive and context-sensitive design decisions, and deepen learning processes (Radianti et al., 2020; Makransky & Petersen, 2021). Recent student-centered research also reports that IVR is perceived positively in educational settings, particularly for its realism, engagement, and potential contribution to learning experience and design skills development (Cenani et al., 2025). More specifically, IVR has been associated with creativity, communication, spatial awareness, and the generation of design alternatives, while also supporting rapid visualization and evaluation during early-stage design processes (Chang et al., 2022; Lombard & Ditton, 1997; Aldrich, 2009).

From the perspective of learning theories, VR signals a shift toward embodied and constructivist modes of knowledge production. Spatial understanding emerges through interaction, movement, and situated engagement rather than detached observation. VR environments operationalize this condition by enabling direct interaction with space, allowing users to construct meaning through experience rather than representation alone (Sanchez-Vives & Slater, 2005). In this regard, IVR should not be reduced to a visualization aid, but understood as an active environment of experiential communication and spatial learning.

The significance of VR becomes even more pronounced in the context of interior architecture. Interior spaces are environments defined by human scale, proximity, materiality, and atmosphere. Immersive environments enable these qualities to be experienced directly, allowing users to evaluate spatial conditions in ways that approximate physical experience. This demonstrates that VR serves not only as a representational tool but also as a medium for spatial validation and experiential assessment.

At the same time, the integration of IVR into design processes is not without constraints. Traditional VR workflows are often introduced in later stages of design due to modeling requirements, technical infrastructure, and time-intensive content production (Portman et al., 2015). Recent educational research further indicates that the effectiveness of IVR environments depends on factors such as interface design, navigational usability, and the overall structure of user interaction (Milovanovic et al., 2017). In addition, studies have identified limitations related to cognitive load, learning complexity, and attention management in immersive environments, which may affect learning outcomes and user performance (Makransky & Petersen, 2021; Elme et al., 2022; Ipsita et al., 2024). Challenges associated with the integration of IVR into design education and workflow adaptation have also been noted (Selzer et al., 2019). These issues indicate that IVR cannot be treated as an automatically seamless replacement for conventional design media.

This also explains why the relationship between IVR and traditional tools remains unresolved. While immersive environments have been shown to support spatial understanding and exploratory engagement with design representations, traditional sketching practices continue to be valued for their immediacy, flexibility, and capacity to support early-stage ideation (Simmons, 2019). IVR should therefore be understood less as a substitute for existing tools than as a complementary medium that reconfigures the structure of design thinking through immersion, embodiment, and real-time interaction.

From a mediation perspective, VR does not eliminate representation; rather, it transforms its nature. The boundary between visual depiction and spatial simulation becomes increasingly permeable, and representation evolves from a static image into a temporal and experiential process. However, existing studies tend to address this transformation primarily in terms of user experience, pedagogy, or visualization performance, without systematically explaining how immersive environments connect to earlier representational stages such as linguistic input and AI-generated imagery. This reveals a critical gap in understanding experiential mediation as part of a broader, multilayered system of architectural representation.

Despite this extensive body of research, immersive virtual reality is predominantly examined as an isolated experiential medium rather than as part of a broader representational system. The relationship between immersive experience and preceding stages of representation—particularly AI-generated imagery and linguistic input—remains insufficiently theorized. This gap limits the ability to conceptualize IVR as an integral mediation layer within a continuous and multilayered process of spatial meaning construction.

Toward a Layered Mediation Model in Interior Architecture

While artificial intelligence restructures the transition between language and image, immersive virtual reality transforms the transition between image and spatial experience. Considered together, these technologies do not operate as independent tools but as sequential mediation layers within an expanded representational system. Rather than functioning as parallel or isolated domains, they establish a continuous chain of transformations in which spatial meaning is progressively reinterpreted across representational stages. Their convergence shifts architectural representation from a linear transmission process into a stratified chain of transformations operating across interconnected domains.

Within this expanded structure, spatial meaning is progressively constructed through multiple stages, including linguistic articulation, algorithmic interpretation, visual synthesis, geometric reconstruction, immersive staging, and embodied experience. Representation thus emerges not as a singular act of depiction but as a cumulative process in which meaning is continuously reformulated across different media and cognitive regimes. Each stage does not merely transmit information but actively reconfigures the status of spatial meaning, introducing new constraints, interpretations, and possibilities.

This layered condition reveals a fundamental transformation in how design knowledge is produced and evaluated. AI-generated images provide probabilistic and data-driven interpretations of spatial intent, while immersive environments enable these interpretations to be experientially tested and reinterpreted. Representation, in this sense, becomes a dynamic system of mediation in which outputs are not final but remain open to iterative refinement across successive layers. This transformation shifts representation from the production of stable outputs toward the continuous negotiation of meaning across domains.

In the context of interior architecture, this transformation gains particular significance. Interior space is inherently relational, defined by bodily proximity, perceptual sensitivity to scale, and material conditions. Even minor deviations in proportion or spatial coherence can directly affect comfort, usability, and experiential quality. While generative AI systems can produce visually compelling yet metrically ambiguous spatial constructs, immersive environments reveal discrepancies related to scale, depth, and spatial continuity through direct experience. This highlights a critical tension between visual plausibility and spatial validity, positioning interior architecture as a key domain in which the limitations of image-based representation become particularly evident. This indicates that representation in interior architecture cannot be evaluated solely through visual fidelity but must also be assessed through experiential validation.

The integration of AI and IVR therefore introduces a recursive feedback structure into the design process. Spatial intent articulated through language is translated into visual form via AI, experienced and evaluated within immersive environments, and subsequently reformulated through conceptual and linguistic adjustments. Representation shifts from a linear production sequence into a feedback-driven and iterative system in which each stage informs and transforms the others. In this sense, representation becomes a recursive system of mediation in which production and evaluation are no longer separable processes but mutually embedded operations.

Despite this emerging condition, existing literature largely treats artificial intelligence and immersive virtual reality as separate domains of inquiry. AI-focused research primarily addresses visual generation, creativity, and data-driven processes, whereas VR studies emphasize immersion, perception, and user experience. Studies that systematically examine how these domains operate as sequential and interdependent mediation layers within a unified representational system remain limited.

As a result, the transformation of representation into a multilayered and continuous system of mediation remains only partially theorized.

This fragmentation points to the need for a conceptual framework capable of explaining how spatial meaning is constructed across these interconnected layers. In response, the following section introduces the AI–IVR Mediated Framework, which conceptualizes architectural representation as a multilayered communicative system operating across linguistic, visual, geometric, and experiential domains. Rather than proposing a fixed workflow, the framework aims to provide an analytical structure through which the evolving relationships between these domains can be examined. Through this framework, the study aims to articulate how spatial meaning is progressively produced, stabilized, and transformed within contemporary design processes.

GEN-AI+IVR FRAMEWORK

The preceding discussions have demonstrated that artificial intelligence and immersive virtual reality should be understood not as isolated tools, but as interrelated mediating systems that restructure how spatial meaning is produced, translated, and experienced. While artificial intelligence operates at the interface between language and image, immersive virtual reality transforms the relationship between image and spatial experience. Considered together, these two domains shift architectural representation from a linear sequence of production into a layered and relational system in which meaning is progressively constructed across multiple transformations.

Conceptually, this framework is developed through a synthesis of existing literature and an interpretive reconstruction of emerging design workflows. It does not describe a fixed or implemented pipeline, but rather proposes an analytical model that articulates how spatial meaning is transformed across successive representational stages.

The AI–IVR mediated framework proposed in this study conceptualizes representation as a multilayered epistemic structure rather than a singular act of depiction. Within this structure, spatial meaning does not move directly from intention to experience but unfolds through a sequence of interconnected stages, including linguistic encoding, algorithmic interpretation, visual stabilization, volumetric inference, spatial reconstruction, immersive staging, and embodied interpretation. Each of these stages operates as both a transformation and a threshold, redefining the status of spatial meaning as it transitions between different representational domains. Rather than being fixed at any single point, meaning is continuously rearticulated, and authorship is redistributed across human intention and computational processes.

The process begins with the construction of linguistic intent, where spatial ideas are articulated through text. At this stage, the designer encodes atmosphere, materiality, scale, and spatial relationships within a semantic structure. Spatial meaning exists here as language, without visual or geometric form, yet this stage is not merely descriptive. Language functions as a generative system that establishes the parameters and constraints for all subsequent transformations, positioning it as the foundational layer of representation.

This linguistic structure is then interpreted through algorithmic processes, where generative models produce visual outputs based on probabilistic associations derived from large-scale datasets. The resulting image stabilizes a particular interpretation of the input, rendering spatial qualities visible for the first time. However, this stabilization should be understood as contingent rather than definitive. The image emerges from the interaction between dataset patterns, learned visual tendencies, and the semantic structure of the prompt, making authorship inherently distributed. At this stage, representation remains within a two-dimensional domain, operating as a visually coherent yet metrically indeterminate construct.

A critical shift occurs in the transition to volumetric approximation, where image-based representations are translated into three-dimensional form. This process generates a spatial scaffold through inferred depth, surface continuity, and geometric relationships. Technically, this transition may involve emerging approaches such as depth estimation models, neural radiance fields (NeRF), Gaussian splatting techniques, or panoramic reconstruction workflows, which infer spatial structure from image-based data. While these methods vary in precision and computational requirements, they share a common principle of reconstructing spatial continuity from probabilistic visual information rather than explicit geometric modeling.

While this introduces spatial continuity, the resulting structure remains provisional and unstable in terms of ergonomics, construction logic, and spatial organization. Issues such as spatial inconsistency, geometric distortion, and AI-induced hallucination effects often emerge at this stage, revealing the limitations of purely image-based inference. This stage therefore functions as an intermediate layer in which meaning transitions from visual composition toward spatial formation, without yet achieving architectural coherence.

The stage of spatial reconstruction introduces a disciplinary intervention in which architectural knowledge is reinserted into the process. Here, the designer reorganizes the generated geometry according to principles of scale, proportion, circulation, and habitability. This transformation does not merely correct geometric inconsistencies; it redefines the epistemic status of the model by translating a probabilistic and visually derived construct into an architecturally grounded spatial system. Representation thus shifts from visual plausibility toward spatial coherence and tectonic validity.

Following reconstruction, the model is prepared for immersive interaction through its integration into real-time environments. This step extends representation into a temporal and interactive domain, where spatial information is no longer static but unfolds through movement and user engagement. The transition from static model to interactive environment marks a shift in how representation operates, transforming it into a performative system.

Within immersive environments, representation acquires an experiential dimension. The user is positioned not as an observer but as a participant situated within space, and spatial meaning is constructed through movement, orientation, and embodied perception. At this stage, representation is no longer confined to visual interpretation but becomes a condition that is directly experienced. Spatial qualities such as scale, proximity, and circulation are evaluated through bodily engagement, allowing inconsistencies that may remain invisible in earlier stages to become perceptually evident.

This experiential condition introduces a critical feedback mechanism. Spatial decisions that appear visually coherent may reveal limitations when experienced, transforming representation into a system of evaluation as well as production. In multi-user environments, this process expands into an intersubjective domain, where spatial meaning is collectively negotiated and reinterpreted. This highlights that experiential validation operates not only as a perceptual test but also as a critical interpretive layer within the design process.

The final stage involves translating experiential feedback back into linguistic and conceptual adjustments. Observations derived from immersion are reformulated into new prompts and design decisions, reinitiating the process. Representation thus becomes recursive rather than linear, operating as a continuous cycle in which spatial meaning is repeatedly produced, tested, and transformed. This recursive structure suggests that design thinking increasingly operates as an iterative dialogue between human intention, computational generation, and embodied experience.

In this sense, the AI–IVR mediated framework redefines architectural representation as a dynamic system of communication distributed across multiple layers. Meaning is not fixed but continuously reconstructed as it moves between language, algorithms, geometry, and experience. Rather than prescribing a fixed workflow, the framework provides a conceptual model for understanding how these transformations operate across different design contexts, including studio-based experimentation, computational workflows, and emerging pedagogical environments. This approach positions representation as an open-ended process and establishes experiential validation as a central component of design thinking.

CONCEPTUAL DEMONSTRATION

To clarify how the proposed framework operates beyond theoretical abstraction, this section presents a conceptual demonstration that traces the transformation of spatial meaning across all layers of the system. This demonstration does not represent a fully implemented or validated technical pipeline; rather, it functions as an analytical scenario constructed to explicate the sequential and iterative logic of the proposed framework. Its aim is to reveal how representation is reconfigured at each stage and how meaning shifts as it moves between different domains.

Figure 4 illustrates the transition from linguistic articulation to AI-generated imagery, from image to volumetric model, and from model to immersive virtual experience, while highlighting the recursive feedback loop that reconnects experiential evaluation to conceptual reformulation. Unlike conventional linear workflows, the process operates as a closed iterative system in which each stage actively reinterprets spatial meaning rather than merely transmitting information. The figure should therefore be read not as a representation of a single project outcome, but as a diagrammatic synthesis of potential representational states within the proposed framework. The visual outputs, geometric models, and immersive environments shown in the figure should therefore be understood as successive representational states through which meaning is progressively constructed, tested, and transformed.

Figure 4. Conceptual demonstration of the AI–IVR framework showing the cyclical transformation from linguistic input to immersive experience through iterative feedback

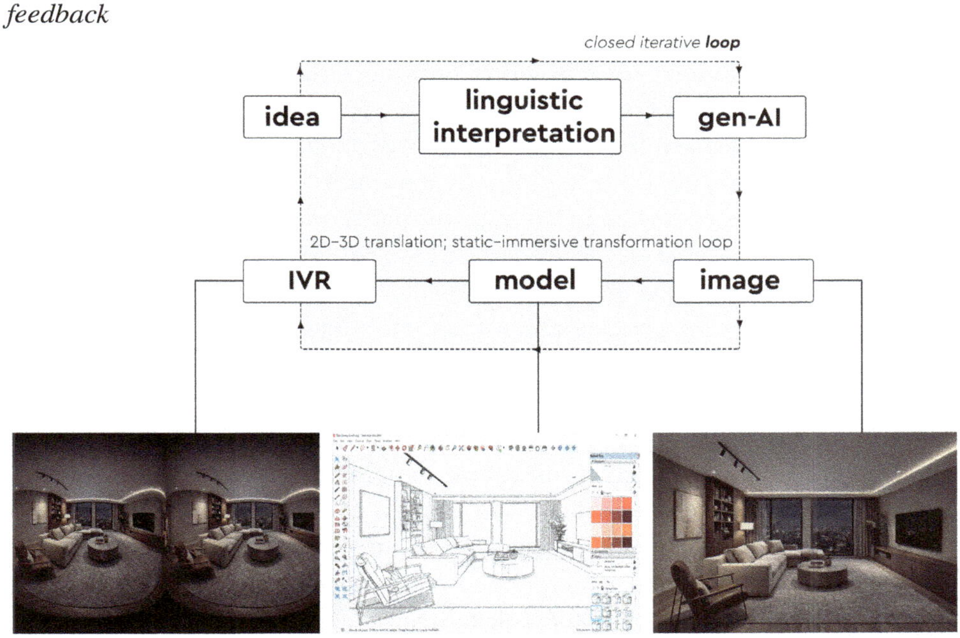

The demonstration begins with the articulation of a compact interior space through language. Spatial qualities such as atmosphere, light conditions, material tactility, enclosure, and circulation density are defined textually. At this initial stage, spatial meaning exists as a semantic construct, and the design process operates as a form of linguistic configuration. This highlights that spatial ideas are not initially geometric but conceptual, structured through language before any visual or spatial manifestation emerges.

When this linguistic construct is translated into a visual representation through generative AI systems, spatial meaning becomes perceptible for the first time. The generated image stabilizes a particular interpretation of the articulated intent, rendering depth, material relations, and atmosphere visible. However, this stabilization remains probabilistic, as multiple visual outcomes can emerge from the same input. This variability indicates that representation at this stage operates within a field of possibilities rather than as a fixed depiction, transforming the image into an exploratory interface rather than a confirmatory output.

The transition from image to three-dimensional form introduces a fundamental transformation. Through volumetric approximation, the spatial construct becomes navigable, allowing the user to conceptually enter the space. Yet this stage also reveals a critical gap between visual coherence and spatial validity, as geometries derived from visual data often lack structural and ergonomic consistency. In line with the framework discussed earlier, this stage may involve intermediate processes such as depth inference, panoramic reconstruction, or neural rendering techniques, each of which introduces its own limitations in terms of spatial accuracy and continuity. This demonstrates that algorithmic generation does not inherently align with architectural reasoning and that each stage reinterprets rather than preserves meaning.

This instability is addressed in the stage of spatial reconstruction, where architectural knowledge reorganizes the generated model into a coherent spatial system. Through adjustments to scale, proportion, circulation, and structural logic, the designer transforms a speculative geometric construct into a habitable environment. This stage represents a key epistemic shift, as meaning is translated from a probabilistic visual condition into a disciplined architectural framework.

When the reconstructed model is transferred into an immersive environment, representation undergoes another transformation. Space is no longer observed externally but experienced internally, and meaning is constructed through embodied interaction. Movement, orientation, and perception replace visual framing as the primary mechanisms through which space is understood, extending representation into an experiential domain. In this context, interior architectural qualities such as lighting gradients, material perception, enclosure, and spatial compression become directly perceptible, reinforcing the role of immersion as a critical evaluative layer.

Within this immersive condition, perceptual inconsistencies become directly observable. Spatial configurations that appear convincing in images may reveal limitations when experienced, such as disproportionate scale, restricted circulation, or spatial imbalance. This demonstrates that representation functions not only as a means of production but also as a system of evaluation, where meaning is continuously reassessed through experience. This evaluative function highlights that experiential validation is not a supplementary step, but an integral component of the representational process itself.

The feedback generated through this experience is then translated back into linguistic and conceptual adjustments, reconnecting the process to its point of origin. This transformation closes the loop, establishing representation as a recursive system in which spatial meaning is continuously rearticulated across iterations. Through this recursive mechanism, design operates as an ongoing negotiation between intention, computation, and experience.

This conceptual demonstration reveals that the AI–IVR mediated framework is not simply a model of technological integration but a redefinition of representational logic in architectural thinking. Particularly within interior architecture, where spatial perception is shaped by proximity, scale, and material sensitivity, this layered and recursive structure becomes critical. Representation should therefore be understood not as a mechanism for producing fixed outcomes, but as a dynamic system of mediation in which meaning is continuously constructed, evaluated, and transformed across interconnected domains.

CONCLUSION

This study has examined the intersection of artificial intelligence and immersive virtual reality as a structural and epistemic transformation in the communicative architecture of interior representation. The discussion has demonstrated that AI and IVR should not be understood merely as tools that extend visualization techniques or accelerate production processes. Rather, these technologies reorganize the conditions through which spatial meaning is structured, transmitted, and evaluated. In this context, representation shifts from a passive mechanism of transmission into a layered system of mediation that actively shapes how interior space is conceived, produced, and experienced.

Architectural representation has historically functioned as the primary interface between design intention and spatial legibility. Through drawings, models, and renderings, spatial ideas have been translated into visual form. However, within AI–IVR mediated environments, this translation no longer occurs as a singular act. Instead, it unfolds as a structured sequence of transformations, where linguistic articulation precedes image formation, image formation precedes volumetric inference, and volumetric inference precedes spatial reconstruction and immersive experience. Spatial meaning becomes progressively constructed across these layers, requiring representation to be understood as a process of transformation rather than direct translation.

Within this condition, the AI–IVR Mediated Framework proposed in this study renders this chain explicit and analytically accessible. Representation is reconceptualized as a cumulative process in which spatial meaning emerges through the interaction between semantic encoding, algorithmic inference, geometric construction, disciplinary calibration, and embodied evaluation. Each layer redefines the status of the design proposition while redistributing interpretive authority between human intention and computational systems. Representation thus becomes an epistemic field in which meaning is continuously negotiated rather than a fixed outcome.

The conceptual demonstration has illustrated how this process operates at the scale of interior space, revealing that visual plausibility does not guarantee spatial coherence. AI-generated images may produce compelling atmospheres while containing dimensional ambiguities, and geometrically reconstructed models may reveal perceptual inconsistencies when experienced immersively. These transitions demonstrate that spatial meaning is continuously stabilized, destabilized, and recalibrated across successive stages. Representation therefore functions as an iterative system of evaluation as much as production.

Taken together, these findings establish three key contributions of the study. First, the research conceptualizes generative artificial intelligence and immersive virtual reality as sequential and interdependent mediation layers within a unified representational system. Second, it reconceptualizes architectural representation as a multilayered, iterative, and feedback-driven process rather than a linear chain of transformations. Third, it situates this transformation within the specific constraints of interior architecture, emphasizing the necessity of experiential validation in the construction of spatial meaning.

This condition gains particular significance within interior architecture, where spatial perception is shaped by proximity, scale, materiality, and bodily orientation. Even minor deviations in proportion or spatial organization can fundamentally alter experience. As a result, discrepancies between algorithmic inference and embodied perception become immediately perceptible, positioning interior space as a critical domain for examining AI–IVR mediated representation.

Within this layered system, artificial intelligence operates as a linguistic–visual interface that restructures how design intention is externalized, while immersive virtual reality functions as an experiential environment that transforms how spatial propositions are perceived and evaluated. Their convergence produces a representational condition characterized by continuous translation, iterative adjustment, and feedback-driven transformation. Spatial meaning emerges not within a single medium, but through its movement across semantic, visual, geometric, and experiential domains.

This transformation also signals a broader shift in design thinking. Rather than following a fixed sequence of representation, the design process unfolds as a recursive dialogue between linguistic articulation, algorithmic generation, spatial calibration, and immersive validation. Design intention is no longer contained within a singular authorial act but becomes distributed across interconnected systems of mediation.

From a pedagogical perspective, this shift suggests that representational literacy must extend beyond drawing and modeling toward the ability to operate across multiple domains of mediation. Designers must be capable of articulating spatial intent linguistically, interpreting algorithmic outputs critically, reconstructing spatial systems with disciplinary knowledge, and evaluating design propositions through experience. Accordingly, design education moves toward the active management of layered representational processes rather than the production of static outputs.

At a broader theoretical level, the framework raises questions concerning authorship, agency, and epistemic responsibility within computational design environments. As generative and immersive systems become more integrated, the production of spatial meaning increasingly depends on the interaction between human and machine processes, requiring new approaches to understanding control, interpretation, and decision-making.

At the same time, the study acknowledges several limitations. The proposed framework remains conceptual and has not been empirically validated through implemented workflows or user-based studies. Future research may therefore focus on testing the framework through design studio experiments, comparative workflow analyses, and user-centered evaluations in immersive environments. In addition, further investigation is required into the technical integration between AI-generated imagery and spatial reconstruction processes, particularly in relation to emerging methods such as neural rendering and real-time volumetric modeling.

In conclusion, the convergence of artificial intelligence and immersive virtual reality marks a fundamental transformation in architectural representation. Representation is no longer confined to visual depictions of space but evolves into a multilayered system of experiential communication structured through successive processes of mediation. Spatial meaning is not directly transferred from conception to experience; it is progressively encoded, interpreted, constructed, and embodied across interconnected layers.

The central question therefore shifts from the level of visual realism toward the continuity, coherence, and interpretability of spatial meaning across these transformations. Within this context, the AI–IVR Mediated Framework positions representation as a dynamic system of transformation and establishes experiential visual communication as a critical paradigm for contemporary interior architecture. Spatial design can thus be reconsidered not as the production of fixed forms, but as the ongoing construction of meaning through layered processes of translation, interpretation, and embodied validation.

REFERENCES

Aldrich, C. (2009). *Learning Online with Games, Simulations, and Virtual Worlds: Strategies for Online Instruction.* Jossey-Bass.

Banh, L., & Strobel, G. (2023). Generative artificial intelligence. *Electronic Markets, 33*(63), 1–17. DOI: 10.1007/s12525-023-00680-1

Brade, S., Wang, B., Sousa, M., Oore, S., & Grossman, T. (2023). Promptify: Text-to-image generation through interactive prompt exploration with large language models. In *Proceedings of the 36th Annual ACM Symposium on User Interface Software and Technology* (pp. 1–14). https://doi.org/DOI: 10.1145/3586183.3606725

Carpo, M. (2003). *Digital Tectonics.* Wiley.

Carpo, M. (2011). *The Alphabet and the Algorithm.* MIT Press.

Cenani, S., Durmazoğlu, M. Ç., Gürer, E., Kutlu, Z., & Dane, G. (2025). Designing in an immersive virtual reality environment: Implications for design education. In De Paolis, L. T., Arpaia, P., & Sacco, M. (Eds.), Lecture notes in computer science: Vol. 15738. *Extended Reality: XR Salento 2025* (pp. 113–126). Springer., DOI: 10.1007/978-3-031-97769-5_9

Chang, Y. S., Kao, J. Y., & Wang, Y. Y. (2022). Influences of virtual reality on design creativity and design thinking. *Thinking Skills and Creativity, 46*, 101127. Advance online publication. DOI: 10.1016/j.tsc.2022.101127

Christou, C. (2020). Virtual reality for learning: A review of current trends. In *Virtual Reality: Concepts and Technologies.* CRC Press.

Dwivedi, Y. K., Kshetri, N., Hughes, L., Slade, E. L., Jeyaraj, A., Kar, A. K., Baabdullah, A. M., Koohang, A., Raghavan, V., Ahuja, M., Albanna, H., Albashrawi, M. A., Al-Busaidi, A. S., Balakrishnan, J., Barlette, Y., Basu, S., Bose, I., Brooks, L., Buhalis, D., & Wright, R. (2023). Opinion paper: So what if ChatGPT wrote it? Multidisciplinary perspectives on opportunities, challenges and implications of generative conversational AI for research, practice and policy. *International Journal of Information Management, 71*, 102642. DOI: 10.1016/j.ijinfomgt.2023.102642

Elgammal, A., Liu, B., Elhoseiny, M., & Mazzone, M. (2017). CAN: Creative adversarial networks, generating "art" by learning about styles and deviating from style norms. In *Proceedings of the 8th International Conference on Computational Creativity* (pp. 96–103).

Elme, L., Jørgensen, M. L., Dandanell, G., Mottelson, A., & Makransky, G. (2022). Immersive virtual reality in STEM: Is IVR an effective learning medium and does adding self-explanation after a lesson improve learning outcomes? *Educational Technology Research and Development*, *70*(5), 1601–1626. DOI: 10.1007/s11423-022-10139-3 PMID: 35873274

Evans, R. (1997). *Translations from Drawing to Building and Other Essays*. MIT Press.

Floridi, L., & Chiriatti, M. (2020). GPT-3: Its nature, scope, limits, and consequences. *Minds and Machines*, *30*(4), 681–694. DOI: 10.1007/s11023-020-09548-1

Gökdemir, G., & Kayan, H. Z. (2025). Artificial intelligence as a linguistic interface in interior design education: Reconceiving design tools as communication media. *International Journal of Architectural Computing*, 14780771251352955. Advance online publication. DOI: 10.1177/14780771251352955

Horvath, A.-S., & Pouliou, P. (2024). AI for conceptual architecture: Reflections on designing with text-to-text, text-to-image, and image-to-image generators. *Frontiers of Architectural Research*, *13*(3), 593–612. DOI: 10.1016/j.foar.2024.02.006

Hou, N., Nishina, D., Sugita, S., Jiang, R., Kindaichi, S., Oishi, H., & Shimizu, A. (2024). Virtual reality space in architectural design education: Learning effect of scale feeling. *Building and Environment*, *248*, 111060. Advance online publication. DOI: 10.1016/j.buildenv.2023.111060

Ipsita, A., Patel, M., Unmesh, A., & Ramani, K. (2024). Authoring instructional flow in iVR learning units to promote outcome-oriented learning. *Computers & Education: X Reality, 5*. https://doi.org/DOI: 10.1016/j.cexr.2024.100074

Kaleja, P., & Kozlovska, M. (2017). Virtual reality as innovative approach to the interior designing. *Selected Scientific Papers – Journal of Civil Engineering, 12*(1), 109–116. https://doi.org/DOI: 10.1515/sspjce-2017-0010

Klapperich, C. M., Sato, K., & Forlizzi, J. (2020). How do tools shape interaction? DIY practices and material engagement. *Personal and Ubiquitous Computing*. Advance online publication. DOI: 10.1007/s00779-020-01452-w

Kolarevic, B. (2003). *Architecture in the Digital Age: Design and Manufacturing*. Taylor & Francis.

Kolarevic, B. (2025). Generative AI technologies and architectural design education. In *On Architecture: Crosscutting and Fusion of Disciplines (OA2025 Proceedings)* (pp. 117–122). DOI: 10.60152/2m4jkgsf

Lin, C. Y. (2025). Bridging AI-generated imagery and 3D modeling: Addressing spatial inconsistency and controllability in design workflows. *Computer Aided Design*, *224*, 629–639.

Lombard, M., & Ditton, T. (1997). At the heart of it all: The concept of presence. *Journal of Computer-Mediated Communication*, *3*(2), 0. Advance online publication. DOI: 10.1111/j.1083-6101.1997.tb00072.x

Makransky, G., & Petersen, G. B. (2021). The cognitive affective model of immersive learning (CAMIL): A theoretical research-based model of learning in immersive virtual reality. *Educational Psychology Review*, *33*(3), 937–958. DOI: 10.1007/s10648-020-09586-2

Manovich, L. (2023). *AI aesthetics*. Strelka Press. https://manovich.net/index.php/projects/ai-aesthetics

Mills, K. A., & Brown, A. (2022). Immersive virtual reality (VR) for digital media making: Transmediation is key. *Learning, Media and Technology*, *47*(2), 179–200. DOI: 10.1080/17439884.2021.1952428

Milovanovic, J., Moreau, G., Siret, D., & Miguet, F. (2017). Virtual and augmented reality in architectural design and education: An immersive multimodal platform to support architectural pedagogy. In *Proceedings of the 17th International Conference on Computer-Aided Architectural Design Futures (CAAD Futures 2017)* (pp. 513–532).

Picon, A. (2010). *Digital Culture in Architecture: An Introduction for the Design Professions*. Birkhäuser.

Portman, M. E., Natapov, A., & Fisher-Gewirtzman, D. (2015). To go where no man has gone before: Virtual reality in architecture, landscape architecture and environmental planning. *Computers, Environment and Urban Systems*, *54*, 376–384. DOI: 10.1016/j.compenvurbsys.2015.05.001

Radianti, J., Majchrzak, T. A., Fromm, J., & Wohlgenannt, I. (2020). A systematic review of immersive virtual reality applications for higher education: Design elements, lessons learned, and research agenda. *Computers & Education*, *147*, 103778. DOI: 10.1016/j.compedu.2019.103778

Ritz, L. T., & Buss, A. R. (2016). A framework for aligning instructional design strategies with affordances of CAVE immersive virtual reality systems. *TechTrends*, *60*(6), 549–556. DOI: 10.1007/s11528-016-0085-9

Rombach, R., Blattmann, A., Lorenz, D., Esser, P., & Ommer, B. (2022). High-resolution image synthesis with latent diffusion models. In *Proceedings of the IEEE/CVF Conference on Computer Vision and Pattern Recognition (CVPR)* (pp. 10684–10695). https://doi.org/DOI: 10.1109/CVPR52688.2022.01042

Sanchez-Vives, M. V., & Slater, M. (2005). From presence to consciousness through virtual reality. *Nature Reviews. Neuroscience*, *6*(4), 332–339. DOI: 10.1038/nrn1651 PMID: 15803164

Selzer, M. N., Gazcon, N. F., & Larrea, M. L. (2019). Effects of virtual presence and learning outcome using low-end virtual reality systems. *Displays*, *59*, 9–15. DOI: 10.1016/j.displa.2019.04.002

Simmons, S. (2019). Drawing in the digital age: Observations and implications for education. *Arts*, *8*(1), 1–18. DOI: 10.3390/arts8010033

Slater, M., & Wilbur, S. (1997). A framework for immersive virtual environments (FIVE): Speculations on the role of presence in virtual environments. *Presence (Cambridge, Mass.)*, *6*(6), 603–616. DOI: 10.1162/pres.1997.6.6.603

Steuer, J. (1992). Defining virtual reality: Dimensions determining telepresence. *The Journal of Communication*, *42*(4), 73–93. DOI: 10.1111/j.1460-2466.1992.tb00812.x

Suchman, L. (2007). *Human–Machine Reconfigurations: Plans and Situated Actions* (2nd ed.). Cambridge University Press.

Uçar, U. E., Gökdemir, G., & Garip, E. (2023). A study of the application of virtual reality technology as an anthropometric measurement tool. *Interaction Design and Architecture(s) Journal (IxD&A), 55*, 194–211. https://doi.org/DOI: 10.55612/s-5002-055-009

Uçar, U. E., & Gürer, E. (2022). Dijital fabrikasyon süreçlerinde sanal gerçekliğin kitlesel bireyselleştirmeye dönük kullanımı. *Journal of Computational Design*, *3*(1), 19–38. DOI: 10.53710/jcode.1062205

Chapter 10
Cognitive Divergence in Design Communication:
Human Reasoning and Artificial Intelligence in Interior Architecture

Gözde Gökdemir
http://orcid.org/0000-0002-6717-6241
Istanbul Technical University, Turkey

ABSTRACT

Artificial intelligence (AI) introduces a new cognitive condition in design communication, where human interpretative reasoning operates alongside computational processes. This chapter examines this relationship through distinct cognitive mechanisms and discusses how design thinking is transformed through the interaction between textual narrative and AI-mediated visualization. To investigate this framework, a speculative design workshop conducted in interior architecture education is presented, analyzing how narrative-based human reasoning and AI-generated imagery interact within a shared design process. The findings indicate that while human cognition enables interpretative depth and conceptual expansion, artificial intelligence supports rapid ideation and variation through computational visualization, yet may also limit spatial diversity by reinforcing recurring tendencies. This interaction reveals a cognitive divergence between human reasoning and artificial computation, redefining how design ideas are generated, transformed, and communicated within hybrid cognitive environments.

DOI: 10.4018/979-8-2600-2711-0.ch010

ARTIFICIAL INTELLIGENCE AND THE TRANSFORMATION OF DESIGN COMMUNICATION

Artificial intelligence (AI) is increasingly transforming the cognitive and communicative structure of contemporary design practice (Almaz et al., 2024; Ploennigs & Berger, 2023). In design disciplines, AI-based systems are being integrated into various stages of the design process, including idea generation, conceptual development, variation production, and visual representation (Ko et al., 2023; Pena et al., 2021; Samad et al., 2024; Shreya and Kumar, 2024). While these developments expand the productive capacity of design, they also restructure the communicative environments in which design thinking evolves. As a result, design processes increasingly take place within hybrid cognitive environments where human reasoning and computational systems operate together.

This emerging condition redefines the role of the designer as an active mediator between interpretative thinking and algorithmic processes, shaping how ideas are translated, negotiated, and materialized within dynamic design environments. This shift has been increasingly discussed in recent literature, where generative AI is no longer understood merely as a tool, but as an active cognitive and creative participant in the design process. Within this perspective, AI systems are conceptualized as thinking partners that participate in ideation and decision-making processes, while also becoming embedded within the infrastructural conditions of design practice, reshaping how authorship, judgement, and design capability are defined (Fleischmann, 2026; Valentine et al., 2026).

Design disciplines have traditionally progressed through practices in which thinking develops through representation and narrative. Sketches, diagrams, and other textutal and visual mediums enable designers to externalize ideas and explore relationships between concepts, materials, and spatial configurations (Nussbaumer & Guerin, 2008). These tools function not only as means of expression but also as cognitive environments for interpretation, reflection, and conceptual exploration, allowing design thinking to continuously evolve through iterative interactions between ideas, representations, and contextual conditions. In this sense, the dynamic space in which design thinking is produced can be defined as design cognition, a concept referring to the mental processes through which knowledge is constructed and transformed, particularly through interaction with representations and problem-solving activities (Ball & Christensen, 2019; Cross, 2001; Neisser, 1967). The integration of artificial intelligence into design processes introduces a new paradigm into this cognitive structure, as the underlying organization of mental processes that shape how designers generate, relate, and develop ideas through representation and interaction. This transformation reflects a broader shift from tool-based interaction toward distributed cognitive systems in which aspects of ideation and evaluation are partially externalized. Within this context, generative AI systems can be understood as active participants in creative reasoning processes, repositioning the designer's role from sole creator to curator and mediator of AI-generated possibilities (Fleischmann, 2026). Designers increasingly interact with AI systems through language-based interfaces, translating conceptual intentions into computational processes with textual prompts. These interactions generate outputs that directly participate in the development of design ideas, positioning design communication within a hybrid cognitive space where interpretative thinking intersects with computational production forming a shared domain of interaction in which design ideas are developed, negotiated, and transformed through both human and computational processes.

This transformation makes visible the fundamental cognitive difference between human reasoning and artificial computation. Human design thinking operates through a multi-layered structure in which analytical reasoning and imagination-based interpretation work together, whereas AI systems rely on computational mechanisms based on data patterns (Fetzer, 1990; Hunt, 1975). The differing modes of functioning of these two cognitive structures produce a distinct cognitive divergence within design communication, as the differentiation between the ways in which human reasoning and computational systems construct, process, and translate design knowledge. This condition becomes particularly evident in the discipline of interior architecture, where spatial imagination and visual narrative play a central role. Interior architecture design involves the development of spatial atmospheres and experiential qualities through both textual and visual representations. The integration of AI-supported systems into this process expands the ways in which spatial ideas are generated and communicated (Gökdemir & Kayan, 2025).

In order to examine how this cognitive divergence operates within concrete design processes, it becomes necessary to situate these theoretical considerations within a structured experimental context. Such a context allows the interaction between interpretative reasoning and computational mechanisms to be observed, traced, and evaluated through design practice. In this context, the study examines a speculative design workshop in order to explore how the cognitive difference between human reasoning and artificial intelligence becomes visible within design practice. Conducted with 18 interior architecture students, the workshop invited participants to develop spatial scenarios for the year 2050 and express these ideas through both narrative and visual representations. The process was structured as a multi-layered design workflow beginning with textual narratives, evolving through visual explorations, and continuing with AI-supported visualization. This structure enables the observation of how interpretative reasoning and computational production operate at different stages of the design process and influence one another.

In this respect, the workshop functions as both a pedagogical exercise and an experimental research setting for examining how different cognitive mechanisms interact within a single design process. The classification of the workshop as an experimental research setting is grounded in its deliberately structured design. The process was organized as a sequence of clearly defined stages, each corresponding to different modes of design production, including human-centered reasoning, hybrid human–AI interaction, and AI-mediated visualization. This staged structure made it possible to observe how different cognitive mechanisms become visible and interact within the same design process.

In addition, the workshop was conducted under consistent conditions across all participants, including a shared design brief, temporal framework, and production steps. The systematic collection of textual, visual, and AI-generated outputs throughout the process enabled the tracing of how design ideas evolve across different representational modes. In this sense, the workshop operates as a structured exploratory environment in which the interaction between human reasoning and computational processes can be examined through design practice. The interplay between narrative-based thinking and AI-generated visualization makes the emerging cognitive divergence in design communication visible, revealing both the productive and limiting aspects of human-AI interaction.

RECONFIGURING DESIGN COGNITION IN INTERIOR ARCHITECTURE

This section establishes the theoretical framework of the study by critically examining the cognitive mechanisms that structure design communication. In this context, the increasingly intensified interaction between human reasoning and artificial intelligence in contemporary design processes is approached as an encounter between two fundamentally distinct modes of production operating through different cognitive logics. Within this framework, the first subsection addresses human reasoning in the context of design cognition, discussing interpretative thinking as a core component of spatial idea generation in design process. The second subsection examines how AI-based systems are incorporated into the cognitive processes of design and evaluates their role in design communication from a cognitive perspective. The third subsection focuses on the integration of AI within interior architecture, approaching the discipline as a representational and narrative-based thinking environment, and examines how language-based interaction and AI-mediated visualization reconfigure the relationship between design thinking and its modes of expression.

When these perspectives are considered together, the distinction between the complex, interpretative nature of human reasoning and the computational, linear operation of AI becomes evident. This encounter both describes a cognitive divergence emerging in spatial design processes and establishes a theoretical framework for understanding how this divergence actively reconfigures design thinking itself.

HUMAN REASONING IN DESIGN COGNITION

Human reasoning in design cognition operates as an interpretative and generative process through which ideas are formed, developed, and acquire meaning. In design disciplines, thinking progresses through a reflective interaction between emerging ideas, representations, and contextual conditions (Schön, 1983). As conceptualized by Schön's notion of reflection-in-action, this process unfolds as a dynamic dialogue in which thinking and making occur simultaneously and continuously inform one another. In this sense, the designer is not only solving a problem but also actively reframing and transforming the problem situation itself.

The literature on design cognition demonstrates that designers develop a mode of reasoning that integrates both analytical and creative processes, allowing problem and solution spaces to co-evolve (Cross, 2023; Razzouk & Shute, 2012). This co-evolutionary process indicates that design problems are not fixed or fully defined at the outset; they are progressively constructed through interactions with representational tools and design actions. Accordingly, design thinking is understood not as a linear problem-solving process that follows predefined steps, but as an open-ended cognitive field in which meaning is continuously constructed, negotiated, and transformed. Within this process, design tools function as both representational media and dynamic cognitive environments in which thinking takes place. Through sketches, diagrams, and other visual compositions, designers externalize ideas, test relationships, and iteratively develop design concepts (Cross, 2023). This process of externalization extends thinking beyond a purely mental activity, enabling it to unfold through material and visual representations. As a result, thinking and making become intertwined, and representation is positioned as a cognitive interface through which reasoning is enacted, reorganized, and expressed. This process enables an active exchange between internal thought processes and external representations, shaping and transforming design ideas.

The cognitive pattern that emerges through this process indicate that design thinking is shaped through tools and representations as well as through the interaction of different cognitive mechanisms. In this respect, a defining characteristic of human design cognition lies in the simultaneous operation of multiple cognitive structures. According to the cognition theory developed by Blanco (1980), human thinking emerges through the interaction of two distinct modes of logical organization: symmetric logic and asymmetric logic. Asymmetric logic operates through differentiation, classification, and causal reasoning, whereas symmetric logic enables equivalence, generalization, and relational expansion by loosening the boundaries between part and whole. This dual structure forms the foundation of design thinking. While the asymmetric mechanism plays a determining role in structuring relations, organizing decisions, and concretizing design, the symmetric mechanism enables metaphorical thinking, associative connections, and speculative imagination by establishing links between concepts and images. Through this interaction, designers are able to engage with, transform, and multiply conditions that are not yet fully defined through representational means.

In this context, design cognition is understood as a non-linear field of thinking in which meaning is continuously reconstructed and expanded, as opposed to a linear problem-solving process (Teal, 2010). This non-linear structure allows multiple layers of knowledge and cognitive processes to interact simultaneously. Within such an environment, designers explore multiple possibilities in parallel and develop ideas through relational modes of thinking. As a result, the design process acquires a dynamic structure characterized by iterations, deviations, and reorientations, rather than following a fixed trajectory.

Taken together, these characteristics define human reasoning as a multi-layered and non-linear cognitive process in which different logical mechanisms operate simultaneously through interpretation, iteration, and exploration. This structure brings together analytical structuring and imagination-based projection, revealing the nature of design thinking. It also provides a theoretical foundation for understanding the cognitive divergence that emerges in its encounter with artificial computation, which will be discussed in the following section.

ARTIFICIAL COMPUTATION IN DESIGN COMMUNICATION

The integration of artificial intelligence into design processes is transforming both the operational dimension of design communication and its underlying cognitive structure. Designers increasingly interact with algorithmic systems, which function as cognitive participants within the design process. As a result, design communication evolves within hybrid cognitive environments where human reasoning and computational processes functioning in conjunction. In this context, the concepts of artificial intelligence and computational intelligence offer distinct yet interrelated theoretical frameworks. Artificial intelligence refers to a broad field encompassing human-like reasoning, learning, and problem-solving processes, whereas computational intelligence denotes a subset of this field that focuses on data-driven, adaptive, and learning-based approaches (Engelbrecht, 2003). Within this scope, methods such as artificial neural networks, evolutionary algorithms, swarm intelligence, and fuzzy systems provide the capacity for pattern recognition, relational inference, and generalization in complex and uncertain problem domains (Kruse et al., 2022). These capabilities enable the simultaneous exploration of multiple possibilities and support the development of alternative solutions through data-driven relationships in design processes.

A significant portion of contemporary AI systems, particularly in the context of generative models, is grounded in data-driven learning processes aligned with computational intelligence approaches (Goodfellow et al., 2015). These systems learn patterns and relationships within large-scale data environments and reorganize these learned associations to produce visual and textual outputs. In this sense, AI functions as a contributor of production within design processes.

When considered alongside human design cognition, these systems reveal distinct cognitive orientations. Human reasoning operates through a multi-layered structure shaped by experience, context, and meaning-making processes, whereas AI systems contribute through the organization and transformation of learned data relationships. This distinction establishes an interactive field in which both systems operate within the same design process while exhibiting different modes of cognition and production. Within design processes, AI-based systems identify patterns within data spaces, organize the relationships among them, and generate outputs based on these structured associations. This process, supported by learning and adaptation, enables the configuration of relationships and their expression in visual and textual forms. Consequently, design outputs emerge through the transformation and reorganization of data-driven relationships.

This transformation calls for a reconsideration of the relationships between narrative, representation, and visualization in design communication. In human design cognition, narrative and representation function as active cognitive environments in which thinking unfolds. In contrast, within AI systems, this process operates through the computational structuring of relationships between inputs and outputs (Morozov, 2023). Designers articulate their intentions through textual inputs, while the system processes these inputs based on learned relationships to generate visual and textual outcomes. This interaction redefines the role of language and modes of expression within the design process. This cognitive configuration also can be more comprehensively understood through the interplay of symmetrical and asymmetrical mechanisms. Computational systems provide strong capacities for structuring relationships, maintaining distinctions, and organizing outputs. Human reasoning, in turn, complements this structure through conceptual expansion, associative thinking, and meaning-making processes. These two orientations coexist within the design process, offering distinct yet interrelated cognitive contributions.

Within this framework, artificial intelligence introduces increased speed, variation, and production capacity into design communication while simultaneously transforming its cognitive foundations. The interaction between human reasoning and the data-driven operations of AI systems constitutes a dynamic field in which different cognitive mechanisms converge. This condition suggests that design communication should be reconsidered not only through the lens of tools but also through the interaction of diverse cognitive structures.

ARTIFICIAL INTELLIGENCE IN INTERIOR ARCHITECTURE

A discipline can be understood as a holistic and systematic structure formed through the interaction of objects, methods, principles, definitions, and tools (Foucault, 1970). Within this framework, interior architecture emerges as a multi-layered discipline that brings together theoretical knowledge and practice-based knowledge within the design process. It constitutes a field in which spatial meaning is constructed and reconstructed through processes of interpretation and representation. The discipline operates through an interconnected structure involving conceptualization, spatial organization, material articulation, and the production of atmosphere (Brooker & Stone, 2010; Ching & Binggeli, 2012). Within this structure, design thinking develops through iterative processes of translation. Historically, this process has been shaped by visually oriented modes of thinking, where sketches, technical drawings, and physical models have functioned as primary tools guiding the production and evolution of design knowledge (Ganshirt, 2020). In the current context, the integration of artificial intelligence systems, particularly generative models, into the design process introduces a new phase of transformation in this cognitive structure. This transformation extends beyond the introduction of new tools and points toward a reconfiguration of how knowledge is produced, mediated, and interpreted within the discipline. It suggests a shift from stable representational logics toward more fluid, adaptive, and interaction-based modes of design thinking. In this sense, design processes increasingly operate through dynamic exchanges between human intention and computational generation.

Artificial intelligent systems operate through language-based inputs and data-driven inference processes, enabling the transformation of textual expressions into spatial imagery. This transformation establishes a new interaction field that reconfigures the cognitive structure of interior architectural design processes. Interpretative and context-sensitive human reasoning encounters computational processes based on pattern recognition, probabilistic inference, and data-driven association within the same production domain. This encounter redefines how spatial ideas are constructed, discussed, and evaluated. In this sense, interior architecture gains visibility as a hybrid cognitive field in which thinking and algorithmic production operate together.

Contemporary applications of artificial intelligence do not correspond to fixed stages within the interior architectural design process but emerge as flexible modes of use that assume different functional roles. In this context, artificial intelligence provides a composite interaction space that supports conceptual production, expands spatial imagination, and opens design decisions to evaluation. The construction of conceptual frameworks and the development of narrative scenarios through text-based inputs constitute a significant component of this interaction. Generative systems make different possibilities of spatial relationships visible through visualization and variation production (Samad et al., 2024; Shreya & Kumar, 2024). In addition, they contribute to the reinterpretation of design across different parameters through processes such as spatial analysis, performance evaluation, and the processing of environmental data (Li et al., 2025; Starowicz & Zielinski, 2024). When considered together, these modes of use indicate that artificial intelligence operates within the design process through a network of interconnected functional roles, moving beyond a linear structure.

This transformation, which introduces a new cognitive layer into the design process, can also be examined through interior architecture education. Its implications within design education are directly related to how the use of artificial intelligence is structured within a pedagogical framework. Recent studies indicate that the pedagogical quality of interaction with artificial intelligence depends on its definition within clearly established frameworks (Fleischmann, 2025; Longo & Albano, 2025; Rhee & Oh, 2025; Zawacki-Richter et al., 2019). In this context, the integration of artificial intelligence into the design process requires an approach structured through clearly defined tasks, established boundaries of use, and mechanisms of critical evaluation. Maintaining the decision-making role of the designer while positioning artificial intelligence as an interface that intensifies idea generation and supports alternative production forms the basis of this approach. Accordingly, interaction with artificial intelligence evolves into a learning environment that is consciously directed and continuously examined.

Design education offers a learning environment in which processes of thinking, production, and evaluation are constructed simultaneously. Within this context, the structured integration of artificial intelligence tools into this environment positions design students as agents who construct spatial ideas through language, test these ideas through generative systems, and reinterpret the resulting outputs. This process requires the development of awareness regarding how design knowledge is produced and directed. In this sense, artificial intelligence should be understood as a cognitive interface that reorganizes the formation and expression of design thinking. Based on this theoretical framework, this study develops a speculative design workshop to investigate the interaction between human reasoning and AI-mediated production processes. The workshop provides an experimental research setting that enables the observation of the cognitive interaction between interpretative human thinking and computational production processes within the design studio environment.

THE SPECULATIVE DESIGN WORKSHOP

The workshop was conducted during the spring semester of 2024-2025 with 18 undergraduate students enrolled in the Interior Architecture Department at Istanbul Technical University. The participants were selected from final-year students due to their relatively advanced proficiency in professional terminology, design knowledge, and conceptual production processes. This ensured that the language used in interacting with artificial intelligence, as well as the articulation of design intent, could be expressed in a more informed and structured manner.

Within the scope of the workshop, participants were asked to develop a speculative healing space projection for the year 2050. The selection of this temporal framework aimed to partially detach the design process from existing references, thereby encouraging speculative thinking and enabling the development of alternative spatial possibilities. This future-oriented construct pushed both human reasoning and AI-based production beyond predefined visual and typological conventions, foregrounding interpretative and conceptual generation. At the same time, the 2050 perspective provided a context in which human-artificial intelligence interaction becomes an integral component of spatial experience, allowing this relationship to be directly addressed within the design process. This framework thus established the central problem field that structured both the narrative production and the subsequent stages of visual exploration and AI-mediated visualization.

The workshop was structured as a progressive process composed of sequential design steps that both inform and transform one another. This structure frames the design process not as a singular act of production, but as a multi-layered field of thinking and making in which different cognitive mechanisms are activated. Each step operates within a distinct design mode, enabling the interaction between human reasoning and the generative logic of artificial intelligence to be differentiated and observed within the design process. At the same time, the process was organized to include a gradual transformation between the textual and visual languages of design; design thinking initiated through textual expression progressively evolved toward visual representation.

All data generated throughout the workshop were collected and systematically recorded via the university's official digital submission platform. This structure enabled the simultaneous tracking of students' textual productions, visual outputs, and their interactions with artificial intelligence systems, making it possible to analyze the design process through final outputs as well as through the evolving modes of communication developed during the process.

To analyze the student works, a qualitative interpretative framework was employed, combining thematic analysis and visual content analysis. The textual manifestos, collage compositions, and AI-generated visualizations were treated as interconnected layers of design production and examined in relation to one another. The analysis followed an iterative process in which recurring patterns, conceptual structures, and representational transformations were identified across different stages of the design workflow.

Thematic analysis was applied to the manifesto texts in order to identify underlying conceptual orientations, such as problem framing, spatial imagination, and relational thinking. In parallel, visual content analysis was used to examine how these conceptual structures were translated, transformed, or altered within collage productions and AI-generated images. Particular attention was given to the degree of alignment between initial design intentions and subsequent visual outputs, as well as to the shifts introduced through human-AI interaction. Rather than evaluating the works in terms of aesthetic quality, the analysis focused on tracing the transformation of design ideas across textual and visual domains, making it possible to reveal the cognitive transitions and divergences emerging between human reasoning and computational production.

The interpretation of the data was conducted through a process-oriented and comparative reading of the design outputs. Rather than treating the student works as isolated artefacts, the analysis focused on how each project evolved across different stages of the workshop, tracing the transformation of design ideas from textual narratives to visual representations and AI-generated outputs.

In this context, interpretation was guided by examining shifts in conceptual clarity, relational thinking, and the alignment between initial design intentions and subsequent visual outcomes. Particular attention was given to moments of divergence, where AI-generated representations introduced reinterpretations, distortions, or extensions of the original ideas. This approach enabled the identification of both continuities and discontinuities within the design process, making the interaction between human reasoning and computational production more visible.

The workshop was structured around three main design stages: manifesto and infography production based on a 2050 projection, collage-based visual representation, and AI-mediated spatial visualization. These stages were designed to correspond to different design modes, namely human-centered reasoning, human-AI interaction, and AI-based production. The primary artificial intelligent tool employed in this process was ChatGPT. This choice was informed by its relatively higher performance in interpreting textual inputs, restructuring them, and transforming them into design-relevant outputs.

The first stage of the workshop focuses on the production of textual narratives, establishing a context in which conceptual thinking and interpretative reasoning are intensified. The second stage develops a hybrid exploratory environment in which textual narratives are reinterpreted through visual research processes, enabling transitions between different modes of representation. The final stage involves AI-mediated visualization, where spatial ideas constructed textually are translated into visual representations. Considered together, these stages make it possible to trace how design thinking is transformed across different cognitive structures.

This structured process is directly aligned with the theoretical framework discussed in the previous sections. Each stage of the workshop corresponds to a distinct cognitive mode, making it possible to observe how different cognitive structures operate and interact within the design process. The transition from textual narratives to visual representations and AI-generated outputs reflects the transformation of design thinking across multiple cognitive domains. The progression of the design process across different cognitive modes allows for the observation of both distinctions and intersections between human reasoning and artificial computation within a controlled environment. In particular, the interaction between interpretative reasoning and computational production renders the notion of cognitive divergence observable within the design process, as differences in meaning construction, representation, and transformation become visible across stages. Furthermore, the gradual transformation between textual and visual design languages provides an experimental ground for examining how spatial ideas are reconstructed across different modes of reasoning. Within this context, representation functions as a cognitive interface through which design ideas are translated, negotiated, and reconfigured between human and artificial systems. In this sense, the workshop functions as both a pedagogical exercise and an experimental research framework for investigating the cognitive difference emerging in contemporary design communication. The following subsections present a detailed account of the workshop stages and student outputs, illustrating the production processes through the works of three students.

Although the workshop involved 18 participants, the analysis presented in this study focuses on three selected student cases. These cases were identified through a purposive sampling approach based on their capacity to represent distinct cognitive orientations and variations observed across the dataset. The selected examples reflect different modes of conceptualization, narrative construction, and visual translation, enabling a focused and in-depth examination of how design thinking evolves across textual, visual, and AI-mediated stages.

This approach provides analytically rich cases through which the interaction between human reasoning and artificial intelligence is clearly articulated. By concentrating on representative and diverse examples, the study traces the transformation of design ideas with greater clarity and depth while foregrounding variation across the dataset.

SCENARIO-BASED MANIFESTO AND INFOGRAPHY PRODUCTION

The initial step of the constructed workshop focuses on the production of manifestos in order to activate human-centered reasoning within the design process. In this stage, students are asked to develop spatial scenarios for the year 2050 and to articulate these scenarios through text-based expressions, situated within the context of potential environmental, societal, and technological transformations. Subsequently, students translate their manifestos into infographic representations that visually communicate their conceptual frameworks.

The process is deliberately structured to proceed without the use of any artificial intelligence tools, relying solely on the participants' own reasoning processes. This approach foregrounds conceptual production and language-based modes of expression at the outset of the design process. Thinking and articulating through text enables the development of spatial ideas that have not yet been formally fixed, allowing them to evolve in an open, flexible, and multi-layered manner. In this context, the manifesto operates as a cognitive framework in which the conceptual structure is established and the design intention begins to take shape. Through their manifestos, students construct speculative scenarios that reinterpret spatial atmosphere, user experience, and the notion of healing. An example of student work can be examined in Figure 1 (Figure 1).

Figure 1. Manifesto and infography design by Student I

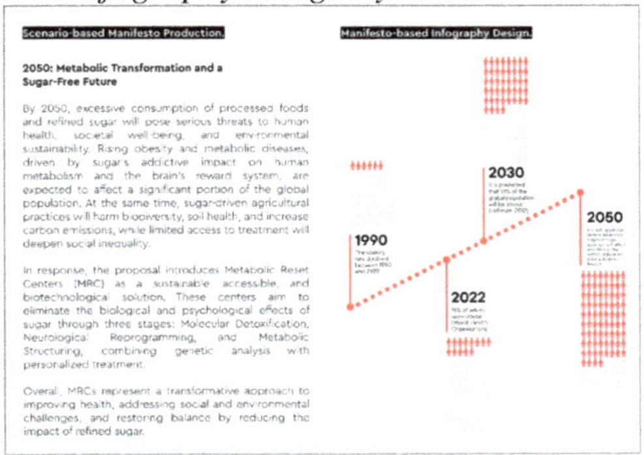

The manifesto presented in Figure 1 establishes a scenario-based conceptual framework that positions the healing space at the intersection of biological, neurological, and environmental processes. The text defines the effects of sugar consumption on individual health, social structures, and ecological systems as a multi-layered problem context, and proposes a holistic spatial solution through Metabolic Reset Centers in response to this condition.

The conceptual structure constructed within the manifesto does not approach space as a static physical environment; it defines it as a continuously operating transformation system that interacts with the user. A direct relationship is established between spatial organization and biotechnological intervention. This indicates that the student constructs the spatial idea not merely through physical arrangement, but through the interrelated notions of process, system, and interaction.

The causal relationships articulated within the text establish a strong connection between the problem definition and the proposed solution, revealing the effective operation of the analytical dimension of conceptual thinking. At the same time, the future-oriented scenario extends beyond existing healthcare systems, making visible the capacity for conceptual expansion and the generation of alternatives. In this respect, the manifesto clearly demonstrates the human capacity for relational thinking, structuring, and conceptual transformation.

Figure 2. Manifesto and infography design by Student II

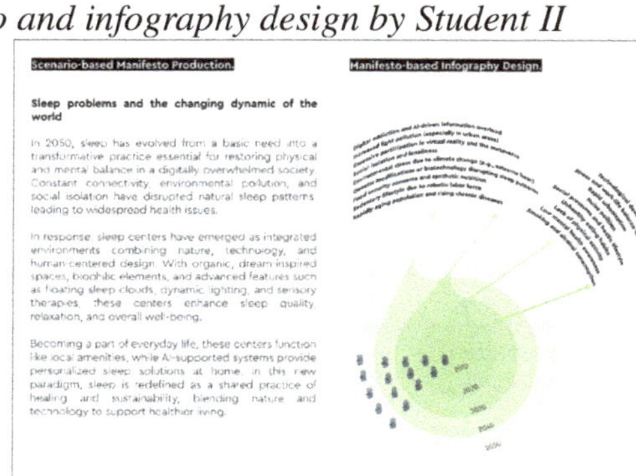

The manifesto presented in Figure 2 develops an approach that defines the healing space through experience, perception, and psychological balance (Figure 2). The text reframes sleep from being a basic necessity into a transformative practice that restores equilibrium within a digitized and overstimulated society. In this context, space is conceived as a structure that evolves in interaction with the user, becomes sensorially enriched, and produces effects through atmosphere.

The conceptual structure established in the text does not primarily rely on a causal problem-solution relationship; it advances through experiential transformation and modes of living. This indicates that the student develops the spatial idea through an interpretative, relational, and atmosphere-oriented mode of thinking. In this way, the manifesto makes visible the human capacity for meaning-making grounded in experience. A similar approach can also be observed in another student work presented in Figure 3 (Figure 3).

Figure 3. Manifesto and infography design by Student III

Third manifesto presents a holistic approach that defines the healing space through the interrelations between health, food production, and ecological sustainability. The text conceptualizes future health environments not as treatment-oriented facilities, but as dynamic systems where production, and everyday life practices intersect. The conceptual framework constructed within the text brings together systemic relationships and daily practices, addressing the spatial idea at both organizational and behavioral levels. This reveals the student's capacity to engage in relational thinking and to establish multi-scalar connections within the process of conceptual production.

When the three manifestos are evaluated together, it becomes evident that students approach the notion of healing space through diverse conceptual orientations. This diversity demonstrates that the language-based production process expands design thinking toward multiple conceptual trajectories, moving beyond a singular solution. These productions also clearly reveal the human capacity for establishing relationships, transforming concepts, and generating alternative scenarios. Through textual productions, students engage with spatial ideas across different scales and contexts, allowing design thinking to expand across conceptual, experiential, and systemic orientations. In this regard, manifesto production is a formative stage in which diverse cognitive orientations become visible. Accordingly, manifesto, as an extension of human reasoning, opens up a field in which conceptual construction, relational thinking, and meaning-making processes operate together. Within this process, students establish connections between different concepts, translate abstract ideas into spatial scenarios, and construct multi-layered narrative structures. This network of relationships provides a guiding framework for the spatial representations to be developed in subsequent stages of the design process.

This phase foregrounds interpretative reasoning and speculative construction, enabling participants to develop their spatial ideas through conceptual structures prior to generating direct visual solutions. Through manifestos, students define the foundational approach of their projects, articulate the themes they engage with, and establish the direction of the design process.

From the perspective of the theoretical framework of the study, manifesto production represents the initial stage in which human reasoning can be most explicitly observed within design communication. At this stage, spatial ideas are shaped through linguistic expression and conceptual construction, forming the foundational narrative structure of the projects. At the same time, this process prepares a conceptual ground for the subsequent transformation of these textual structures into visual representations.

VISUAL TRANSLATION OF SPATIAL NARRATIVES: MANIFESTO-BASED COLLAGE DESIGN

In the second step of the workshop, the textual narratives produced during the manifesto phase were transformed into visual compositions, and scenario-based collage studies were developed. The collage method functioned as a tool that supports associative and interpretative modes of thinking within design cognition. The combination of different visual fragments enabled spatial ideas to evolve not through a linear process, but within a fragmented and relational structure.

In this process, a hybrid cognitive environment was established in which human reasoning and AI-supported visual exploration practices operated together. During the collage production, students shared their conceptual ideas with the AI tool and subsequently evaluated the generated visuals together with their own digital interventions through their individual interpretative perspectives. In this way, design thinking acquired a hybrid structure based on human-machine collaboration, moving back and forth between textual constructs and visual production.

From this perspective, the collage stage functioned as an intermediate layer in which the transformation between textual narrative and visual representation takes place. Accordingly, the conceptual ideas developed during the manifesto phase began to evolve into spatial narratives through visual imagery, establishing a foundation for the subsequent stage of AI-based spatial visualization. In this context, three representative examples of students' collage productions are presented in Figure 4.

Figure 4. Manifesto-based collage design by students

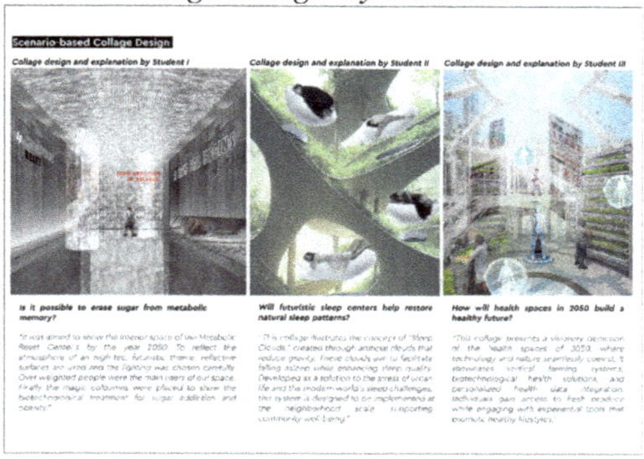

Figure 4 illustrates how three distinct 2050 scenarios developed during the manifesto phase are restructured through collage production. When considered together, these examples demonstrate that collage reconfigures textual narratives through multiple interpretative strategies, generating diverse visual equivalents. While students maintain the conceptual directions established in the manifesto phase, they expand and diversify these ideas through the possibilities offered by the visual language.

A significant observation in this stage is that AI-supported tools do not function as direct design generators, but rather as catalysts for visual exploration and variation. Human reasoning operates as the primary mechanism that guides the process by determining which visual elements are selected, how they are related, and within which conceptual framework they are evaluated. In contrast, artificial intelligence accelerates the process, multiplies alternatives, and expands the field of visual exploration. At the same time, the visuals generated by AI were not directly adopted as final outputs. Instead, students reworked the generated material through digital post-production using tools such as Adobe Photoshop and Adobe Illustrator. Through processes of editing, layering, and compositional transformation, the visual outputs were reinterpreted and reconstructed. This approach enabled the production to move beyond a tool-driven output, incorporating an additional layer shaped by students' interpretative capacities and imagination.

In this context, the collage stage mediates between textual narrative and visual representation, acting as a site of transformation. Design thinking, at this stage, develops through processes of selection, association, and reconstruction within a hybrid cognitive structure. Textual ideas are translated into spatial atmospheres through visual imagery, establishing a critical foundation for the subsequent stage of AI-based spatial visualization.

AI-BASED SPATIAL VISUALIZATION

In the third step of the workshop, the conceptual and visual content developed during the preceding manifesto and collage production phases was translated into interior visual representations through the use of AI-based image generation tools. This phase unfolded within an AI-mediated design mode, in which the design language advanced primarily through visual representation.

Within the theoretical framework of this study, this stage constitutes a critical threshold for observing how design communication operates through a computational logic of production. Artificial intelligent systems transform the conceptual orientations and visual references defined by the designer into spatial images through algorithmic generation processes. In this context, the designer no longer produces the spatial idea directly through drawing or modeling; they assume a role that defines, constrains, and directs the generative process through textual prompts and visual inputs. Consequently, design production is reconfigured as a computational process in which parameters are specified and outcomes are subsequently interpreted.

This transformation makes it possible to concretely observe how the conceptual framework developed during the manifesto and collage stages is reinterpreted and visually stabilized through artificial intelligence. At the same time, this phase demonstrates that representation operates as an active layer of mediation in which spatial meaning is produced, transformed, and rearticulated. Sample student works produced at this stage are presented in Figure 5 (Figure 5).

Figure 5 illustrates how three distinct conceptual orientations developed during the manifesto and collage production steps are transformed into spatial visualizations through artificial intelligence. An examination of the images reveals that artificial intelligence demonstrates a strong capacity for visual synthesis, particularly in the generation of atmosphere, the use of lighting, the articulation of material effects, and the establishment of spatial coherence. Spatial relationships at multiple scales, user-space interactions, and programmatic organizations can be produced as integrated scenes within a relatively short time frame. This indicates that AI-based tools not only accelerate the production process but also enable the rapid testing of alternative spatial scenarios.

Figure 5. AI-driven visualization by students

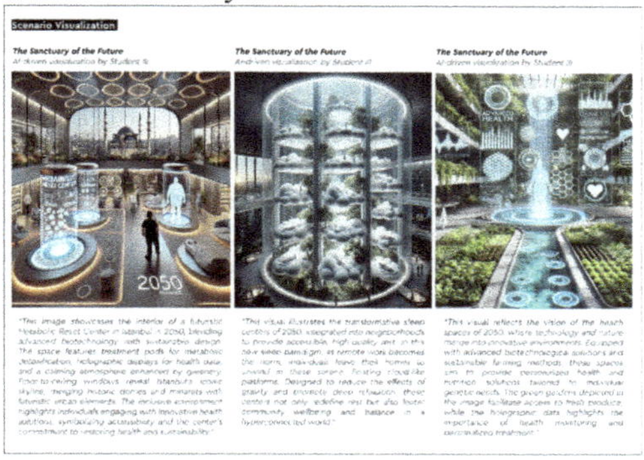

Nevertheless, this mode of production also reveals a set of limitations. The images generated by artificial intelligence do not always fully correspond to the conceptual framework articulated by the students during the manifesto stage. In particular, instances were observed in which the intended spatial atmosphere, experiential continuity, and user-oriented spatial configurations were not consistently reflected in the visual outputs. This results in a partial misalignment between conceptual intention and visual representation.

Although AI-generated imagery is often visually compelling, it does not consistently achieve conceptual accuracy or experiential sensitivity. Moreover, the generative logic of artificial intelligence systems tends to prioritize aesthetic coherence and visual impact, which can at times lead to a superficialization of conceptual depth in favor of striking visual effects. The more controlled and relational structure established during the collage phase becomes partially dissolved at this stage, and the influence of designer intervention may remain limited. This condition indicates a partial shift of control over representation from the human subject toward algorithmic systems.

In this context, the AI-based visualization process can be understood not merely as a tool that enhances production capacity, but as a critical threshold that redefines the relationships between conceptual intention, control, and representation. While human reasoning within the design process maintains its interpretive, relational, and speculative character, artificial intelligence functions through a computational logic of visual synthesis. The interaction between these two distinct cognitive structures gives rise to both a productive potential and specific zones of tension. Accordingly, the AI-mediated spatial visualization stage does not only expand the capacity for visual production; it also provides an experimental setting in which the cognitive dissonance between human interpretive thinking and AI-driven computation becomes explicitly visible.

CONCLUSION

This study conceptualizes contemporary design communication as a hybrid cognitive field structured through the interaction between human reasoning and artificial intelligence. At its core lies the recognition that these two systems operate through fundamentally different cognitive logics. Human reasoning manifests as a multi-layered, interpretative, and non-linear process shaped by relational thinking, conceptual expansion, and meaning-making. This structure produces a mode of thinking in which design problems are not fixed or predefined; rather, they are continuously reconstructed, transformed, and multiplied throughout the process. In contrast, artificial intelligence operates through computational mechanisms grounded in data-driven pattern recognition, probabilistic inference, and the transformation of inputs into outputs. The encounter between these two modes of cognition gives rise to a condition of cognitive divergence that actively restructures how design thinking is constructed, represented, and communicated.

Within this theoretical framework, the speculative design workshop presented in this study provides an experimental setting in which this cognitive divergence becomes concretely observable through the transformation of design ideas across textual, visual, and AI-mediated stages. The staged structure of the workshop makes it possible to trace how distinct cognitive structures, previously defined in the theoretical framework, operate and interact across different phases of the design process. The findings indicate that design thinking evolves through differentiated yet interconnected cognitive modes corresponding to distinct stages of the process. The manifesto production step foregrounds human-centered reasoning, enabling the development of diverse conceptual frameworks through narrative production. At this stage, design unfolds as an open-ended domain of thought that has not yet been formally fixed, directly reflecting the interpretative and non-linear nature of human cognitive structure.

The collage step introduces a hybrid environment in which human interpretation and AI-supported visual exploration interact, allowing conceptual ideas to be reconfigured through relational, fragmented, and associative visual structures. In this sense, the stage operates as a dynamic cognitive space in which different representational modes intersect and transform one another. The final stage of AI-based spatial visualization represents a mode of production in which these conceptual and visual inputs are translated into spatial imagery through computational processes, making the shift toward data-driven and pattern-based reasoning processes explicitly visible.

When these three steps are considered together, a distinct cognitive dialectic emerges between human reasoning and artificial intelligence, reflecting the cognitive divergence outlined in the theoretical framework. While human cognition offers interpretative depth, relational thinking, and the capacity for speculative expansion, artificial intelligent systems demonstrate strong capabilities in rapid visual synthesis, the generation of variations, and the organization of complex spatial relationships. However, this interaction does not merely produce a complementary relationship; it also reveals specific zones of tension. The study shows that although AI-generated outputs are visually coherent and compelling, they do not always fully align with the conceptual intentions established through human reasoning. This misalignment becomes particularly evident in the representation of atmosphere, experiential continuity, and user-centered spatial configurations. Such conditions expose the limitations of computational systems in capturing experiential nuance and conceptual specificity, while also indicating a partial shift of control over representation from the human designer toward intelligent systems.

In this context, the study contributes to the theoretical reconsideration of design communication by repositioning representation from a passive medium of transfer to a dynamic layer of mediation. Representation operates as an interface for conveying ideas and for progressively producing, transforming, and stabilizing spatial meaning across different stages of the design process. The integration of artificial intelligence into this structure further transforms the ontological status of representation. It shifts the production of meaning from a direct act of transmission to a negotiated, rearticulated, and continuously reconstructed process between human and algorithmic systems. This condition signals a cognitive shift that calls for a reconsideration of the relationships between subject, tool, and representation in design.

From a pedagogical perspective, the findings indicate that AI-based design environments hold significant potential for expanding both the cognitive and expressive capacities of interior architecture education. The structured progression from textual narrative to visual representation enables students to navigate between different modes of thinking, supporting both conceptual production and visual exploration. At the same time, this process allows students to articulate their design intentions more clearly, test these intentions, and iteratively reassess them through multiple variations. However, the findings also demonstrate that the integration of artificial intelligence into interior architecture education cannot be reduced to the acquisition of technical skills alone. It must be framed within a broader context of critical thinking, conceptual awareness, and epistemic responsibility. Preserving the interpretative agency of the designer and cultivating a critical distance toward the generative logic of artificial intelligence systems become essential in this regard.

Nevertheless, several limitations of the study should be acknowledged. The research is based on a specific workshop conducted within a single institutional context and relies on a limited set of artificial intelligence tools. Variations in technological platforms, data environments, and pedagogical approaches may produce different outcomes. Furthermore, the study primarily focuses on the relationship between conceptual production and visual representation, while broader issues such as authorship, originality, and the ethical implications of AI-mediated design remain underexplored. These concerns become increasingly critical as the role of artificial intelligence in design processes expands. Future research should therefore comparatively examine the impact of different AI systems on design cognition, investigate how long-term engagement with AI reshapes design thinking, and explore how ethical and epistemic dimensions can be systematically integrated into design education.

Building upon these insights, it is important to consider how this cognitive divergence may evolve as artificial intelligence systems become more deeply embedded in everyday design practices. As designers engage with AI as an active component of the ideation process, the boundaries between authorship, interpretation, and generation become increasingly fluid. This transformation points toward a co-creative paradigm in which design outcomes emerge through iterative interactions between human cognition and algorithmic processes. In this context, design practice expands toward a relational and process-oriented understanding, where meaning develops through continuous negotiation. Accordingly, there is a growing need for methodological frameworks that can engage with this evolving interaction in a critical and structured manner within both design research and education.

In conclusion, the integration of artificial intelligence into interior architecture design processes extends beyond the expansion of existing representational tools, fundamentally redefining the cognitive and communicative conditions of design. By rendering visible the cognitive divergence between human reasoning and artificial intelligence, this study positions AI-mediated design not as a fixed and resolved paradigm, but as a dynamic and open-ended field of interaction in which meaning, control, and authorship are continuously negotiated and reconfigured.

REFERENCES

Almaz, A. F., El-Agouz, E. A. E., Abdelfatah, M. T., & Raafat, I. (2024). The future role of artificial intelligence design's integration into architectural and interior design education is to improve efficiency, sustainability, and creativity. *Civil Engineering and Architecture*, *12*(3), 1749–1772. DOI: 10.13189/cea.2024.120336

Ball, L. J., & Christensen, B. T. (2019). Advancing an understanding of design cognition and design metacognition: Progress and prospects. *Design Studies*, *65*, 35–59. DOI: 10.1016/j.destud.2019.10.003

Blanco, I. M. (1980). *The The Unconscious as Infinite Sets: An Essay in Bi-logic*. Routledge.

Brooker, G., & Stone, S. (2010). *What Is Interior Design?* Rotovision.

Ching, F. D. K., & Binggeli, C. (2012). *Interior Design Illustrated*. John Wiley & Sons.

Cross, N. (2001). Designerly ways of knowing: Design discipline versus design science. *Design Issues*, *17*(3), 49–55. DOI: 10.1162/074793601750357196

Cross, N. (2023). *Design Thinking: Understanding How Designers Think and Work*. Bloomsbury Publishing. DOI: 10.5040/9781350305090

Engelbrecht, A. (2003). *Computational Intelligence: An Introduction*. John Wiley &Sons.

Fetzer, J. H. (1990). *Artificial Intelligence: Its Scope and Limits*. Springer. DOI: 10.1007/978-94-009-1900-6

Fleischmann, K. (2025). The commodification of creativity: Integrating generative artificial intelligence in higher education design curriculum. *Innovations in Education and Teaching International*, *62*(6), 1843–1857. DOI: 10.1080/14703297.2024.2427039

Fleischmann, K. (2026). From tools to thinking partners: Cognitive and pedagogical shifts in design education through generative AI. *Arts and Humanities in Higher Education*, *0*(0), 14740222261420495. Advance online publication. DOI: 10.1177/14740222261420495

Foucault, M. (1970). The order of discourse. In Young, R. (Ed.), *Untying the Text* (pp. 52–64). Routledge.

Ganshirt, J. (2020). *Tools for Ideas: Introduction to Architectural Design*. Birkhäuser. DOI: 10.1515/9783035622089

Gökdemir, G., & Kayan, H. Z. (2025). Artificial intelligence as a linguistic interface in interior design education: Reconceiving design tools as communication media. *International Journal of Architectural Computing*, *0*(0), 14780771251352955. Advance online publication. DOI: 10.1177/14780771251352955

Goodfellow, I., Bengio, Y., & Courville, A. (2015). *Deep Learning*. MIT Press.

Hunt, E. B. (1975). *Artificial Intelligence*. Academic Press. DOI: 10.1016/B978-0-12-362340-9.50006-9

Ko, J., Ennemoser, B., Yoo, W., Yan, W., & Clayton, M. J. (2023). Architectural spatial layout planning using artificial intelligence. *Automation in Construction*, *154*, 1–18. DOI: 10.1016/j.autcon.2023.105019

Kruse, R., Mostaghim, S., Borgelt, C., Braune, C., & Steinbrecher, M. (2022). *Computational Intelligence: A Methodological Introduction*. Springer Nature. DOI: 10.1007/978-3-030-42227-1

Li, Y., Chen, H., Yu, P., & Yang, L. (2025). A review of artificial intelligence in enhancing architectural design efficiency. *Applied Sciences (Basel, Switzerland)*, *15*(3), 1–22. DOI: 10.3390/app15031476

Longo, G. M., & Albano, S. (2025). Bridging creativity and technology: Integrating generative AI into architectural pedagogy through hybrid frameworks. In T. Ahram, W. Karwowski, C. Martino, G. Bucchianico, V. Maselli (Eds.), *Intelligent Human Systems Integration*, (pp. 318-330). AHFE International. DOI: 10.54941/ahfe1005837

Morozov, E. (2023, March 12). The problem with artificial intelligence? It's neither artificial nor intelligent. *The Guardian*. https://www.theguardian.com/commentisfree/2023/mar/30/artificial-intelligence-chatgpt-human-mind

Neisser, U. (1967). *Cognitive Psychology*. Appleton-Century-Crofts.

Nussbaumer, L. L., & Guerin, D. A. (2008). The relationship between learning styles and visualization skills among interior design students. *Journal of Interior Design*, *26*(2), 1–15. DOI: 10.1111/j.1939-1668.2000.tb00355.x

Pena, M. L. C., Carballal, A., Rodrigues-Fernandez, N., Santos, I., & Romero, J. (2021). Artificial intelligence applied to conceptual design: A review of its use in architecture. *Automation in Construction*, *124*, 1–30. DOI: 10.1016/j.autcon.2021.103550

Ploennigs, J., & Berger, M. (2023). AI art in architecture. *AI in Civil Engineering*, *2*(8), 1–11. DOI: 10.1007/s43503-023-00018-y

Razzouk, R., & Shute, V. (2012). What is design thinking and why is it important. *Review of Educational Research*, *82*(3), 330–348. DOI: 10.3102/0034654312457429

Rhee, J., & Oh, E. (2025). Pedagogy explorations into alternative use of generative AI in design studios. *Technology | Architecture + Design, 9*(1), 84-97. DOI: 10.1080/24751448.2025.2475714

Samad, A., Izani, M., Razak, A., & Rosli, M. (2024). Enhancing creative design: integrating artificial intelligence into interior design education at the university of sharjah. In *Proceedings of the International Visualization, Informatics and Technology Conference (IVIT).* Kuala Lumpur, Malesia. DOI: 10.1109/IVIT62102.2024.10692963

Schön, D. A. (1983). *The Reflective Practitioner: How Professionals Think in Action.* Basic Books.

Shreya, H. R., & Kumar, T. (2024). Artificial intelligence tools and chatbots for design education. In Senjyu, T., So-, C., & Joshi, A. (Eds.), *Smart Trends in Computing and Communications* (pp. 207–396). Springer Nature., DOI: 10.1007/978-981-97-1313-4_33

Starowicz, A., & Zieliński, M. (2024). Sustainable acoustics: The impact of AI on acoustics design and noise management. *Technical Sciences*, *27*, 193–209. DOI: 10.31648/ts.10297

Teal, R. (2010). Developing a (non-linear) practice of design thinking. *International Journal of Art & Design Education*, *29*(3), 294–302. DOI: 10.1111/j.1476-8070.2010.01663.x

Valentine, L., Liu, W., Zhang, L., Bofylatos, S., Christer, K., & Cruickshank, L. (2026). The new normal? AI in design practice, education, and research. *The Design Journal*, *29*(2), 293–298. DOI: 10.1080/14606925.2026.2636392

Zawacki-Richter, O., Marín, V. I., Bond, M., & Gouverneur, F. (2019). Systematic review of research on artificial intelligence applications in higher education-where are the educators? *International Journal of Educational Technology in Higher Education*, *16*(1), 39. DOI: 10.1186/s41239-019-0171-0

Compilation of References

Abidin, C. (2021). Mapping internet celebrity on TikTok. *Social Media + Society*.

Adorno, T. W., & Horkheimer, M. (2002). *Dialectic of enlightenment: Philosophical fragments* (Jephcott, E., Trans.). Stanford University Press. (Original work published 1947)

Aggarwal, C. C. (2018). *Neural Networks and Deep Learning: A Textbook*. Springer International Publishing. DOI: 10.1007/978-3-319-94463-0

Aguera y Arcas, B. (2016, February 23). *Art in the Age of Machine Intelligence*. Medium. Retrieved September 21, 2024, from https://medium.com/artists-and-machine-intelligence/what-is-ami-ccd936394a83

Akay, A. (2007). Toplumbilim, görsel kültür özel sayısı. *Toplum ve Bilim*, •••, 22.

Alaqlobi, O., Alduais, A., Qasem, F., & Alasmari, M. (2024). Artificial intelligence in applied (linguistics): A content analysis and future prospects. *Cogent Arts & Humanities*, *11*(1), 1–19. DOI: 10.1080/23311983.2024.2382422

Al, B. (2019). The concept of generative art and digital creativity in visual arts. *Design Informatics*, *1*(2), 78–91.

Albano, C. (2022). Out of Breath: Vulnerability of Air in Contemporary Art. University of Minnesota Press, 2022. DOI: 10.5749/9781452968193

Albano, C. (2021). To 'Hold In-Common' in the Midst of Clouds' Drift. *Performance Research*, *26*(7), 38–43. DOI: 10.1080/13528165.2021.2059286

Aldrich, C. (2009). *Learning Online with Games, Simulations, and Virtual Worlds: Strategies for Online Instruction*. Jossey-Bass.

Alexander, B. (2017). *The New Digital Stotytelling*. Bloomsbury Publishing. DOI: 10.5040/9798400690839

Alexander, B., & Levine, A. (2008). Web 2.0 Storytelling: Emergence of a New Genre. *EDUCAUSE*, *43*(6), 41–56.

Alleyne, A. (2018, October 25). *A sign of things to come? AI-produced artwork sells for $433K, smashing expectations*. CNN. Retrieved November 18, 2024, from https://edition.cnn.com/style/article/obvious-ai-art-christies-auction-smart-creativity/index.html

Almaz, A. F., El-Agouz, E. A. E., Abdelfatah, M. T., & Raafat, I. (2024). The future role of artificial intelligence design's integration into architectural and interior design education is to improve efficiency, sustainability, and creativity. *Civil Engineering and Architecture*, *12*(3), 1749–1772. DOI: 10.13189/cea.2024.120336

Alpaydın, E. (2020). *Introduction to Machine Learning*. MIT Press.

Amoris, A. (2025). *The art of artificial intelligence: New frontiers of creativity*. CBF Publishing.

Anadol, R. (2021). *Machine Hallucinations- Nature Dreams* [AI installation]. Retrieved January 22, 2026, from https://refikanadol.com/works/machine-hallucinations-nature-dreams/

Anthony, L. F. W., Kanding, B., & Selvan, R. (2020). CarbonTracker: Predicting the Carbon Footprint of Training Deep Learning Models. *arXiv*. DOI: 10.48550

Arantes, P., Sa, V. J., Veiga, P. D. D., & Fernandes-Marcos, A. (Eds.). (2019). *Proceedings of the 9th International Conference on Digital and Interactive Arts*. Portugal. 2019. New York: Association for Computing Machinery. ACM ISBN: 978-1-4503-5273-4 978-1-4503-7250-3.

Aristotle. (2006). Retorik (M. Çiftkaya, Çev.). İmge Kitabevi Yayınları. (Original work published ca. 350 B.C.E.)

Aronsson, S., & Solsjo, C. (2022). *Transmedia Storytelling & Web 4.0 - an upcoming love story*. Jonkoping.

Artut, S. (2017). *Variable* [Electronic sculpture]. Zilberman Gallery.

Aslan, E. (2019). Yapay zekâ resimleri ve sanatın başkalaşan mecrası üzerine. *Güzel Sanatlar Enstitüsü Dergisi*, (42), 231–242. DOI: 10.32547/ataunigsed.516382

Auger, J. (2013). Speculative design: Crafting the speculation. *Digital Creativity (Exeter)*, *24*(1), 11–35. DOI: 10.1080/14626268.2013.767276

Aykut, A. (2013). Güncel sistemden estetik eğitimine bir öneri: Görsel kültür kuramı. *Electronic Turkish Studies*, *8*(9), 705–714. DOI: 10.7827/TurkishStudies.5280

Aziz, A. (2015). *Sosyal bilimlerde araştırma ve yöntem teknikleri*. Nobel Akademik Yayıncılık Eğitim Danışmanlık.

Bak Herrie, M., Maleve, N. R., Philipsen, L., & Bryld Staunæs, A. (2024). Democratization and generative AI image creation: Aesthetics, citizenship, and practices. *AI & Society*, *40*(5), 3495–3507. DOI: 10.1007/s00146-024-02102-y

Ball, L. J., & Christensen, B. T. (2019). Advancing an understanding of design cognition and design metacognition: Progress and prospects. *Design Studies*, *65*, 35–59. DOI: 10.1016/j.destud.2019.10.003

Banh, L., & Strobel, G. (2023). Generative artificial intelligence. *Electronic Markets*, *33*(63), 1–17. DOI: 10.1007/s12525-023-00680-1

Barale, A. (2024). *The art of artificial intelligence: Philosophical keywords*. Cambridge Scholars Publishing.

Barrat, J. (2025). *The Intelligence Explosion: When AI Beats Humans at Everything*. St. Martin's Press.

Barthes, R., Greimas, A. J., Bremond, C., Eco, U., Gritti, J., Morin, V., Metz, C., Todorov, T., & Genette, G. (2011). *Análise Estrutural da Narrativa* (7th ed.). Editora Vozes.BBC (Ed.). *Digital Stories*. Retrieved 2025, from BBC Capture Wales: Retrieved from March 02, 2026, https://www.bbc.co.uk/wales/audiovideo/sites/galleries/pages/digitalstorytelling.shtml

Barthes, R. (1977). The death of the author. In *Image, music, text* (Heath, S., Trans.; pp. 142–148). Hill and Wang.

Barthes, R. (1977). The death of the author. In *Image–music–text* (pp. 142–148). Hill and Wang.

Barthes, R. (1982). *Empire of Signs* (Howard, R., Trans.). Hill and Wang. (Original work published 1970)

Başak, R. (2021). Görsel sanatlar eğitiminde ideoloji tartışmaları temelinde görsel kültür kuramı ve materyal kültürü. *E-Kafkas Journal of Educational Research*, *8*(2), 198–221. DOI: 10.30900/kafkasegt.957360

BBC (Ed.). (n.d.). *Digital Stories*. Retrieved 2025, from BBC Capture Wales: Retrieved from March 02, 2026, https://www.bbc.co.uk/wales/audiovideo/sites/galleries/pages/digitalstorytelling.shtml

Beguš, N., Metahaven, & Beguš, G. (2026). Latent spacecraft: Brains, GANs, Finnegans. Antikythera: Journal for the Philosophy of Planetary Computation. DOI: 10.1162/ANTI.5KP1

Beinin, J. (1994, March/April). Marxism and Postmodernism. *Middle East Report*, 187–188.

Belkhir, L., & Elmeligi, A. (2018). Assessing ICT global emissions footprint: Trends to 2040 & recommendations. *Journal of Cleaner Production*, *177*, 448–463. DOI: 10.1016/j.jclepro.2017.12.239

Bender, E. M., Gebru, T., McMillan-Major, A., & Shmitchell, S. (2021). On the dangers of stochastic parrots: Can language models be too big? In *Proceedings of the 2021 ACM Conference on Fairness, Accountability, and Transparency* (pp. 610–623). Association for Computing Machinery. DOI: 10.1145/3442188.3445922

Bender, E. M., & Hanna, A. (2025). *The AI Con: How to Fight Big Tech's Hype and Create the Future We Want*. Harper/The Bodley Head.

Benjamin, W. (1994). O narrador: considerações sobre a obra de Nikolai Leskov. In *Magia e técnica, arte e política: ensaios sobre literatura e história da cultura* (Vol. 1. Série Obras Escolhidas, pp. 197-221). São Paulo: Brasiliens.

Berkhout, F., & Hertin, J. (2001). Impacts of Information and Communication Technologies on Environmental Sustainability: Speculations and Evidence. *Report to the OECD*. Retrieved January 22, 2026, from https://www.oecd.org/dataoecd/4/6/1897156.pdf

Berners-Lee, T. (1989). Information Management: A Proposal. CERN. Geneva: CERN.

Berney, M., Ouaazki, A., Macko, V., Kocher, B., & Holzer, A. (2024). Care-based eco-feedback augmented with generative AI: Fostering pro-environmental behavior through emotional attachment. In *Proceedings of the CHI Conference on Human Factors in Computing Systems (CHI '24),* May 11-16, 2024, USA. DOI: 10.1145/3613904.3642296

Bilgin, N. (2006). *Sosyal bilimlerde içerik analizi: Teknikler ve örnek çalışmalar*. Siyasal Kitabevi.

Blanco, I. M. (1980). *The The Unconscious as Infinite Sets: An Essay in Bi-logic*. Routledge.

Bleecker, J. (2022). Design Fiction. In Carta, S. (Ed.), *Machine Learning and the City*. DOI: 10.1002/9781119815075.ch47

Boden, M. A. (2016). *AI: Its nature and future*. Oxford University Press.

Brade, S., Wang, B., Sousa, M., Oore, S., & Grossman, T. (2023). Promptify: Text-to-image generation through interactive prompt exploration with large language models. In *Proceedings of the 36th Annual ACM Symposium on User Interface Software and Technology* (pp. 1–14). https://doi.org/DOI: 10.1145/3586183.3606725

Brain, T. (2019). *Asunder* [AI installation]. Tega Brain Studio. Retrieved January 22, 2026, from https://tegabrain.com/Asunder

Brain, T. (2021). *Synthetic Messenger* [Art project]. Retrieved January 25, 2026, from https://tegabrain.com/Synthetic-Messenger

Brain, T., & Lavigne, S. (2021). The Battle to Control the Carbon Media Cycle, *Ding Magazine*. Retrieved January 25, 2026, from https://dingdingding.org/issue-4/the-battle-to-control-the-carbon-media-cycle/

Braun, V., & Clarke, V. (2006). Using thematic analysis in psychology. *Qualitative Research in Psychology*, *3*(2), 77–101. DOI: 10.1191/1478088706qp063oa

Braun, V., & Clarke, V. (2021). To saturate or not to saturate? Questioning data saturation as a useful concept for thematic analysis. *Qualitative Research in Sport, Exercise and Health*, *13*(2), 201–216. DOI: 10.1080/2159676X.2019.1704846

Brooker, G., & Stone, S. (2010). *What Is Interior Design?* Rotovision.

Brown, T., Mann, B., Ryder, N., Subbiah, M., Kaplan, J. D., Dhariwal, P., Neelakantan, A., Shyam, P., Sastry, G., Askell, A., Agarwal, S., Herbert-Voss, A., Krueger, G., Henighan, T., Child, R., Ramesh, A., Ziegler, D., Wu, J., Winter, C., Hesse, C., Chen, M., Sigler, E., Litwin, M., Gray, S., Chess, B., Clark, J., Berner, C., McCandlish, S., Radford, A., Sutskever, I., & Amodei, D. (2020). Language Models are Few-Shot Learners. *Advances in Neural Information Processing Systems 33 (NeurIPS 2020)*. Retrieved November 18, 2024, from https://arxiv.org/abs/2005.14165

Bucher, T. (2012). Want to be on the top? Algorithmic power and the threat of invisibility on Facebook. *New Media & Society*, *14*(7), 1164–1180. DOI: 10.1177/1461444812440159

Buhl, N. (2023, September 21). *OpenAI's DALL-E 3 Explained: Generate Images with ChatGPT*. Encord. Retrieved November 18, 2024, from https://encord.com/blog/openai-dall-e-3-what-we-know-so-far/

Burke, S. (2008). *The Death and Return of the Author* (3rd Edition ed.). Edinburgh University Press. DOI: 10.1515/9781474482172

Canan, S., & Acungil, M. (2018). *Dijital gelecekte insan kalmak*. Nefes Yayıncılık.

Candemir, T. (2006). *"Çağdaş Teknolojinin Sanat Dallarına Etkileri Ve Yardımcı Yazılımlarla Bilgisayarda Resim Yapmak"*. 6 th International Educational Technology Conference, (pp.357-365).

Cardenas Cordova, D., Kelly, N., & Rezayan, L. (2025). A systematic literature review of the speculative design process and a proposed framework for speculative design. *Design Science, 11*, e38. DOI: 10.1017/dsj.2025.10030

Carey, J. (2005). *What good is art?* Vakıfbank Cultural Publications.

Carpo, M. (2003). *Digital Tectonics*. Wiley.

Carpo, M. (2011). *The Alphabet and the Algorithm*. MIT Press.

Cave, S., & Dihal, K. (2019). Hopes and fears for intelligent machines in fiction and reality. *Nature Machine Intelligence*, *1*(2), 74–78. Retrieved November 18, 2024, from. DOI: 10.1038/s42256-019-0020-9

Çelebi, B. (2021). *The effect of machines on art and the transformation of the artist from the 20th century to the present* (Master's thesis). Sakarya University, Sakarya, Turkey.

Cenani, S., Durmazoğlu, M. Ç., Gürer, E., Kutlu, Z., & Dane, G. (2025). Designing in an immersive virtual reality environment: Implications for design education. In De Paolis, L. T., Arpaia, P., & Sacco, M. (Eds.), Lecture notes in computer science: Vol. 15738. *Extended Reality: XR Salento 2025* (pp. 113–126). Springer., DOI: 10.1007/978-3-031-97769-5_9

Cesar & Lois. (2018). *Degenerative Cultures* [Artwork]. Retrieved January 22, 2026, from https://cesarandlois.org/digitalfungus/

Chakrabarty, D. (2009). The climate of history: Four theses. *Critical Inquiry*, *35*(2), 197–222. DOI: 10.1086/596640

Chang, Y. S., Kao, J. Y., & Wang, Y. Y. (2022). Influences of virtual reality on design creativity and design thinking. *Thinking Skills and Creativity*, *46*, 101127. Advance online publication. DOI: 10.1016/j.tsc.2022.101127

Cheng, K., & Neisch, P. (2022). A new perspective on eclectic attributes in architecture: Taking eclectic architecture in Beijing and Hong Kong as an example. *Journal of Asian Architecture and Building Engineering*, *22*(3), 1126–1145. DOI: 10.1080/13467581.2022.2074017

Cheng, M. (2022). The creativity of artificial intelligence in art. In *Proceedings of the 2021 Summit of the International Society for the Study of Information. Proceedings*, *81*(1), 110. Retrieved January 22, 2025, from. DOI: 10.3390/proceedings2022081110

Ching, F. D. K., & Binggeli, C. (2012). *Interior Design Illustrated.* John Wiley & Sons.

Chmielewski, D., & Hu, K. (2023, August 10). Disney creates task force to explore AI and cut costs - sources. *Reuters.* Retrieved November 18, 2024, from https://www.reuters.com/technology/disney-creates-task-force-explore-ai-cut-costs-sources-2023-08-08/

Christou, C. (2020). Virtual reality for learning: A review of current trends. In *Virtual Reality: Concepts and Technologies.* CRC Press.

Çoban, İ. (2025). *Substance- Essence* [Film]. Istanbul. Retrieved 10.02.2026 https://filmfreeway.com/Essence998

Çoban, İ. (2026, March 10). *Interview on the role of artificial intelligence in art and design* [In-depth interview by the author]. Personal Archive.

Cohen, H. (1994). The further exploits of Aaron, painter. *Stanford Humanities Review*, *2*(4), 141–158.

Crawford, K. (2021). *Atlas of AI: Power, Politics, and the Planetary Costs of Artificial Intelligence.* Yale University Press.

Crawford, K. (2021). *Atlas of AI: Power, politics, and the planetary costs of artificial intelligence.* Yale University Press. DOI: 10.2307/j.ctv1ghv45t

Creswell, J. W. (2014). *Research design: Qualitative, quantitative, and mixed methods approaches* (4th ed.). SAGE.

Creswell, J. W., & Poth, C. N. (2018). *Qualitative inquiry and research design: Choosing among five approaches* (4th ed.). SAGE.

Cross, N. (2001). Designerly ways of knowing: Design discipline versus design science. *Design Issues*, *17*(3), 49–55. DOI: 10.1162/074793601750357196

Cross, N. (2023). *Design Thinking: Understanding How Designers Think and Work.* Bloomsbury Publishing. DOI: 10.5040/9781350305090

Cubitt, S. (2015). Integral waste. *Theory, Culture & Society*, *32*(4), 133–145. DOI: 10.1177/0263276414537316

Cubitt, S. (2017). *Finite Media- Environmental Implications of Digital Technologies.* Duke University Press.

Cucuzzella, C. (2021). Making the invisible visible: Eco-art and design against the anthropocene. *Sustainability (Basel)*, *13*(7), 3747. DOI: 10.3390/su13073747

Cunningham, S., & Craig, D. (2019). *Social media entertainment.* NYU Press.

Curtis, D. J. (2009). Creating inspiration: The role of the arts in creating empathy for ecological restoration. *Ecological Management & Restoration, 10*(3), 174–184. DOI: 10.1111/j.1442-8903.2009.00487.x

Dakamsih, N., Alshunnag, M., & Alkayid, A. (2025). When Stories Get a Visual Voice: AI-Generated Images, a Visual Pedagogy for Enhancing Student Engagement and Critical Analysis in World Literature. *Educational Process: International Journal, 18*(1), e2025416. DOI: 10.22521/edupij.2025.18.416

Danto, A. (1964). The art world. *The Journal of Philosophy, 61*(19), 571–584. DOI: 10.2307/2022937

Danto, A. C. (2013). *What is art?* (Baransel, Z., Trans.). Sel Yayıncılık.

Darian, S. (1979). The role of redundancy in language and language teaching. *System, 7*(1), 47–59. DOI: 10.1016/0346-251X(79)90022-8

Davis, P., Napole, A., Reddy, C., Palepu, S. K., Wu, A. Q., Mannam, S. S., Gajjar, A. A., Jabarkheel, R., Ajmera, S., Ahmad, H., Scott, K. W., Sioutas, G., Shekhtman, O., Kandregula, S., Rahmani, R., Catapano, J. S., Burkhardt, J. K., & Srinivasan, V. M. (2025). Systematic evaluation of AI-based text-to-image models for generating medical illustrations in neurosurgery: A multi-stage comparative study. *Clinical Neurology and Neurosurgery, 257*, 109039. DOI: 10.1016/j.clineuro.2025.109039 PMID: 40614319

de Carvalho Souza, M. E., & Weigang, L. (2025). Grok, Gemini, ChatGPT and DeepSeek: Comparison and applications in conversational artificial intelligence. *Inteligencia Artificial, 2*(1). Advance online publication. DOI: 10.5281/zenodo.14885243

Deleuze, G., & Guattari, F. (1993). *What is philosophy?* (Ilgaz, T., Trans.). YKY.

Demos, T. J. (2016). *Decolonizing Nature, Contemporary Art and the Politics of Ecology*. Sternberg Press.

Dickie, G. (1969). Defining art. *American Philosophical Quarterly, 6*(3), 253–256.

Dickie, G. (2001). *Art and value*. Blackwell Publishers.

Diffuse The Rest. (2022, September 5). Hugging Face. Retrieved November 18, 2024, from https://huggingface.co/spaces/huggingface-projects/diffuse-the-rest

Dingli, A. S. (2015). Who Are the Digital Natives? In *The New Digital Natives*. Springer-Verlag., DOI: 10.1007/978-3-662-46590-5_2

DiSalvo, C. (2012). *Adversarial design*. MIT Press. DOI: 10.7551/mit-press/8732.001.0001

Duchamp, M. (1973). *The writings of Marcel Duchamp* (Sanouillet, M., & Peterson, E., Eds.). Da Capo Press.

Dunne, A., & Raby, F. (2007). Technological dreams series: No.1, robots. Kunst-museen Krefeld; MoMA permanent collection. https://dunneandraby.co.uk/content/projects/10/0

Dunne, A. (1999). *Hertzian tales: An investigation into the critical and aesthetic potential of the electronic product as a post-optimal object*. RCA CRD Research Publications.

Dunne, A., & Raby, F. (2001). *Design noir: The secret life of electronic objects*. Birkhäuser.

Dunne, A., & Raby, F. (2013). *Speculative everything: Design, fiction, and social dreaming*. MIT Press.

Dwivedi, Y. K., Kshetri, N., Hughes, L., Slade, E. L., Jeyaraj, A., Kar, A. K., Baab-dullah, A. M., Koohang, A., Raghavan, V., Ahuja, M., Albanna, H., Albashrawi, M. A., Al-Busaidi, A. S., Balakrishnan, J., Barlette, Y., Basu, S., Bose, I., Brooks, L., Buhalis, D., & Wright, R. (2023). Opinion paper: So what if ChatGPT wrote it? Multidisciplinary perspectives on opportunities, challenges and implications of generative conversational AI for research, practice and policy. *International Journal of Information Management*, *71*, 102642. DOI: 10.1016/j.ijinfomgt.2023.102642

Elgammal, A. (2018, October 26). *AI-Art-Creative-Process* [Graph]. The Conversation. Retrieved February 15, 2026 https://theconversation.com/when-the-line-between-machine-and-artist-becomes-blurred-103149

Elgammal, A. (2019). *AI Is Blurring the Definition of Artist*. American Scientist. Retrieved November 18, 2024, from https://www.americanscientist.org/article/ai-is-blurring-the-definition-of-artist

Elgammal, A., Liu, B., Elhoseiny, M., & Mazzone, M. (2017). CAN: Creative adversarial networks, generating "art" by learning about styles and deviating from style norms. In *Proceedings of the 8th International Conference on Computational Creativity* (pp. 96–103).

Elme, L., Jørgensen, M. L., Dandanell, G., Mottelson, A., & Makransky, G. (2022). Immersive virtual reality in STEM: Is IVR an effective learning medium and does adding self-explanation after a lesson improve learning outcomes? *Educational Technology Research and Development*, *70*(5), 1601–1626. DOI: 10.1007/s11423-022-10139-3 PMID: 35873274

Engelbrecht, A. (2003). *Computational Intelligence: An Introduction*. John Wiley &Sons.

European Parliament. (2025, February 19). *EU AI Act: first regulation on artificial intelligence Topics*. European Parliament. Retrieved May 5, 2025, from https://www.europarl.europa.eu/topics/en/article/20230601STO93804/eu-ai-act-first-regulation-on-artificial-intelligence

Europeana. (2019). Retrieved 2025, from Europeana: https://www.europeana.eu/

Evans, R. (1997). *Translations from Drawing to Building and Other Essays*. MIT Press.

Fakhar, A. (2024, January 11). *Religious Ethics in the Age of Artificial Intelligence and Robotics: Exploring Moral Considerations and Ethical Perspectives*. AI and Faith. Retrieved May 5, 2025, from https://aiandfaith.org/insights/religious-ethics-in-the-age-of-artificial-intelligence-and-robotics-exploring-moral-considerations-and-ethical-perspectives/

Fetzer, J. H. (1990). *Artificial Intelligence: Its Scope and Limits*. Springer. DOI: 10.1007/978-94-009-1900-6

Filimowicz, M. (2023). *AI and the Future of Creative Work Algorithms and Society*. Routhledge. DOI: 10.4324/9781003299875

Fleischmann, K. (2025). The commodification of creativity: Integrating generative artificial intelligence in higher education design curriculum. *Innovations in Education and Teaching International*, *62*(6), 1843–1857. DOI: 10.1080/14703297.2024.2427039

Fleischmann, K. (2026). From tools to thinking partners: Cognitive and pedagogical shifts in design education through generative AI. *Arts and Humanities in Higher Education*, *0*(0), 14740222261420495. Advance online publication. DOI: 10.1177/14740222261420495

Floridi, L., & Chiriatti, M. (2020). GPT-3: Its nature, scope, limits, and consequences. *Minds and Machines*, *30*(4), 681–694. DOI: 10.1007/s11023-020-09548-1

Ford, C., Gardner, D., Horgan, L. E., Liu, C., Tsaasan, A. M., Nardi, B., & Rickman, J. (2017, May). Chat speed op pogchamp: Practices of coherence in massive twitch chat. In *Proceedings of the 2017 CHI conference extended abstracts on human factors in computing systems* (pp. 858-871). DOI: 10.1145/3027063.3052765

Forensic Architecture. (2020). *Cloud Studies* [Artwork]. Retrieved January 22, 2026, from https://forensic-architecture.org/investigation/cloudstudies

Foss, S. K. (2005). Theory of visual rhetoric. In Smith, K., Moriarty, S., Barbatsis, G., & Kenney, K. (Eds.), *Handbook of visual communication: Theory, methods, and media* (pp. 141–152). Lawrence Erlbaum.

Foucault, M. (1970). The order of discourse. In Young, R. (Ed.), *Untying the Text* (pp. 52–64). Routledge.

Franco, F. (2022). *The Algorithmic Dimension: Five Artists in Conversation*. Springer International Publishing. DOI: 10.1007/978-3-319-61167-9

Froehlich, J., Findlater, L., & Landay, J. (2010). The design of eco-feedback technology. In *Proceedings of the SIGCHI Conference on Human Factors in Computing Systems*. New York: ACM Press. DOI: 10.1145/1753326.1753629

Fuchs, C. (2012). Towards Marxian Internet Studies. *Marx is Back-The Importance of Marxist Theory and Research for Critical Comm, 10*(2). 392-412.

Fuchs, C. (2014). *Digital Labour and Karl Marx*. Routhledge. DOI: 10.4324/9781315880075

Fuchs, C., & Mosco, V. (Eds.). (2015). *Marx in the Age of Digital Capitalism*. Brill.

Gabrys, J. (2016). *Program Earth: Environmental Sensing Technology and the Making of a Computational Planet*. University of Minnesota Press. DOI: 10.5749/j.ctt1b7x5gq

Gama, N. (2012). *Cinzel Decorative*. Google Fonts. Retrieved from https://fonts.google.com/specimen/Cinzel+Decorative/about?preview.text=Little%20Red%20Riding%20Hood&query=Natanael+Gama

Ganshirt, J. (2020). *Tools for Ideas: Introduction to Architectural Design*. Birkhäuser. DOI: 10.1515/9783035622089

GeSI. (2015). *SMARTer2030: ICT solutions for 21st century challenges*. https://gesi.org/research/smarter2030

Gökdemir, G., & Kayan, H. Z. (2025). Artificial intelligence as a linguistic interface in interior design education: Reconceiving design tools as communication media. *International Journal of Architectural Computing*, 14780771251352955. Advance online publication. DOI: 10.1177/14780771251352955

Göktaş, L. S. (2023). ChatGPT uzaktan eğitim sınavlarında başarılı olabilir mi? Turizm alanında doğruluk ve doğrulama üzerine bir araştırma. *Journal of Tourism and Gastronomy Studies*, *11*(2), 892–905. DOI: 10.21325/jotags.2023.1224

Golder, S., Ahmed, S., Norman, G., & Booth, A. (2017). Attitudes toward the ethics of research using social media data. *Social Science & Medicine*.

Goldhaber, M. H. (1997). The attention economy and the Net. *First Monday*, *2*(4).

Goodfellow, I. J., Pouget-Abadie, J., Mirza, M., Xu, B., Warde-Farley, D., Ozair, S., Courville, A., & Bengio, Y. (2014) Generative Adversarial Nets. *Proceedings of the 27th International Conference on Neural Information Processing Systems,* 2, 2672-2680.

Goodfellow, I., Bengio, Y., & Courville, A. (2015). *Deep Learning*. MIT Press.

Google Gemini Artificial Intelligence Model. (2023, December 06). [Screenshot]. Retrieved February 15, 2026 https://blog.google/technology/ai/google-gemini-ai/?utm_source=tldrai#sundar-note

Graf, C. (2017). Narrating through Images. In Johnston, S. I. (Ed.), *Religion: Narrating Religion* (pp. 157–175). Macmillan Reference USA.

Gramigna, R. (2023). *The visage as text: physiognomy, semiotics, and face reading from antiquity to artificial intelligence*. Chinese Semiotic Studies.

Grau, O., Hoth, J., & Wandl-Vogt, E. (2019). *Digital Art through the Looking Glass: New Strategies for Archiving, Collecting and Preserving in Digital Humanities*. Edition Donau-Universität Krems.

Greenfield, G., Romero, J., & Machado, P. (Eds.). (2021). *Artificial intelligence and the arts: Computational creativity, artistic behavior, and tools for creatives*. Springer International Publishing.

Güçlüer, S. B. (2024). Stuart Hall'un yaklaşımıyla: Medyanın etkisinde Ciguli'nin temsili ve kimliği. *Online Journal of Music Sciences*, *9*(2), 676–687. DOI: 10.31811/ojomus.1522355

Guinness, H. (2023). *The 30+ top AI art generators in 2025*. Zapier. Retrieved May 5, 2025, from https://zapier.com/blog/ai-art-generator/#jasper-art

Gültekin, A. C. (2014). The institutional structure of art activity in Arthur Danto and George Dickie. *FLSF Journal of Philosophy and Social Sciences, 18*, 115–132. Retrieved: 08.02.2026 https://izlik.org/JA23NT44LF

Güney, E., & Yavuz, H. (2020). The role of the artist and the changing concept of art in AI-assisted artistic production. *Journal of Art and Design, 26*, 415–439.

Güney, E., & Yavuz, H. (2020). Yapay Zekâ ile Sanatsal Üretim Pratiğinde Sanatçının Rolü ve Değişen Sanat Olgusu. *Sanat ve Tasarım Dergisi*, (26), 415–439.

Hall, S. (1997a). Introduction. In Hall, S. (Ed.), *Representation: Cultural representations and signifying practices* (pp. 1–12). Sage Publications.

Hamilton, W. A., Garretson, O., & Kerne, A. (2014). Streaming on Twitch: Fostering participatory communities of play. In *Proceedings of the SIGCHI Conference on Human Factors in Computing Systems*. DOI: 10.1145/2556288.2557048

Heidegger, M. (2011). *The origin of the work of art* (Tepebaşlı, F., Trans.). Deki Yayınları. (Original work published 1950)

Heikkurinen, P., & Ruuska, T. (Eds.). (2021). *Sustainability Beyond Technology: Philosophy, Critique, and Implications for Human Organization*. Oxford University Press. DOI: 10.1093/oso/9780198864929.001.0001

Hermerén, G. (2024). *Art and artificial intelligence*. Cambridge University Press. DOI: 10.1017/9781009431798

Herpers, Y. P. (2023). *The art and the artificial intelligence: How the value of real art is increased*. Herpers Publishing International.

Hilty, L. M. (2008). *Information Technology and Sustainability. Essays on the Relationship between ICT and Sustainable Development*. Books on Demand, Norderstedt.

Hilty, L. M., & Aebischer, B. (2015). ICT for Sustainability: An Emerging Research Field. In Hilty, L., & Aebischer, B. (Eds.), *ICT Innovations for Sustainability. Advances in Intelligent Systems and Computing* (Vol. 310, pp. 3–36). Springer. DOI: 10.1007/978-3-319-09228-7_1

Hintze, A., Proschinger Åström, F., & Schossau, J. (2025). Autonomous language-image generation loops converge to generic visual motifs. *Patterns, 7*(1), 101451. DOI: 10.1016/j.patter.2025.101451 PMID: 41583980

Horton, D., & Wohl, R. R. (1956). Mass communication and para-social interaction. *Psychiatry, 19*(3), 215–229. DOI: 10.1080/00332747.1956.11023049 PMID: 13359569

Horvath, A.-S., & Pouliou, P. (2024). AI for conceptual architecture: Reflections on designing with text-to-text, text-to-image, and image-to-image generators. *Frontiers of Architectural Research, 13*(3), 593–612. DOI: 10.1016/j.foar.2024.02.006

Horváthová, K. (2017). Redundancy in the verbal communication of teachers in primary education. *Journal of Language and Cultural Education, 5*(3), 93–107. DOI: 10.1515/jolace-2017-0030

Hou, N., Nishina, D., Sugita, S., Jiang, R., Kindaichi, S., Oishi, H., & Shimizu, A. (2024). Virtual reality space in architectural design education: Learning effect of scale feeling. *Building and Environment, 248*, 111060. Advance online publication. DOI: 10.1016/j.buildenv.2023.111060

Hunt, E. B. (1975). *Artificial Intelligence*. Academic Press. DOI: 10.1016/B978-0-12-362340-9.50006-9

Hu, T.-E. (2015). *A Prehistory of the Cloud*. The MIT Press. DOI: 10.7551/mitpress/9780262029513.001.0001

Hutcheon, L. (1989). *The Politics of Postmodernism*. Routhledge.

Inie, N., Falk, J., & Selvan, R. (2025). How CO2STLY Is CHI? The carbon footprint of generative AI in HCI research and what we should do about it. In *Proceedings of the 2025 CHI Conference on Human Factors in Computing Systems* (CHI '25). New York, USA, Article 206, 1-29. DOI: 10.1145/3706598.3714227

Ipsita, A., Patel, M., Unmesh, A., & Ramani, K. (2024). Authoring instructional flow in iVR learning units to promote outcome-oriented learning. *Computers & Education: X Reality, 5*. https://doi.org/DOI: 10.1016/j.cexr.2024.100074

Irwin, T. (2015). Transition Design: A Proposal for a New Area of Design Practice, Study, and Research. *Design and Culture, 7*(2), 229–246. DOI: 10.1080/17547075.2015.1051829

Islam, A. (2023, March). *A History of Generative AI: From GAN to GPT-4*. Marktechpost. Retrieved May 5, 2025, from https://www.marktechpost.com/2023/03/21/a-history-of-generative-ai-from-gan-to-gpt-4/

Jameson, F. (1991). *Postmodernism, or, The cultural logic of late capitalism*. Duke University Press. Retrieved May 5, 2025, from https://web.education.wisc.edu/halverson/wp-content/uploads/sites/33/2012/12/jameson.pdf

Jameson, F. (1998). *The cultural turn: Selected writings on the postmodern, 1983–1998*. Verso.

Jana, M., & Banerjee, S. (2025). *Artificial intelligence and contemporary media.* Notion Press.

Jenkins, H. (2006). *Convergence culture: Where old and new media collide.* NYU Press.

Jenkins, H., Ford, S., & Green, J. (2013). *Spreadable media: Creating value and meaning in a networked culture.* NYU Press.

Jeon, B. (2024). Studies of Artificial Intelligence (AI) Cinema: The necessity for studying AI film making methodologies that apply iconography, semiotics, and film semiotics theories. *The Korean Journal of Arts Studies.*

Jiang, H., Brown, L., Cheng, J., Artist, A., Khan, M., Gupta, A., Workman, D., Hanna, A., Flowers, J., & Gebru, T. (2023, 08 08-10). AI Art and its Impact on Artists. *AAAI/ ACM Conference on AI, Ethics, and Society*, 12. DOI: 10.1145/3600211.3604681

Johannessen, L. K., Keitsch, M. M., & Pettersen, I. N. (2019). Speculative and critical design — Features, methods, and practices. *Proceedings of the 22nd International Conference on Engineering Design (ICED19)* (pp. 1623–1632). Cambridge University Press. DOI: 10.1017/dsi.2019.168

Johnson, H., & Shaw, J. S. (2005). *Glossary of digital art and printmaking.* Digital Art Practices & Terminology Task Force. Retrieved: 05.03.2026 https://www.bermangraphics.com/dapttf/GlosDigArt.pdf

Jones, N. (2018). How to stop data centres from gobbling up the world's electricity. *Nature, 561*(7722), 163–166. DOI: 10.1038/d41586-018-06610-y PMID: 30209383

Junior, F. (2021). *Entre Lendas e História - Narrativas que Representam a Identidade de São Luís.* Appris Editora.

Kaleja, P., & Kozlovska, M. (2017). Virtual reality as innovative approach to the interior designing. *Selected Scientific Papers – Journal of Civil Engineering, 12*(1), 109–116. https://doi.org/DOI: 10.1515/sspjce-2017-0010

Kalpokienė, J., & Kalpokas, I. (2023). Creative encounters of a posthuman kind – anthropocentric law, artificial intelligence, and art. *Technology in Society, 72*, 102197. DOI: 10.1016/j.techsoc.2023.102197

Kara, D. (2003). Sanat Eğitiminde Disiplinlerarası Sanat. *Yapı Mimarlık Tasarım Kültür Sanat*, 108-112.

Kaya, Y. (2017). Güncel Sanatta Yeni Bir Yaklaşım Olarak "Melezlik". *Sanat ve Tasarım Dergisi*, (20), 165–182. DOI: 10.18603/sanatvetasarim.370751

Kitchin, R. (2014). *The Data Revolution: Big Data, Open Data, Data Infrastructures & Their Consequences*. Sage Publications. DOI: 10.4135/9781473909472

Klapperich, C. M., Sato, K., & Forlizzi, J. (2020). How do tools shape interaction? DIY practices and material engagement. *Personal and Ubiquitous Computing*. Advance online publication. DOI: 10.1007/s00779-020-01452-w

Ko, J., Ennemoser, B., Yoo, W., Yan, W., & Clayton, M. J. (2023). Architectural spatial layout planning using artificial intelligence. *Automation in Construction, 154*, 1–18. DOI: 10.1016/j.autcon.2023.105019

Kolarevic, B. (2025). Generative AI technologies and architectural design education. In *On Architecture: Crosscutting and Fusion of Disciplines (OA2025 Proceedings)* (pp. 117–122). DOI: 10.60152/2m4jkgsf

Kolarevic, B. (2003). *Architecture in the Digital Age: Design and Manufacturing*. Taylor & Francis.

Kong, F. (2020). Application of artificial intelligence in modern art teaching. [iJET]. *International Journal of Emerging Technologies in Learning, 15*(13), 1863–1870. DOI: 10.3991/ijet.v15i13.15351

Kovalova, M., Alforova, Z., Sokolyuk, L., Chursin, O., & Obukh, L. (2022). The digital evolution of art: Current trends in the context of the formation and development of metamodernism. *Amazonia Investiga, 11*(56), 114–123. DOI: 10.34069/AI/2022.56.08.12

Kowert, R., & Daniel, A. J. (2021). The one-and-a-half sided parasocial relationship. *Journal of Gaming & Virtual Worlds, 13*(2), 121–143.

Kruse, R., Mostaghim, S., Borgelt, C., Braune, C., & Steinbrecher, M. (2022). *Computational Intelligence: A Methodological Introduction*. Springer Nature. DOI: 10.1007/978-3-030-42227-1

Lambert, J., & Hessler, B. (2018). *Digital Storytelling: Capturing lives, creating community* (5th ed.). Routledge. DOI: 10.4324/9781351266369

Latour, B. (2004). *Politics of Nature: How to Bring the Sciences into Democracy* (Porter, C., Trans.). Harvard University Press. DOI: 10.4159/9780674039964

Leach, N. (Ed.). (1997). *Rethinking architecture: A reader in cultural theory*. Routledge.

LeCun, Y., Bengio, Y., & Hinton, G. (2015, May 27). Deep Learning. *Nature, 521*(7553), 436–444. DOI: 10.1038/nature14539 PMID: 26017442

Lee-Morrison, L. (2021). Finding pictures in the Sky: Machinic visions of cloudscapes. In *Proceedings of Politics of the Machines- Rogue Research 2021 (POM 2021)* (pp. 344-350). British Computer Society. DOI: 10.14236/ewic/POM2021.46

Lenoir, B. (2005). *The work of art* (Derman, A., Trans.). Yapı Kredi Publications.

Lenzerini, F. (2011). Intangible Cultural Heritage: The living culture of peoples. *European Journal of International Law*, *22*(1), 101–120. DOI: 10.1093/ejil/chr006

Leufkens, S. (2022). Measuring redundancy: The relation between concord and complexity. *Linguistics Vanguard : Multimodal Online Journal*, *9*(s1), 95–106. Advance online publication. Retrieved January 22, 2025, from. DOI: 10.1515/lingvan-2020-0143

Leufkens, S. C. (2020). A functionalist typology of redundancy. *Revista da Abralin*, *19*(3), 79–103.

Lewis, T. (2014, December 4). A brief history of artificial intelligence. *LiveScience*. Retrieved: 20.03.2026 https://www.livescience.com/49007-history-of-artificial-intelligence.html

Lin, C. Y. (2025). Bridging AI-generated imagery and 3D modeling: Addressing spatial inconsistency and controllability in design workflows. *Computer Aided Design*, *224*, 629–639.

Lin, Z., Wang, Z., Liu, Q., Zhang, X., & Liu, J. (2026). Narratology meets text-to-image: A survey of consistency in AI generated storybook illustrations. *Artificial Intelligence Review*, *59*(2), 83. DOI: 10.1007/s10462-025-11482-6

Liu, B. (2023). Arguments for the rise of artificial intelligence art: Does AI art have creativity, motivation, self-awareness and emotion? *Arte. Individuo y Sociedad*, *35*(3), 811–822. DOI: 10.5209/aris.83808

Li, Y., Chen, H., Yu, P., & Yang, L. (2025). A review of artificial intelligence in enhancing architectural design efficiency. *Applied Sciences (Basel, Switzerland)*, *15*(3), 1–22. DOI: 10.3390/app15031476

Lombard, M., & Ditton, T. (1997). At the heart of it all: The concept of presence. *Journal of Computer-Mediated Communication*, *3*(2), 0. Advance online publication. DOI: 10.1111/j.1083-6101.1997.tb00072.x

Longo, G. M., & Albano, S. (2025). Bridging creativity and technology: Integrating generative AI into architectural pedagogy through hybrid frameworks. In T. Ahram, W. Karwowski, C. Martino, G. Bucchianico, V. Maselli (Eds.), *Intelligent Human Systems Integration*, (pp. 318-330). AHFE International. DOI: 10.54941/ahfe1005837

López-Varela Azcárate, A. (2023). Intermedial semiotics in the age of artificial intelligence. Challenges and opportunities for the arts. *Techno Humanities*, *3*(2), 108–116. DOI: 10.1016/j.techum.2024.04.001

Lyotard, J.-F. (1984). *The postmodern condition: A report on knowledge* (Bennington, G., & Massumi, B., Trans.). University of Minnesota Press.

Lyotard, J.-F. (1994). *Das postmoderne Wissen: ein Bericht* (Engelmann, P., Ed.). Passagen-Verlag.

Makransky, G., & Petersen, G. B. (2021). The cognitive affective model of immersive learning (CAMIL): A theoretical research-based model of learning in immersive virtual reality. *Educational Psychology Review*, *33*(3), 937–958. DOI: 10.1007/s10648-020-09586-2

Malmodin, J., & Lundén, D. (2018). The energy and carbon footprint of the global ICT and entertainment & media sectors 2010-2015. *Sustainability*, *10*(9), 3027. DOI: 10.3390/su10093027

Manovich, L. (2023). *AI aesthetics*. Strelka Press. https://manovich.net/index.php/projects/ai-aesthetics

Manovich, L. (2001). *The language of new media*. MIT Press.

Manovich, L. (2001). *The Language of New Media*. MIT Press.

Marx, K. (2012). *Economic and Philosophic Manuscripts of 1844*. Dover Publications.

Maxwell, R., & Miller, T. (2012). *Greening the Media*. Oxford University Press.

Mayer-Schönberger, V., & Cukier, K. (2013). *Big Data: A Revolution That Will Transform How We Live, Work, and Think*. Houghton Mifflin Harcourt.

Mayring, P. (2000). Qualitative content analysis. *Forum Qualitative Sozialforschung / Forum: Qualitative. Social Research*, *1*(2), 20.

Mayring, P. (2015). Qualitative content analysis: Theoretical background and procedures. In Bikner-Ahsbahs, A., Knipping, C., & Presmeg, N. (Eds.), *Approaches to qualitative research in mathematics education (ss* (pp. 365–380). Springer. DOI: 10.1007/978-94-017-9181-6_13

Mazzone, M., & Elgammal, A. (2019, February 21). Art, Creativity, and the Potential of Artificial Intelligence. Retrieved May 5, 2025, from https://www.mdpi.com/2076-0752/8/1/26

Mbembe, A. (2020). *The Universal Right to Breathe* (C. Shread, trans.), Critical Enquiry. Retrieved January 22, 2026, from https://critinq.wordpress.com/2020/04/13/the-universal-right-to-breathe/

McCorduck, P. (1991). *Aaron's Code: meta-art, artificial intelligence, and the work of Harold Cohen*. W.H. Freeman.

McCormack, J., & d'Inverno, M. (Eds.). (2012). *Computers and Creativity*. Springer Berlin Heidelberg. DOI: 10.1007/978-3-642-31727-9

McLuhan, M. (1965). *Understanding media: The extensions of man*. McGraw-Hill.

Meier, A. (2015). A Digital Waterfall That Illuminates the Threat of Air Pollution, *Hyperallergic*. Retrieved from https://hyperallergic.com/a-digital-waterfall-that-illuminates-the-threat-of-air-pollution/

Metahaven [Kruk, V., & van der Velden, D.]. (2011). Facestate. Walker Art Center; Graphic Design: Now in Production exhibition. https://walkerart.org/magazine/metahavens-facestate

Mich, L., & Garigliano, R. (2023). ChatGPT for e-tourism: A technological perspective. *Information Technology & Tourism*, *25*(1), 1–12. DOI: 10.1007/s40558-023-00248-x

Miles, M. (2014). *Eco-aesthetics: Art, Literature and Architecture in a Period of Climate Change*. Bloomsbury Academic.

Miller, J. (2022, December). *The Rebirth of the Author*. Medium. Retrieved May 5, 2025, from https://jjosephmiller.medium.com/the-rebirth-of-the-author-ca6bcc085c89

Miller, C. H. (2019). *Digital Storytelling - A creator's guide to interactive entertainment*. Routledge. DOI: 10.1201/9780429440045

Mills, K. A., & Brown, A. (2022). Immersive virtual reality (VR) for digital media making: Transmediation is key. *Learning, Media and Technology*, *47*(2), 179–200. DOI: 10.1080/17439884.2021.1952428

Milovanovic, J., Moreau, G., Siret, D., & Miguet, F. (2017). Virtual and augmented reality in architectural design and education: An immersive multimodal platform to support architectural pedagogy. In *Proceedings of the 17th International Conference on Computer-Aided Architectural Design Futures (CAAD Futures 2017)* (pp. 513–532).

Mirzoeff, N. (2015). *How to see the world*. Pelican Books.

Mitchell, W. J. T. (1994). *Picture theory: Essays on verbal and visual representation*. University of Chicago Press.

Moll, J. (2018). *CO2GLE* [Art project]. Retrieved January 22, 2026, from https://www.janavirgin.com/CO2/

Moll, J. (2019). *The Hidden Life of an Amazon User* Ret [Art project]. Retrieved January 22, 2026, from https://www.janavirgin.com/AMZ/

Moll, J. (2022). *Inanimate Species* [Art project]. Retrieved January 22, 2026, from https://www.janavirgin.com/INANIMATESPECIES/inanimate_works.html

Morozov, E. (2023, March 12). The problem with artificial intelligence? It's neither artificial nor intelligent. *The Guardian*. https://www.theguardian.com/commentisfree/2023/mar/30/artificial-intelligence-chatgpt-human-mind

Morozov, E. (2013). *To Save Everything, Click Here: Technology, Solutionism, and the Urge to Fix Problems that Don't Exist*. Public Affairs.

Morris, C. W. (1938). Foundations of the theory of signs. In O. Neurath (Ed.), International Encyclopedia of Unified Science (pp. 1–59). Chicago University Press., https://www.mpi.nl/publications/item2364493/foundations-theory-signs, Retrieved February 15, 2026, from.

Mou, L. (Ed.). (2024). *Artificial intelligence for art creation and understanding*. CRC Press. DOI: 10.1201/9781003406273

Moura, F. T. (Ed.). (2024). *Artificial intelligence, co-creation and creativity: The new frontier for innovation*. Taylor & Francis. DOI: 10.4324/9781003453901

Moura, F. T., Castrucci, C., & Hindley, C. (2023). Artificial intelligence creates art? An experimental investigation of value and creativity perceptions. *The Journal of Creative Behavior*, *57*(4), 534–549. DOI: 10.1002/jocb.600

Mul, J. d. (1999). *Romantic Desire in (Post)modern Art and Philosophy*. State University of New York Press.

Müller, B. (2024). Design against the machine: The role of generative AI tools in design education [Practitioner report]. https://borism.medium.com/design-against-the-machine-72648374aec1

Murray, J. (2017). *Hamlet on the Holodeck: The Future of Narrative in Cyberspace*. MIT Press.

Ndalianis, A. (2003). Architectures of the senses: Neo-Baroque entertainment spectacles. In D. Thorburn & H. Jenkins (Eds.), *Rethinking media change: The aesthetics of transition* (pp. 355–374).[1] The MIT Press.

Near Future Laboratory [Bleecker, J., Girardin, F., Byrne, E., & Foster, N.]. (2012). TBD catalog: The design fiction product catalog for the normal ordinary everyday near future. Near Future Laboratory.

Near Future Laboratory [Bleecker, J.]. (2024). A newspaper from an artificially intelligent (near) future. Near Future Laboratory.

Neisser, U. (1967). *Cognitive Psychology*. Appleton-Century-Crofts.

Neuman, W. L. (2014). *Social research methods: Qualitative and quantitative approaches I*. Yayınodası Yayıncılık.

Nugent, C. (2018, August 20). *Can Artificial Intelligence Create Art? Buyers Think So*. Time. Retrieved November 18, 2023, from https://time.com/5357221/obvious-artificial-intelligence-art/

Nussbaumer, L. L., & Guerin, D. A. (2008). The relationship between learning styles and visualization skills among interior design students. *Journal of Interior Design*, *26*(2), 1–15. DOI: 10.1111/j.1939-1668.2000.tb00355.x

Østvold, M., Paulsen, M., & Trondsen, J. K. (2024). Speculative design through the lens of AI. *Proceedings of the 26th International Conference on Engineering and Product Design Education (EPDE2024)* (pp. 627–632). Aston University. DOI: 10.35199/EPDE.2024.106

Oswald, L. R. (2020). *Doing semiotics: A research guide for marketers at the edge of culture* (E-book ed.). OUP Oxford.

Özselçuk, S. K. (2023). A critical study on the use of AI algorithms in digital art: Refik Anadol's *Machine Memories: Space*. *International Journal of Economic and Administrative Academic Research*, *3*(1), 1–21.

Palinkas, L. A., Horwitz, S. M., Green, C. A., Wisdom, J. P., Duan, N., & Hoagwood, K. (2015). Purposeful sampling for qualitative data collection and analysis in mixed method implementation research. *Administration and Policy in Mental Health*, *42*(5), 533–544. DOI: 10.1007/s10488-013-0528-y PMID: 24193818

Papacharissi, Z. (2015). *Affective publics: Sentiment, technology, and politics*. Oxford University Press.

Parikka, J. (2019). *Working for Systems that Do Not Do the Work*. Retrieved January 22, 2026, from https://www.janavirgin.com/AMZ/parikka.html

Parikka, J. (2015). *A Geology of Media*. University of Minnesota Press. DOI: 10.5749/minnesota/9780816695515.001.0001

Pasquinelli, M. (Ed.). (2015). *Alleys of Your Mind: Augmented Intelligence and Its Traumas*. Meson Press.

Patton, M. Q. (2015). *Qualitative research & evaluation methods: Integrating theory and practice* (4th ed.). SAGE.

Paul, C. (2015). *Digital Art* (3rd ed.). Thames & Hudson.

Pearl, M. (2023, September 21). *OpenAI just demoed its most sophisticated image generator yet, DALL-E 3*. Mashable. Retrieved September 21, 2024, from https://in.mashable.com/tech/60582/openai-just-revealed-dall-e-3-its-newest-image-generator

Pena, M. L. C., Carballal, A., Rodrigues-Fernandez, N., Santos, I., & Romero, J. (2021). Artificial intelligence applied to conceptual design: A review of its use in architecture. *Automation in Construction, 124*, 1–30. DOI: 10.1016/j.autcon.2021.103550

Pepi, M. (2020). How does a human critique art made by AI? *Art in America, 108*(4), 26–29. https://www.artnews.com/art-in-america/features/creative-ai-art-criticism-1202686003/

Pericliev, V. (2015). On Redundancy in Describing Linguistic Systems. In Bolić, P. A., & Tselinska, D. A. (Eds.), *Proceedings of the 13th International Conference on the Lexical-Functional Grammar* (pp. 125–136). CSLI Publications.

Perrault, C. (1697). *Histoires ou Contes du Temps Passé.*

Peters, B., & Peters, T. (2013). *Inside smartgeometry: Expanding the architectural possibilities of computational design*. Wiley. DOI: 10.1002/9781118653074

Picon, A. (2010). *Digital Culture in Architecture: An Introduction for the Design Professions*. Birkhäuser.

Pirim, A. G. H. (2006). Yapay zekâ. *Yaşar Üniversitesi E-Dergisi, 1*(1), 81–93.

Plato. (2022). Republic (Translated by S. Eyüboğlu and M. A. Cimcoz). Türkiye İş Bankası Cultural Publications. (Original work written around 380 BC)

Ploennigs, J., & Berger, M. (2023). AI art in architecture. *AI in Civil Engineering, 2*(8), 1–11. DOI: 10.1007/s43503-023-00018-y

Portman, M. E., Natapov, A., & Fisher-Gewirtzman, D. (2015). To go where no man has gone before: Virtual reality in architecture, landscape architecture and environmental planning. *Computers, Environment and Urban Systems*, *54*, 376–384. DOI: 10.1016/j.compenvurbsys.2015.05.001

Power, A. J. (Ed.). (2020). *The Birth and Death of the Author: A Multi-Authored History of Authorship in Print*. Taylor & Francis. DOI: 10.4324/9780429459023

Privitera, A. G., Fontana, F., & Geronazzo, M. (2024). The Role of Audio in Immersive Storytelling: A Systematic Review in Cultural Heritage. *Multimedia Tools and Applications*, *84*(16), 16105–16143. DOI: 10.1007/s11042-024-19288-4

Programme, P. V. (n.d.). *Insight through first-person stories...* Retrieved 2025, from Patient Voices: https://www.patientvoices.org.uk/

Psomadaki, O. I., Dimoulas, C. A., Kalliris, G. M., & Paschalidis, G. (2019). Digital storytelling and audience engagement in cultural heritage management: A collaborative model based on the Digital City of Thessaloniki. *Journal of Cultural Heritage*, *36*, 12–22. DOI: 10.1016/j.culher.2018.07.016

Purves, T. (2005). *What we want is free*. State University of New York Press.

Radford, A., Kim, J. W., Hallacy, C., Ramesh, A., Goh, G., Agarwal, S., Sastry, G., Askell, A., Mishkin, P., Clark, J., Krueger, G., & Sutskever, I. (2021, February 26). *Learning Transferable Visual Models From Natural Language Supervision*. arXiv. Retrieved November 18, 2024, from https://arxiv.org/abs/2103.00020

Radianti, J., Majchrzak, T. A., Fromm, J., & Wohlgenannt, I. (2020). A systematic review of immersive virtual reality applications for higher education: Design elements, lessons learned, and research agenda. *Computers & Education*, *147*, 103778. DOI: 10.1016/j.compedu.2019.103778

Radsch, C. (2024, October 9). *Dismantling AI Data Monopolies Before it's Too Late | TechPolicy.Press*. Tech Policy Press. Retrieved October 9, 2024, from https://www.techpolicy.press/dismantling-ai-data-monopolies-before-its-too-late

Rayner, A. (2016, March 28). Can Google's Deep Dream become an art machine? *The Guardian*. Retrieved: 15.01.2026 https://www.theguardian.com/artanddesign/2016/mar/28/google-deep-dream-art

Razzouk, R., & Shute, V. (2012). What is design thinking and why is it important. *Review of Educational Research*, *82*(3), 330–348. DOI: 10.3102/0034654312457429

Reichardt, J. (1968). *Cybernetic serendipity: The computer and the arts*. Studio International.

Rhee, J., & Oh, E. (2025). Pedagogy explorations into alternative use of generative AI in design studios. *Technology | Architecture + Design, 9*(1), 84-97. DOI: 10.1080/24751448.2025.2475714

Ribeiro, M., & Almeida, M. (2024). Methodology to develop Web Storytelling Applications. In D. Raposo, J. Neves, R. Silva, L. C. Castilho, & R. Dias, *Advances in Design, Music and Arts III* (pp. 426-436). SPRINGER. DOI: 10.1007/978-3-031-73705-3_32

Ritz, L. T., & Buss, A. R. (2016). A framework for aligning instructional design strategies with affordances of CAVE immersive virtual reality systems. *TechTrends, 60*(6), 549–556. DOI: 10.1007/s11528-016-0085-9

Rizvic, S., Djapo, N., Alispahic, F., Hadzihalilovic, B., Cengic, F., Imamovic, A., & Boskovic, D. (2017). Guidelines for interactive digital storytelling presentations of cultural heritage. *9th International Conference on Virtual Worlds and Games for Serious Applications (VS-Games)* (pp. 253-259). Athens: IEEE. DOI: 10.1109/VS-GAMES.2017.8056610

Robhestand1. (2024, October). *AI and the Commodification of Art: Protecting Creative Integrity*. A.I. in Screen Trade. Retrieved October 8, 2024, from https://aiinscreentrade.com/2024/10/08/ai-and-the-commodification-of-art-protecting-creative-integrity/

Robin, B. R. (2008). Digital Storytelling: A powerful technology tool for the 21st century classroom. *Theory into Practice, 47*(3), 220–228. DOI: 10.1080/00405840802153916

Rodríguez-Fernández, N., Rebelo, S. M., & Martins, T. (Eds.). (2022). *Artificial intelligence in music, sound, art and design: 11th International Conference, EvoMUSART 2022, held as part of EvoStar 2022, Madrid, Spain, April 20–22, 2022, proceedings*. Springer International Publishing.

Rombach, R., Blattmann, A., Lorenz, D., Esser, P., & Ommer, B. (2022). High-resolution image synthesis with latent diffusion models. In *Proceedings of the IEEE/CVF Conference on Computer Vision and Pattern Recognition (CVPR)* (pp. 10684–10695). https://doi.org/DOI: 10.1109/CVPR52688.2022.01042

Rorty, R. (1989). *Contingency, Irony, and Solidarity*. Retrieved October 8, 2024, from DOI: 10.1017/CBO9780511804397

Ryan, M.-L. (2015). *Narrative as Virtual Reality 2: Revisiting Immersion and Interactivity in Literature and Electronic Media*. Johns Hopkins University Press. DOI: 10.1353/book.72246

Rynning, M. (2017). Speculative graphic design: Visual identity branding as a catalyst for change. Nordes 2017: Design + Power. DOI: 10.21606/nordes.2017.042

Sağır, M., Güdül, A., & Taştekin, A. U. A. (2025). Tur rotası oluşturmada yapay zekâ uygulamalarının karşılaştırılması: ChatGPT ve Gemini örneği. *Selçuk Üniversitesi Akşehir Meslek Yüksekokulu Sosyal Bilimler Dergisi*, (19), 1–12.

Salselas, I., & Penha, R. (2019). The role of sound in inducing storytelling in immersive environments. *14th International Audio Mostly Conference: A Journey in Sound.* Nottingham: ACM. DOI: 10.1145/3356590.3356619

Samad, A., Izani, M., Razak, A., & Rosli, M. (2024). Enhancing creative design: integrating artificial intelligence into interior design education at the university of sharjah. In *Proceedings of the International Visualization, Informatics and Technology Conference (IVIT).* Kuala Lumpur, Malesia. DOI: 10.1109/IVIT62102.2024.10692963

Samo, A., & Highhouse, S. (2023). Artificial intelligence and art: Identifying the aesthetic judgment factors that distinguish human- and machine-generated artwork. *Psychology of Aesthetics, Creativity, and the Arts*, *19*(5), 1084–1098. Advance online publication. Retrieved January 22, 2025, from. DOI: 10.1037/aca0000570

Sanchez-Vives, M. V., & Slater, M. (2005). From presence to consciousness through virtual reality. *Nature Reviews. Neuroscience*, *6*(4), 332–339. DOI: 10.1038/nrn1651 PMID: 15803164

Schellmann, H. (2024). *The Algorithm: How AI Can Hijack Your Career and Steal Your Future*. Hachette Books.

Schön, D. A. (1983). *The Reflective Practitioner: How Professionals Think in Action*. Basic Books.

Seering, J., Kraut, R. E., & Dabbish, L. (2017). Shaping pro and anti-social behavior on Twitch through moderation and example-setting. In *Proceedings of the ACM on Human-Computer Interaction*. DOI: 10.1145/2998181.2998277

Selzer, M. N., Gazcon, N. F., & Larrea, M. L. (2019). Effects of virtual presence and learning outcome using low-end virtual reality systems. *Displays*, *59*, 9–15. DOI: 10.1016/j.displa.2019.04.002

Serrat, O. (2017). Storytelling. In O. Serrat, *Knowledge Solutions*. DOI: 10.1007/978-981-10-0983-9_91

Shatto, B., & Erwin, K. (2016). Moving on From Millennials: Preparing for Generation Z. *Journal of Continuing Education in Nursing*, *47*(6), 253–254. DOI: 10.3928/00220124-20160518-05 PMID: 27232222

Shen, Y., & Yu, F. (2021). The influence of artificial intelligence on art design in the digital age. *Scientific Programming*, *2021*(1), 4838957. Retrieved January 22, 2025, from. DOI: 10.1155/2021/4838957

Shermer, M. (2017). Why Artificial Intelligence Is Not An Existential Threat. *Skeptic*, •••, 2.

Shreya, H. R., & Kumar, T. (2024). Artificial intelligence tools and chatbots for design education. In Senjyu, T., So-, C., & Joshi, A. (Eds.), *Smart Trends in Computing and Communications* (pp. 207–396). Springer Nature., DOI: 10.1007/978-981-97-1313-4_33

Shusterman, R. (2009, January). Aesthetics and Postmodernism. *The Oxford Handbook of Aesthetics, Chapter 47*, 771-782.

Silver, D., Huang, A., Maddison, C. J., Guez, A., Sifre, L., van den Driessche, G., Schrittwieser, J., Antonoglou, I., Panneershelvam, V., Lanctot, M., Dieleman, S., Grewe, D., Nham, J., Kalchbrenner, N., Sutskever, I., Lillicrap, T., Leach, M., Kavukcuoglu, K., Graepel, T., & Hassabis, D. (2016). Mastering the game of Go with deep neural networks and tree search. *Nature*, *529*(7587), 484–489. DOI: 10.1038/nature16961 PMID: 26819042

Simmons, S. (2019). Drawing in the digital age: Observations and implications for education. *Arts*, *8*(1), 1–18. DOI: 10.3390/arts8010033

Simon-Shoshan, M. (2013). Narrativity and textuality in the study of stories. *Workshop on Computational Models of Narrative (CMN 2013)*. Hamburg. DOI: 10.4230/OASIcs.CMN.2013.228

Singh, A., & Tholia, S. (2022). Toward the symbiocene through artificial intelligence. *AI & Society*, *39*(2), 805–806. DOI: 10.1007/s00146-022-01546-4

Singla, P. (2024). *Artificial Intelligence in Linguistics Research: Applications in Language Acquisition and Analysis*. NATURALISTA CAMPANO.

Sjöblom, M., & Hamari, J. (2017). Why do people watch others play video games? *Computers in Human Behavior*, *75*, 985–996. DOI: 10.1016/j.chb.2016.10.019

Skjulstad, S., & Rynning, M. (2015). Graphic design speculations: Teaching visual identity for water sustainability within a speculative design framework. Cumulus Mumbai 2015 Conference Proceedings. https://www.researchgate.net/publication/286040232

Slater, M., & Wilbur, S. (1997). A framework for immersive virtual environments (FIVE): Speculations on the role of presence in virtual environments. *Presence (Cambridge, Mass.)*, *6*(6), 603–616. DOI: 10.1162/pres.1997.6.6.603

Snijders, C., Matzat, U., & Reips, U.-D. (2012). Big Data': Big gaps of knowledge in the field of Internet. *International Journal of Internet Science*, *7*(1), 1–5.

Socio-Economic Development Index (SEGE). (2025). *T.C. Sanayi ve Teknoloji Bakanlığı*. Retrieved February 15, 2026 https://www.sanayi.gov.tr/merkez-birimi/b94224510b7b/sege

Solomon, L. H. G., & Baio, C. (2022). When do we stop being human? Prefiguring nonanthropocentric thinking. *Leonardo*, *55*(5), 445–450. DOI: 10.1162/leon_a_02246

Srnicek, N. (2017). *Platform Capitalism*. Polity Press.

Srnicek, N. (2017). Platform Capitalism. *Polity*.

Starowicz, A., & Zieliński, M. (2024). Sustainable acoustics: The impact of AI on acoustics design and noise management. *Technical Sciences*, *27*, 193–209. DOI: 10.31648/ts.10297

Steuer, J. (1992). Defining virtual reality: Dimensions determining telepresence. *The Journal of Communication*, *42*(4), 73–93. DOI: 10.1111/j.1460-2466.1992.tb00812.x

Stokes, J., Greene, R., Paul, R., de Rugy, V., Camp, E., & Petti, M. (2023, January 19). Don't Let Disney Monopolize A.I.-Generated Art. *Reason Magazine*. Retrieved January 22, 2025, from https://reason.com/2023/01/19/dont-let-disney-monopolize-a-i-generated-art/

Storm, J. A. J. (2021). *Metamodernism: The Future of Theory*. University of Chicago Press. Retrieved January 22, 2025, from DOI: 10.7208/chicago/9780226786797.001.0001

Striphas, T. (2015). Algorithmic culture. *European Journal of Cultural Studies*, *18*(4-5), 395–412. DOI: 10.1177/1367549415577392

Suchman, L. (2007). *Human–Machine Reconfigurations: Plans and Situated Actions* (2nd ed.). Cambridge University Press.

Taylor, G. D. (2014). *When the machine made art: The troubled history of computer art*. Bloomsbury Academic.

Teal, R. (2010). Developing a (non-linear) practice of design thinking. *International Journal of Art & Design Education*, *29*(3), 294–302. DOI: 10.1111/j.1476-8070.2010.01663.x

Tikhonova, E., Zavolskaya, O., & Mekeko, N. (2025). Stylistic Redundancy and Wordiness in Introductions of Original Empirical Studies: Rhetorical Risks of Academic Writing. *Journal of Language and Education*, *11*(2), 125–136. DOI: 10.17323/jle.2025.27389

Tomalin, M. (2025). Multimodal social semiotics and the challenge of artificial intelligence. *Multimodality & Society*, *5*(2), 223–244. Advance online publication. Retrieved January 22, 2025, from. DOI: 10.1177/26349795251327939

Tonkinwise, C. (2014). To save everything, click here: The folly of technological solutionism. *Journal of Design History*, *27*(1), 111–113. DOI: 10.1093/jdh/ept034

Toprak, A. (2020). Transformation of AI algorithms into digital installations. *Yeni Düşünceler E-Refereed Journal*, *14*, 47–59.

Uçar, U. E., Gökdemir, G., & Garip, E. (2023). A study of the application of virtual reality technology as an anthropometric measurement tool. *Interaction Design and Architecture(s) Journal (IxD&A), 55*, 194–211. https://doi.org/DOI: 10.55612/s-5002-055-009

Uçar, U. E., & Gürer, E. (2022). Dijital fabrikasyon süreçlerinde sanal gerçekliğin kitlesel bireyselleştirmeye dönük kullanımı. *Journal of Computational Design*, *3*(1), 19–38. DOI: 10.53710/jcode.1062205

UNESCO. (2003a). *Text of the Convention for the Safeguarding of the Intangible Cultural Heritage.* Paris: UNESCO. Retrieved from https://ich.unesco.org/en/convention

UNESCO. (2003b). *Manual on Oral Traditions and Expressions.* UNESCO, Paris. Retrieved from https://ich.unesco.org/doc/src/00114-EN.pdf

Valdivia Alonso, D. (2026). Imagining AI futures in mainstream cinema: Socio-technical narratives and social imaginaries. *AI & Society*. Advance online publication. DOI: 10.1007/s00146-026-02880-7

Valentine, L., Liu, W., Zhang, L., Bofylatos, S., Christer, K., & Cruickshank, L. (2026). The new normal? AI in design practice, education, and research. *The Design Journal*, *29*(2), 293–298. DOI: 10.1080/14606925.2026.2636392

van Dijk, J. (2020). *The digital divide*. Polity Press.

Venkatesan, R., & Li, B. (2017). *Convolutional Neural Networks in Visual Computing: A Concise Guide*. CRC Press. DOI: 10.4324/9781315154282

Vergil, H., Kaplan, M., İbrahim, M. M., Hasan, A. D., & Khan, A. U. I. (2025). *Beyond Algorithms: Artificial Intelligence's Impact and Applications in Economics and Finance*. Ibn Haldun University.

Vermeulen, T., & van den Akker, R. (2010). Notes on Metamodernism. *Journal of Aesthetics & Culture*, *2*(1), 1–14. Retrieved January 22, 2025, from https://www.tandfonline.com/doi/epdf/10.3402/jac.v2i0.5677?needAccess=true. DOI: 10.3402/jac.v2i0.5677

Vidal, M., Smith, T., Rotta, T., & Prew, P. (Eds.). (2019). *The Oxford Handbook of Karl Marx*. Oxford University Press. DOI: 10.1093/oxfordhb/9780190695545.001.0001

Vidugirytė, I. (2022). Lotman and the Baroque. *Semiotika*, *17*(32), 164–177.

Vincent, J. (2023). AI art tools Stable Diffusion and Midjourney targeted with copyright lawsuit. *The Verge*. Retrieved January 22, 2025, from https://www.theverge.com/2023/1/16/23557098/generative-ai-art-copyright-legal-lawsuit-stable-diffusion-midjourney-deviantart

Vinuesa, R., Azizpour, H., Leite, I., Balaam, M., Dignum, V., Domisch, S., Felländer, A., Langhans, S. D., Tegmark, M., & Fuso Nerini, F. (2020). The role of artificial intelligence in achieving the sustainable development goals. *Nature Communications*, *11*(1), 233. DOI: 10.1038/s41467-019-14108-y PMID: 31932590

Wands, B. (2006). *Art of the digital age* (Akınhay, O., Trans.). Akbank Publications.

Warhol, A. (1964). *Brillo Boxes*. Philadelphia Museum of Art. Retrieved April 5, 2026, from https://www.philamuseum.org/objects/89204

Waters, J. K. (2025). *Meta AI Releases Open Source Machine Learning Library to Tackle Dataset Management Challenges*. Campus Technology. Retrieved January 22, 2025, from https://campustechnology.com/Articles/2025/01/22/Meta-AI-Releases-Open-Source-Machine-Learning-Library.aspx

Weatherbed, J. (2024, January 9). Artists keep rallying against creative companies for using AI. *The Verge*. Retrieved January 22, 2025, from https://www.theverge.com/2024/1/9/24031468/wacom-wizards-of-the-coast-mtg-artists-against-generative-ai

Weitz, M. (1956). The role of theory in aesthetics. *The Journal of Aesthetics and Art Criticism*, *15*(1), 27–35. DOI: 10.1111/1540_6245.jaac15.1.0027

Weizman, E. (2019). *Forensic Architecture: Violence at the Threshold of Detectability*. Zone Books.

Weston, G. (2023, March 22). *The rise of Web3 Storytelling*. (101 Blockchains) Retrieved February 22, 2024, from 101 Blockchains: https://101blockchains.com/web3-storytelling/

Williams, M. L., Burnap, P., & Sloan, L. (2017). Towards an ethical framework for publishing Twitter data in social research. *Sociological Research Online*. PMID: 29276313

Winegard, E. (2019). The role and significance of digital media technologies in the dissemination of art and design. (Master's thesis). Istanbul University, Istanbul, Turkey.

Wissner-Gross, A. (2016). *Datasets Over Algorithms*. Edge. Retrieved October 8, 2024, from https://www.edge.org/response-detail/26587

Wittel, A. (2012). Digital Marx: Toward a Political Economy of Distributed Media. Triple C. Communication Capitalism & Critique. *Open Access Journal for Global Sustainable Information Society*, *10*(2), 313–333.

Wittgenstein, L. (2007). *Philosophical Investigations* (Barışcan, H., Trans.). Metis Publishing. (Original work published 1953)

Wohn, D. Y., & Guo, M. (2021). Understanding digital audiences in livestreaming. *Journal of Computer-Mediated Communication*.

Woodcock, J., & Johnson, M. R. (2019). The affective labor of live streaming on Twitch. *Television & New Media*, *20*(8), 813–823. DOI: 10.1177/1527476419851077

Wulf, T., Schneider, F., & Beckert, S. (2021). Exploring parasocial interaction with streamers.

Wutich, A., Beresford, M., & Bernard, H. R. (2024). Sample sizes for 10 types of qualitative data analysis: An integrative review. *Qualitative Research*.

Yin, R. K. (2018). *Case study research and applications: Design and methods* (6th ed.). SAGE.

Yurtseven, N. B. (2023). Wakandalının Kültürel Kimliği: Black Panther Filmi Üzerine Bir Temsil İncelemesi. *4. BOYUT Medya ve Kültürel Çalışmalar Dergisi*, *0*(23), 1–21. DOI: 10.26650/4boyut.2023.1340900

Yusa, I. M. M., Yu, Y., & Sovhyra, T. (2022). Reflections on the use of artificial intelligence in works of art. *Journal of Aesthetics, Design, and Art Management*, *2*(2), 152–167. Advance online publication. Retrieved January 22, 2025, from. DOI: 10.58982/jadam.v2i2.334

Zawacki-Richter, O., Marín, V. I., Bond, M., & Gouverneur, F. (2019). Systematic review of research on artificial intelligence applications in higher education-where are the educators? *International Journal of Educational Technology in Higher Education*, *16*(1), 39. DOI: 10.1186/s41239-019-0171-0

Zee. (2025). *Artificial Intelligence Apps Gain Global Popularity, Report Finds*. TechRound. Retrieved January 22, 2025, from https://techround.co.uk/news/ai-apps-global-popularity/

Zhang, Y., Fu, J., Lai, J., Deng, S., Guo, Z., Zhong, C., Tang, J., Cao, W., & Wu, Y. (2024). Reporting of ethical considerations in qualitative research utilizing social media data. *Journal of Medical Internet Research*. PMID: 38758590

Zylinska, J. (2020). *AI Art. Machine Visions and Warped Dreams*. Open Humanities Press.

About the Contributors

And Algül, born in 1973, graduated from Bilkent University, took his master's degree from Marmara University, and completed his PhD at Yeditepe University. He is working at Üsküdar University, Faculty of Communication, Department of Visual Communication Design Studies, conducts studies about Virtual Reality, Informatics Society, Surveillance Society, Technological Determinism, Social Media, New Media, Interaction, Culture, Society, Design, Digital Games and Communication Tools.

***

Mehmet Emin Arkci was born in Istanbul in 2000. He completed his high school education at Florya Final Anatolian High School between 2013 and 2018. During his high school years, he achieved district-level rankings in various poetry recitation competitions. He continued to earn similar achievements throughout his undergraduate education, becoming the Tekirdağ provincial champion for two consecutive years in the poetry recitation competition titled "Bir Şiir Bir Nefes", organized by the Ministry of Youth and Sports of the Republic of Türkiye. In 2019, he was admitted to the Department of Electrical and Electronics Engineering at İnönü University Faculty of Engineering. After studying there for a period of time, he left the program. Between 2020 and 2024, he completed his undergraduate degree as an honor student in the Department of International Relations at Tekirdağ Namık Kemal University, Faculty of Economics and Administrative Sciences. During this period, he worked as a paid theatre actor at an organization called Trakya Cultural Center and actively took part in student clubs at his university as both an executive member and a founding member. Since 2020, Arkcı has been working professionally as a voice-over artist, and his voice has been featured in various commercials and digital game productions. He is currently continuing his master's education at Çanakkale Onsekiz Mart University, Institute of Graduate Studies, within the Department of

New Media and Communication. He also serves as a volunteer at the COMU Social Responsibility Project Coordination Office.

Tamer Bayrak, born in Istanbul in 1988, completed his undergraduate degree at Istanbul Kültür University, Faculty of Communication, Department of Communication Design. He earned his Master's degree from Istanbul Kültür University's Institute of Social Sciences, Communication Design Program, and his doctorate from Istanbul Aydın University's Institute of Social Sciences, Department of Public Relations and Publicity, with a thesis on New Media and Eye Tracking technology. Bayrak is a faculty member at Çanakkale Onsekiz Mart University, Faculty of Communication, Department of New Media and Communication. He has directed short films, and his research interests include Virtual Reality Technologies, Eye Tracking Techniques, Brain Wave Analysis, New Media, Digital Games, Technological Determinism, Social Media, Surveillance Societies, Research Methods, Media Literacy, Technological Obesity, Gamification, Artificial Intelligence, and Communication.

İhsan Eken received his B.A. in Visual Communication Design from İstanbul Commerce University (2009) and his M.A. in Advertising and Brand Communication Management from Bahçeşehir University (2011). He earned his Ph.D. in Media and Communication Studies from İstanbul Commerce University, focusing on mobile accessibility for visually impaired users through a usability approach. He is currently an Associate Professor at İstanbul Medipol University. His research examines the transformative impact of digitalization on communication and visual culture, with particular emphasis on user behavior in digital environments, AI-assisted content production, and information reliability. His areas of expertise include usability, UX/UI design, digital media, 3D modeling, animation, and artificial intelligence. He has published in national and international peer-reviewed journals and contributes to academia through teaching and the supervision of graduate theses.

İpek Fatma Ertan received her B.A. in Painting from the Faculty of Fine Arts at Marmara University and her M.A. in Graphic Design from İstanbul Arel University, where she also completed her Proficiency in Art. Her doctoral-level thesis, "The Use of Three-Dimensional Design and Virtual Reality: The Case of Göbekli Tepe," explores the integration of 3D design and immersive technologies within a cultural heritage context. Ertan began her academic career as a lecturer at İstanbul Gelişim University and Beykent University, and later served as an Assistant Professor at Iğdır University. She subsequently held the position of Associate Professor and Head of the Department of Cartoon and Animation at Üsküdar University. She is currently an Associate Professor in the Department of Media and Visual Arts at

İstanbul Medipol University. Her research adopts an interdisciplinary approach to digital visuality, animation, and the integration of emerging technologies into artistic production processes. Her areas of specialization include 2D/3D animation, digital game design, virtual and augmented reality applications, motion graphics, and artificial intelligence. Her recent work particularly focuses on the integration of artificial intelligence into visual arts and digital games, generative AI, algorithmic art practices, and the use of game engines such as Unreal Engine in creative production workflows. In addition, her research interests encompass the historical and theoretical dimensions of animation cinema, as well as the preservation of intangible cultural heritage in digital environments. Ertan has published extensively in national and international peer-reviewed journals and has authored books and conference papers. Alongside her research and teaching at undergraduate and graduate levels, she contributes to academic knowledge production through the supervision of master's theses, supporting the scholarly development of emerging researchers.

Toni Gameiro (b. 2004) holds a degree in Communication Design and Audiovisual Media from the School of Applied Arts of the Polytechnic Institute of Castelo Branco (ESART-IPCB). For his final degree project, he developed a comprehensive game concept, integrating narrative structure with visual mechanics. He currently operates as a Web and Graphic Designer, focusing on the intersection of digital branding and interactive media. His professional trajectory is directed toward specialization in Animation and Game Design, with a particular interest in environment-building and character mechanics.

Gözde Gökdemir completed her master's thesis at Istanbul Technical University through the International Master of Interior Architectural Design Program (IMIAD). She completed her PhD in Interior Architecture at Mimar Sinan Fine Arts University. Since 2019, she has been continuing her academic career at Istanbul Technical University, Department of Interior Architecture.

Christo Kaftandjiev is a Professor, Ph.D., and Doctor Habilis of marketing semiotics, and digital and AI marketing communications Faculty of Journalism, Sofia University, Bulgaria. Professor Kaftandjiev conducts seminars in many European and Asian universities and at more than 150 business conferences, advertising festivals, trade expos, and other events across Europe and Asia. Christo is the author of numerous SCOPUS and World of Science articles and 10 books on these topics, including: "The Language of Advertising. Graphics and Text"; "Visual Communications", "The Texts of Print Advertising"; "Harmony in Advertising Communication", "The Images of Women in Advertising", "Absolut Semiotics in an Absolut World", "Heroes and Beauties in Advertising", "Mythological

Archetypes in Advertising", "Integrated Marketing Communications", "Marketing communications during the Black Plague (Coronovirus 19)". Kaftandjiev is the Editor-in-Chief of the American Journal of Linguistics.

Özge Kaya is a lecturer in the Department of Cartoon and Animation at Üsküdar University in Istanbul. She holds a Proficiency in Art degree from Yıldız Technical University, Department of Art and Design. Her research focuses on cultural heritage, visual communication design, human-computer interaction, and the creative processes of artificial intelligence. She is particularly interested in how AI technologies transform design applications, user experience, and the dynamics of human-agent collaboration. Her interdisciplinary approach brings together design theory, communication sciences, and technology studies.

Yasemin Kayabaşı is a graphic designer and academic. She is an Assistant Professor at Burdur Mehmet Akif Ersoy University, Faculty of Art and Design, in the Department of Digital Game Design. She also teaches in the Departments of Visual Communication Design and Animation, focusing on design education that bridges creativity, critical thinking, and technology. Her research and creative practice explore the intersections of graphic design, interaction design, game design, character design, concept development, and speculative design, with a particular interest in integrating artificial intelligence, augmented reality, and digital illustration into contemporary design processes.

Lara Marques (b. 2004) graduated in Communication and Audiovisual Design from the Higher School of Applied Arts of the Polytechnic Institute of Castelo Branco in 2025. With a foundational background in Visual Arts, her work focuses primarily on Editorial Design and UX/UI. She approaches design through a practical and organized methodology, translating abstract creative concepts into clear and functional visual solutions. Her experience includes the production of diverse audiovisual content and the strategic development of digital communication. She has worked on adapting brand identities for a range of high-impact platforms, including social media, digital catalogs, and professional presentations. Currently, her interests lie in exploring the intersection between visual design, digital media, and contemporary marketing strategies.

Hiba Narmouq graduated with a bachelors degree in Architecture from the German Jordanian University. She is a student in the non-thesis master's program in Visual Communication Design at Üsküdar University. Her research interests include architecture, scenography, art and visual studies.

Madalena Ribeiro (b. 1970) holds a PhD in Computer Engineering from the University of Beira Interior, a master's degree in Electrical and Computer Engineering (Informatics) from the University of Lisbon (Instituto Superior Técnico), and a degree in Mathematics from the University of Coimbra, specializing in Computer Graphics. She completed her final project at Fraunhofer IGD (Germany) under an ERASMUS scholarship. She began her academic career in 1995 at the Polytechnic Institute of Castelo Branco and has been an Adjunct Professor at the School of Applied Arts since 2005. Her teaching includes web design and development, interaction, programming for the arts, interface design, and augmented reality. Her research focuses on color and color vision deficiency, augmented reality, web-based storytelling, and digital approaches to cultural heritage within the TECHN&ART - IPCB research center.

Kader Sürmeli is a Professor in the Department of Art at Yıldız Technical University. She holds a PhD in Fine Arts Education from Ondokuz Mayıs University. Her research interests encompass visual culture, digital arts, and graphic design. She has supervised numerous master's and doctoral theses on digital design, visual communication, and technology-mediated artistic expression.

Ezgi Tokdil is a faculty member in the Department of Fine Arts Education at Burdur Mehmet Akif Ersoy University, Turkey. Her research and artistic practice explore the intersections of visual culture, ecology, and technology. She focuses on digital environmentalism, artificial intelligence, and the aesthetic contradictions of sustainability discourses. Drawing on media ecology and posthuman theory, she investigates the entanglements between digital aesthetics, ecological awareness, and cultural memory in the age of environmental crisis. In addition to her academic pursuits, she is the editor-in-chief of ArtDesign Journal and the editor of the International Journal of Communication and Art. She also serves as a field editor and editorial board member in various other journals.

Uğur Efe Uçar graduated from Istanbul Technical University with a degree in Interior Architecture and completed international master's studies within the IMIAD program at ITU and Hochschule für Technik Stuttgart. He received his PhD in Architectural Design Computing Programme from Istanbul Technical University. He works as a Research Assistant at ITU, Faculty of Architecture, Department of Interior Architecture. His research focuses on computational design, virtual reality, generative systems, and the integration of vernacular architectural knowledge into contemporary design processes. His work explores design as a communicative and linguistic system, particularly through AI-assisted methodologies and immersive environments.

Index

A

B

C

D

E

G

H

I

www.ingramcontent.com/pod-product-compliance
Ingram Content Group UK Ltd.
Pitfield, Milton Keynes, MK11 3LW, UK
UKHW050844101026
15624UKWH00018B/535

9 798260 027110